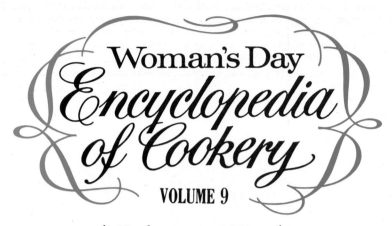

Woman's Day
Encyclopedia of Cookery
VOLUME 9

in 12 volumes—over 2,000 pages—
with more than 1,500 illustrations in color,
1,000 entries and 8,500 recipes
1,200 menus, 50 specialty cook books
and a host of delightful features by distinguished food writers.

Prepared and edited by the Editors of Woman's Day
Editor: EILEEN TIGHE
Managing Editor: EVELYN GRANT   *Food Editor:* GLENNA MCGINNIS
Art Consultant: HAROLD SITTERLE   *Photographic Editor:* BEN CALVO
Associates: OLIVIA RISBERG, CHARLOTTE SCRIPTURE,
CAROLYN STORM, JOHANNA BAFARO

SPECIAL PROJECT STAFF
Editor: NIKA STANDEN HAZELTON   *Art Director:* LEONARD A. ROMÁGNA
Associates: L. GERALDINE MARSTELLER, HELEN FEINGOLD,
SUSAN J. KNOX, INEZ M. KRECH

FAWCETT PUBLICATIONS, INC.   NEW YORK

THIRD EDITION

Printed in U.S.A. by
FAWCETT-HAYNES PRINTING CORPORATION
Rockville, Maryland

Table of Contents

VOLUME 9

PECTIN TO PURÉE

Definitions and 830 Recipes
How to buy, store, prepare, cook, and serve •
Nutritive Food Values • Caloric Values

To help you plan more varied meals
with the recipes in this volume

Foreword

To the best of our knowledge, no work of this magnitude ever has been undertaken by any author, editor, or publisher in America. The editors of Woman's Day, with a special staff of experts, present to you this Encyclopedia of Cookery, a comprehensive and colorful library on all culinary matters. The twelve-volume encyclopedia contains in its 2,000 pages over 8,500 recipes from all over the world, 1,500 food illustrations in color, 1,200 menus, 50 special cook books and over 1,000 food definitions. In addition, there are full details about all foods, their nutritive and caloric values, how to buy, serve, prepare, and cook them. There is a history of food and cooking, articles on nutrition, diet, entertaining, menu planning, herbs and spices. Every topic of culinary interest is covered. Five years of intensive work have gone into its preparation, backed by twenty-five years of food and cookery experience in the publication of Woman's Day.

We think you will find this Encyclopedia of Cookery the most complete and authoritative work ever published on the subject. It is a library for everyone who cares about good food and the fine art of preparing it.

The Editors

PECTIN—A water soluble substance present in the cell walls of citrus fruits, apples, and sugar beets. When properly combined with sugar and acid, it forms a jelly and is used in the making of jams and jellies to gel them. The commercial liquid pectin is made from apple pectin; the powdered pectin is made from citrus or apple pectin.

Commercially prepared pectin in dry and liquid forms can be added to fruits and vegetables which themselves have only small amounts of natural pectin and acid in order to produce a firmer jam, jelly, or preserve. Also the addition of commercial pectin eliminates the need for long cooking to concentrate a jam and jelly to the point of proper consistency; use of pectin therefore results in a greater yield. Pectins are used commercially in the production of candies, drugs, and textiles. Use as directed on bottle or package.

PEEL—When used as a noun, "peel" refers to the outer skin of such fruits and vegetables as apples and potatoes. As a verb "to peel" means to remove the outer peel, skin, or rind of food.

At times the peelings can be used and cooked separately as in candied orange and grapefruit peels. Apple peelings can be added to stewed fruits for added flavor, lemon peel added to black coffee, etc.

PEMMICAN—North American Indian cake made of dried and pounded meat mixed with melted fat and various berry and herb seasonings. Originally, it was made of dried buffalo meat or venison. The paste was then shaped into cakes and carried in rawhide bags. This wholesome substance, which was light and easy to carry, could be taken on long trips without spoiling, and it packed a lot of nourishment for the space it occupied.

Different Indian tribes had different recipes. All were based on some sort of "jerky," a meat that was not jerked at all, but rather dried or smoked. A companion of La Salle in his explorations through the Northwest in 1669-70 reports on the making of jerky: "In the woods where there is no salt the meat is cut in very thin slices and spread on a gridiron raised three feet from the ground, covered with small wooden switches on which you spread your meat. Then a fire is made underneath the gridiron, and the meat is dried on the fire and smoked until there is no longer any moisture in it and it is

dry as a piece of wood." The meat used might be deer, buffalo, rabbit, squirrel, antelope, beef, or whatever other game was available in the area. Bear fat was the most popular fat, but each Indian tribe added its own special seasonings. Wild grapes and cherries, corn, beans, and herbs were used. Maple syrup was recommended by some. A nonspicy pemmican was also used by the people of Tibet and a modern kind of pemmican, using beef and raisins, was carried on Arctic and other expeditions.

Pennsylvania Dutch Cookery

Eating is serious business in Pennsylvania Dutch country, that fertile and lovely region in the east of the state which has at its heart five counties: York, Lancaster, Lebanon, Berks, and Lehigh. Pennsylvania is a state settled by people of many of the old-world countries, who still remember the ways of their forebears. None do so more than the Pennsylvania Dutch, the descendants of many Protestant religious sects that have come over from Germany since the 17th century to seek and find religious freedom in William Penn's humanitarian colony. The "Dutch" has nothing to do with Holland Dutch; it is a corruption of the dialect word *Deitsch* or *Deutsch,* which means "German." The people we know as Pennsylvania Dutch are of Germanic origin, and their ways of living, especially as expressed in their language, a German dialect, in the food, the arts, and occasionally in the costumes, are a carry-over from the 18th- and 19th-century German farm or small-town life. These people were, and are, conservative folks, clinging not only to their religious beliefs, but also to their homespun ways of farming and living.

Religion was the mainspring of their lives. The various denominations of Mennonites, the Moravians, the "church people," the Brethren, Schwenkfelder and other "plain people," and the Amish kept their religious distinctions, which also were expressed in their ways of dressing and the varying degrees with which they accepted the pleasures and progress

of the plain American world around them. These outward distinctions have now well-nigh disappeared, except among the Amish, with the "plain" dress of their women that is without ornament, including flowers, even on their wedding days. The heavily bearded men wear black suits of an old-fashioned cut, brightened by dazzling white shirts, or electric blue or purple shirts. Even the little children wear these clothes, and as you drive around the Pennsylvania Dutch country, you see the black- or straw-hatted men and boys and the bonneted women and girls driving in their buggies, closed ones for married couples, open ones for bachelors, for the true Amish shun automobiles.

The Pennsylvania Dutch started as farmers, and they are still farmers. Blessed with some of the best land in the United States, their farms are wonders of care and beauty. They speak of the love of owners for their land, of their understanding of it, and of the land's gratitude. The bounty of the land is for all to see in the farmers' markets, in the roadside stands, where the most beautiful vegetables and fruits, preserves, pickles, hams and sausages, cheese and butter are displayed as if to make a model picture for an artist to paint. It follows that people who work hard on the land also rejoice in its fruits on their own tables. To set a good table is the pride of any Pennsylvania Dutch woman, and a good table is a table bountiful beyond belief to outsiders.

This is the land of the shoofly pie, not a pie as we know it, but more a dunking coffeecake; of crisp funnel cakes, batter pushed through a funnel into hot fat and the most delicious fried cake there ever was; of lemon sponge and vanilla pie and endless other pies; smoked sausages such as the superlative Lebanon bologna; chicken corn soup; noodle dishes, fat, egg-rich, golden homemade noodles, these; the many rich irresistible cookies; fresh and dried corn dishes; vegetables and salads with a robust taste; hams and chicken; sauerkraut and pork galore, including the famous *schnitz und gnepp,* dried apples, ham, and dumplings cooked together.

The substantial nature of Pennsylvania Dutch food is alleviated by the renowned "seven sweets and seven sours," the pickles and relishes that are one of the great features of the region. They are the pride of the housewives, and their pride is well deserved, for the chowchow, corn relish, bread and butter pickles, and all the others with which the farm women cover the empty white places on their tablecloths, are delicious. However, they will admit themselves that they seldom serve all fourteen pickles at one meal.

Pennsylvania Dutch cookery is cookery for people who work hard outdoors in all weather, who like to eat flavorful well-seasoned food in quantity. The cooking reflects the German origin of the people; it has been said if a historian really wants to know what German rural and small-town life was like in the 18th and early 19th centuries, he would find it still somewhere in the Pennsylvania Dutch country, especially among the Amish.

APPETIZERS, RELISHES, AND PRESERVES

CHOWCHOW

- 2 cups diced peeled cucumbers
- 2 cups green beans, cut into 1-inch lengths
- 2 cups shelled Lima beans
- 2 cups kernel corn, cut from cob
- 1 cup sliced celery
- 1 cup seeded chopped green peppers
- 1 cup seeded chopped red peppers
- ½ cup tiny whole onions
- 1½ teaspoons powdered mustard
- 1 cup sugar
- 2 cups cider vinegar

Cook vegetables separately and then combine after draining. Add mustard and sugar to vinegar. Bring mixture to boil. Add vegetables and bring to boil again. Spoon mixture into sterilized jars. Seal and cool. Makes about 6 pints.

PEPPER CABBAGE

- 1 cup chopped celery
- 2 cups chopped green peppers
- 1 medium head cabbage, cored and chopped
- 2 tablespoons vinegar
- Salt and pepper to taste

Combine all ingredients in a large saucepan and cook over medium heat, stirring occasionally to prevent sticking. Cook until vegetables are tender. Pour into sterilized glasses. Seal and cool. Makes about 3 pints.

GREEN-TOMATO MUSTARD PICKLE

- 1 peck green tomatoes
- 2 pounds small white onions
- 6 sweet red peppers, diced
- 1 medium cauliflower, broken into small flowerets
- 1 cup salt
- Mustard Sauce
- 1 dozen sour pickles, sliced

Slice tomatoes and onions into large kettle. Add peppers and cauliflower. Add salt and mix through vegetables with hands. Let stand overnight. Heat vegetables, but do not boil. Drain off liquid. Add Mustard Sauce and bring to boil. Add pickles and simmer for a few min-

utes. Pour into hot sterilized jars, and seal. Makes about 5 pints.

Mustard Sauce

- 4 ounces powdered mustard
- 1 tablespoon turmeric
- 1 cup all-purpose flour
- 1 cup sugar
- 3½ quarts white vinegar
- 1 tablespoon celery seed
- 1 tablespoon mustard seed

Mix dry ingredients. Add a little of the vinegar, stirring to a smooth paste. Add remaining vinegar and seeds. Cook, stirring constantly, until thickened.

PHILADELPHIA VEGETABLE RELISH

- 3 cups minced cabbage
- 1 cup minced celery
- 1 cup minced green pepper
- ½ cup minced sweet red pepper
- 2 tablespoons salt
- 1½ cups white vinegar
- 2 tablespoons mustard seed
- 2 tablespoons sugar

Combine vegetables. Sprinkle with salt, cover, and store in refrigerator overnight. Next day, drain thoroughly and put in glass jars. Mix remaining ingredients, and bring to boil. Pour over vegetables, cover, and store in refrigerator. This will keep for about 1 week. Makes about 1½ quarts.

PENNSYLVANIA DUTCH APPLE BUTTER

- 2 quarts cider
- 3½ pounds cooking apples
- 3 cups sugar
- 2 teaspoons each of ground allspice and cloves
- 1 tablespoon ground cinnamon
- ¼ teaspoon salt

Boil cider for 15 minutes. Add apples, cut into eighths. Cook until very tender. Force through a sieve to remove peels and seeds. Return to kettle; add sugar, spices, and salt. Simmer slowly until thick, stirring frequently to prevent burning. Pour into jars or crock. Makes about 4 pints.

SOUPS

CHICKEN RIVVEL CORN SOUP

- 1 stewing chicken (about 4 pounds), cut up
- 3½ quarts boiling water
- 2 onions, chopped
- 1 cup chopped celery and leaves
- 8 ears of sweet corn, shucked
- 2 hard-cooked eggs, shelled and sliced
- Salt and pepper
- 1 cup all-purpose flour
- 1 egg, well beaten
- ¼ cup milk

Cook chicken at a simmer in boiling water for 3 hours, or until tender. Remove chicken pieces and strain broth. Add onions, celery, and corn cut from the cobs to the broth. Remove chicken meat from bones, and cube. Add cubes to soup. Cook until vegetables are tender.

Just before serving, add hard-cooked eggs and season with salt and pepper to taste. Mix flour with egg and milk. Rub mixture with a fork until it crumbles. Drop crumbs slowly into soup. Cook, covered, without stirring, over low heat for 7 minutes. Serve immediately. Makes 6 servings.

PFLAUMENSUPPE (Prune Soup)

- 1½ cups dried prunes
- 7 cups water
- 2 cups raisins
- 1 cup sugar
- ⅔ cup all-purpose flour
- ½ teaspoon salt
- 3½ cups milk

Add prunes to water and cook until just tender. Add raisins and cook until plumped and tender. Add ¾ cup of the sugar and cook for an additional 5 minutes. Mix remaining sugar with flour and salt. Gradually stir in milk. Gradually stir mixture into fruit mixture. Cook over low heat, stirring constantly, until smooth and thickened. Add more milk if soup is too thick. Makes 6 to 8 servings.

POTATO SOUP WITH BACON AND BROWNED BREAD CUBES

- 4 large potatoes, peeled and diced
- 1 large onion, peeled and diced
- 6 cups water
- 6 bacon strips, diced
- 2 cups bread cubes
- ¾ cup heavy cream
- Salt and pepper

Cook potatoes and onion in water until tender. Fry bacon until crisp. Remove bacon pieces and brown bread cubes in fat until golden. Add cream to soup and season with salt and pepper to taste. Put some bread cubes and bits of crisp bacon into each soup bowl and fill bowls with hot soup. Serve immediately. Makes 6 servings.

PEPPER POT SOUP WITH DUMPLINGS

- Bones from beef or veal
- ½ pound tripe, diced
- 6 cups water
- ½ bay leaf
- 1½ teaspoons salt
- ⅛ teaspoon pepper
- 3 onions, diced
- 2 potatoes, diced
- 2 carrots, diced
- ½ cup diced celery
- ½ green pepper, diced
- 2 tablespoons fat
- Dumpling Batter, page 1355
- Few sprigs of parsley, chopped

Put bones and tripe in kettle with water, bay leaf, salt, pepper, and one third of the onion. Bring to boil and simmer, covered, for 2 hours. Cook remaining onion, potato, carrot, celery, and green pepper in fat for 5 minutes. Remove bones from soup mixture and add vegetables. Cover, and simmer for 30 minutes longer. Drop Dumpling Batter by spoonfuls into simmering soup. Cover and cook for 15 minutes. Sprinkle with parsley. Makes 4 servings.

MAIN DISHES

OYSTER-POTATO PIE

Line a long baking pan with pastry. Pre-cook potatoes and dice or slice. Arrange alternate layers of potatoes and oysters; dot with butter. Season with salt and pepper to taste. Put on top crust and bake in preheated moderate oven (350°F.) for 30 minutes.

Baked Meat Pie

Use recipe for Oyster-Potato Pie; add chopped meat instead of oysters. Also add sliced onion. Season only slightly with salt and pepper.

BEEF MOUNDS WITH NOODLES

1 can (8 ounces) tomato sauce
¾ pound ground beef
2 slices dry bread
½ cup hot water
   Dash of cayenne
½ teaspoon onion salt
4 cups hot cooked noodles
2 tablespoons chopped parsley

Beat tomato sauce into beef. Soak bread in water, and add to first mixture with remaining ingredients except noodles and parsley. Shape mixture into 4 mounds in shallow baking pan. Bake in preheated hot oven (400°F.) for about 20 minutes. Remove beef mounds. Mix noodles and parsley with drippings in pan. Put noodles in serving dish, and top with beef mounds. Makes 4 servings.

GEBRATENE KALBSLEBER
(Baked Calf's Liver)

4 slices of calf's or beef liver, ¾ inch thick
1½ cups soft bread crumbs
2 tablespoons butter or margarine, melted
3 tablespoons chopped onion
1 small egg, well beaten
¼ pound fresh pork, ground
   Salt, pepper, and crumbled dried marjoram to taste
4 slices of bacon

Wash liver and pat dry. With a sharp knife cut a pocket into the side of each slice. Mix remaining ingredients except bacon and use mixture to stuff liver slices. Put stuffed slices in a well-greased shallow baking dish. Top each slice with a strip of bacon. Cover and bake in preheated moderate oven (350°F.) for 50 to 60 minutes, or until liver is tender. If desired, make a gravy with the pan drippings. Serve with currant jelly. Makes 4 servings.

SCHNITZ UND GNEPP
(Dried Apples and Raised Dumplings)

1 small smoked ham (about 3 pounds)
1 package active dry yeast or 1 cake compressed yeast
¼ cup water*
1 tablespoon sugar
1 teaspoon salt
4¾ cups milk
1 tablespoon butter
3 cups wheat flour (bread flour)
3 cups sweet apple schnitz (dried apple slices)
   Brown sugar

Cook ham in water to cover for 1½ hours. Sprinkle or crumble yeast into water. *Use very warm water (105°F. to 115°F.) for dry yeast; use lukewarm (80°F. to 90°F.) for compressed. Let stand for a few minutes, then stir until dissolved. Add sugar and salt to dissolved yeast. Let stand until mixture bubbles. Heat ¾ cup of the milk, add butter, and stir until melted. Cool to lukewarm. Stir in yeast mixture. Beat in flour until smooth and well blended. Knead on floured board. Put in warm place and let rise until doubled in bulk. Punch down and form into small balls. Let balls rise for about 1 hour. While yeast balls are rising, add sweet apple *schnitz* to ham. Cook for 1 hour longer, or until ham is tender. Remove meat and be sure there are at least 1½ inches of broth. If less, add water to make 1½ inches. Drop yeast balls (dumplings) into boiling broth (apple *schnitz* are in broth, too) and cover tightly. Cook over medium heat gently for 25 to 30 minutes. DO NOT REMOVE COVER DURING THIS TIME. At the end of 30 minutes, dumplings should be nicely raised. Remove dumplings and keep warm. Add the remaining 4 cups milk to broth. Add brown sugar to taste. Reheat, but do not boil. Apple *schnitz* and gravy are eaten on dumplings with sliced ham. Makes 6 to 8 generous servings.

SWEET-AND-SOUR HAM WITH VEGETABLES

1 onion
3 or 4 potatoes
   Salt
1 slice fully cooked ham (1½ pounds)
2 teaspoons powdered mustard
¼ cup firmly packed brown sugar
2 tablespoons vinegar

Cut onion and potatoes into chunks. Cook in small amount of lightly salted water until tender; drain. Sprinkle ham with mustard, brown sugar, and vinegar. Broil one side, turn, spoon pan juice over the top, and broil until lightly browned. Put ham on serving platter. Pour ham drippings over drained potatoes and onion, and toss for 1 minute over low heat. Serve around ham. Makes 3 or 4 servings.

SCRAPPLE

4 pigs' knuckles
1 pound lean pork
1 large onion, stuck with 3 cloves
3 quarts water
1 tablespoon salt
1 teaspoon pepper
1 teaspoon ground sage
3 cups cornmeal
   All-purpose flour
   Butter or bacon fat

Over low heat, cook pigs' knuckles, pork, and onion in water for 2½ hours, or until meat almost falls off bones. Drain; reserve broth. Strain broth through fine sieve or three thicknesses of cheesecloth, and chill. Remove fat. Separate meat from bones and force through fine blade of food chopper or whirl in electric blender. Measure 2 quarts of broth and pour into large kettle. Add meat, salt, pepper, and sage to broth. Bring to boil. Combine cornmeal with remaining quart of broth. Stir into boiling mixture and cook over medium heat until thickened, stirring constantly. Cook, covered, over lowest possible heat for about 20 minutes, stirring often. Pour into 2 loaf pans (9 x 5 x 3 inches). Cool, and chill. To serve, cut scrapple into slices, coat with flour, and brown in hot butter. Makes 16 servings.

Note: Scrapple keeps for about 1 week if wrapped in moisture-proof paper, and stored in the refrigerator.

PICKLED PIGS' FEET OR SOUSE

6 pigs' feet
   Boiling water
3 cups cider vinegar
2 tablespoons salt
½ teaspoon pepper
15 whole cloves
1 tablespoon broken cinnamon sticks
1½ cups chopped bread and butter pickles

Scrape and clean pigs' feet. Add boiling water to cover. Cook until pigs' feet are tender, for about 4 hours. Remove meat from bones, and cube. Reserve 3 cups broth. Add vinegar, salt, pepper, and spices to broth. Simmer for 30 minutes. Put meat and chopped pickles into a shallow dish. Pour broth over mixture. Chill until firm. Cut into slices and serve with dark bread. Makes 6 servings.

PIGS' KNUCKLES AND SAUERKRAUT WITH CARAWAY DUMPLINGS

1½ quarts sauerkraut
6 pigs' knuckles, fresh or corned
1 onion, chopped
1 cup water
   Caraway Dumpling Batter

Put sauerkraut and pigs' knuckles in kettle. Sprinkle with chopped onion and add water. Simmer, covered, until tender, about 2½ hours. Drop Caraway Dumpling Batter by tablespoonfuls on top; cover and cook for 15 minutes. Makes 6 servings.

Note: Serve some dill pickles with it.

Caraway Dumpling Batter

1½ cups sifted all-purpose flour
1 teaspoon baking powder
½ teaspoon salt
1 teaspoon sugar
1 egg, beaten
⅓ cup water
2 tablespoons butter or margarine, melted
1 tablespoon caraway seeds

Mix dry ingredients. Add combined egg, water, and melted butter. Mix until dry ingredients are moistened. Stir in caraway seeds.

JELLIED VEAL

Knuckle of veal
1 tablespoon whole mixed pickling spice
1 tablespoon salt
2 bay leaves
1 onion, sliced
2 hard-cooked eggs
6 stuffed olives, sliced

Have butcher cut veal into 3 or 4 pieces. Cover with cold water, bring slowly to boil, and remove scum. Add seasonings and onion. Simmer, covered, for 2½ to 3 hours, until meat is very tender. Remove meat and bones from broth. Strain broth and cook down until it measures about half. Chop meat fine. Put a little broth in oiled bowl or loaf tin. Arrange slices of eggs and olives in pretty pattern. Put in refrigerator until broth is set. Combine meat and remaining broth, pour into mold, and chill for several hours until set. Unmold; garnish with sprigs of fresh herbs and sliced cucumbers, if desired. Makes 8 servings.

FRANKFURTERS AND NOODLES

1 onion, chopped
¼ cup butter or margarine
1 can (19 ounces) tomatoes
4 ounces wide noodles
1 teaspoon sugar
4 frankfurters, cut into 1-inch pieces
½ cup grated Cheddar cheese
Salt and pepper to taste

Cook onion in the butter in skillet until golden. Add tomatoes, noodles, and sugar. Bring to boil and simmer, uncovered, for 20 minutes, stirring frequently. Add remaining ingredients, and heat. Makes 4 servings.

BOILED POTPIE

1 stewing chicken (3 pounds)
2 quarts water
2 teaspoons salt
4 potatoes, quartered
1 onion, diced
1 tablespoon minced parsley
Pepper
Dough Squares

Cover chicken with the water, add the salt, and stew until almost tender. Add potatoes, onion, parsley, and pepper to taste. Drop Dough Squares into boiling broth, one by one, covering whole top of stew. When half of squares have been added, stir before adding the rest. Cover tightly and continue boiling for 20 minutes, or until squares have a "spongy" texture when cut with a fork. Makes 6 to 8 servings.

Dough Squares

2 eggs
1 tablespoon shortening
1 teaspoon baking powder
½ teaspoon salt
1½ cups (about) all-purpose flour

Mix first 4 ingredients with spoon. Then add flour until stiff enough to roll out to ⅛-inch thickness; cut into squares. Drop into boiling broth. A few drops of yellow food coloring can be added to dough if desired.

SWEET-POTATO SAUSAGE CAKES

1 pound bulk sausage
2 teaspoons salt
4 cups shredded raw sweet potatoes

Combine all ingredients and blend well. Put in 1- to 1½-quart casserole. Bake, covered, in preheated moderate oven (350°F.) for about 45 minutes, uncovering for last 15 minutes. Makes 8 servings.

VEGETABLES, MEAT ACCOMPANIMENTS, AND SALADS

STEWED POTATOES

1 medium onion, sliced
2 tablespoons butter or margarine
2 cups diced potato
Salt and pepper
1½ cups boiling water
2 teaspoons all-purpose flour

Cook onion in the butter for 2 or 3 minutes. Add remaining ingredients except flour. Bring to boil, cover, and simmer for 15 minutes, or until potatoes are tender. Thicken with the flour blended with a little cold water. Add more salt and pepper to taste. Makes 4 servings.

POTATOES AND TURNIPS

3 large baking potatoes
2 cups mashed cooked turnip
3 tablespoons butter or margarine
Hot milk
Salt and pepper

Scrub potatoes. Bake in preheated very hot oven (450°F.) for 45 minutes, or until done. Cut potatoes into halves lengthwise and scoop out pulp. Add turnip and butter, and mix well. Beat in enough hot milk to make mixture light and fluffy. Season with salt and pepper to taste, and pile lightly into potato shells. Put back in oven to brown lightly. Makes 6 servings.

BERKS COUNTY POTATO FILLING

1 cup mashed potatoes
2 eggs, beaten
1 cup milk
4 slices of bread
1 small onion, diced
2 tablespoons butter or margarine
Salt and pepper to taste

Thoroughly mix mashed potatoes and eggs, using a fork. Add milk and set aside. Cut bread into ½-inch cubes and brown with onion in the butter. Stir onion and bread into potato mixture and add seasonings. Turn into a greased cas-

Funnel Cakes or Plowlines

serole and bake in preheated moderate oven (375°F.) for 1 hour. Makes 6 servings.

Note: This is served as a vegetable.

BOOVA SHENKEL
(Filled Noodles)

2½ cups all-purpose flour
½ teaspoon baking powder
Salt
3 tablespoons shortening
1 egg, well beaten
Water
Potato Filling
Butter

Sift flour with baking powder and ½ teaspoon salt. Cut in shortening until mix-

Pennsylvania Dutch Apple Butter

Chowchow

Corn Pie

ture is crumbly. Add egg and enough water (about ¾ cup) to make a dough with the consistency of piecrust. On a lightly floured board roll out dough into 6- to 8-inch circles. Put ⅛ of the Potato Filling on each round. Moisten edges of dough with water. Fold dough over filling and press edges together. These will have the shape of half-moons. Drop filled noodles into boiling salted water or broth and simmer for 30 minutes. Remove from broth and drain. Heat butter in a large skillet and brown filled noodles until golden on both sides. Makes 8 servings.

Potato Filling

4 cooked potatoes, peeled and mashed
½ teaspoon salt
   Dash of pepper
3 tablespoons butter or margarine, melted
¼ cup minced onion
2 tablespoons minced parsley
2 eggs, well beaten
¼ cup dry bread crumbs
¼ cup minced celery

Mix all ingredients thoroughly and fill noodles as directed.

FRIED APPLES

6 cooking apples
¼ cup butter
   Brown sugar

Quarter and core apples, but do not peel. Melt butter in frying pan. Place apples skin side down in pan. Sprinkle generously with sugar, add a little water, cover, and cook very slowly until tender and candied. Eat hot. Makes 6 servings.

CORN PIE

8 slices of bacon, cut into halves
2 cups fine dry bread crumbs
1 green pepper, seeded and minced
2 cups chopped fresh tomatoes
3 cups uncooked fresh corn kernels cut from the cob
1½ teaspoons salt
¼ teaspoon pepper
1 teaspoon sugar

Put 4 slices of the bacon in the bottom of a shallow 2-quart casserole. Top with half of bread crumbs. Add in layers green peppers, tomatoes, and corn, which have been seasoned with salt, pepper, and sugar. Sprinkle remaining bread crumbs over top, and cover with remaining bacon. Bake in preheated moderate oven (375° F.) for 1 hour, or until top is lightly browned. Makes 6 servings.

SOUR GREEN BEANS

- 4 cups cooked green beans, cut into 1-inch lengths
- 1/3 cup cider vinegar
- 1/3 cup water
- 1/3 cup firmly packed light brown sugar
- 1/2 teaspoon salt
- 1/4 teaspoon pepper

Drain beans. Simmer vinegar with water and brown sugar for 5 minutes. Add beans, salt, and pepper. Bring to a boil and serve. Makes 6 to 8 servings.

DRIED CORN

- 2 cups dried corn
- Water
- 1 teaspoon salt
- 2 teaspoons sugar
- 3/4 cup light cream

Cover dried corn with water. Add salt and simmer until corn is tender and water absorbed. Add sugar and cream. Reheat but do not boil. Makes 6 to 8 servings.

WILTED LETTUCE

- 6 slices of bacon
- 6 to 8 green onions
- 1 tablespoon sugar
- 1/3 cup vinegar
- 1/2 teaspoon pepper
- 2 or 3 heads garden lettuce, washed and leaves separated

Cut bacon into small pieces and fry in skillet until crisp. Remove bacon to drain on paper towels. Slice onions, both bulbs and tops, into bacon fat in skillet. Add sugar, vinegar, and pepper. Cook for 2 or 3 minutes; pour over lettuce in salad bowl, mixing lightly. Top with crisp bacon. Serve immediately. Makes 4 to 6 servings.

DANDELION SALAD

- 1 1/2 pounds dandelion greens
- 1/4 pound bacon, diced
- 3/4 cup light cream
- 3 eggs, well beaten
- 1 tablespoon sugar
- 1/3 cup cider vinegar
- 1 1/2 teaspoon salt
- 1 teaspoon paprika

Wash and trim dandelion greens. Drain well and place in a salad bowl. Fry bacon until crisp. Remove crisp pieces and drain off all but 3 tablespoons of the bacon fat. Add cream and blend well. Beat eggs with sugar, vinegar, salt, and paprika. Gradually stir into cream mixture. Cook over low heat, stirring constantly, until slightly thickened. Pour hot dressing over dandelion greens and toss well. Sprinkle with crisp pieces of bacon. Makes 6 servings.

POOR MAN'S GRAVY

- 3 tablespoons butter or margarine
- 3 tablespoons all-purpose flour
- 2 cups milk or water
- Salt and pepper

Melt butter and stir in flour. Cook over low heat, stirring constantly, until flour is dark brown. Gradually stir in milk and cook over low heat, stirring constantly, until sauce is smooth and thickened. Season to taste. Serve spooned over new potatoes cooked in their jackets. Makes about 2 cups.

GRANDMOTHER STOUGHTON'S TOMATO GRAVY

In an iron skillet put a big spoonful of butter. Let melt. Fill pan with peeled and slivered vine-ripened tomatoes. Sprinkle with flour from shaker. Cover with clabbered milk. Turn heat very low; cook long, brown slowly. Fill pan with clabbered milk, let simmer until thick, don't touch, don't stir. Add more butter now and then. Dunk or use as gravy.

BREADS

FRANCES CLARK'S ROLLS

- 1 package active dry yeast or 1 cake compressed yeast
- 1/2 cup water*
- 2/3 cup shortening
- 1 cup milk, scalded
- 1/2 cup sugar
- 1 teaspoon salt
- 2 eggs, beaten
- 5 cups (about) all-purpose flour

Sprinkle or crumble yeast into water. *Use very warm water (105°F. to 115° F.) for dry yeast; use lukewarm (80°F. to 90°F.) for compressed. Let stand for a few minutes, then stir until dissolved. Put shortening in milk and stir until melted. Add sugar, salt, and eggs. Combine with yeast in big bowl. Add half of flour, beat hard, and let stand until bubbly. Add rest of flour, more if necessary to form dough. Knead, put in greased bowl, cover, and set in refrigerator to rise. Shape rolls as desired, let rise, and bake in preheated hot oven (400°F.) for 10 to 15 minutes. Makes about 3 dozen.

WELSCH KORNKUCHE
(Corn Cake)

- 4 cups yellow cornmeal
- Water (about 2 1/4 cups)
- 1/2 package active dry yeast or 1/2 cake compressed yeast
- 1/2 cup water*
- 1 teaspoon salt
- 3 eggs, well beaten
- 1 1/2 teaspoons baking soda

Mix cornmeal with water until of the consistency of thick applesauce. Sprinkle or crumble yeast into water. *Use very warm water (105°F. to 115°F.) for dry yeast; use lukewarm (80°F. to 90°F.) for compressed. Let stand for a few minutes, then stir until dissolved. Add dissolved yeast and salt to cornmeal and let stand, covered, overnight. Beat well and stir in remaining ingredients. Spoon mixture into a well-greased loaf pan (9 x 5 x 3 inches). Bake in preheated moderate oven (350°F.) for 1 hour. Unmold and cool slightly. Cut into slices and serve. Makes 8 servings.

BUCKWHEAT CAKES

- 1 package active dry yeast or 1 cake compressed yeast
- 1/2 cup water*
- 2 1/2 cups buckwheat flour
- 1 teaspoon salt
- 2 tablespoons blackstrap molasses
- 2 cups buttermilk
- 1/2 teaspoon baking soda

Sprinkle or crumble yeast into water. *Use very warm water (105°F. to 115° F.) for dry yeast; use lukewarm (80°F. to 90°F.) for compressed. Let stand for a few minutes, then stir until dissolved. Put flour and salt in bowl; add molasses, buttermilk, and yeast. Mix well and cover. Let stand overnight. In the morning add baking soda. Bake on hot greased griddle. Makes fifteen 5-inch cakes. If there is a cupful or more batter left, keep covered in refrigerator overnight to use as starter for the next batch. Next morning add 1/2 cup lukewarm water, 1/4 teaspoon each of salt and baking soda, and 1 cup buckwheat flour. Mix well.

SOUR-MILK GRIDDLE CAKES

- 1 cup sifted all-purpose flour
- 1/4 teaspoon cream of tartar
- 1/2 teaspoon each of baking soda and salt
- 1 egg, beaten
- 1 cup thick sour milk or buttermilk
- 1 teaspoon melted butter

Sift dry ingredients. Combine last 3 ingredients, add to dry ingredients, and stir until smooth. Brown on hot greased griddle. Makes twelve 4-inch griddle cakes.

STICKY CINNAMON BUNS

- 1 package active dry yeast or 1 cake compressed yeast
- 1/3 cup water*
- 1/2 cup shortening
- 3/4 cup milk, scalded
- 3 1/2 cups (about) sifted all-purpose flour
- 1 teaspoon salt
- 10 tablespoons (about 2/3 cup) granulated sugar
- 2 eggs
- 1 cup light corn syrup
- 1/4 cup soft butter
- 3/4 cup firmly packed light brown sugar
- 2 teaspoons ground cinnamon
- 1/2 cup hickory or black walnut meats
- 1/4 cup dried currants

Sprinkle or crumble yeast into water. *Use very warm water (105°F. to 115°

F.) for dry yeast; use lukewarm (80°F. to 90°F.) for compressed. Let stand for a few minutes, then stir until dissolved. Add shortening to milk, cool to lukewarm, and add yeast. Add 1½ cups of the flour, the salt, and 2 tablespoons granulated sugar. Beat until smooth. Cover, set bowl in warm place, and let stand until spongy and bubbly. Add eggs, one at a time, and add remaining granulated sugar. Beat in about 2 cups of the flour, enough to make a soft dough. Turn out on floured board and knead for about 10 minutes, until smooth and elastic. Return to greased bowl, cover, and let rise until doubled in bulk. Punch dough down, turn out on floured board, let stand for 5 minutes.

Meanwhile grease two 9-inch square cake pans and pour ½ cup syrup into each pan. Divide dough into halves. Roll one half to rectangle (9 x 14 inches), spread with half of the butter, and sprinkle with half of the brown sugar, cinnamon, nuts, and currants. Roll as a jelly roll; cut into nine 1-inch slices. Arrange cut side down in pan of syrup. Repeat with second portion of dough.

Cover pans of buns; let rise in warm place until doubled in bulk. Bake in preheated moderate oven (350°F.) for 35 minutes. Turn out of pans immediately and place on trays, bottom side up, before syrup hardens. Makes 18 buns.

DUMPLING BATTER
1 cup all-purpose flour
1 tablespoon melted shortening
½ teaspoon each of salt and
   baking powder
½ cup milk

Mix ingredients. For richer dumplings beat 1 egg and add enough milk to make cup half full. Drop by tablespoonfuls on top of simmering stew. Cover and cook for 15 minutes.

DESSERTS

RHUBARB PUDDING
1 egg
⅛ teaspoon salt
1 cup granulated sugar (or less for
   frozen rhubarb)
3 cups diced fresh or frozen rhubarb
¼ cup butter or margarine
¾ cup all-purpose flour
½ cup firmly packed brown sugar

Beat egg until thick and lemon-colored with salt and granulated sugar; pour over rhubarb. Put in well-buttered 8-inch square pan. Over the top sprinkle a *streusel* made by rubbing the butter into the flour and brown sugar. Bake in preheated moderate oven (350°F.) for about 45 minutes. Serve slightly warm, plain or

with cream, if desired. Makes 6 servings.

CINNAMON FLOP
3 tablespoons melted butter or
   margarine
1½ cups sugar
2 eggs, well beaten
2¼ cups all-purpose flour
2 teaspoons baking powder
1 cup milk
1 cup firmly packed dark brown sugar
¼ cup butter or margarine
   Plenty of ground cinnamon

Mix melted butter with sugar. Beat in eggs. Sift flour with baking powder and add alternately with the milk, beginning and ending with the flour. Spread mixture in a well-buttered 9-inch square pan. Sprinkle top with brown sugar, dot with butter, and sprinkle with ground cinnamon. Bake in preheated hot oven (400°F.) for about 30 minutes. Serve warm, cut into squares. Makes one 9-inch square.

STEAMED MOLASSES PUDDING
2 cups sifted all-purpose flour
½ teaspoon salt
½ teaspoon each of ground cinnamon
   and nutmeg
¼ teaspoon each of ground cloves and
   ginger
1 teaspoon baking soda
1 egg, slightly beaten
1 cup molasses
½ cup cold water
½ cup each of diced candied fruit and
   white raisins

Mix flour, salt, spices, and baking soda. Combine egg, molasses, and water; pour into dry ingredients; mix thoroughly. Stir in candied fruit and raisins. Pour into 2 greased 1-pound coffee tins. Cover and steam for 3 to 4 hours. Serve hot with lemon sauce.

PIES

AMISH VANILLA PIE
Pastry for 1-crust 9-inch pie,
unbaked

Liquid:
½ cup firmly packed brown sugar
1 tablespoon all-purpose flour
1 egg, well beaten
¼ cup dark corn syrup
1 teaspoon vanilla extract
1 cup water

Crumbs:
1 cup all-purpose flour
½ cup firmly packed light brown sugar
½ teaspoon cream of tartar
½ teaspoon baking soda
2 tablespoons butter
2 tablespoons lard or shortening

Line 9-inch pie pan with the pastry. Combine the ingredients for the liquid mixture in the order given, mixing after each addition and adding the water very gradually. Bring to a full rolling boil,

then set aside to cool. Combine ingredients for the crumbs, using hands to blend. Pour cooled cooked liquid into the unbaked pastry; top with crumbs. Bake in preheated moderate oven (350°F.) for 40 minutes, or until firm. Makes 6 to 8 servings.

SOUR-CREAM HUCKLEBERRY PIE
Pastry for 1-crust 9-inch pie, unbaked
1 quart huckleberries
½ to ¾ cup sugar
1 tablespoon all-purpose flour
   Few grains of salt
1 cup dairy sour cream
   Juice of ½ lemon

Line pie pan with pastry. Put washed and well-drained berries in crust. Mix sugar, flour, and salt; amount of sugar depends upon sweetness of berries. Add sour cream and lemon juice. Pour over huckleberries. Bake in preheated hot oven (425°F.) for 10 minutes, reduce heat to slow (325°F.) and bake for 30 minutes longer. Cool before serving. Makes 6 servings.

LEMON STRIP PIE
Pastry for 1-crust 9-inch pie, unbaked
1 tablespoon butter
½ cup sugar
   Grated rind and juice of 1 small
   lemon
1 egg, well beaten
2 tablespoons all-purpose flour
½ cup white corn syrup
½ cup water
   Sweet Dough for strips

Line pie pan with pastry, fluting a high edge. Cream butter and gradually stir in sugar; add lemon rind and juice, egg, and flour. Stir in corn syrup and gradually stir in water. Pour this mixture into lined pie pan. Roll Sweet Dough on lightly floured board to the size of the top of the pie. Cut into 1-inch strips. Place dough strips over the filling, about ¼ inch apart, taking care not to cross them, just placing strips on top of filling. Bake in preheated moderate oven (350°F.) for 40 minutes. Cool thoroughly before serving. Makes 6 to 8 servings.

Sweet Dough
Cream 1 tablespoon lard with 2 tablespoons light brown sugar. Beat in 1 small egg, well beaten. Stir in about ¾ cup all-purpose flour mixed with ½ teaspoon baking powder. Knead on a lightly floured board.

FUNERAL PIE
Pastry for 2-crust 9-inch pie, unbaked
3 tablespoons cornstarch
½ cup sugar
1¾ cups water
2½ cups seedless raisins
2 tablespoons fresh lemon juice
1 teaspoon grated lemon rind
½ teaspoon salt
2 tablespoons butter

Line pie pan with pastry. Mix cornstarch with sugar. Gradually stir in water. Add raisins and cook over low heat, stirring constantly, until mixture thickens. Remove from heat and stir in remaining ingredients. Pour mixture into pie pan. Cover with top crust, slit crust to allow steam to escape, and seal edges with water. Bake in preheated hot oven (400° F.) for 30 minutes. Serve warm. Makes 6 to 8 servings.

SPICY SHOOFLY PIE

Pastry for 1-crust 9-inch pie, unbaked

Crumb Mixture:

- ¾ cup all-purpose flour
- ½ cup firmly packed brown sugar
- ½ teaspoon each of salt and ground cinnamon
- ⅛ teaspoon each of ground ginger, nutmeg, and cloves
- 2 tablespoons shortening

Liquid:

- ½ cup molasses
- 1 egg, well beaten
- ½ teaspoon baking soda
- ¾ cup hot water

Line pie pan with pastry. Combine ingredients for crumb mixture, using hands to blend. Combine ingredients for liquid and pour into pastry. Top with crumbs. Bake in preheated hot oven (400°F.) for 10 minutes. Reduce heat to slow (325°F.); continue baking for about 30 minutes, or until firm. Makes 6 to 8 servings.

CAKES AND COOKIES

FUNNY CAKE

Pastry for 1-crust 9-inch pie, unbaked

Lower part:

- ½ cup sugar
- ⅓ cup cocoa
- ⅓ cup hot water
- ½ teaspoon vanilla extract

Upper part:

- ⅔ cup sugar
- ⅓ cup shortening
- 1 egg, well beaten

Sour Green Beans **Pigs' Knuckles and Sauerkraut with Caraway Dumplings** **Spicy Shoofly Pie**

⅔ cup milk
1 teaspoon baking powder
1 cup sifted all-purpose flour
1 teaspoon vanilla extract

Line pie pan with pastry. Mix sugar with cocoa, hot water, and vanilla. Pour mixture into pie pan. Mix sugar with shortening. Beat in egg and milk. Stir in baking powder and flour. Stir in vanilla. Beat until smooth. Pour mixture over cocoa mixture. Bake in preheated moderate oven (350°F.) for 40 minutes, or until top springs back when lightly touched. Makes 6 to 8 servings.

FUNNEL CAKES OR PLOWLINES
3 eggs, well beaten
2 cups milk
4 cups sifted all-purpose flour
⅓ cup sugar
½ teaspoon salt
1 tablespoon baking powder
Fat or oil for deep frying
Confectioners' sugar

Beat eggs with milk and gradually beat in flour, sugar, salt, and baking powder. Beat until very smooth. Holding the opening of a funnel closed, fill the funnel with the batter. Open the end of the funnel and allow dough to run out in a stream into deep hot fat (375°F. on a frying thermometer). Move the funnel to make a pattern, starting at the center of the pan and swirling batter outward in a circle. Fry for 2 or 3 minutes, or until brown. Drain on absorbent paper and sprinkle with confectioners' sugar. Makes about 30 cakes, depending on size.

BLOTCH KUCHA OR SUGAR LEB CAKE
⅓ cup butter or margarine
⅓ cup lard
1½ cups firmly packed light brown sugar
2 eggs
1 cup buttermilk
3 cups all-purpose flour
1 teaspoon baking powder
½ teaspoon baking soda
1 cup coarsely chopped walnuts

Cream butter and lard until light and fluffy. Gradually beat in sugar. Beat 1 egg and stir into mixture. Gradually stir in buttermilk. Sift flour with baking powder and baking soda. Add dry ingredients to creamed ingredients. Blend well. Spread mixture in a well-greased jelly-roll pan (15 x 10 inches). Beat remaining 1 egg and spread over top of the cake. Sprinkle with nuts. Bake in preheated moderate oven (350°F.) for about 30 minutes, or until top springs back when touched lightly. Cut into 3- x 2-inch pieces.

APEA CAKE
4 cups sifted all-purpose flour
2 teaspoons baking powder
1 teaspoon baking soda (scant)
2 cups firmly packed light brown sugar
1 cup lard (scant)
1 egg, well beaten
Milk

Sift flour with baking powder and baking

soda. Stir in brown sugar. Cut in lard until mixture is crumbly. Beat egg in cup and fill cup with milk. Add milk and egg to dry ingredients. Pour mixture into 2 greased and floured 8-inch layer-cake pans. Bake in preheated moderate oven (375°F.) for 25 to 30 minutes. Unmold and cool on rack. Use as a breakfast cake. Makes 10 to 12 servings.

SOUR-CREAM SUGAR CAKES
¾ cup shortening and butter combined
2 cups sugar
3 eggs
1 cup dairy sour cream
4 cups sifted all-purpose flour
1 teaspoon each of baking soda, baking powder, and salt

Cream shortening and butter with sugar. Add eggs, one at a time, mixing thoroughly. Add sour cream alternately with last 4 ingredients mixed together. Drop by tablespoons onto greased and floured cookie sheets. Sprinkle lightly with sugar. Bake in preheated moderate oven (350°F.) for 10 minutes, or until golden. Makes about 4 dozen cookies, depending on size.

POTATO OR RAISED CAKE
1 cup shortening
1 cup mashed potatoes
1 cup sugar
1 egg
1 cup milk and potato water or plain water
1 package active dry yeast or 1 cake compressed yeast
1 cup water*
1 tablespoon salt
7 cups sifted all-purpose flour
Molasses
Crumb Topping

Mix well shortening, mashed potatoes, sugar, and egg. Heat milk to lukewarm and add to potato mixture. Sprinkle or crumble yeast into water. *Use very warm water (105°F. to 115°F.) for dry yeast; use lukewarm water (80°F. to 90° F.) for compressed. Let stand for a few minutes, then stir until dissolved. Add dissolved yeast and salt to potato mixture. Add flour, a few cupfuls at a time. When dough clings together and leaves side of bowl, turn out on a heavily floured board and knead until smooth and elastic. Then put in greased bowl and let rise until doubled in bulk. Cut into 6 portions. Flatten dough and put each round in a well-buttered 8-inch pie pan. Let rise again until doubled.

Using finger, punch holes around top of cake. Dribble about 1 tablespoon molasses into holes and around top of cake. Sprinkle with Crumb Topping. Dribble a little more molasses over top. Bake in preheated moderate oven (350° F.) for 25 to 30 minutes. Makes 6 cakes, 6 servings each.

Crumb Topping
2 cups sifted all-purpose flour
⅔ cup firmly packed dark brown sugar
½ cup shortening
Pinch of salt

Mix until ingredients are crumbled.

OLD-FASHIONED MOLASSES COOKIES
1 cup soft butter or margarine
1 cup sugar
2 eggs
1 cup molasses
4 cups all-purpose flour
1 teaspoon each of salt, baking soda, and ground ginger

Cream butter and sugar until light. Beat in eggs. Add molasses and sifted dry ingredients. Mix well. Chill for 2 to 3 hours. Roll out on lightly floured board to ⅛-inch thickness. Cut with floured 3½-inch cookie cutter. Bake in preheated moderate oven (375°F.) for about 10 minutes. Makes about 3 dozen.

YORK HERMITS
1 cup butter
2½ cups sifted all-purpose flour
1 teaspoon baking soda
½ teaspoon salt
1½ cups sugar
3 eggs, slightly beaten
¾ pound seeded raisins
2 cups mixed nuts, the bigger the variety the better

Work butter into flour, baking soda, and salt. Add sugar. Beat in eggs, one at a time. Add raisins and nuts and mix well. Drop by teaspoonfuls onto greased cookie sheets. Bake in preheated moderate oven (375°F.) for about 10 minutes. Makes about 3 dozen cookies, depending on size.

FASTNACHTS
3 packages active dry yeast or 3 cakes compressed yeast
¾ cup water*
2 cups milk, scalded and cooled to lukewarm
2 eggs, beaten
½ cup sugar
2 teaspoons salt
¼ cup shortening
7 cups (about) sifted all-purpose flour
Cooking oil

Sprinkle or crumble yeast into water in large bowl. *Use very warm water (105° F. to 115°F.) for dry yeast; use lukewarm (80°F. to 90°F.) for compressed. Let stand for a few minutes, then stir until dissolved. Add next 5 ingredients and mix. Add enough flour to make a stiff dough. Let rest for 10 minutes. Turn out on lightly floured board and knead until smooth. Roll into a rectangle ¾ inch thick. Cut with a floured doughnut cutter, or cut into 2-inch squares. Let rise for 10 minutes. Fry in deep hot oil (350°F. on frying thermometer) until just delicately browned on both sides. Drain on absorbent paper and cool. Roll in granulated sugar if desired. Store airtight. Makes 4 dozen fastnachts.

PENUCHE, PANOCHA, or PENUCHI

—This is a candy made from brown sugar which is cooked to the soft-ball stage (234° to 240°F. on a candy thermometer), cooled to lukewarm, and then beaten until smooth and creamy. It can be either dropped by teaspoonfuls onto a cookie sheet and allowed to harden, or poured into a pan and cut into squares like fudge. The surface of the cookie sheet or pan should be buttered.

The name of the candy comes from the Mexican-Spanish *panocha,* meaning raw sugar. Nuts are often added to penuche.

PECAN PENUCHE

2½ cups firmly packed
    dark brown sugar
1 cup evaporated milk, undiluted
⅛ teaspoon salt
3 tablespoons butter
    or margarine
1 cup chopped pecans
1 teaspoon vanilla extract

Cook sugar, milk, salt, and butter in a saucepan. Cook to soft-ball stage (236° F. on a candy thermometer). Let cool slightly; stir in nuts and extract. Beat until creamy. Pour into buttered 8-inch-square pan. Cut into 1-inch squares. Makes 64 pieces.

PEPPER (Capsicum)—The many-seeded fruit of a genus of herbs or shrubs which originated in tropical America, and was first cultivated by pre-Incan tribes over 2,000 years ago. The capsicum family is a very large one, and its fruits vary in size, shape, color, and pungency. In general the members of the family can be divided into two types: the sweet, larger-fruited, bell or bull-nose peppers; and the smaller-fruited, hotter, and more pungent chili and cayenne peppers. Sweet peppers are green at maturity but turn red as they continue to mature, and are found in food stores in both stages. Some are long, comparatively slender, and pointed. Others are short, chunky, and wide. One heart-shape and particularly sweet-flavored variety, the pimiento, is widely used for commercial canning. Sweet peppers are eaten raw in salads, cooked as a vegetable, and used as an ingredient in many meat and vegetable dishes.

The more pungent varieties, too, can be purchased green, yellowish-green, or red, although most generally they are used in the red stage. They range in size from the small chili varieties to peppers almost as large as the sweet types, but they tend to have thinner flesh than sweet peppers. Sometimes they are strung and dried; occasionally the entire plant, with peppers attached, is dried. They are also dried and crushed. These hotter pepper varieties are used whole to make vinegars and pickles. In Mexican, Caribbean, and South American cuisines they are often combined with other ingredients in cooked dishes. *Chili con carne* is perhaps the best known in the United States.

The condiments paprika, chili powder, cayenne or red pepper, and crushed red pepper (also called pizza pepper) are all made from dried and ground or crushed peppers of various degrees of pungency.

Availability—All year round, with peak months from June through November. The most popular sweet varieties are the California Wonder, a large, smooth, dark-green type which turns crimson as it matures and is short, chunky, and wide; Chinese Giant, another chunky type, noted for its mild flavor, bright scarlet coloring and 4-ridged fruit; pimiento, a sweet-flavored heart-shape variety; Ruby King, long and thin with thick flesh and bright red when ripe; Sunnybrook, which resembles a somewhat flattened tomato and is about 3 inches in diameter.

Among the widely available pungent types are the cayenne peppers which bear fruits about 5 inches long, often curled and twisted and noted for their hot flavor; and slender hot chilies, yellowish-green or red in color. Tabasco, a small-fruited variety measuring 1½ inches in length, and about ⅜ of an inch in diameter is widely grown and available throughout the southern states.

Also available are canned pimientos, whole or in broken pieces; hot pepper sauce; pickled hot peppers, both red and green; and dried hot peppers, both whole and crushed. Dried hot peppers are also found in mixed pickling spice; and pimiento is used in stuffed olives. Stuffed green peppers are available frozen.

Purchasing Guide—Good quality peppers must be mature, firm, well-shaped, thick-fleshed for their variety, and of good color and fresh appearance. Avoid shriveled, limp, tough, blemished peppers. Pale color denotes immaturity and these should be avoided.

Storage—Peppers should be refrigerated, covered.

☐ Refrigerator shelf, raw: 4 to 5 days
☐ Refrigerator shelf, cooked: 1 to 2 days
☐ Refrigerator frozen-food compartment, prepared for freezing: 2 to 3 months
☐ Freezer, prepared for freezing: 1 year

Nutritive Food Values—Red and green peppers are a good source of vitamin C, some vitamin A (red peppers contain more vitamin A than green) as well as small quantities of calcium, phosphorus, iron, sodium, magnesium, thiamin, riboflavin, and niacin.

☐ Green, 3½ ounces, raw = 22 calories
☐ Green, 3½ ounces, boiled and drained = 18 calories
☐ Red, raw = 31 calories
☐ Pimientos, canned, solids and liquids = 27 calories

Basic Preparation—Wash. Cut off tops and remove seeds and ribs. Peppers may be left whole, or cut into halves, strips, rings or dices.

☐ **To Stuff and Bake**—If peppers are to be stuffed and baked, they should first be cooked in boiling salted water for 5 minutes. Drain; stuff; bake in preheated moderate oven (375°F.) for 25 to 30 minutes.

☐ **To Freeze**—(Peppers lose their crispness when frozen, but can still be used very satisfactorily for cooking.) Wash peppers and remove seeds and membranes. Cut into halves, slice, or dice. Scald halves for 3 minutes; sliced and diced 2 minutes. Chill, package, and freeze. Peppers can also be packed and frozen without scalding. Pimiento peppers can be peeled easily if first roasted in preheated hot oven (400°F.) for 3 or 4 minutes, or until peel is charred. Peel can then be rubbed off. Cool peeled pimientos and pack dry. Hot peppers can be washed and packaged without scalding.

HAMBURGER PEPPER STEAKS

2 pounds ground beef
2 tablespoons butter or margarine
¼ cup soy sauce
2 tablespoons sherry
1 tablespoon cornstarch
2 teaspoons sugar
½ cup water
4 green peppers, cut into eighths

Shape meat into 6 oval steaks. Brown lightly in margarine. Mix remaining ingredients except peppers and pour over meat. Add green peppers. Cover; cook over medium heat for 8 to 10 minutes, or until meat is of desired doneness and peppers are still crisp. Makes 6 servings.

BEEF-AND-RICE STUFFED PEPPERS

4 large green peppers
½ pound ground beef
1 small onion, minced
1 cup cooked rice

½ teaspoon salt
⅛ teaspoon paprika
¼ teaspoon each of celery seeds, curry
powder, and Worcestershire
¼ cup soft bread crumbs, buttered

Wash peppers; remove stem ends, seeds, and membranes. Cook in 1 cup boiling salted water for 5 minutes; drain. Brown beef and onion, stirring with fork. Add remaining ingredients except bread crumbs; mix well. Fill peppers with meat mixture; top with crumbs. Bake in preheated moderate oven (350°F.) for about 30 minutes. Makes 4 servings.

HASH-STUFFED PEPPERS WITH CABBAGE

4 large sweet green peppers
2 cans (16 ounces each) corned-beef hash
2 tablespoons butter or margarine
1 onion, chopped
2 cans (8 ounces each) tomato sauce
½ cup water
2 teaspoons dark brown sugar
Salt and pepper to taste
1 small head green cabbage, cut into quarters

Cut tops from green peppers and remove seeds and membranes. Cook for 4 or 5 minutes in boiling water; drain. In skillet sauté corned-beef hash, stirring often. Remove peppers and fill with hash. Melt butter in same skillet and sauté onion until golden; add tomato sauce, water, and brown sugar; season with salt and pepper. Add stuffed peppers and wedges of cabbage. Cover and cook slowly until cabbage is tender. Top each pepper with some sauce, or with ketchup. Makes 4 servings.

GREEN-PEPPER-AND-BEEF OVEN STEW

2 pounds beef stew meat
¼ cup all-purpose flour
4 teaspoons salt
1 garlic clove, chopped fine
3 tablespoons shortening
1½ cups water
5 medium-size green peppers
2 cups sliced onions
2 cups diced tomatoes
¼ cup chopped parsley
½ teaspoon pepper

Trim meat and discard excess fat. Cut meat into 1-inch cubes. Blend flour with salt and mix with the meat. Brown with garlic in hot shortening. Turn into 2-quart casserole. Add water. Cover and cook in preheated slow oven (325°F.) for 1¼ hours. Wash green peppers, cut out stems, and remove seeds and membranes. Cut peppers into 1½-inch pieces. Add to beef along with onions, tomatoes, parsley, and pepper. Cover; return to oven and cook for 20 minutes longer, or until vegetables are tender. Serve hot. This stew should be eaten the day it is made, because the green pepper has a tendency to fade on standing overnight. Makes 6 servings.

VEAL AND PEPPER LONG BOYS

French bread
Butter
1½ pounds veal cutlet, ½ inch thick
All-purpose flour
Salt and pepper
1 onion, chopped
3 tablespoons salad oil
Pinch of ground marjoram
¼ cup water
3 green peppers, quartered

Cut bread into four 6-inch lengths. Split; spread with butter. Pound cutlet to ¼-inch thickness. Cut into pieces to fit bread. Sprinkle with flour, salt, and pepper. Fry onion in oil until brown. Push aside. Brown veal; sprinkle with marjoram. Add water; cover and simmer for 30 minutes. Add green peppers and simmer for 15 minutes longer, or until veal and peppers are tender. Arrange meat and peppers on each Long Boy. Makes 4 servings.

CORN-STUFFED PIMIENTOS

1¼ cups drained canned whole-kernel corn
¾ cup soft bread crumbs
1 tablespoon chili sauce
1 teaspoon instant minced onion
3 tablespoons butter or margarine, melted
Salt and pepper to taste
4 to 6 well-drained canned pimientos

Mix corn and crumbs. Blend chili sauce and onion and add to corn mixture. Add remaining ingredients except pimientos. Put pimientos in shallow baking dish or pie pan and stuff with corn mixture. Bake in preheated hot oven (400°F.) for 10 to 15 minutes. Makes 4 to 6 servings.

PEPPERS STUFFED WITH RICE AND CHEESE

4 large sweet red peppers
1 cup uncooked rice
1 onion, minced
2 tablespoons butter or margarine
¾ cup water
½ pound American cheese
Salt and pepper
2 tablespoons chopped parsley

Select large peppers. Cut into halves and remove seeds. Put in boiling water and cook for 5 minutes. Drain, reserving liquid. Cook rice in boiling salted water until tender; drain. Cook onion in butter. Add water and cheese; stir until melted and blended. Stir in rice; season with salt and pepper to taste. Add parsley. Fill pepper halves. Put on rack in skillet or kettle with 1½ cups reserved pepper liquid; cover and simmer for about 15 minutes. Makes 4 servings.

ANCHOVY-STUFFED PEPPERS

4 sweet green peppers
2 cans (2 ounces each) rolled anchovy fillets with capers
¼ cup chopped onion
1 small garlic clove

¼ cup chopped pitted ripe olives
1 tablespoon minced parsley
4 cups soft bread crumbs
⅓ cup grated cheese
Salt and pepper

Cut thin slice from stem end of peppers and remove seeds and membranes. Cover peppers with boiling salted water; simmer for 5 minutes and drain. Drain oil from anchovies and sauté onion and garlic in the oil until onion is golden. Remove from heat, discard garlic, and add remaining ingredients except anchovies. Reserve 4 anchovies for tops of peppers and chop the rest. Add to crumb mixture and mix well. Season with salt and pepper. Fill peppers with anchovy mixture; top each with an anchovy, and place in baking dish with a little water. Bake in preheated moderate oven (350°F.) for 30 minutes. Makes 4 servings.

CREOLE STUFFED PEPPERS

4 large sweet green peppers
1 pound ground beef
2 cups cooked rice
½ teaspoon monosodium glutamate
Seasoned salt and pepper to taste
Creole Sauce

Split peppers; wash and remove seeds and membrane. Parboil for 5 minutes; drain. Cook beef until it loses red color. Pour off fat. Mix beef, rice, and seasonings. Add ¼ cup Creole Sauce. Pack peppers with mixture and put them in large shallow baking dish. Pour about 1½ cups Sauce around peppers. Cover; bake in preheated moderate oven (350°F.) for 45 minutes. Serve with remaining Creole Sauce, heated. Makes 8 servings.

Creole Sauce

Cook 1 chopped onion and ½ cup diced celery in 2 tablespoons butter for 5 minutes. Add 1 can (15½ ounces) spaghetti sauce, 1 can (8 ounces) tomato sauce, 1 cup water, 1 bay leaf, 2 whole cloves, and salt and pepper to taste. Simmer for 15 minutes. Makes about 3 cups.

FRIED EGGPLANT AND PIMIENTO LONG BOYS

Split 6-inch lengths of French bread, or use French rolls. Brush with olive oil and sprinkle with garlic salt. Cover one half with overlapping slices of panfried eggplant. On the other half put slices of pimiento.

SAUTÉED GREEN PEPPER STRIPS

6 large sweet green peppers
Boiling water
3 tablespoons cooking oil
Seasoned salt and pepper

Wash peppers, and remove seeds and membranes. Cut peppers in strips. Cover with boiling water and cook, covered, for 3 minutes. Drain, and sauté slowly in hot oil until lightly browned. Season to taste with salt and pepper. Makes 4 servings.

GRILLED GREEN PEPPERS

4 medium sweet green peppers
½ cup French dressing
Chopped green onion

Wash peppers, cut into quarters, and remove seeds and membrane. Put in dish, cover with French dressing, and marinate overnight. Cook outdoors in hinged broiler until peppers are tender. Or broil in range. Put in hot serving dish, and pour marinade over top. Sprinkle with green onion. Makes 4 servings.

PEPPERS AND TOMATOES

2 sweet green peppers, quartered
2 tablespoons butter
  or margarine
4 tomatoes, quartered
  Salt and pepper

Cook peppers in butter for 2 minutes. Add tomatoes, cover, and cook over low heat for about 10 minutes, stirring twice. Season with salt and pepper to taste. Makes 4 servings.

PEPPER SALAD, ITALIAN STYLE

Place sweet green peppers over direct heat of gas or electric stove. As the side exposed to the heat scorches, turn to scorch evenly on all sides. With sharp knife and using fingers also, remove scorched skin of peppers under running cold water. Cut off stems and remove seeds and membranes. Wash peppers and pat dry on paper towels. Cut into even strips. Place in flat bowl. Sprinkle with salt and pepper to taste and add olive oil, about 2 teaspoons for each pepper.

To make a popular Italian antipasto, arrange pepper strips on individual plate. Top with 2 anchovy fillets, arranged crosswise. Sprinkle with pepper, olive oil, and capers to taste. No salt is needed since the anchovy fillets and the capers are salty.

EGG, PEPPER, AND CHEESE SANDWICHES

Mix 4 chopped hard-cooked eggs with a little chopped green pepper and grated American cheese. Moisten with mayonnaise. Season with salt and pepper. Spread between slices of bread. Spread both sides of sandwiches with softened butter or margarine. Grill slowly until browned on both sides. Makes about 6 sandwiches.

MEXICAN CHILI SALSA

1 can (4 ounces) peeled green chilies, chopped
4 tomatoes, peeled, seeded, and diced
1 sweet green pepper, finely chopped
2 green onions, sliced
2 tablespoons red wine vinegar
½ teaspoon salt
¼ teaspoon each of pepper and crumbled dried oregano

Mix all ingredients. Chill well. Makes about 2 cups.

Note: A Mexican *salsa* or sauce of sweet and hot chilies makes a good cold relish to serve with meat or fish. If you prefer a hotter relish, add crushed dried hot chilies.

PEPPER RELISH

4 each medium, sweet green and red peppers
¾ cup vinegar
1 box powdered fruit pectin
3½ cups sugar

Cut open peppers and discard seeds and membranes. Put peppers through food chopper, using medium blade. Drain, and discard about half of juice. Measure 2 cups peppers with remaining juice into large saucepan. Add vinegar. Stir in pectin and bring to a hard boil over high heat, stirring. At once stir in sugar. Bring to a full rolling boil and boil hard for 1 minute, stirring. Remove from heat and skim off foam. Alternately stir and skim for 5 minutes to cool slightly and prevent any floating. Ladle into hot sterilized jars and seal. Makes about four ½-pint jars.

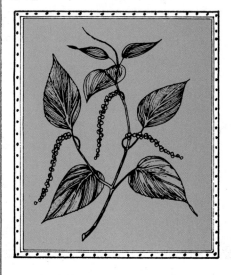

PEPPER (Piper nigrum)—The fruit of the pepper plant, a perennial climbing shrub indigenous to the forests of southwestern India, but now widely cultivated in warm countries throughout the world. It is the most popular spice in the world, for its familiar companion, salt, is not a spice at all but a mineral. The word "pepper" has been traced back through Greek to the Sanskrit *pippali*.

Both black and white pepper come from the dried berry of the same vine, which can grow up to twenty feet in its wild state and climbs on tree trunks like ivy. The berries for black pepper are picked when they are unripe and reddish in color. They grow on catkins, with about fifty berries to a spike. They are dried in the sun or smoked. When the spike is dry the berries are rubbed off, winnowed, and packed and shipped as the familiar black peppercorns. They are small reddish-brown or black pellets, with a wrinkled surface. They are sometimes cracked or ground before being sold, or can be ground by the user in a pepper mill as needed. This is perhaps the best system, for the whole berries keep their flavor longer than the ground ones.

The berries which will make white pepper are picked when they are slightly riper than those for black pepper. They are then fermented in piles or soaked in water to make it easy to remove the outer coating of the seed. Sometimes this coat is rubbed off by machine. The inner part is then shipped as white pepper. As might be expected white pepper is not as pungent as black pepper. Often the two are ground and mixed together to obtain certain degrees of hotness.

Pepper, whether black or white, or the now uncommon Long Pepper of Java, has long been esteemed as one of the world's most valuable spices. We take its availability for granted now, but it has not always been so plentiful. Black pepper was traded for centuries between India and Europe and was as precious as gold. In 408 A.D. when Rome was sacked by the Goths, the king of the Goths, Alaric, demanded as the city's ransom 3,000 pounds of pepper, as well as gold and silver.

After one of the battles won by the Crusaders busy with liberating the Holy Lands from their Moslem conquerors, the people of Genoa received more than 16,000 pounds of pepper as their share of the booty. And the subsequent sale of it made them rich.

Pepper was the most prized of all spices during the Middle Ages. The spice was so precious that it was often used as money. People received their pay in pepper or paid their rents with it. The guards who worked on the docks of medieval London had their pockets sewed up by anxious merchants so that they could not steal the rare spice.

The constant cry for pepper and its high price was one of the factors that induced the canny Portuguese explorers to look for an all-sea route to the Indies, where the treasure grew. Vasco da Gama, sailing around the Cape of Good Hope in South Africa, found such a route. By reaching the home of pepper, India's Malabar coast, he took the pepper trade away from the people of Genoa and Venice who had monopolized the overland routes by which it had traveled from the East. To compete with the Portuguese, other countries founded companies that dealt in spices, such as the Dutch, English, Danish, and French East

India companies.

The uses of pepper were not limited to the kitchen. A 15th-century English remedy recommended: "Take nine peppercorns for aching loins." The Middle Ages were the times of great plagues, and pepper was said to ward them off. Later-day people have sometimes argued that if you swallow a whole peppercorn every morning immediately upon arising for a week, severe cases of ague may be cured.

Pepper has played an important part in American history. Soon after the Revolution, an enterprising ship's captain from Salem, Massachusetts, managed to outwit the Dutch merchants who at that time monopolized the pepper trade. The wily Yankee arranged to trade directly with the growers in the East Indies, and on his first voyage brought back 150,000 pounds of pepper which he then sold at a 700 per cent profit. This was the start of the trade which was to make Salem a great shipping center, and the young United States a commercially active trading country.

There is a story that George Washington was instrumental in the devising of Philadelphia Pepper Pot Soup. The legend is that the tripe-based dish was created by a desperate chef for Washington and his troops at Valley Forge during the winter of 1777-1778. There was nothing available but tripe, peppercorns, and scraps, and Washington demanded something hot and cheering. The cook, who was from Philadelphia, named his solution after his hometown.

Pepper is available as whole peppercorns, cracked, coarsely or finely ground. Whole pepper remains flavorful for decades; ground pepper loses its aroma quickly and should not be stored for more than a month. Freshly ground pepper tastes best in all foods.

Use pepper in almost all foods except those with sweet flavors. Unlike other spices, pepper does not mask the flavor of foods but rather adds pungency which enhances and gives zest to any dish. Use white pepper where black specks are not desired, as in white sauces, clear soups, mashed potatoes, etc. Use whole in soups, stews, and pickling.

PEPPERGRASS (Lepidium sativum)—
Garden cress and shepherd's purse are other names for this annual spring herb. The plant grows to maturity very quickly; from seed to eating takes about three weeks. The flavor is similar to watercress and like watercress, it is used as a garnish or in salads.

PEPPERMINT (Mentha piperita)—An aromatic perennial herb found wild in damp lowland areas in the temperate zones of Europe, Asia, and America. It has a cool refreshing flavor. Peppermint is an important plant crop less for its leaves, which are used for flavoring, than for its oil. This oil is made by steam distillation after the crop, in full blossom, is dried and it is used widely for gum, candy, dentifrices, and other pharmaceutical preparations. Over one million pounds of peppermint oil are produced yearly in the United States from crops grown in Michigan, Indiana, and the Pacific Northwest States.

Peppermint, which, like spearmint, is a variety of the mint family, was grown for medicinal purposes in the medieval herb gardens of the monastic establishments of Europe. It is mentioned around 820 A.D. in the garden catalog of the great Abbey of St. Gall in Switzerland, one of the centers of medieval learning, whose library to this day, both architecturally and culturally, is one of the glories of Europe. The oil became so valuable that the mint herb was used for tithing.

The popularity of peppermint depends not only on its flavor, but also on its pleasant odor, which conjures up visions of cool streams and shady glens.

Oil of peppermint can be purchased in drugstores. It is widely used in medicines, dental preparations, and chewing gums. Peppermint extract is available wherever flavorings are sold. Extracts are made from oil of peppermint, about 85 percent alcohol, and water. Combination extracts made from peppermint and spearmint are also available. Peppermint oil and extract are used for flavoring mint candies, frostings, jelly, cakes, ice cream and other desserts, and beverages.

PEPPERMINT CHIFFON PIE
1 envelope unflavored gelatin
¾ cup sugar
¼ teaspoon salt
1 cup milk
4 eggs, separated
½ teaspoon each of vanilla and peppermint extracts
Red food coloring
Vanilla-Wafer Crust

In top part of double boiler mix gelatin, ¼ cup of the sugar, and the salt. Add milk and egg yolks, and beat slightly to blend. Put over simmering water and cook, stirring constantly, until mixture thickens and coats a metal spoon. Remove from heat; add flavorings and a few drops of food coloring. Chill until thickened but not firm. Beat egg whites until foamy; gradually add remaining sugar and beat until stiff but not dry. Fold into gelatin mixture. Pile lightly into Vanilla-Wafer Crust and chill until firm. Serve plain or spread with sweetened whipped cream. If desired, sprinkle with shaved chocolate.

Vanilla-Wafer Crust
Mix 1¼ cups finely crushed vanilla-wafer crumbs and ⅓ cup soft (not melted) butter or margarine. Using back of spoon, press mixture firmly and evenly on bottom and sides of buttered deep 9-inch pie pan. Press edge with finger tips to extend a little above pan. Bake in preheated moderate oven (350°F.) for about 10 minutes. Chill.

MARBLED PEPPERMINT-CHOCOLATE CREAM
1 package (3 ounces) vanilla pudding and pie filling
½ cup sugar
2 cups milk
1 cup heavy cream, whipped
3 drops oil of peppermint
Green food coloring
½ cup semisweet chocolate pieces, melted

Mix pudding, sugar, and milk in saucepan. Cook, stirring, until smooth and thickened. Cool; pour into freezing tray and chill. Fold in whipped cream and flavoring. Add just enough coloring to tint mixture a delicate green. Put in freezing tray and freeze until partially frozen. Swirl in chocolate to give a marbled effect; freeze until firm. Makes 6 servings.

PEPPERMINT FREEZE
1 envelope unflavored gelatin
2 cups milk
¾ cup crushed peppermint candy
2 eggs, slightly beaten
1 cup heavy cream, whipped
Red food coloring

Sprinkle gelatin on milk in top part of double boiler. Add candy and put over simmering water. Heat, stirring, until candy is dissolved. Pour slowly into eggs, stirring. Put back in double boiler and cook, stirring constantly, until mixture thickens and coats a metal spoon. Remove from heat and chill until thickened

Chili Baked Ocean Perch

but not firm. Fold in whipped cream and add a few drops of food coloring. Pour into freezing tray and freeze until firm. Serve with chocolate sauce, if desired. Makes 6 servings.

PEPPERMINT TAFFY

2 cups light corn syrup
1 tablespoon butter
  or margarine
1 tablespoon vinegar
  Peppermint extract

Put all ingredients except flavoring in large heavy saucepan. Bring to boil, and cook until a small amount of mixture forms a hard ball when dropped in very cold water (254°F. on a candy thermometer). Pour onto a large buttered platter. As edges cool, turn mixture toward center with a spatula. When just cool enough to handle, make a hollow in center of taffy and add a few drops of flavoring. Gather up taffy and pull until light, using a little butter to grease hands while pulling. Twist into a long rope and cut into pieces with scissors. Wrap each piece in wax paper and store in a cool dry place. Makes about 1¼ pounds.

PEPPERONE—This highly spiced dry sausage is of Italian origin. It is made from coarsely ground beef and pork mixed with salt, coarsely ground black pepper, cayenne, and garlic. The mixture is cured and then stuffed into casings and linked in pieces ten to twelve inches long. The sausage is then air-dried at moderate temperatures for three to four weeks.

PERCH—A widely distributed, spiny-finned fresh-water food fish. In the United States it is found in the eastern section of the country and also abounds in the Great Lakes and the streams and lakes of the upper Mississippi valley. Known also as the yellow, barred, or ring perch, they are carnivorous, voracious, and prolific. Perch grow to a large size in still brackish waters of bays and inlets. They are distinctively colored with an olive back lightening along the sides to golden yellow. A perch has six or eight dark vertical bands on its sides and its fins are orange and red.

The pike-perch is a genus closely related to the perch family, but showing some resemblence to the pike in its elongated body shape. One of the best-known species of this group is the wall-eyed pike, a famous game fish living in deep pools with clear moving water and found throughout the United States with the exception of the far West and the deep South. Another species of pike-perch is the sauger or sand pike.

The name perch is also widely applied to many other spiny-finned fish, including some salt-water varieties. Among the latter are the so-called "ocean perch" which belong to the sea-bass and rock-fish family.

Perch is a mild fish, with firm white coarse flesh and a delicate flavor.

Availability and Purchasing Guide—Perch and pike-perch are available fresh or frozen, whole or filleted. Select fresh fish with firm flesh, clear full eyes, red gills, and a shiny skin.

Frozen fillets of ocean perch are available.

Storage—Wrap in moisture-proof paper

or place in a tightly covered container in coldest part of refrigerator.

Keep frozen fish solidly frozen until ready to use. Once thawed, do not refreeze; use immediately.

☐ Refrigerator shelf, raw: 1 to 2 days

☐ Refrigerator shelf, cooked: 3 to 4 days

☐ Refrigerator frozen-food compartment, prepared for freezing: 2 to 3 weeks

☐ Freezer, prepared for freezing: 1 year

Nutritive Food Values—Good source of protein.

☐ Yellow perch, 3½ ounces, raw = 91 calories

☐ Pike-perch, 3½ ounces, raw = 93 calories

☐ Ocean perch, Atlantic, 3½ ounces, raw = 88 calories

☐ Ocean perch, Pacific, 3½ ounces, raw = 95 calories

Basic Preparation—Remove scales, if any. Eviscerate and remove head and tail. Fillet or prepare whole or cut into desired shape. Wash thoroughly and pat dry. Cook fish over low heat, for shortest possible time, to keep it moist and tender.

☐ **To. Broil**—Wash split whole fish quickly in cold water. Wipe fillets with a damp cloth or paper towel. Thaw frozen fish just before using. Put fish on greased broiler rack and brush with melted butter or other fat. Sprinkle with salt and pepper. Broil about 3 inches from heat for 8 to 12 minutes, or until fish flakes easily when tested with a fork. Brush again with butter during broiling.

☐ **To Panfry or Sauté**—Wipe fish with a damp cloth or paper towel. Thaw frozen fish just before using. Cut fillets into serving pieces. Leave small fish whole. Dip fish into undiluted evaporated milk or beaten egg and roll in mixture of equal parts of flour and cornmeal, seasoned with salt and pepper. Or roll in flour, dip in egg, then roll in fine dry bread crumbs or cracker crumbs. Heat enough fat in skillet to cover bottom and sauté fish for 3 to 5 minutes on each side, turning carefully with fork or turner. Add more fat as needed.

☐ **To Deep Fry**—Wipe fish with a damp cloth or paper towel. Thaw frozen fish just before using. Cut fillets into serving pieces. Leave small fish whole. Roll in seasoned flour and dip into a mixture of slightly beaten egg and water, allowing 2 tablespoons cold water to each egg. Roll in fine dry bread crumbs or cracker meal. For a thicker crust, coat twice with egg and crumbs. Arrange a few pieces of fish in frying basket just to cover the bottom; do not overlap. Fry in hot deep fat (370°F. on a frying thermometer) until golden brown. Drain.

☐ **To Bake**—Have whole fish cleaned and dressed but not split. Head and tail may be left on. Wash fish and wipe dry. Fillets may also be baked. Thaw frozen fish just before using. Put fish in a shallow baking pan and brush with soft butter or margarine. Season with salt and pepper. Bake in preheated hot oven (400°F.) for 10 to 15 minutes, or until fish flakes easily with a fork.

☐ **To Poach**—Fillets are best for poaching. Wipe fish with a damp cloth or paper towel. Thaw frozen fish just before using. Pour about 2 cups water into a large skillet. Add 1½ teaspoons salt, 1 slice of lemon or 1 tablespoon vinegar, 1 slice of onion separated into rings, a few parsley sprigs or celery leaves, ¼ teaspoon peppercorns, and 1 bay leaf. Boil for 5 minutes. Reduce heat and add fish. Cover and simmer for 5 to 10 minutes, or until fish flakes easily with a fork. Serve hot with butter. Or cool in the broth, chill, and serve with mayonnaise.

☐ **To Steam**—Use a trivet or rack or even a small colander in a covered pan. Either whole fish or fillets may be steamed. Wash whole fish or wipe fillets with a damp cloth or paper towel. Thaw frozen fish just before using. Put on a greased small rack in a large saucepan. Sprinkle fillets with salt and pepper. Add enough boiling water to reach just below top of rack. Don't allow the water to touch the fish. Cover tightly; bring to boil, reduce heat and steam for about 10 minutes to the pound, or until fish flakes easily with a fork.

☐ **To Freeze**—Remove scales, eviscerate, and remove head and tail. Wash thoroughly and drain. Fillet fish if desired. Dip fish into a brine solution of ¼ cup salt and 4 cups cold water for 20 to 30 seconds. Drain. Wrap fish in moisture-vapor-proof wrapping, excluding as much air as possible. Seal.

PERCH, MEXICAN STYLE

1½ pounds perch fillets
½ cup fine dry bread crumbs
1 small onion, grated
¼ cup soft butter
or margarine
1 teaspoon chili powder
⅛ teaspoon each of thyme
and pepper
¾ teaspoon salt
Lemon wedges

Wipe fillets with damp cloth and arrange in a shallow baking dish. Blend remaining ingredients except lemon wedges and spread on fish. Bake in preheated very hot oven (450°F.) for about 25 minutes. Garnish with lemon wedges. Makes 4 servings.

CHILI BAKED OCEAN PERCH

Put 1 pound partially thawed frozen ocean-perch fillets in shallow baking dish. Mix ¾ cup chili sauce, ¼ cup dry red wine, and 2 tablespoons instant minced onion. Spread on fish and sprinkle with ¾ cup grated American cheese. Bake in preheated very hot oven (450°F.) for 15 to 20 minutes. Makes 2 servings.

DEVILED OCEAN-PERCH FILLETS

Separate 1 pound partially thawed frozen ocean-perch fillets; put on broiler rack. Spread with mixture of 2 tablespoons each of prepared mustard, ketchup, and horseradish; 1 tablespoon cooking oil; salt to taste. Broil. Makes 4 servings.

PERCOLATOR—A coffeemaker which, by its own steam pressure forces boiling water up a hollow stem and into a basket holding ground coffee. The water drips back down into the pot through this ground coffee, to continue boiling and rising until the liquid reaches the desired strength. Percolators can be either electric or non-electric. When electric, the desired strength can be pre-selected because the percolating is thermostatically controlled. Non-electric percolators do not stop percolating automatically so that the coffeemaking must be carefully timed for good results.

PERSIMMON—A warm-weather fruit of which there are two species of importance. One of them, the common or American persimmon, *Diospyros virginiana,* is native from Connecticut and southern Iowa to Florida and Texas. This species produces a small, pulpy fruit which can vary in size from a half to two inches in diameter, is yellow or orange with a reddish cheek and has large seeds embedded in its soft flesh.

The second species, *D. Kaki,* is known as the Oriental or Japanese persimmon. A native of China and Korea, it was introduced to the United States in the second half of the 19th century. It is grown commercially in Florida and California, and to a lesser extent throughout the south. The tree can reach forty or more feet in height; its fruit grows to some three inches in diameter. Some varieties have large seeds in the semi-transparent pulp; other varieties are seedless. When ripe the fruit somewhat resembles a tomato in size and surface texture, and is reddish-orange in color. The taste is deliciously sweet, with a faint acid tinge, but persimmons must be ripe to be edible.

Persimmons are eaten out-of-hand and used in salads and puddings.

Availability and Purchasing Guide—Persimmons are in season from October to February. Select clean, plump fruit with smooth, glossy skin. The stem cap should be attached. The fruit should be soft but firm.

Nutritive Food Values—Contains fair quantities of vitamin C and good quantities of vitamin A.

☐ American, 3½ ounces, raw = 127 calories

☐ Japanese, 3½ ounces, raw = 77 calories

Storage—Persimmons ripen best in a cool, dark, dry place. When ripe, refrigerate and eat as soon as possible.

☐ Fresh, refrigerator shelf: 1 to 2 days

☐ Frozen, refrigerator frozen-food compartment, prepared for freezing: 2 to 3 months

☐ Frozen, freezer, prepared for freezing: 1 year

Basic Preparation—Persimmons are eaten with a spoon. Wash and chill before serving. Cut into halves and serve with lemon or lime; or à la mode with vanilla ice cream.

☐ **To Freeze**—Select soft ripe fruit. Peel and cut into pieces. Press pulp through a sieve. To 4 cups pulp add ⅛ teaspoon ascorbic acid and mix well. If desired, add 1 cup sugar to 4 cups pulp. Pack in containers, leaving ½-inch headspace. Seal.

PERSIMMON, GRAPEFRUIT, AND POMEGRANATE SALAD

2 ripe persimmons
1 large grapefruit, cut into segments
1 pomegranate
Salad greens
Cream Dressing

Peel persimmons. Begin at blossom end and work toward the stem so that the fruit may retain its shape. Cut into sections the size of grapefruit segments. Cut pomegranate into quarters. Remove seeds. Remove white membranes between seeds. Place salad greens in bowl or on 4 individual salad plates. Arrange overlapping persimmon and grapefruit sections on greens. Sprinkle with pomegranate seeds. Serve with Cream Dressing. Makes 4 servings.

Cream Dressing

Combine 1 cup heavy sweet cream or dairy sour cream, 2 tablespoons fresh lemon juice, 1 tablespoon sugar or honey, and ¼ teaspoon salt. Blend thoroughly.

PERSIMMON PULP

Choose soft ripe fruit with a transparent skin. Only ripe fruit is sweet; unripe persimmons have an acid taste and pucker the mouth. Peel and strain pulp. Or mash, removing seeds. If the pulp is not used immediately, stir 1 tablespoon fresh lemon juice into each 2 cups pulp, to prevent discoloration.

COLD PERSIMMON PUDDING

2 cups Persimmon Pulp (above)
1 cup sugar
1 tablespoon fresh lime or lemon juice
1 teaspoon fresh lemon juice
⅔ cup heavy cream, whipped
Ground ginger

Combine all ingredients except ginger. Place in glass serving dish and chill. Sprinkle with ginger just before serving. Makes 4 servings.

PERSIMMON À LA MODE

With the point of a sharp knife, cut through the skins of ripe persimmons and peel back skin like petals, without removing the stem. Place persimmons on individual serving plates. Fill petals with vanilla ice cream. Garnish with sprigs of mint, if available. Allow 1 persimmon for each serving.

PERSIMMON ICE

2 cups Persimmon Pulp (above)
1 cup sugar
1 tablespoon fresh lime or lemon juice

Blend all ingredients. Freeze in refrigerator tray or rotary freezer. If possible, serve on fresh grape leaves. Makes 4 servings.

BAKED PERSIMMON PUDDING

1 cup sifted all-purpose flour
½ teaspoon salt
½ teaspoon baking soda
¾ cup sugar
1 cup Persimmon Pulp (above)
2 eggs, beaten
1 cup milk
½ teaspoon grated lemon rind
2 tablespons butter or margarine

Sift together flour, salt, baking soda, and sugar. Add Persimmon Pulp to the flour mixture along with remaining ingredients. Mix well. Turn batter into a well-greased, lightly floured baking dish (8 x 8 x 2 inches). Bake in preheated moderate oven (350°F.) for 50 minutes, or until pudding is done. Serve warm with whipped cream, hard sauce, or lemon sauce. Makes 6 servings.

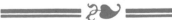

PETITE MARMITE—A meal-in-one soup that is a specialty of all French restaurants. The literal translation is "small pot." The dish is so called because it is served in the small earthenware pot in which it is cooked.

Essentially, a *petite marmite* is a beef broth made with a large piece of lean beef, marrow bones, poultry giblets, carrots, turnips, leeks, little onions, celery, and cabbage. Sometimes a small chicken is added to the ingredients. The *petite marmite* is served with toasted French bread, and sometimes grated Parmesan cheese is added to the soup.

There are as many recipes for a *petite marmite* as there are people who make it. Basically, the success of the dish rests on its containing a good quantity of many well-flavored ingredients which makes a full-bodied, nourishing soup and main dish.

PETITE MARMITE, I

6 carrots, peeled and sliced
3 leeks, sliced
3 white turnips, peeled and quartered
2 pounds chicken backs and necks
2½ pounds of beef shin
2½ pounds of beef bones
3 quarts cold water
2 tablespoons salt
½ teaspoon peppercorns
1 teaspoon herb seasoning
1 quart shredded cabbage
Grated Parmesan cheese
French bread

Put first 9 ingredients in a large soup kettle. Cover, bring to a boil, reduce heat, and simmer for about 4½ hours. Skim occasionally. Take out chicken pieces, meat and bones. Remove meat from bones and return meat to soup. Add herb seasoning and cabbage. Cook for 10 minutes longer. Serve with grated cheese and French bread. Makes about 4 quarts.

PETITE MARMITE, II

3 medium onions, sliced
1 tablespoon butter
2 pounds beef chuck in one piece
2 pounds beef soup bones
1 stewing chicken (about 5 pounds)
3 quarts water
Salt
2 bay leaves
8 peppercorns
Few parsley sprigs
½ teaspoon crumbled dried thyme
2 whole cloves
1 cup diced celery
4 carrots, diced
3 leeks, white part only, sliced
¼ small green cabbage, slivered
1 package (10 ounces) frozen peas
Pepper
Grated cheese

Brown onions in butter in large kettle. Add beef, bones, chicken, water, 1 tablespoon salt, bay leaves, peppercorns, parsley, thyme, and cloves. Bring to boil, and simmer, covered, for 4 hours, or until meats are tender. Remove meats, cool, and slice thin. Cook remaining vegetables for garnish until barely tender in a little boiling salted water. Drain. Strain soup mixture and reheat. Season to taste with salt and pepper. Put some vegetables and meat slices in individual

marmites or soup bowls. Cover with broth. Serve with grated cheese. Makes 6 to 8 servings.

PETITS FOURS—A French term describing fancy little cookies or small iced and decorated cakes.

How to Cook Superbly:

Petits Fours

by Helen Evans Brown

*F*our means oven, in French, and *petit* is small. So a *petit four,* to a Frenchman, means a little something from the oven, or a little baked delicacy. *Petits fours secs* include many little pastries, such as macaroons, Florentines, Madeleines, *langues du chats, tuiles,* actually any fancy little pastry or cookie. *Petits fours glacés,* on the other hand, are tiny iced cakes, variously colored and flavored and daintily decorated. It is these that most of us think of as *petits fours,* and as something that only a skilled pastry chef can produce. That last is just not so. Even though it is a bit of a project, any venturesome cook can make iced *petits fours* that can be served with pride at the fanciest party. And think what a hit and how much money they'd raise at the church bazaar! The nicest thing about this venture into the art of the *pâtissier* is that it can be done in three, even four, stages, so the fascinating pursuit can be stretched into odd moments for a week or more. And once you've achieved the *petits fours,* you've also learned three classic recipes for pastry making: *fondant, génoise,* and *crème au beurre* (buttercream). Because

this is a time-consuming project, I have given recipes large enough for seven to nine dozen *petits fours.* The surplus may be frozen but the icing will lose a little of its sheen. To restore this, brush the *petits fours* very lightly with a watercolor brush that has been dipped into water and shaken dry.

EQUIPMENT

Besides the ordinary kitchen measures, spoons, knives, spatulas, pans, and cake racks, you'll need a heavy pan and a pastry brush for making syrup, a large fireproof bowl and a shallow pan (17 x 11 inches) for the *génoise,* and a French whip, rotary eggbeater, or electric mixer for the buttercream. It's also nice to have a candy thermometer for both the fondant icing and the buttercream, and a sharp round cookie cutter about 1½ inches in diameter.

FONDANT

Fondant, which is used for many candies as well as for the glossy, smooth icing that is so characteristic of *petits fours glacés,* may be made a week or more before using. In fact it really should be made at least a day in advance of using, so that it will have time to ripen.

Ingredients:
- 5 cups granulated sugar
- ¾ cup hot water
- ¼ cup light corn syrup

Method:
Combine sugar, water, and corn syrup in a heavy saucepan and stir over low heat until the sugar is completely dissolved and the mixture looks clear. Dip the pastry brush into cold water and wash down the sides of the saucepan so that any of the sugar there will be removed. This is important. Turn up heat and boil syrup rapidly without stirring, washing down the sides of the pan again if necessary. When the syrup has reached 240°F. on your candy thermometer, remove from heat. If you have no thermometer, drop a little syrup into a cup of cold water; if you can form it into a soft ball with the fingers it is ready. If not, cook a little longer, but be careful not to overcook. Let the syrup stand for a minute, then pour onto a marble slab or a large platter that has been rinsed with cold water. The syrup should be no more than 1 inch thick. When it has cooled so that it is comfortable to the touch, start scraping the edges into the middle with a spatula or wooden spoon. Work constantly until entire mixture is thick and white. Then, taking a little at a time, knead it into a soft, smooth paste. As each piece is finished, cover with a cloth wrung out in cold water. When all is kneaded, put in a jar and cover tightly. This will hold at room temperature for 2 weeks.

GÉNOISE FINE

This *pâte à génoise* is a butter sponge-cake that is used for making many famous cakes (*gâteaux*), either large or small.

Ingredients:
- ¾ cup butter
- 6 large eggs
- 1 cup sugar
- 1 cup sifted cake flour
- ¼ teaspoon salt
- 1 teaspoon vanilla extract or 1 teaspoon grated lemon rind

Method:
Grease a shallow pan (17 x 11 inches) and line with wax paper. Clarify the butter. To do this, melt it slowly, skim off the foam that rises, and let the butter stand for at least 5 minutes; then pour very carefully into a cup, discarding the white sediment at the bottom. You should have almost 5 ounces (just over ½ cup) of clear, yellow oil; this is clarified butter. Put it aside. Set the oven at moderate (350°F.). Put the eggs and the sugar in a large bowl and place the bowl over a pan of hot, not boiling, water. Heat,

whipping occasionally, until the mixture is warm, not hot. It should be about 110°F., comfortable when a little is poured on the inside of your wrist. Remove from heat and start beating. If you have an electric beater, do it at high speed for 10 minutes; a rotary beater will take twice as long if done vigorously, and a hand whip will take from 15 to 25 minutes depending upon your speed. At any rate, the mixture should increase 2½ to 3 times in volume, and will become fluffy and very light in color. It will be so thick that it will level out very slowly. Have ready the flour sifted with the salt, and the cooled butter to which you've added the vanilla or lemon rind. Sprinkle the flour evenly over the mixture, pour the butter on top, and fold in very quickly but thoroughly, taking care not to overmix, thus losing volume. Pour into prepared pan and spread evenly. Bake for 25 minutes, or until beautifully browned. When pressed lightly with a finger, it should spring back. Turn out on a cake rack (you may have to put two together for this size pan) and quickly peel off the paper. Allow to cool thoroughly, preferably overnight.

CRÈME AU BEURRE (Buttercream)

This rich butter filling can be used for innumerable fancy desserts as well as for the *petits fours*. It will keep a long time in the refrigerator or can be frozen, in which case it may have to be beaten again to restore its fluffiness.

Ingredients:
- 1 cup sugar
- ⅓ cup hot water
- ¼ teaspoon cream of tartar
- 8 egg yolks
- 1 cup soft, not melted, butter

Method:
Mix sugar, water, and cream of tartar and cook in exactly the same way as the syrup for the fondant. While it is cooking, beat the egg yolks until light and fluffy, preferably with an electric mixer. When the syrup reaches 240°F., or forms a soft ball in cold water, remove from the heat and pour very gradually into the egg yolks, beating constantly. If you use a rotary beater you'll need help; a whip may be managed alone. Continue beating until the mixture is cool and very thick and fluffy. Add the softened butter, a little at a time, and continue beating until smooth. Cover and keep until needed.

TO MAKE PETITS FOURS

☐ **Shaping the Cakes**—Using a very sharp knife, trim the crusts from the *génoise,* then cut into small fancy shapes, using a ruler as a guide and measure. Cut squares, oblongs, diamonds, and triangles. Use the cookie cutter for rounds and, if you wish, other cookie cutters

such as crescents, ovals, or bells (for a wedding, maybe!). The pieces should be small to be in proportion to the cake's thickness of about 1 inch. If you want larger cakes, make them higher by layering 2 pieces together with buttercream filling. This recipe will make from 80 to 100 small cakes.

☐ **Filling the Cakes**—The buttercream can be flavored in numerous ways: grated orange or lemon rind; vanilla or almond extract; melted and cooled unsweetened chocolate; cocoa; instant coffee, or any liqueur such as Cointreau, Grand Marnier, brandy, rum, Curaçao, coffee liqueur, or kirsch. Add these to taste. To fill the cakes, slice a layer off the top, scoop out some of the inside, fill with flavored buttercream, and replace top; or split cake into 2 or 3 layers and put together again with buttercream between. Buttercream may also be spread on the sides of the cakes, after which they should be rolled in finely chopped nuts. The tops should be iced with fondant (see below). Another tricky way to use buttercream is to ice the top of the cake with it, then chill it thoroughly. It may then be covered with a thin layer of cool fondant.

☐ **Icing the Cakes**—When the cakes are filled, arrange them on a cake rack, leaving plenty of space around each one. Place the rack on a cookie sheet. Divide the fondant into as many parts as you wish flavors of icing. Working with 1 part at a time, put the fondant in the top part of a double boiler over hot, not boiling, water. Add a discreet amount of vegetable coloring and enough liquid (water, flavoring extract, brandy or other liqueur, strong coffee, or melted unsweetened chocolate) to make the fondant thin enough to pour easily over the top and sides of the cakes, but not so thin that it won't completely mask them. At first you'd better take it easy, adding only a few drops of liquid at a time. Keep stirring over the hot water, but don't overheat or the icing will lose its gloss. Just before using, stir in a few drops of slightly beaten egg white. The full amount of icing will take the white of a medium egg; gauge amount accordingly. Try testing a spoonful over a cake, or over a piece of bread if you don't want to risk one of your precious *petits fours!* You'll soon be able to tell when it has reached the proper consistency. Now pour the icing over the cakes or, if you prefer, spoon it over. It should cover the top and run evenly down the sides. The surplus will fall onto the cookie sheet below and can be scraped up and reused.

Sometime the *petits fours* are glazed before icing to prevent crumbs from marring the smooth surface. This is done by beating egg white slightly with an equal amount of confectioners' sugar and brushing the mixture on the sides of the cakes, or by melting strained apricot jam and brushing while still hot on the cakes. In either case, they should be allowed to dry thoroughly before proceeding with the icing. This step is not essential.

☐ **Decorating the Petits Fours**—Here you're on your own and the possibilities are endless. Little silver dragées, tiny pieces of angelica or glacéed cherries or citron, crushed candied violet or rose leaves, slivers of almonds, or chopped pistachio nuts are suggestions. Also the fondant, when put into a pastry gun with a writing tube or a paper cornucopia with the tip snipped off, may be piped on in stripes, curlicues, spirals, or even initials. And if you are good at cake decorating, you can make dainty flowers and leaves. When the icing has set, trim the bottoms of the cakes of any surplus icing and, as a finishing and professional touch, put each *petit four* in a little fluted paper cup, available at bakery suppliers or perhaps from your neighborhood pastry shop.

PFEFFERNÜSSE

PFEFFERNÜSSE—A German word, literally translated as "pepper nut," and used to describe a spicy traditional Christmas cookie. The inclusion of black pepper among the spices used explains its name. Usually the cookie is shaped, let stand overnight, baked, and then allowed to ripen before serving.

PFEFFERNÜSSE

3 cups sifted all-purpose flour
¾ teaspoon each of salt, baking powder, ground allspice, mace, and cardamom
¼ teaspoon black pepper
¾ teaspoon baking soda
⅛ teaspoon ground aniseed
1 cup honey
3 tablespoons shortening
1 egg
Frosting

Sift dry ingredients. Heat honey (do not boil). Add shortening. Cool. Beat in egg. Stir in dry ingredients just until blended. Let dough stand for 10 minutes to stiffen enough to handle easily. Shape into 1-inch balls. Place on lightly greased cookie sheets. Bake in preheated moderate oven (350°F.) for 13 to 15 minutes. Cool; frost. Store airtight for a week to ripen. Makes 5 dozen.

Frosting

Combine 1 egg white, 2 teaspoons honey, and ¼ teaspoon ground aniseed. Gradually add 1½ cups sifted confectioners' sugar, beating until smooth. Put 12 to 14 cookies in a bowl, add 2 tablespoons frosting, and stir to frost all sides of cookies. Lift out with a fork onto rack. Repeat until all are frosted.

ALMOND PFEFFERNÜSSE

5 eggs
2 cups firmly packed brown sugar
Grated rind of 1 lemon
3 tablespoons strong coffee
5½ cups sifted all-purpose flour
2 teaspoons baking powder
½ teaspoon each of salt, black pepper, mace, and nutmeg
1 teaspoon each of cloves and allspice
1 tablespoon cinnamon
⅛ teaspoon ground cardamom
1 cup ground almonds
½ cup chopped citron
¼ teaspoon aniseed
Apricot brandy

Beat eggs until thick. Gradually beat in sugar. Add remaining ingredients, except brandy; mix well. Chill. Shape into rolls 1 inch in diameter. Cut slices ½ inch thick. Let stand in cool place to dry overnight. Turn cookies over and put a drop of brandy on each to make cookies pop and become rounded. Bake in preheated slow oven (300°F.) for about 20 minutes. Makes 8 dozen. Store airtight.

PHEASANT—A highly prized and beautiful game bird which is closely related to the partridge and the quail. The *Phasianidae* family to which these birds belong numbers about 165 species. The male pheasants are large, handsome birds, resplendent with brilliant plumage; female birds are smaller and less brilliant. The flesh is succulent, with a flavor somewhere between poultry and venison. The succulence depends on how long the bird has been hung. Eaten at precisely the right moment, the flesh is tender and highly flavorsome.

Pheasants came originally from Asia, but they are bred in a great variety of places, from semidesert steppes to dense jungles up to a height of 16,000 feet or more in the very cold mountains of central Asia. These exquisite birds have inspired artists and gourmets alike. Pheasants in full plumage are a standard subject of still lifes, especially those by Dutch and Flemish painters. In a great variety of dishes, pheasants have graced the tables of the kings and nobles of Europe, and of the rich in America, for the pheasant is a symbol of opulent living.

Pheasants are usually shot as game birds, but they can be purchased frozen, either in full plumage or plucked. A young bird has short round claws and should be roasted. An older bird should be marinated and cooked in moist heat. A cock ranges from two and three-quarters to five pounds, while a hen, which is plumper and more tender, weighs from two to three pounds.

Since these birds when wild do not have much fat covering, they should be covered with bacon or salt pork while roasting. If the pheasants are shot, they should be hung for four days in warm weather or for ten to twelve days in cold weather. Hang the pheasant by the neck. When the tailfeathers can be plucked easily, the bird is ready for plucking and cooking. The shooting season for pheasant is from October to February.

Caloric Value

☐ 3½ ounces, raw, flesh only = 162 calories

STUFFED ROAST PHEASANT

1 pheasant (3 to 4 pounds)
½ pound bulk sausage meat
1 tart green apple, peeled, cored, and chopped
¼ cup chopped parsley
1 egg, well beaten
Salt and pepper
3 slices of bacon
½ cup sherry
1 tablespoon red currant jelly
1½ tablespoons fresh lemon juice

Wash pheasant and pat dry. Mix sausage meat with apple, parsley and egg. Season with salt and pepper. Stuff bird with this mixture. Put bird on a rack in a shallow roasting pan. Cover breast of the bird with bacon. Roast in preheated moderate oven (350°F.) for 1 hour, or until bird is almost tender. Pour off excess fat. Mix remaining ingredients and pour over bird. Baste with pan juices several times and continue roasting for 15 minutes, or until bird is tender. Makes 3 or 4 servings.

BRAISED PHEASANT WITH SAUERKRAUT

1 pheasant (about 5 pounds)
Marinade
About 3⅓ cups (one 1-pound, 11-ounce can) sauerkraut
2 cups beef bouillon
½ teaspoon caraway seeds
1 cup dry white wine
3 or 4 juniper berries
Shortening
Salt and pepper

Let pheasant marinate overnight. Drain sauerkraut and add bouillon, caraway seeds, and wine. Crush juniper berries and add them or, optionally, 3 tablespoons gin. Simmer for 1 hour.

Meanwhile drain pheasant and cut it into pieces. Brown in hot shortening, seasoning with salt and pepper to taste. When pieces are well browned, put in casserole; top with prepared sauerkraut and liquid; cover. Cook in preheated moderate oven (350°F.) until bird is tender. It will take from 30 minutes to 1 hour, depending on the pheasant. Serve with baked potatoes (or fried mush or hominy) and glasses of chilled white wine. Makes 4 servings.

Marinade

1 cup white wine
2 cups hot water

1 medium onion stuck with cloves
2 cardamom seeds, crushed

Combine all ingredients and pour over pheasant.

SAUTÉED PHEASANT

Singe bird and cut into serving pieces. (If cooking an older bird, first marinate overnight using Marinade recipe above; wipe the pieces dry.) Fry bacon, or use cooking oil as grease, and sauté bird, turning frequently, until well-browned. Add 1 or 2 sliced onions and salt and pepper to taste. Add 1 cup dry white wine, cover, and reduce the heat. Simmer for 30 minutes to 1 hour; test by sticking fork into leg joint to make sure bird is tender. Serve with wild rice, cranberry relish, and fresh kale.

PHILIPPINE COOKERY

by William Clifford

Americans who visit Manila feel more at home there than anywhere else in the Far East. Western influence in the Philippines has been profound, especially during the four centuries of Spanish colonial rule that preceded the American period. Filipinos say it was a little like living four hundred years in a convent followed by fifty years in Hollywood. Convent training has a permanent effect, and the Philippines is the only Christian country of Asia. Educated Filipinos speak and write in English or Spanish. They bear Spanish names, do Spanish dances, eat Spanish food.

Actually the purely Spanish element in Philippine society forms a thin upper crust, as do purely Spanish dishes like *paella*. But one expert estimates that the cooking of the country owes about one third of its ideas to Spain, and Spanish culinary terms are common in Tagalog, the national language. Some examples include *litson* (*lechón de leche,* suckling pig), *potsero* (*puchero,* stew pot), *pritada* (*fritada,* a fried dish), *relyeno* (*relleno,* stuffed), *torta* (*tortilla,* omelet), *karne* (*carne,* meat), *escabetse* (*escabeche,* pickled), *gisado* (*guisado,* stewed), *letse plan* (*leche flan,* custard pudding), *nata de pinya* (*nata de piña,* pineapple cream).

China must be credited with another share of the origins of modern Filipino cooking. Wheat and rice noodles, soy sauce, bean curd, bean sprouts, egg rolls, steamed foods—all come from China. The United States has contributed less to the national cuisine, though in Manila people enjoy hamburgers and hot dogs, ice cream and Coca-Cola.

What's left at the heart of Filipino cooking is the indigenous Tagalog or national cuisine, which is a first cousin to the Indonesian and Malay, just as the 7,000 islands of the Philippines are a northward extension of Malaysia and Indonesia. The indigenous cooking is much more than a mere extension, however. One of its distinctive features is the frequent combination of meat and fish or of two meats in the same dish, as in chicken and pork *adobo* (see recipes). Another is the very extensive use of pork, which is forbidden the Moslem Indonesians and Malays. Filipinos do much frying, both in lard and coconut oil. Many foods are first cooked with water until tender, then finished by frying, the opposite of our practice of browning in fat, then adding water to make a stew.

Favorite meats after pork are chicken, beef, and goat. Cockfighting is the national sport, and every important village has a ring with bleachers. Since the loser of every cockfight ends up in the stew pot, there's quite a bit of rooster simmering over village fires all the time.

Being a nation of tropical islands, the Philippines naturally feed on everything that swims in the surrounding waters. Ocean fish of all sorts, squid, oysters, clams, large and small shrimps abound. The Moro fishermen who live in the south eat giant turtles and turtle eggs. They also collect birds' nests and beautiful pearls in the islands of the Sulu Archipelago, which are said to number 3,000. Besides the Moros, who are Moslems, the big southern island, Mindanao, harbors both pygmies and tree dwellers. On Luzon, north of Manila, live the Igorot aborigines, who managed to escape even the pervasive influence of Spain.

All Filipinos eat rice. All who live near the sea enjoy the many uses of the coconut. Pineapples, papayas, and bananas lead the long list of other tropical fruits. A small citrus fruit called *calamansi* is the sweeter equivalent of lemons and limes. Cooks make liberal use of it, together with coconut milk, garlic, red peppers, ginger, and turmeric. They also season with salty liquids made from soybeans (*toyo,* which is Tagalog for soy sauce), shrimp (*hipon*), and anchovy or other fish, as well as salty fermented shrimp paste (*bagoong*).

Many Filipinos enjoy a hearty early breakfast that includes fish and rice, and perhaps a cup of chocolate in place of coffee or tea. Country people take their main meal at noon, but city dwellers tend to wait until late at night, as in most tropical islands and in Spain. After the midday siesta comes the *merienda,* an afternoon snack as important to Filipinos as an Englishman's tea. Besides a refreshing drink it offers fritters, turnovers, steamed cakes, and sweetmeats of all sorts, all equally acceptable the next morning for breakfast. When the tropical sun goes down, Filipinos begin to think about dinner and a drink of *tuba* (fermented palm sap), or rum, or their world famous San Miguel beer.

Four meals a day may do for every day, but when there's someone to entertain or a fiesta to celebrate, the serious feasting really begins. Fragrant white sampaguita, frangipani, and scarlet hibiscus adorn the boards that groan with the weight of barbecued suckling pigs, roasted chickens, whole sweet-and-sour fish, rolls of stuffed beef, nourishment to give the guests strength for a tango followed by a cha-cha-cha, or for another round of the intricate bamboo pole dance, where if you miss a step the bamboos come crashing together on your ankles. Women come dressed in their largest puffed sleeves and finest silks; men sport embroidered pineapple-fiber shirts. A major holiday like Christmas goes on for as much as three weeks of feasting, at the end of which everybody takes a good long afternoon nap before returning with relish to four meals a day.

ESCABETSENG APAHAP
(Sweet-and-Sour Sea Bass)

1 sea bass (2 pounds)
 Salt
 Oil for frying
1 medium onion, sliced
2 garlic cloves, sliced
½ teaspoon minced fresh gingerroot
2 tablespoons lard
¼ cup vinegar
3 tablespoons brown sugar
1 small red pepper, seeded and quartered
¼ pound small mushrooms, sliced
 Water
1 tablespoon cornstarch

Rub the fish inside and out with salt. Deep fry in oil heated to 375°F. on a frying thermometer for about 5 minutes (not quite done); drain. Sauté onion, garlic, and gingerroot in lard. Mix vinegar and brown sugar with salt to taste; add this mixture with red pepper, mushrooms, and ½ cup water to sautéed onion. When mixture boils, add drained fish, cover, and simmer for 5 minutes. Remove fish. Add cornstarch mixed with ½ cup cold water, and stir until thickened. Pour over fish. Makes 3 or 4 servings.

RELYENONG HIPON
(Stuffed Shrimps)

The egg-roll wrappers used here can be bought ready-made from Chinese grocers. To make your own, mix 2 cups all-purpose flour with ½ teaspoon salt and 1 cup water or a little less. Knead well and roll out paper-thin on floured board. Or press out a small ball of the dough into a thin sheet on a medium hot lightly greased griddle and lift it up quickly, trimming off any thin edges that get crisp. The aim is to dry the dough partially, not to cook it.

- 1 cup ground pork, sautéed until done
- ¼ cup chopped green onion Salt and pepper
- 12 giant shrimps, shelled, partially cooked, and deveined, but with tails left on
- 12 egg-roll wrappers Fat for deep frying

Mix pork, green onion, and salt and pepper to taste. Pack some of mixture into back of each shrimp where sand vein has been removed, deepening opening if necessary. Wrap in egg-roll wrappers and deep fry in fat heated to 375°F. on a frying thermometer until golden brown. Serve hot. Makes 4 to 6 servings.

TAPANG BAKA
(Cured Beef)

Often called simply *tapa*, this dish can also be made with pork (*tapang baboy*). It may be served with a small dish of vinegar for dipping, or with rice. It makes a good appetizer with a cold drink. In the Philippines the meat would be hung out to dry in the sun, but in the following recipe it is cured in the refrigerator.

- 1 tablespoon salt
- 1 teaspoon saltpeter
- 1 teaspoon pepper
- 2 pounds lean beef such as flank steak, cut across grain into thin slices Lard or cooking oil

Rub salt, saltpeter, and pepper on meat. Leave in refrigerator for 3 days or more, draining off any liquid that accumulates. Deep fry in lard heated to 375°F. on a frying thermometer. Makes 6 servings.

MORCON
(Stuffed Rolled Beef)

The beef for this dish must be a lean thin sheet or sheets, such as beef prepared for making braciola, or flank steak pounded so that it is nowhere more than ¼ inch thick.

- 2 pounds beef, cut and pounded into a thin sheet or sheets
- ¼ cup fresh lemon juice
- 2 tablespoons soy sauce
- 2 garlic cloves, minced
- ½ teaspoon pepper
- ½ pound cooked smoked ham, cut into thin strips
- 2 hard-cooked eggs, cut into eighths
- 2 tablespoons minced salt pork or bacon
- 2 tablespoons raisins
- 12 green olives, pitted and chopped
- 2 cups water
- 1 medium onion, sliced
- ¼ cup vinegar
- 1 can (8 ounces) tomato sauce

Spread beef out flat and season with lemon juice, soy sauce, garlic, and pepper. Arrange strips of ham and eggs; sprinkle with salt pork, raisins, and olives. Roll up and tie with string. Make sure ends are tight. Place in pan with the water, the onion, vinegar, and tomato sauce. Cover and simmer for 1 hour, or until tender. Slice and serve with sauce from pan. Makes 6 to 8 servings.

LITSONG BABOY
(Barbecued Suckling Pig)

The pig is often stuffed with tamarind leaves and always served with Liver Sauce. The sour taste of tamarind is a hard one for which to find a substitute, but try the following:

- 1 suckling pig, about 10 pounds
- ½ cup dried prunes
- ½ cup fresh lime juice Liver Sauce

Have the pig dressed for roasting. Cut prunes into halves and soak in lime juice for about 1 hour. Rub prunes and juice in cavity of pig and truss with skewers or string. Roast on rotisserie over charcoal or on rack in roasting pan in preheated moderate oven (350°F.) for about 4 hours. If done in the oven, pour 2 cups boiling water over pig and baste every 15 minutes. Serve with Liver Sauce. Makes 8 to 10 servings.

Liver Sauce

- 1 pork liver
- 1 small onion, minced
- 1 garlic clove, minced
- ¼ cup lard
- ¼ cup vinegar
- ¼ cup firmly packed brown sugar
- ¼ cup water
- 1 teaspoon pepper Salt

Broil liver for about 10 minutes on each side. Force through food chopper, using medium blade. Sauté onion and garlic in the lard until golden. Add vinegar, sugar, water, and pepper, and simmer for 5 minutes. Stir in ground liver, heat, and add salt to taste.

PAKSIW NA LITSON
(Sour Pork Stew)

This dish is made with leftover suckling pig or any roast pork. Uncooked pork may be substituted for the roast pork and Liver Sauce, but then the seasonings and cooking time must both be increased and the sauce thickened with a little cornstarch. Philippine vinegars, which may be made from coconut water or sugar cane, vary in acid. You may dilute vinegar with water if you prefer less acidity.

- 4 cups diced roast pork
- ½ cup Liver Sauce (at left)
- ¾ cup vinegar
- ¼ cup firmly packed brown sugar
- ¼ cup soy sauce
- 1 garlic clove, minced
- 1 bay leaf
- 1 teaspoon crumbled dried oregano
- ½ teaspoon ground cinnamon
- 6 whole cloves

Combine all ingredients and simmer for 30 minutes, adding a little water if necessary. Because of the vinegar and the seasoning already in the meat and Liver Sauce, you probably don't need salt and pepper, but add them if you like. Serve hot or cold. Makes 6 servings.

ADOBONG MANOK AT BABOY
(Chicken and Pork)

This is the national dish, and it is made by simmering, then browning, not the other way around. Two other operations are optional, marinating at the beginning and adding Coconut Milk at the end. It's also common practice to make adobo with just chicken or pork, but the combination is best.

- 2 pounds boneless pork, cut into large cubes
- 1 cup vinegar (diluted if desired)
- 2 garlic cloves, minced
- 1 teaspoon peppercorns
- 1 bay leaf Water
- 1 frying chicken (3½ pounds), cut into 2-inch pieces (chop through bone) Lard for frying
- 1 cup Coconut Milk (page 1370) Salt

Combine pork, vinegar, garlic, pepper, and bay leaf. Add 1 cup water, cover, and cook slowly for 1 hour. Add chicken and cook for 30 minutes longer, adding more water as it becomes necessary. When pork and chicken are tender, remove pieces from liquid and fry in lard until brown. Return to liquid, add Coconut Milk and salt to taste, and simmer for 5 minutes. Makes 8 servings.

For additional variety *adobo* can be colored red with annatto seeds or yellow with turmeric. Pineapple and tomatoes may be added to chicken for *adobo a la monja,* or it may be made with squid (*adobong pusit*) or bamboo shoots, pork, and shrimps (*adobong labong*).

PANSIT GISADO
(Fried Stewed Noodles)

- ½ cup each of julienne cooked shrimps, chicken, ham, and pork
- 1 onion, sliced
- 4 garlic cloves, sliced
- ¾ cup lard or cooking oil
- 2 tablespoons soy sauce
- 2 tablespoons patis*
- 2 cups shredded cabbage
- 1 pound fine egg noodles or rice noodles
- 2 limes, sliced thin

Fry shrimps, chicken, ham, and pork with onion and garlic in ¼ cup lard for 3 minutes. Drain, and reserve half of mixture. Add soy sauce, *patis,* and cabbage to the remainder; cover, and cook for 5 minutes, or until cabbage is tender. Cook noodles for 2 minutes in boiling unsalted water; drain. Fry all at once in remaining lard until light brown. Break up and add to cabbage mixture. Serve garnished with lime slices and reserved meats and shrimps. Makes 6 servings.
Patis is a liquid fish sauce and is sold in oriental food stores.

GINATAN
(Sweet Fruits and Roots)
This supercarbohydrate dessert should include diced breadfruit (nangka) *and taro root* (gabi) *if you can get them, but it stands up well with more easily available ingredients.*

- 2 cooking bananas, sliced
- 1 medium sweet potato, peeled and diced
- 1 medium yam, peeled and diced
- ½ cup sugar
- ¼ teaspoon salt
- 3 tablespoons quick-cooking tapioca
- 2 cups thin Coconut Milk (below)
- ½ cup Coconut Cream (below)
- 1 lime

Combine all ingredients except Coconut Cream and lime, and cook over low heat until tender. Add Coconut Cream and juice of ½ lime just before removing from heat. Cut remaining ½ lime into 8 thin slices and put one on each serving. Makes 8 servings.

LETSE PLAN
(Custard Pudding)
There isn't very much fresh milk in the Philippines because there aren't enough cows, but a lot of what there is goes into this favorite dessert.

- ¾ cup firmly packed brown sugar
- 3 tablespoons water
- 2 cups milk
- 1 cup granulated sugar
- 8 egg yolks
- 1 teaspoon grated lemon rind

Dissolve brown sugar in the water and cook until sugar caramelizes. Line a 1-quart casserole or 8 small custard cups evenly with the caramel. Scald milk and cool. Blend in granulated sugar, egg yolks, and lemon rind. Pour into lined casserole or cups. Place in pan of water and bake in preheated moderate oven (350°F.) for 1¼ hours, or until firm. Cool. Makes 8 servings.

Coconut Water, Milk, and Cream
Coconut water is what comes out of a green coconut. It is very refreshing to drink on a hot day in the tropics, but is not much used in cooking, except some-

Relyenong Hipon   **Ginatan**

Adobong Manok at Baboy

times for soaking a fish to take out some of the fishiness. Coconut Milk and Cream have to be made by you from shredded or grated coconut, and you can do it with either water or milk, hot or cold, in as little as 5 minutes or overnight. If you want the milk for a sweet dish such as *Ginatan* you can use the packaged shredded coconut (sweetened) available in all food stores. But if the dish is not meant to be sweet, you must either try to find unsweetened packaged coconut or make your own from whole coconuts.

In the tropics everyone knows how to chop open a coconut and every kitchen has a special coconut grater. If you're not so lucky, try this: Punch holes in two of the "eyes" at the end of the coconut and drain off any liquid. Place nut in moderate oven (350°F.) for 15 minutes or until shell cracks. Hit with kitchen mallet or hammer until all of shell breaks off. Pare off the brown skin and grate or shred the white meat.

With 2 cups of shredded coconut use 1 cup fresh scalded milk or water brought to a boil. Pour liquid over coconut, let stand for 15 minutes, and squeeze through a cheesecloth. This gives Coconut Cream. Pour another cup or more of milk or water on the same coconut meat, let stand again for 15 minutes, and squeeze dry. This gives Coconut Milk. Discard shredded coconut. The more liquid the weaker the Coconut Milk. If you let the second liquid stand in the refrigerator overnight before squeezing you will perhaps get a stronger milk. If you make Coconut Cream with cream instead of milk, then chill it, you can whip it.

PICCALILLI—A pickle relish made with chopped green tomatoes, red and green peppers, onions, sugar, vinegar pickling spices, and often cabbage. Sometimes called "Indian pickle" because of its origin in the East Indies.

PICCALILLI
1 quart chopped green tomatoes
2 sweet green peppers, chopped
2 sweet red peppers, chopped
2 large mild onions, chopped
1 small cabbage, chopped
½ cup salt
2 cups vinegar
2¼ cups firmly packed dark brown sugar
2 tablespoons mixed pickling spice or prepared mustard

Mix vegetables and salt, and let stand overnight. Drain and press out liquid. Add vinegar and sugar. Tie spice in a cheesecloth bag and add to mixture. Bring to boil and simmer until mixture is clear and slightly thickened. Pour to overflowing into hot sterilized jars and seal. Makes about 3 pints.

PICKLES—Although any food or food mixture preserved in salt and/or an acid liquid can properly be considered a pickle, usage of the noun, "pickle," is commonly confined to a few of the most often pickled vegetables and fruits. Among these favorites are cucumbers, cauliflower, onions, and watermelon. These pickles have long been popular with Americans. In the days of the old country store, every store had its huge pickle barrel with crunchy preserved cucumbers in it. Pickles were considered to be necessary accompaniments to the heavy foods of those times. During the California Gold Rush pickles were carried to the coast and sold for a high figure of eleven dollars a jar.

Americans love pickles, in any form. Watermelon pickle, for instance, is a delicacy first made in America. Other popular pickles are green tomato, dill, sweet, and bread-and-butter. Pickles go so well with sandwiches that an old American saying, "Apple pie without cheese/Is like a kiss without a squeeze," has been parodied to: "Bread and butter without a pickle/Is like an itch without a tickle."

Many kinds of pickles are available commercially. Among them are the sour pickles which include whole sour pickles, mixed pickles, chowchow and mustard pickles, onions, green beans, carrots, and cauliflower; dill pickles which include the genuine dill pickles prepared by natural fermentation, fresh dill pickles, processed dill pickles, and whole or sliced Polish-style dill pickles; and a great variety of sweet pickles including whole cucumbers in many different sizes, sweet dill pickles, mixed sweet pickles, pickled peaches, crabapples, pears, cantaloupe, and watermelon rind.

TO MAKE PICKLES
■ **Ingredients**—Use only fresh, firm, not too ripe fruits and vegetables. Cucumbers and green tomatoes should be small to medium in size and freshly gathered. If possible, pickle them within 24 hours of picking.

Use a good clear standard vinegar, free from sediment, one with 4 per cent to 6 per cent acidity. Strength of vinegar

is usually shown on the bottle label. If vinegar or brine is too weak, the pickles will spoil or become soft. Distilled white vinegar is best for preserving the color of foods. This is particularly true of fruit pickles. It also helps to maintain crispness in cucumber pickles.

Use a pure granulated salt for pickling. Any granulated salt containing less than 1 per cent chemicals added to prevent caking is satisfactory. Flake salts (dairy salt used in making butter, cheese salt, or kosher salt) are satisfactory for brining, but you'll need to use 1½ times the amounts called for in the recipe. Flake salts are available from feed- and farm-supply stores if you can't find them in your food store.

Use soft water if possible. Large amounts of calcium and other salts found in many hard waters may interfere with the fermentation and pickling processes. High iron content in water may cause pickles to darken. If hard water must be used, boil, skim off scum and let water stand for 24 hours. Ladle water off the top, leaving the sediment in the bottom.

Use whole spices for most cooked pickles. They keep their flavor longer. They can also be tied in a cloth to cook with other ingredients and be removed later. Spices packed in the jars with pickles will turn them dark.

Don't use coloring agents. Don't heat cucumbers in a copper kettle to give a dark green color. Heating vinegar in copper produces poisonous copper acetate. Don't add copper sulfate or vitriol.
■ **Equipment**—Use enamelware, aluminum, stainless steel, or glass utensils for pickling. Don't use a galvanized pail.

Use only perfect jars. Discard chipped or cracked ones. Don't use zinc lids. Sharp acid foods like pickles will eat into metal if they touch it directly.

For brining, you'll need a crock or stone jar; clean, thin white cloth; a heavy plate or round board cut to fit inside of crock and coated with paraffin; clean stones or paraffined bricks to hold cover down.

For sterilizing jars before filling and processing after filling, a large kettle or old-fashioned wash boiler is essential. It should have a rack or hardwood platform inside, preferably with dividers so that jars do not touch and room for the water to circulate beneath the jars.

Household scales are helpful but not absolutely necessary.

DILL PICKLES
Wash medium cucumbers and soak overnight in a brine made in a proportion of 1½ cups salt and 4 quarts of water. For 10 pounds of cucumbers prepare a canning brine of 10 quarts water, 1 quart vinegar, and 2 cups salt; boil for 10

minutes. Let this brine stand overnight. Next day, drain cucumbers and pack tightly in sterilized jars with small bunches of dill. If desired, 1 cup grated horseradish and 1 cup mustard seed may be used with the dill. Put a small amount of each in each jar. Add a small hot red pepper to each jar, if desired. Cover cucumbers with the cold canning brine, being sure brine completely covers them. Put on cap, screwing band tight. These will ferment for 3 or 4 days. When fermentation (bubbling) has ceased, store without removing screw bands.

DILL PICKLES (Kosher Style)

Wash medium cucumbers and soak for 24 hours in a brine made in a proportion of 1 cup salt and 2 quarts water. Remove from brine and dry. For 2 to 3 pounds cucumbers make a vinegar solution of 2 cups white vinegar and 3 cups water. Add 2 tablespoons mixed pickling spice and several small bunches of dill. Bring to a boil. Add cucumbers and remove from heat. Into each clean quart jar, put 2 garlic cloves and 2 small hot red peppers. Pack cucumbers tightly in jar with at least one small bunch of the dill. Bring vinegar solution to boil and pour over cucumbers, being sure liquid completely covers them. Seal at once.

FRESH DILL PICKLES (Kosher Style)

30 to 36 cucumbers (3 to 4 inches long)
3 cups vinegar
3 cups water
6 tablespoons salt
Fresh or dried dill
Garlic cloves
Mustard seed

Wash cucumbers. Make a brine of the vinegar, water, and salt. Bring to boil. Put a generous layer of dill, ½ to 1 sliced garlic clove, and 1½ teaspoons mustard seed in each clean quart jar. Pack cucumbers tightly in jars. When half filled with cucumbers, add another layer of dill and complete packing. Fill jars to within ½ inch of the top with boiling brine. Put caps on jars, screwing bands tight. Process for 5 minutes in boiling water bath. Pickles will shrivel some after processing. They will later plump in sealed jar.

CRISP BREAD-AND-BUTTER PICKLES

1 gallon sliced cucumbers
8 medium-size onions
2 large sweet red or green peppers
½ cup coarse salt
1 cup water
2½ cups sugar
2½ cups vinegar
1 tablespoon mustard seed
½ teaspoon each of ground turmeric and whole cloves

Slice cucumbers into paper-thin slices, leaving the peel on. Slice onions into thin rings. Cut peppers into thin rings or strips. Dissolve coarse salt in the water and pour over the sliced vegetables. Put some ice on top of cucumbers. Use about 1 quart crushed ice; it is the ice and salt that give an almost brittle, crisp pickle. Let stand for 3 hours, weighted with a plate. Drain.

Combine sugar, vinegar, and spices and bring to a boil. Add drained vegetables and heat to the boiling point. Don't boil. Pack into sterilized jars, fill to overflowing, and seal. Makes 6 pints.

CAULIFLOWER PICKLES

2 medium heads cauliflower
2 cups tiny white onions
¾ cup salt
Ice cubes
2 quarts white vinegar
1¼ cups sugar
2 teaspoons ground turmeric
2 tablespoons mustard seed
1 tablespoon celery seed
1 hot red pepper

Divide cauliflower into flowerets. There should be 2 quarts. Scald and peel onions. Add salt to vegetables; mix with ice cubes; cover with more ice cubes. Let stand for 3 hours. Drain. Mix remaining ingredients in large kettle; bring to boil, stirring to dissolve sugar. Add cauliflower and onions. Cook for 10 minutes, or until tender but not soft. Pack in hot sterilized pint jars. Reheat liquid to boiling; pour over vegetables and seal; Makes 5 pints.

DILLY GREEN-BEAN PICKLES

½ gallon (or 2 pounds) green beans
Salt
4 cups vinegar
1 cup sugar
2 tablespoons mixed pickling spices, tied in a bag
2 garlic cloves
Heads of dried or fresh dill

Wash beans well before stringing. Snip off tops. Leave beans whole in a size that fits the jars. Soak in ice water for 30 minutes. Make a brine to cover, using 1 tablespoon salt to each quart water. Bring to a boil. Boil for approximately 20 minutes, or until tender. Drain well. Place beans back in pan and add vinegar, sugar, spice bag, and garlic. Simmer for 10 minutes. Pack beans standing upright into hot sterilized jars. Cover with the hot vinegar solution. Place a head or so of dill on the top. Seal. Makes 2 quarts.

OKRA PICKLES

2 pounds tender fresh okra
5 pods hot red or green pepper
5 garlic cloves, peeled
4 cups white vinegar
½ cup water
6 tablespoons salt
1 tablespoon celery seed or mustard seed (optional)

Wash okra and pack into hot sterilized jars. Put 1 pepper pod and 1 garlic clove in each jar. Bring remaining ingredients to boil. Pour over okra and seal. Let stand for 8 weeks before using. Makes 5 pints.

Note: If pepper pods are not available, use ¼ teaspoon crushed dried hot red pepper for each jar.

ONION PICKLES

2 quarts small white onions
½ cup salt
2 tablespoons mixed pickling spice
1 cup sugar
4 cups white vinegar

Pour boiling water to cover over onions and let stand for 2 minutes. Drain, cover with cold water, and peel. Add the salt and let stand in water to cover overnight. Rinse in cold water and drain. Tie spice in a cheesecloth bag and boil for 10 minutes with the sugar and vinegar. Remove spice bag, add onions, and bring to a boil. Put onions in hot sterilized jars and fill to overflowing with the syrup. Makes about 6 pints.

CRYSTAL TOMATO PICKLES

2½ pounds green or underripe tomatoes
4½ teaspoons slaked lime powder (buy in drugstore)
Water
1¾ cups sugar
2 cinnamon sticks
½ teaspoon ground nutmeg
2 pieces whole dried gingerroot
½ teaspoon salt
2 cups white vinegar

Cut tomatoes into ¼-inch slices and put in bowl. Dissolve lime in 4 cups water and add to tomatoes. Stir. Let stand overnight in refrigerator. Next day, drain; rinse tomatoes in several changes of cold water; drain again. In kettle mix sugar, spices tied in cheesecloth bag, salt, vinegar, and ½ cup water. Bring to boil and boil for 5 minutes. Add tomatoes and cook, uncovered, for 20 minutes, or until syrup is thick and tomatoes clear. Pack into hot sterilized jars and seal. Makes 2½ pints.

GREEN TOMATO PICKLE

2¼ pounds green tomatoes
6 ounces onions (about 4 medium)
2 tablespoons salt
¾ teaspoon each of celery seed, mustard seed, and whole allspice
Small piece of gingerroot
1 garlic clove
1 dried hot red pepper
1¼ cups vinegar
¾ teaspoon powdered mustard
½ teaspoon curry powder
1 pound apples
½ cup firmly packed brown sugar
1 cup granulated sugar
2 tablespoons chopped pimiento

Wash and stem tomatoes. Peel onions. Slice tomatoes and onions thinly. Sprinkle salt over vegetables in layers. Let stand overnight. In the morning drain thoroughly. Tie whole spices, garlic, and dried red pepper in cheesecloth bag; add to vinegar along with mustard and curry powder. Peel and core apples, grate on coarse grater, and add to vinegar and spices. Bring quickly to boil and simmer for 1 minute. Add sugars; mix well; add well-drained tomatoes and onions. Bring again to boil. Add pimiento; simmer for 15 minutes. Remove spice bag. Pack pickle into hot sterilized jars. Seal. Makes 2½ pints.

DILL GREEN-TOMATO PICKLES
(Kosher Style)
Small firm green tomatoes
Garlic cloves
Celery stalks
Sweet green peppers, quartered
2 quarts water
1 quart vinegar
1 cup salt
Dill to taste

Pack tomatoes into sterilized quart jars. To each jar, add 1 garlic clove, 1 celery stalk, and 4 quarters of green pepper. Mix remaining ingredients and boil for 5 minutes. Pour into filled jars and seal at once. This amount of liquid fills about 6 quarts.

WATERMELON PICKLE
Rind from 1 large watermelon
Water
Salt
Pickling Syrup
1 lemon, sliced thin

Trim off green skin and pink meat from watermelon rind. Cut rind into 1-inch squares or small oblong pieces. Measure; there should be 4 quarts. Cover with cold salted water (¼ cup salt to 2 quarts water) and let stand overnight. Drain, cover with fresh cold water, and simmer until tender. Drain. Add to Pickling Syrup with lemon. Bring to boil and simmer for 1 hour, or until clear. Remove spice bag and pack pickle in hot sterilized jars and seal. Makes about 4 pints.

Pickling Syrup
Mix 2 quarts cider vinegar, 2 cups water, and 4 pounds (9 cups) sugar in large preserving kettle. In cheesecloth bag tie 2 tablespoons each of whole cloves and allspice, 1 piece gingerroot, and 3 tablespoons cracked cinnamon. Add spices to first mixture, bring to boil, and boil rapidly for 5 minutes.

ZUCCHINI PICKLES
2 pounds small zucchini
2 medium onions
¼ cup salt
2 cups white vinegar
1 cup sugar
1 teaspoon each of celery seeds, mustard seeds, and ground turmeric
½ teaspoon powdered mustard

Wash zucchini. Cut unpeeled zucchini and peeled onions into very thin slices and drop into crock or bowl. Cover with water and add salt. Let stand for 1 hour; drain. Mix remaining ingredients and bring to boil. Pour over zucchini and onion. Let stand for 1 hour. Put in kettle and bring to boil and cook for 3 minutes. Pack into hot sterilized jars and seal. Makes 3 pints.

CARROT PICKLES
2 to 3 bunches small carrots
Water
1 cup sugar
2 cups vinegar
1 teaspoon salt
1 cinnamon stick
1 tablespoon mixed pickling spice

Cook carrots in small amount of boiling water until tender. Drain and remove skins. Leave small carrots whole; cut larger ones into pieces as desired. Mix sugar, vinegar, 1½ cups water, and the salt in saucepan. Tie spices in a cheesecloth bag; add to vinegar mixture. Boil for 5 to 8 minutes. Pack carrots into hot sterilized pint jars, leaving ½-inch headspace. Remove spice bag from syrup and reheat syrup to boiling. Pour, boiling hot, over carrots, leaving ½-inch headspace. Adjust caps. Process in boiling-water bath for 30 minutes. Makes about 3 pints.

MUSTARD PICKLE
1 large head cauliflower, broken into flowerets
1 quart small pickling cucumbers or 1 quart sliced cucumber
1 quart small white onions, peeled
2 red peppers, sliced
1 cup salt
¼ cup powdered mustard
½ cup firmly packed brown sugar
1 cup water
1 quart vinegar
½ teaspoon celery seed
2 teaspoons mustard seed
1 teaspoon each of whole cloves and allspice
¼ cup all-purpose flour
1 teaspoon turmeric

Arrange vegetables in layers in large bowl or enamel preserving kettle, sprinkling each layer with salt. Let stand overnight. Drain. Mix mustard and sugar in large preserving kettle. Add water, vinegar, and seeds. Add cloves and allspice tied in cheesecloth bag. Bring to a boil. Add vegetables, bring again to boil and simmer until tender. Mix flour and turmeric into a paste with a little cold water. Add to pickles and cook for 5 minutes longer. Remove spice bag. Pack pickles into hot sterilized jars and seal. Makes 4 or 5 pints.

OLIVE-OIL CUCUMBER-ONION PICKLE
4 pounds (8 medium) cucumbers
2 pounds onions
Salt
Water
2 quarts cider vinegar
3 pounds (6¾ cups) sugar
2 tablespoons each of celery seed and mustard seed
2 tablespoons turmeric
2 tablespoons grated horseradish
½ cup olive oil

Thinly slice unpeeled washed cucumbers and peeled onions into crock or large bowl, sprinkling each layer generously with salt. Let stand overnight. Drain, and rinse with cold water. Drain again. Bring remaining ingredients except oil to boil. Add vegetables and simmer until cucumbers are transparent. Remove from heat and let stand until cold. Add oil and pack into sterilized jars; seal. Makes 6 or 7 pints.

MIXED SWEET PICKLES

2 medium heads cauliflower
2 sweet red peppers, cut into strips
2 green peppers, cut into strips
1 pound onions, cut into wedges
4 cups white vinegar
2 cups sugar
½ cup light corn syrup
1 tablespoon each of mustard and celery seed
1 teaspoon whole cloves
¼ teaspoon ground turmeric
2 tablespoons salt

Break cauliflower into flowerets; there should be 2 quarts. Cook in a small amount of unsalted water for 5 minutes; drain. Combine remaining ingredients and bring to boil. Add cauliflower; simmer for 2 minutes. Pack into hot sterilized jars; seal. Makes 6 pints.

CRYSTAL MIXED PICKLES

Remove label from 1 jar (12 ounces) sweet mixed pickles. Drain juice and thoroughly fill jar with sugar, about 1½ cups, being sure all space between pickles is filled. Insert table knife in jar to make more room for sugar. Let stand for a few minutes and add more sugar if possible. Put lid on securely. Put in refrigerator and invert jar. Turn jar occasionally so that sugar dissolves and pickles crystallize. After a week, refrigeration is not necessary.

PICKLE, TO—A process by which food is preserved in salt, an acid liquid such as vinegar, or sugar, or in any combination of the three. Technically speaking a pickle is either the brine used or any food so preserved. However, in everyday usage the word pickle is generally restricted to those vegetables and fruits which have, over the years, made the most popular pickles: cucumbers, onions, and watermelon rind, for example. The word relish is used to describe such pickled fruits and vegetables when they are chopped.

Pickling is one of the four most popular means of keeping food from spoiling; the others are canning, freezing, and dehydrating. Historically, pickling is one of the oldest methods of food preservation known to man. Some four thousand years ago the Chinese knew of the preservative qualities of salt brine. The

Babylonians pickled their fish. Since earliest times, in fact, vinegar and salt, or both together, have been used as preservatives for fish and meats.

The ancient Greeks and Romans used pickling in many ways. Apicius, an early Roman writer, gives many recipes for pickling. In answer to the question of "how to keep pork or beef skin and cooked trotters," he writes: "Put in mustard which is prepared with vinegar, salt, and honey, so that it is covered, and use when required." Turnips are to be soaked in honey, vinegar, and myrtle berries, or in honey, vinegar, and salt. This recipe is still followed in Near Eastern cookery.

All European countries learned how to pickle and all of them still pickle fish, meats, and vegetables. The pickled herrings of Scandinavia and German pork and sauerkraut are prime examples.

PICKLED PIGS' FEET

8 pigs' feet
½ onion, sliced
½ carrot, sliced
⅛ teaspoon peppercorns
   Few sprigs of parsley
½ bay leaf
½ teaspoon salt
1 cup vinegar
3 cups water

Clean pigs' feet thoroughly. Leave whole or split into halves. Combine with remaining ingredients in kettle, bring to boil and simmer, covered, until tender. Cool. Makes 4 servings.

SPICED PICKLED BEETS

9 pounds small bunch beets with tops
   Water
2 cups sugar
1 tablespoon whole allspice
2 cinnamon sticks
1½ teaspoons salt
3½ cups vinegar

Wash and drain beets. Leave 2 inches of stems and the taproots. Cover with boiling water and cook until tender. Drain and peel. There should be about 3 quarts. Bring remaining ingredients and 1½ cups water to boil and simmer for 15 minutes. Pack beets into hot sterilized pint jars, leaving ½-inch headspace. If necessary, cut larger beets into halves. Remove cinnamon sticks from liquid and bring liquid to boiling. Pour, boiling hot, over beets, leaving ½-inch headspace. Adjust caps. Process pints in boiling-water bath for 30 minutes. Makes about 6 pints.

PICKLED EGGS

12 eggs
4 cups cider vinegar
1 tablespoon peppercorns
1 tablespoon whole allspice
1 tablespoon whole cloves
1 tablespoon green gingerroot, minced
1 teaspoon salt

Cover eggs with cold water, and bring to

a rapid boil. Cover, and let stand for 15 minutes. Drain, and cover with cold water. Remove shells. Bring remaining ingredients to a boil, and simmer for 10 minutes. Put eggs into hot sterilized jars, and strain hot liquid over them. Seal and keep in a cool place.

PICKLED APPLE SLICES

1 can (1 pound, 4 ounces) apple slices
½ cup vinegar
½ cup water
½ cup sugar
1 tablespoon mixed pickling spice
½ lemon, sliced thin
½ cup golden raisins

Drain liquid from apples into saucepan. Add vinegar, water, sugar, spice, and lemon. Bring to a boil, and add apples and raisins. Simmer for three minutes. Remove from heat and let stand overnight before using. Makes about 1 quart.

SPICY PICKLED PEACHES

Six 4-inch cinnamon sticks
1 tablespoon whole allspice
2 tablespoons whole cloves
1 piece gingerroot
1 quart cider vinegar
1 quart water
¼ teaspoon salt
8 cups sugar
6 pounds (4 quarts) medium-size firm peaches

Tie spices loosely in a cheesecloth bag and boil with vinegar, water, salt, and sugar for 10 minutes. Add peeled whole peaches, a few at a time, and simmer until tender. When all are done, remove spice bag. Pack peaches into hot sterilized jars, and fill with boiling syrup; seal. Makes about 10 pints.

PICKLED APRICOTS

About 3½ cups (1-pound, 13-ounce can) whole peeled apricots
6 whole allspice
⅓ cup cider vinegar
1 cinnamon stick
   Small piece of gingerroot

Drain apricots, reserving juice. Add remaining ingredients to juice and simmer gently 15 minutes. Add apricots and heat for a few minutes. Serve warm or cold with poultry or pork. Makes about 4 cups.

PICKLED FIGS

4 quarts firm-ripe figs
5 cups sugar
2 quarts water
3 cups vinegar
1 tablespoon each of whole cloves and allspice
2 cinnamon sticks

Peel figs. (If preferred unpeeled, pour boiling water over figs and let stand until cool; drain.) Add 3 cups sugar to the water and cook until the sugar dissolves. Add figs and simmer for 30 minutes. Add remaining sugar and the vinegar. Tie spices in a cheesecloth bag; add to figs. Cook gently until figs are clear. Cover and let stand for 12 to 24 hours in a cool place. Remove spice bag. Heat to simmering and pack into hot sterilized pint jars, leaving ¼-inch headspace. Adjust caps. Process in boiling-water bath for 10 minutes. Makes about 8 pints.

PICKLING SPICE—A blend of different whole spices (allspice, bay leaf, cardamom, celery, chilies, cinnamon, cloves, coriander, dill, fenugreek, gingerroot, mace, mustard, and black pepper are among the most common ingredients) which produces a distinctive, pleasant, spicy, and sweet flavor upon cooking. Pickling spice is packaged premixed in balanced proportions. It is used in pickling and preserving meats, vegetables, and relishes, and to season gravies, sauces, stews, fish, and shellfish.

PICNIC—An occasion, usually held outdoors, where food is eaten under informal circumstances and where a good time is had by all.

Picnics can be as varied as one chooses to make them, from a spur-of-the-moment picnic where everything is bought at the market en route, to the carefully planned barbecue for backyard entertaining.

PICNICS
by James A. Beard

My family upbringing imbued me with a passion for picnics. We lived in western Oregon, a green countryside whose mountains, streams, and beaches provided perfect settings for outdoor dining. Of course, we had many planned affairs: holiday picnics, weekend picnics, birthday picnics, anniversary picnics. But we also picnicked in between times on the spur of the moment. And always, when we traveled, whether by boat, train, or auto, my mother packed imaginative snacks for us to eat as we watched the scenery pass by. One of my fondest memories is our annual trek by train to our summer beach home. Each of us carried a special packaged lunch to be eaten en route. I usually ate mine

on the outdoor observation platform at the end of the train. This was a magic spot, unduplicated in today's closed-in, air-conditioned parlor and buffet cars. I can recall the excitement of sitting on a folding chair on the observation deck with my lunch box on my knees. What would it contain this time? It might be thin, thin slices of moist chicken on even thinner slices of firm homemade bread with parsley butter or mayonnaise. Maybe it would be fine Seville-orange marmalade on well-buttered homemade bread; maybe small fresh rolls stuffed with salad mixture, each roll a new surprise. Maybe there would also be a date bar or a large sugar cookie. Feasting on these tasty tidbits, lulled by the rhythmic clatter of the train, I would feel the wind rushing past and watch the tracks sweep away into a dwindling ribbon. Another favorite boyhood jaunt was an occasional trip on the old river steamer, the *Bailey Gatzert,* that went up the Columbia River to the applegrowing country near Hood River. Along went a hamper for elevenses, which we ate on deck as we churned sedately through the great Columbia gorge. One year's picnic season began with my birthday in May. My mother made arrangements in advance at a popular amusement park on the river. The park had nice stretches of lawn with shade trees and summer picnic houses, and we always reserved the largest summerhouse. We started out, usually twenty to thirty children and adults, early in the day, laden with hampers and many containers. This was before the era of the outdoor grill, but we carted a supply of chafing dishes with alcohol burners. The hot food was frankfurters made to order in a miniature size, and buns to match. We had baskets of sandwiches, salads, relishes, a huge container of homemade ice cream and, of course, a colossal birthday cake.

There was always enough food for two meals. We ate lunch and then spent the afternoon riding the roller coaster and playing games; then we had another snack before packing up to leave.

Memorial Day was our next planned picnic venture. In true American tradition we never let a patriotic holiday go by without listening to speeches and brass bands, and eating lots of food. Memorial Day exercises started in the morning at the nearby Lone Fir Cemetery. Civil War veterans were still numerous and attended in their uniforms, both blue and gray. Spanish-American War veterans, led by my godfather General Summers, turned out in force. Important leaders of the community spoke at length of our country's patriots, promi-

nent ministers led the devotions, and then the band struck up in the bandstand. As the music played we solemnly decorated the graves.

After the ceremonies we all gathered at a nearby park for a communal picnic. Each woman brought food, whatever was her specialty, and it was all spread out on long wooden tables. Strangely enough these mass picnics produced some delectable dishes, and plenty of them.

July Fourth was another holiday picnic. By that time we were at our beach home for the summer. The small town of Seaside, Oregon, three miles away, had a parade, and the loggers who came down from the hills held log-rolling contests. After the fun was over we went home for an evening beach bonfire and picnic, complete with elaborate fireworks: Roman candles, sky rockets, Catherine wheels, giant crackers, and dangling strings of tiny Chinese firecrackers that popped off in rapid succession. We roasted weenies at the fire, popped corn, and toasted marshmallows. Some of the teen-agers strummed their ukuleles and the most daring dashed off into the rough surf for a late-evening dip.

Summer at the beach, it seems to me, was one continuous picnic. Often we even had breakfast on the sand. We located a comfortable spot near a large driftwood log that would shelter us from the wind and then collected smaller pieces of wood for fires. We built two fires, one for toasting foods on sticks and the other, smaller, for simple grills. We took along a basket of fresh fruit, whatever was in season: apricots, plums, dark juicy cherries, ripe red raspberries, or loganberries from the sandy coast soil. These we ate plain. Then there was always country ham and bacon with eggs from the grill, and even little pancakes made from mother's own sour-cream pancake recipe. Some of us toasted bread in the fire. Topping for toast or pancakes was often the wild huckleberries or blackberries of the coast cooked down with sugar until they were syrupy.

When we went into the hills to go berrying, or along the stream to catch crawfish, both regular pastimes at the coast, we took along a hamper with hot baked beans. These were not the Boston variety sweetened with molasses, but a simple garlic-flavored bean dish topped with crumbs and grated cheese. With it went plenty of sandwiches, salads, and pickles.

We went home to the city in time for Labor Day. This was indeed a day for brass bands and parades, and in every park people gathered to hear lengthy speeches extolling the working-man. We children always ate our fill and romped with greater abandon, for this day was the signal of the end of vacation and the end of picnics for months to come.

Yet, if we were blessed with a pleasant Indian summer in the fall, we frequently had a final taste of outdoor living before the winter rains set in. Sometimes we went out to gather mushrooms or hazel-nuts, or to the valley farms to gather the late fruits. Often these treks were arranged on impulse and the picnic hamper was not elaborate. It was apt to contain whatever we had ready pre-pared: a piece of cold roast, some sausages, homemade bread and butter, and a salad. We would pick up fruit at our destination, and buy cider from a local farmer. It was hearty homely fare, but mouth-watering and the perfect selec-tion for robust appetites in crisp fall weather.

As I look back on those boyhood picnicking experiences, I recall what seems to be an endless season of joy and good feasting. We had what I like to term a "good picnic spirit" and I assure you it is a spirit well worth culti-vating, for it combines love of the countryside with rich appreciation of the bounty it offers us. I recommend picnicking as a sure cure for the tensions of our modern world.

BEACH PICNIC

The good beach picnic is easy to tote, easy to eat on the sand without elaborate utensils. Cold Broiled Chicken is finger food. The Pungent French Rolls, finger food again, are really portable salads. (Make them the night before, weight them down a bit, and chill for a truly mellow flavor.) Hearty Baked Pea Beans, carried in an insulated container or re-heated on a small grill, call only for plates and forks. Fruit, cheese, and cookies are all eaten out of hand. Cold drinks packed in ice and good hot coffee complete the picture.

COLD BROILED CHICKEN
BAKED PEA BEANS
PUNGENT FRENCH ROLLS
CHEESE AND BARTLETT PEARS
COOKIES
COFFEE   SOFT DRINKS

COLD BROILED CHICKEN
½ cup soy sauce
1 cup sherry
1 tablespoon paprika
2 garlic cloves, minced
  Dash of hot pepper sauce

6 chickens, split
½ cup cooking oil
  or melted butter

Combine the soy sauce, sherry, paprika, garlic, and hot pepper sauce, and pour over the chicken halves. Let stand for an hour or two, turning occasionally. Re-move the chicken from the marinade and brush each piece with oil. Broil, bone side to the heat, for 13 minutes. Brush with the marinade and broil for 3 more minutes. Turn, and move the chicken a little farther from the broiling unit to prevent the skin side from blistering and burning. Brush skin side with marinade and broil for 12 minutes. Brush again, and continue broiling until tender. Cool the chicken and wrap in aluminum foil for carrying to the picnic site. Makes 12 servings.

BAKED PEA BEANS
2 pounds dried pea beans
1 onion, stuck with 2 cloves
1 bay leaf
1 tablespoon salt
1 pound lean salt pork
1 pound smoked ham
3 onions
3 garlic cloves
2 teaspoons powdered mustard
¼ cup rum

Cover the beans with water and soak overnight. Drain and add fresh water to come 3 inches above the beans. Add the onion stuck with cloves, bay leaf, and salt, and bring to a boil. Boil rapidly for 5 minutes. Skim the top, reduce the heat and simmer until the beans are tender but not mushy. Meanwhile, put the salt pork in water and bring to a boil. Lower the heat and simmer for 25 minutes. Re-move the pork from the water and cut it first into slices, then into small pieces. Cut the ham into strips. Peel and chop the onions and garlic cloves. Blend the mustard with a little bean liquid. Taste the beans for seasoning. Place a layer of the beans in the bottom of a large baking dish. Add a layer of salt pork, ham, onion, and garlic. Repeat the layers end-ing with beans on top. Pour the mustard water over the mixture, and add enough bean liquid to come to the top of the baking dish. Bake in preheated moderate oven (350°F.) for 1½ hours. If more moisture is needed, add more bean liquid. Remove from the oven and pour the rum over the beans. Return to the oven and bake for 45 minutes longer, or until nicely browned and bubbly. Reheat at picnic. Makes 12 servings.

PUNGENT FRENCH ROLLS
12 French rolls
   Olive oil
2 red onions, chopped
2 green peppers, diced
2 cucumbers, peeled and diced
24 anchovy fillets, cut
4 large ripe tomatoes, peeled,

   seeded, and diced
36 pitted black olives, chopped
⅓ cup chopped parsley
¼ cup capers
   Mayonnaise

Split the rolls almost through and brush inside well with olive oil. Mix remaining ingredients, except mayonnaise. Moisten with mayonnaise and fill rolls. Arrange these stuffed rolls in a box or on a plate and provide paper napkins to wrap around them as they are eaten. This dish takes the place of both bread and the salad course. Makes 12 servings.

ROADSIDE PICNIC

A long drive in the country—to the mountains, the coast, or to visit a his-torical site—often calls for a picnic en route. Remember, a roadside lunch is a rather brief break in the day's activity. Keep the menu simple, with foods that pack with the least trouble and are easy to assemble when you eat. Start with the old favorite, good Deviled Eggs. They travel well and please outdoor appetites. The Olive Meat Loaf, really a country pâté, is rich, flavorful, and cuts well for sandwiches. Crisp finger vegetables with a jar of dunk sauce provide salad without mess or fuss. Even the Lemon Squares and melon wedges can be eaten out of hand. Then hot coffee and you are off once more.

SARDINE-STUFFED DEVILED EGGS
OLIVE MEAT LOAF
FINGER SALAD WITH DUNKING SAUCE
FRENCH BREAD AND
SANDWICH ROLLS
LEMON SQUARES WITH
APRICOT GLAZE
MELON WEDGES WITH LIME
COFFEE   MILK

SARDINE-STUFFED DEVILED EGGS
12 hard-cooked eggs
1 can skinless and boneless sardines
2 tablespoons finely minced
   green onion
½ teaspoon salt
   Juice of 1 lemon
½ teaspoon Worcestershire
   Mayonnaise, if necessary
   Ripe olives

Cool eggs quickly under cold running water. Shell and halve the long way. Re-move the yolks carefully and mash. Drain and mash the sardines. Season them with minced onion, salt, lemon juice, and Worcestershire. Beat the mashed egg yolks into the sardine mixture and taste for seasoning. If the mixture needs binding, blend in a little mayonnaise. Using a spoon or knife, fill the egg whites with the sardine mixture; or force the

Beach Picnic

Sandwich and Salad Picnic

Holiday Picnic

mixture through a pastry tube using the rosette attachment. Garnish each stuffed egg with slices of ripe olives.

OLIVE MEAT LOAF

2 pounds ground beef chuck
1 pound ground pork
1 pound ground veal
1 large onion, chopped
1 garlic clove, minced
1 large carrot, ground in blender, or grated
2 eggs
2 teaspoons salt
½ teaspoon pepper
1 cup small stuffed olives, halved
3 slices of bacon
 Sliced stuffed olives for top

Combine meats with onion, garlic, carrot, eggs, salt, and pepper. Mix well. Add halved olives. Shape into oval loaf in shallow baking pan. Top with bacon. Bake in preheated slow oven (325°F.) for about 2 hours. Garnish with sliced olives. Makes 8 to 10 servings.

FINGER SALAD WITH DUNKING SAUCE

Be sure the vegetables are cold and crisp. Use both red and white radishes, small green onions, romaine, cucumber sticks, peeled and halved small carrots, sprigs of watercress, and thinly sliced young turnips. For dunking, use Rémoulade Sauce.

Rémoulade Sauce

1 cup dairy sour cream
1 cup mayonnaise
¼ cup chopped capers
3 tablespoons chopped chives
1 garlic clove, minced
1½ teaspoons paprika
1 tablespoon chopped fresh dill or
2 tablespoons chopped dill pickle
1 tablespoon fresh lemon juice
2 tablespoons chopped parsley

Blend all ingredients and let mellow for 1 or 2 hours. Makes about 2½ cups.

LEMON SQUARES WITH APRICOT GLAZE

For the spongecake:

¼ cup all-purpose flour
¼ cup cornstarch
4 eggs
¼ cup sugar
½ teaspoon vanilla extract
½ teaspoon grated lemon rind

Sift the flour and cornstarch together. Separate the eggs; beat the egg whites until they form soft peaks. Gradually add the sugar and beat until stiff. Stir the egg yolks lightly and stir in 1 cup of the egg whites plus the vanilla and lemon rind. Pour this mixture over the rest of the egg whites, add the flour and cornstarch, and fold all together lightly. Pour into a wax-paper-lined pan (15 x 10 x 1 inches) and bake in preheated hot oven (400°F.) for 10 minutes.

Lemon-Curd Filling:

5 egg yolks
¾ cup sugar
2 large lemons (juice and grated rind)
¼ pound sweet butter

In a heavy saucepan, or the top part of a double boiler, combine the egg yolks, sugar, lemon juice, and grated rind. Cook very slowly (if over water, do not let the water boil), whisking constantly with a wire whisk. As the mixture cooks, add the butter a bit at a time. Continue cooking and whisking until the mixture thickens. Cool thoroughly before using. Lemon curd keeps well; store it in a jar in the refrigerator and it will last for months.

For the Apricot Glaze:

Melt 4 ounces apricot preserves and stir and boil down for 1 minute. Add 2 tablespoons of rum or brandy and cook down for 1 minute. Strain; cool slightly.

To prepare the Squares:

Cut the spongecake into halves lengthwise and spread one half with Lemon-Curd Filling. Top with the second half. Cut into squares, brush with Apricot Glaze, and chill.

HOLIDAY PICNIC

A large holiday gathering is most successful when people fix their own food. Advance preparation is mainly a matter of wise shopping. Be sure to have an ample supply and a wide choice. You will need a good assortment of meats, breads, cheeses, and relishes, and well-seasoned frankfurters for those who like hot sandwiches. The night before or early on the morning of the picnic, bake the ham and set it aside to cool. Make a huge bowl of coleslaw. The recipe given here adds a new twist to this old favorite. Finally, prepare a big freezer of Strawberry Ice Cream. These are really simple tasks taking little time and effort. At the last minute, pack plenty of soft and cooling drinks in jugs and pails of ice and you're set for the big event.

ASSORTED RELISHES AND
CONDIMENTS
HERO LOAVES   PUMPERNICKEL
LONG BUNS AND ROUND BUNS
COLESLAW
FLANK STEAK TERIYAKI
FRANKFURTERS
BAKED HAM   ASSORTED COLD MEATS
CHEESE TRAY OF
CHEDDAR, PROVOLONE, SWISS,
MUENSTER, EDAM
FREEZER OF
STRAWBERRY ICE CREAM
WITH ICE CREAM CONES

Breads: The hero loaves are, of course, for do-it-yourself hero sandwiches. Pumpernickel goes well with cold meats and cheese. Long buns are for frankfurters, and round ones for cold meats.

Coleslaw: Make a simple cabbage slaw and dress it with dairy sour cream and mayonnaise, mixed half and half and seasoned with garlic.

Frankfurters: Choose regular frankfurters and include knackwurst if you like.

Cold Meats: Buy as many different kinds of French, Italian, German, Polish, or other flavorful sausages as you can find in your area and have ham, canned or baked, according to your favorite recipe.

Cheese Tray: Arrange whole cheeses or sections of cheese on a board with a cheese knife and let people cut their own.

FLANK STEAK TERIYAKI

Flanks of choice or prime beef are best for this dish. One flank will serve 3 or 4 persons generously. Have the butcher trim the steaks well. For 3 flanks, prepare the following marinade:

1 cup soy sauce
1 cup sherry
½ cup peanut oil
3 garlic cloves, minced
⅓ cup chopped or grated fresh gingerroot (if not available, use ½ teaspoon ground ginger)

Blend all ingredients and marinate the steaks in the mixture for several hours, turning them occasionally. To grill: broil over brisk coals, allowing 3 to 4 minutes per side for rare; 5 minutes per side for medium. Cut into paper-thin slices, sloping the knife to cut diagonally through the grain of the meat. Each slice can be dipped into heated marinade before going into a sandwich.

FREEZER OF STRAWBERRY ICE CREAM

2 quarts strawberries
2 cups sugar
3 quarts heavy cream
 Pinch of salt

Clean and hull the berries and sprinkle them with sugar. Cover, and let stand for 1½ to 2 hours. Mash them lightly. Mix the cream with the salt and pour into the freezer; freeze until mushy. Remove the cover of the freezer and stir in the strawberries. Re-cover, and continue freezing until solid. Makes almost 1½ gallons.

SANDWICH AND SALAD PICNIC

This menu can be served at an informal backyard picnic, or packed, and carried for a spread in the countryside. Everything is prepared well in advance. (The salads both improve with some mellowing.) Since the food is served cold, it can be arranged on a table and guests can swim, play tennis, or stroll and then help themselves when they wish. Put the tongue and turkey on platters and cut a supply of thin slices ready for sandwich making. Nearby, place thin sliced breads, mayonnaise, and pickles. Another platter of ready-made sandwiches in wax paper and two bowls of the salads make plate-heaping a temptation. Desserts are simple: fresh fruit, and a tasty jelly roll for those with a sweet tooth.

TONGUE SANDWICHES ON RYE BREAD
SLICED TURKEY ON HOMEMADE BREAD
CREAM CHEESE ON WHOLE-WHEAT BREAD
DATE-NUT BREAD SANDWICHES
SALMAGUNDI HERRING SALAD
ITALIAN RICE SALAD
PICKLED ONIONS
HOMEMADE, FRESH DILL PICKLES
JELLY ROLL   FRESH FRUIT   COFFEE

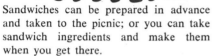

SANDWICHES

Sandwiches can be prepared in advance and taken to the picnic; or you can take sandwich ingredients and make them when you get there.

Tongue: A whole, boiled and skinned beef tongue can be transported to be sliced at the picnic. Carry thinly sliced rye bread and a pot of mustard butter: cream ⅔ cup butter, beat in 1 teaspoon powdered mustard and 2 teaspoons Dijon or diable mustard. Spoon the mixture into a container. Makes about 1 cup.

Sliced Turkey: Carry a whole roasted turkey (or chicken) with carving tools. Take along thinly sliced homemade bread, a pot of unsalted butter and mayonnaise.

Cream Cheese: Cream ½ pound cream cheese. Beat in ½ cup chopped sweet onion (red Italian are excellent) and ¼ cup finely minced parsley; add salt to taste. Butter thin slices of whole-wheat bread and spread with the cheese mixture. Top with second slices of bread. Trim crusts and cut into fingers. This fills 10 to 12 sandwiches.

Date-Nut: Date-nut bread comes in cans. Each can makes 12 to 14 slices. Spread slices with butter, then with creamy cottage cheese, a good marmalade, and sprinkle with coarsely chopped walnuts. Top each with another buttered slice of the bread and press together.

SALMAGUNDI HERRING SALAD
1½ Bismarck herrings, or 2 jars of Bismarck herring
2 cups sliced cold cooked potatoes
1½ cups sliced cold cooked beets
½ cup grated raw carrot
1 cup finely diced cold cooked chicken or veal
½ cup diced raw tart apple

½ teaspoon sugar
¼ cup chopped parsley
1½ cups mayonnaise
Salt and pepper
Dairy sour cream
Sliced sweet gherkins
Chopped fresh dill (optional)
Hard-cooked eggs
Cherry tomatoes

Drain the herring and dice it fine. Mix with the vegetables, meat, and apple. Blend in the sugar, parsley, and mayonnaise, and add salt and pepper to taste. Top with sour cream and garnish with sliced gherkins, dill, and sieved egg yolks. Surround with tomatoes. Makes 12 servings.

Note: You can serve this salad from a jar and pass garnishes.

ITALIAN RICE SALAD
3 cups cooked rice
2 pimientos, cut into strips
1 green pepper, cut into strips
12 green onions, finely cut, or ⅔ cup chopped red Italian onions
1 teaspoon dried or 2 tablespoons fresh basil
18 large stuffed olives, sliced
1½ cups cooked chicken or turkey breasts, cut into julienne strips
18 anchovy fillets, coarsely cut
Garlic flavored French dressing
Tomato wedges
Hard-cooked eggs

Combine the first 8 ingredients. Toss with dressing. Garnish with tomato wedges and quartered eggs. Makes 10 to 12 servings.

A SIMPLY ELEGANT PICNIC

An elegant picnic calls for an elegant setting: the garden perhaps, or a nearby park. Iced *Gazpacho,* a Spanish soup, comes in many versions. This, with chopped vegetables added, has a fresh crunchy texture. The Roast Beef should be gently warm. Condiments and a salad of tiny potatoes go with it, and Strawberry Tarts are a festive finale.

ICED GAZPACHO WITH VEGETABLE, CROUTON, AND HERB GARNISH
WARM ROAST BEEF
FRENCH POTATO SALAD
WITH ONION AND PARSLEY DRESSING
HERB-BUTTERED RYE- AND WHITE-BREAD SANDWICHES
HORSERADISH CREAM
CHOWCHOW   BLACK OLIVES
CURRANT-GLAZED STRAWBERRY TARTS
ICED TEA

ICED GAZPACHO WITH VEGETABLE, CROUTON, AND HERB GARNISH
1 cup blanched almonds
8 ripe tomatoes

3 garlic cloves, chopped
1 cup chopped onion
1 cup coarse French-bread crumbs
Juice of 1 lemon
Salt and pepper
Tomato juice
Hot pepper sauce

Grind almonds in an electric blender. Peel and chop the tomatoes, and blend with the chopped garlic and onion. Grind the bread crumbs in the blender. Combine the ground almonds with some of the tomato mixture, and blend in the blender. Mix this with the rest of the tomatoes and the bread crumbs, add the lemon juice and season to taste with salt and pepper. Add enough tomato juice to make 8 cups; or add more chopped tomatoes. Taste for seasoning and add a healthy dash of hot pepper sauce. Chill and serve in bowls over cubes of frozen tomato juice. Let guests help themselves to the following garnishes (you will need about 1 cup of each to serve 8 persons): Chopped cucumber, tomato, green onion, green pepper, celery, fresh herbs (parsley and fresh basil, if available); tiny croutons of toasted bread. Makes 8 servings.

WARM ROAST BEEF
Choose a 4- to 5-rib roast to serve 8 and have it well trimmed. If you buy ready-packaged meats, you will find ribs already cut and trimmed for the oven. Place the meat on a rack and insert a meat thermometer in the thickest part of the roast, making certain that it does not touch the bone. Roast in preheated slow oven (300°F.) without basting, until the thermometer registers 130°F. As the meat cools down to warm, it will continue cooking with its own heat. This will give you a good rare roast. Remove the meat from the oven to stand and cool, but do not let it get cold. It should be warm and crisp on the outside and warm and juicy-rare in the center. Serve in paper-thin slices with:

Chowchow: The English type made with mustard, turmeric, and spices.

Horseradish Cream: If possible, get fresh horseradish and shred enough root to make 1½ cups. Combine 1 cup of the horseradish with 1 cup dairy sour cream. Season with 1 teaspoon salt and a dash of hot pepper sauce. Sprinkle remaining horseradish over the top.

FRENCH POTATO SALAD WITH ONION AND PARSLEY DRESSING
3 pounds tiny new potatoes
Salt
½ cup dry white wine
1 cup salad oil
⅓ cup vinegar
½ teaspoon freshly ground pepper
1 cup finely chopped green onion
¼ cup chopped parsley
2 pimientos, cut up

Boil the potatoes in their jackets until

just pierceable. Pour cold water over them and peel at once. Cut them into halves or quarters, sprinkle with ½ teaspoon salt and add the white wine. Let stand for 30 minutes. Mix the oil, vinegar, pepper, 1 teaspoon salt, onion, and parsley, and pour over the potatoes. Toss well. Add pimiento. If you want to serve the salad warm, you can heat the oil and vinegar, pour them over the potatoes, and toss thoroughly. Makes 8 servings.

HERB-BUTTERED RYE- AND WHITE-BREAD SANDWICHES
    ⅔ cup sweet butter
    ¼ cup chopped chives
    ¼ cup finely chopped fresh dill
    ½ teaspoon salt
      Freshly ground pepper to taste
    8 slices each of rye and white bread

Cream the butter and beat in the chives, dill, salt, and pepper. Spread 8 slices of bread with this mixture and top with remaining slices to make sandwiches. Trim the crusts and cut into fingers or wedges. Chill until ready to take to picnic.

CURRANT-GLAZED STRAWBERRY TARTS
      Pastry (made with 3 cups flour)
    2 quarts fresh strawberries
    1 jar (16 ounces) currant jelly
    2 cups heavy cream, whipped
      Vanilla extract

Roll pastry to ⅛-inch thickness and bake 24 small tart shells or two 9-inch pie shells. Cool. Fill shells with perfect strawberries, arranging them so they look attractive, points up. Chill in refrigerator. Melt the currant jelly in a heavy saucepan over medium heat. When it is thick and syrupy, spoon over berries so that each berry is coated with jelly. Chill again. Serve with whipped cream flavored to taste with vanilla.

〰 COOKOUT PICNIC 〰

Tired of grilled foods? Then here is a change. Boil lobster tails over a charcoal or wood fire and serve them with mayonnaise and all sorts of relishes. While the seafood cooks, still the hunger pangs with Iced Curried Pea Soup. The Salade Niçoise can include a variety of tidbits. Add your favorites. Red-Cherry Kuchen is a light, tangy sweet, and iced tea a refreshing finish. Serve cool white wine with the lobster, if you enjoy wine with dinner.

ICED CURRIED PEA SOUP
BOILED LOBSTER TAILS
WITH MELTED BUTTER AND
HOMEMADE MAYONNAISE AND
RELISHES
SALADE NIÇOISE
FRENCH BREAD   HARD ROLLS
POTATO CHIPS
RED-CHERRY KUCHEN   ICED TEA

ICED CURRIED PEA SOUP
    2 boxes (10 ounces each) frozen peas
    2 cans condensed consommé
    1 can water
    2 teaspoons curry powder or more,
      to taste
      Salt and pepper

Cook peas according to the package directions but omit salt. Whirl in blender; add consommé and blend until smooth. Add water and curry powder, and blend. Season with salt and pepper to taste and add more curry powder if desired. Makes about 2 quarts, or 8 servings.

BOILED LOBSTER TAILS
Allow 2 lobster tails per person. Carry a good-size kettle to the picnic and fill it almost full with salted water. Bring to a boil. If you like added seasonings, you may put in a peeled onion, a few sprigs of parsley, a garlic clove, and a few peppercorns. When the water boils, plunge in the lobster tails and cook for 7 to 12 minutes. When they are done, remove and put them on a board. Split the lobster tails open with a heavy knife. Serve with melted butter and Homemade Mayonnaise with Relishes: For 8 people allow about 1 quart mayonnaise. Use your favorite mayonnaise recipe, but omit sugar if the recipe calls for it. The sweet is not complementary to the fish or to some of the relishes. Surround the bowl of mayonnaise with any or all of the following and let each one mix his own sauce for the lobster: chopped anchovies, India relish, red pepper relish, chutney, chopped dill pickles, chopped chives or green onions, several types of mustard in jars, chopped hard-cooked eggs, chopped parsley and other fresh herbs, chili sauce.

SALADE NIÇOISE
Make a bed of greens in a large bowl. Combine 3 cans (7 ounces each) of white-meat tuna in chunks, 1 pound whole green beans, cooked and chilled, 8 tomatoes, cut into wedges, and 8 halved hard-cooked eggs. Garnish with anchovy fillets and rings of green pepper and thinly sliced onion. Use 2 good-sized onions. Black olives, either Italian style or California ripe olives, are a tasty addition. Serve the salad with Basil Dressing.

Basil Dressing
    1 cup salad oil
    ⅓ cup vinegar
    ½ teaspoon salt
    1 garlic clove, crushed or finely
      chopped
    4 chopped anchovy fillets
    1½ teaspoons dried basil, or 3
      tablespoons of chopped fresh basil

Blend all ingredients well with a fork and pour over the salad platter just before serving. Makes 8 servings.

RED-CHERRY KUCHEN
For the dough:
    2 packages active dry yeast
    ½ cup warm water
    3 tablespoons sugar
    ½ teaspoon salt
    ½ cup warm milk
    2 eggs, slightly beaten
    1 teaspoon grated orange rind
    2 to 3 cups all-purpose flour
    ¼ cup butter, softened

Dissolve the yeast in the water. Combine the sugar and salt with the warm milk, and add the yeast mixture. Stir well, and add the eggs and orange rind. Add enough flour to make a dough that is soft but still stiff enough to knead thoroughly. Gradually work in the butter with your fingers. Turn the dough out onto a floured board and knead for about 10 minutes, adding more flour, if necessary, to make a soft but firm dough. Place in a buttered bowl, cover with a towel, and put in a warm place to rise. Let rise until doubled in bulk. Punch the dough down, turn it out and work again for 1 to 2 minutes. Divide it into halves and pat out to fit two 9-inch-square baking pans. Or pat it out to fit a long baking pan (15 x 10 x 1 inches). Set aside and let the dough rise for a few minutes.

For the filling:
    ½ to 1 cup sugar
    1 tablespoon cornstarch
    4 cups pitted red sour cherries
    2 tablespoons butter
      Cinnamon

Mix sugar and cornstarch. Add cherries and put on top of the dough. Dot with butter and sprinkle lightly with cinnamon. Bake in preheated moderate oven (350°F.) for 45 to 50 minutes, or until the dough is done and the cherries cooked and bubbly. Makes 12 to 16 servings.

〰 CAMPING PICNIC 〰

When the sun sets and evening breezes blow up around the campsite, appetites grow sharp. But campfire cooking can be an easy task with a supply of processed foods, canned or freeze-dry. Add fresh vegetables and fruits, purchased every day or two near the campsite and you're all set. Chili con Carne is rib-sticking fare. Roasted Corn on the Cob is a natural accompaniment, and toasted sesame-seed butter continues the Southwestern theme. Add raw vegetables for a fresh crisp texture and pickled hot peppers for zest. Then, to cool the mouth, treat your picnickers to luscious slices of watermelon and spice drops.

ROAST-BEEF CHILI CON CARNE
CRACKERS
ROASTED CORN ON THE COB
TOASTED SESAME-SEED BUTTER
CARROTS   GREEN PEPPERS
CUCUMBERS   PICKLED RED PEPPERS
WATERMELON
SPICE DROPS   COFFEE

ROAST-BEEF CHILI CON CARNE

1 envelope tomato-soup mix
3 cups water
1 envelope chili-seasoning mix
1 tablespoon instant minced onion
1 can (12 ounces) roast beef
2 cans (1 pound each) red kidney beans
4 hard-cooked eggs, cut into chunks

Combine first 4 ingredients; simmer for 10 minutes. Add remaining ingredients, except eggs, and simmer for about 5 minutes longer. Add eggs. Makes 6 servings.
Note: If preferred, substitute 2 cans (1 pound each) chili with beans for chili-seasoning mix; reduce water to 2 cups, and use 1 can red kidney beans.

ROASTED CORN ON THE COB

To roast corn over fire: remove silk and close husks. Soak in salted water for about 5 minutes; drain. Roast on grill over hot fire for 10 to 15 minutes, turning frequently. (Or remove husks; put corn in cold water and bring to boil.) Serve with toasted sesame-seed butter made by toasting sesame seeds until lightly browned and mixing with butter.

PIE—Any dish of fish, flesh, fowl, or fruit covered on top with a crust of some sort is a pie. In America, pies are more often than not dessert pies, baked in a shallow pan with a bottom crust. In England, this type of pie is known as a tart. There are many kinds of crusts used for pies: crumbs, meringues, biscuits, as well as regular pastry. There are even pies such as Shepherd's Pie where the "crust" consists of mashed potatoes. Many pies are in fact not covered with a crust at all, but rather baked in some sort of pastry shell leaving the top exposed. There seem to be as many varieties of pie as there are women of many nations who bake pies.

Americans inherit their love of pies from the English. In the 14th century London was full of cookshops selling deep-dish meat pies with a heavy crust. The famous English mince pie, the Christmas pie that Little Jack Horner ate in his corner, is an evolution from these early meat pies. An old English tradition claims that eating twelve mince pies, one each day from Christmas until Twelfth Night, will make the eater happy for twelve months of the year.

When the colonists came to this country they brought with them their love for the English meat pies and dessert tarts. Until the Revolution women continued the custom of baking pies in deep pastry shells covered with a top or "coffin." Sometime after we declared our independence, a thrifty New England housewife realized that flat pies, or "tarts," needed less filling and now the traditional American pie is a flat one.

Several pies are particularly associated with the United States. There is the pumpkin pie, a refinement of the first pumpkin pies which were merely hollowed-out whole pumpkins; the molasses-flavored shoofly pies of the Pennsylvania Dutch; and most famous of all—American apple pie. In the days before refrigeration and freezers, the apples were picked, peeled, quartered, and hung on cords in the kitchen. The dried quarters were used to make pies all through the winter. New Englanders ate them for breakfast. "What is pie for?" asked Emerson when challenged on the custom. In 1902 the *New York Times* blasted an English suggestion that pie be eaten only twice a week. This, said the *Times,* was "utterly insufficient . . . as anyone who knows the secret of our strength as a nation and the foundation of our industrial supremacy must admit. Pie is the American synonym of prosperity, and its varying contents the calendar of the changing seasons. Pie is the food of the heroic. No pie-eating people can ever be permanently vanquished."

TO FREEZE PIES

Main-dish pies, fruit, mince, pumpkin, and chiffon pies all freeze well. Cream and custard pies should not be frozen in home freezers.

■ **To Freeze Pastry**—Pastry may be frozen in a ball, rolled out into circles, or fitted and fluted in a pie pan. Wrap pastry circles with 2 pieces of moisture-proof paper between each 2 layers so that a pastry circle may be removed without thawing the whole batch. Place the stack on a piece of cardboard; wrap in moisture-proof wrapping and seal. Before using a circle of pastry, thaw completely at room temperature, then fit into pie pan and proceed as recipe directs.

■ **Unfilled Piecrust**—Place pastry, shaped in a pie pan and either unbaked or baked, in freezer. Freeze solid before wrapping. After piecrust is frozen solid, remove it from pan and wrap. Minimize breaking by stacking frozen crusts in a cardboard box with crumbled paper between each 2 crusts.

To use frozen unbaked piecrusts to make a baked shell place crust again in pie pan and put in the oven. Ovenproof

glass pie pans should first stand for 5 to 10 minutes at room temperature. Bake as for unfrozen pastry, adding about 5 minutes to the baking time. Prick shell with a fork after 5 minutes of baking.

Baked shells can be thawed at room temperature or heated for about 10 minutes in preheated hot oven (400°F.).

To make a 1-crust pie using a frozen unbaked pie crust, remove it from freezer, place in pie pan, and allow to thaw while preparing filling. Fill and bake as recipe directs.

■ **Filled Pies**—Prepare crust and filling for fruit and chiffon pies as recipe directs using a regular pie pan or an aluminum-foil pan specifically made for freezing. The top crust of fruit pies should not be slit before freezing. The filling of chiffon or similar pies should set completely before freezing. Baked pies must be cooled thoroughly before freezing. Meringues should be omitted. Make them and add them to the pie just before serving.

Protect the tops of baked or unbaked pies by covering them with either a paper plate or aluminum pie pan. Then wrap and seal. Keep pies level until frozen solid. Freeze fragile pies unwrapped until solid, then wrap and seal.

■ **To Thaw Pies**—Thaw chiffon or other pies with unbaked fillings unwrapped in the refrigerator for 1 to 1½ hours. Unwrap unbaked fruit pies and place, while still frozen, in preheated hot oven (425° F.). Bake for 40 to 60 minutes according to the type and size of pie. Slit tops of double-crust pies before baking. Chiffon pies are sometimes eaten while still partially frozen.

Unwrap baked fruit pies and heat them in preheated moderate oven (375°F.) for about 30 minutes, or until center is hot.

■ **To Store Frozen Pies**

● Unbaked fruit pies: 6 to 8 months
● Unbaked main-dish pies: 6 to 8 months
● Unbaked pumpkin, winter-squash, and sweet-potato pies: 4 to 6 months
● Baked pies and pie shells, chiffon pies: 2 months

PIE COOK BOOK

*Recipes for savory meat
and vegetable pies; cake, cream
and custard pies; deep-dish
and jellied pies; and the inimitable
all-American favorite, apple.*

MAIN-DISH PIES

MEAT, FISH, and POULTRY PIES

These can be 1- or 2-crust pies, and sometimes are made with a "crust" of mashed potatoes and no pastry at all. The fillings generally have vegetables added and a seasoned gravy. These pies provide an excellent way to use leftovers.

BEEF AND KIDNEY PIE

- 1 beef kidney (about 1¼ pounds)
  Salt and pepper
- 2 to 3 cups diced cooked beef
- 2 cups beef gravy
- 1 can (1 pound) onions, drained
- 2 potatoes, diced
- 2 carrots, diced
  Standard Pastry for 1-crust
  9-inch pie, unbaked (page 1399)

Remove outer membrane from kidney. Split kidney and cut into cubes. Cover with water. Add salt and pepper to taste and simmer for 1 hour, or until tender. Add next 5 ingredients and simmer until potato and carrot are tender. Season to taste with salt and pepper. Add more liquid if necessary. Pour into 2-quart casserole. Cover with Standard Pastry, rolled ⅛ inch thick. Make a few slits for steam to escape. Bake in preheated hot oven (425°F.) for 20 minutes, or until browned. Makes 4 to 6 servings.

LAMB PIE WITH POPPY-SEED CRUST

- ⅓ cup lamb fat or butter
- ⅓ cup all-purpose flour
- 3 cups lamb broth or bouillon
- 1 teaspoon bottled sauce for gravy
- 1 box (10 ounces) frozen peas
- 1 can (1 pound) onions, drained
- 2 cups cubed roast lamb
  Salt and pepper
- 1 tablespoon poppy seed
- 1 stick of pastry mix

Make gravy with fat, flour, broth, and sauce for gravy. Add vegetables and lamb; season with salt and pepper to taste. Put in 2-quart casserole. Add poppy seed to pastry mix; stir in liquid as directed on pastry-mix label. Roll out on floured board to fit top of casserole. Cut vents to allow steam to escape, and put on lamb mixture. Bake in preheated hot oven (425°F.) for 25 minutes, or until well browned. Makes 6 servings.

INDIVIDUAL MEAT PIES

    Standard Pastry for 2-crust
    9-inch pie, unbaked (page 1399)
- ½ pound ground beef
- 1 small onion, chopped
- ¼ cup chopped green pepper
- 1 teaspoon salt
- ¼ teaspoon pepper
- 1 egg, beaten
- ½ cup milk

Line 2 individual aluminum-foil pie pans with pastry. Brown beef, onion, and green pepper lightly in skillet; add seasonings and divide mixture between 2 pie pans. Mix egg and milk; pour over meat. Arrange ½-inch strips of pastry, rolled ⅛ inch thick, on pies, lattice fashion. Bake in preheated hot oven (425° F.) for about 30 minutes. Makes 2 servings.

SPANISH BEEF PIES

- 1 large onion, chopped
- ½ medium green pepper, chopped
- 1 tablespoon butter
- ½ pound ground beef
- ½ teaspoon salt
- ⅛ teaspoon pepper
- ½ cup canned corn
- ¼ cup each of pitted ripe
  olives and seedless raisins
- 2 boxes (10 ounces each)
  piecrust mix
- 2 hard-cooked eggs
- 1 egg white

Cook onion and green pepper in butter until lightly browned. Add beef and cook, breaking up with fork, until meat loses its red color. Pour off fat, if any. Add remaining ingredients except last 3 and mix well. Prepare piecrust mix and roll, half at a time, to ⅛-inch thickness. Cut twelve 6-inch rounds with a saucer. Put a spoonful of meat mixture on half of each round and top with slice of egg. Brush edges with cold water. Fold over and crimp edges with fork. Cut a few slits in top for steam to escape. Brush with white of egg, slightly beaten. Bake in preheated very hot oven (450°F.) for about 15 minutes. Makes 12 pies.

LAMB SHEPHERD'S PIE

- ½ cup diced celery
- 1 small onion, chopped
- ¼ cup water
- 2 cups diced cooked lamb
- 2 cups gravy
  Few parsley sprigs, chopped
- 1 can (8 ounces) peas, drained
  Salt and pepper
- 2 cups seasoned mashed potatoes
- 2 tablespoons butter or margarine
  Paprika

Cook celery and onion in the water for 5 minutes; do not drain. Mix with lamb, 1 cup of the gravy, parsley, and peas. Put in shallow 1½-quart baking dish. Add salt and pepper to taste. Spread with potato and dot with butter. Sprinkle with paprika. Bake in preheated hot oven (400°F.) for about 30 minutes. Serve with remaining gravy, heated. Makes 4 servings.

COLD VEAL-AND-HAM PIE

- 1 pound boned leg or shoulder of
  veal, sliced very thin
- ½ pound thinly sliced baked or
  boiled ham
- 3 hard-cooked eggs, sliced lengthwise
- 3 tablespoons minced parsley
- 1 teaspoon salt
- ⅛ teaspoon pepper

- ¼ teaspoon each of rosemary,
  marjoram, and thyme
- ½ cup undiluted canned consommé
  Standard Pastry for 1-crust 9-inch
  pie, unbaked (page 1399)

Pound veal slices as thin as possible. Trim fat from ham. Arrange layers of veal, ham, and eggs in 9-inch pie pan, sprinkling each layer with parsley, salt, pepper, and herbs, mixed together. Pour consommé over mixture. Cover with pastry rolled ⅛ inch thick. Make slits in top crust to let steam escape. Bake in preheated hot oven (425°F.) for 15 minutes, or until pastry is golden. Then cover with a double sheet of foil to prevent further browning and reduce heat to moderate (350°F.). Bake for 1 hour longer. Cool. Wrap in foil or plastic and chill for at least 3 hours. Makes 6 servings.

DEEP-DISH HAM PIE WITH CHEESE PASTRY

- ¼ cup butter or margarine
- ¼ cup all-purpose flour
- ¼ teaspoon powdered mustard
- 1 teaspoon instant minced onion
- 2 cups milk
- 1 can (3 ounces) sliced mushrooms,
  undrained
- 2 to 3 cups diced cooked ham
- 1 cup cooked peas
  Salt and pepper
  Cheese Pastry (page 1399)

Melt butter and blend in flour, mustard, and onion. Gradually add milk and cook, stirring constantly, until thickened. Add remaining ingredients except salt and pepper and pastry. Heat and season with salt and pepper to taste. Put in 1½-quart casserole. Roll out Cheese Pastry to ⅛-inch thickness, cut into ½-inch strips, and fit over top of pie, lattice fashion. Bake in preheated hot oven (425°F.) for 20 minutes, or until lightly browned. Makes 4 servings.

SAUSAGE-LEEK PIE

- 2 packages (8 ounces each) brown-
  and-serve sausage links
- 4 leeks or 8 green onions
  Boiling salted water
  Standard Pastry for 2-crust
  9-inch pie, unbaked (page 1399)
- 2 tablespoons butter or margarine
- 2 tablespoons all-purpose flour
  Salt to taste
  Dash of freshly ground
  white pepper
- ½ cup heavy cream
  or evaporated milk
- 1 tablespoon horseradish
- ½ cup pine nuts or pistachio
  nuts, chopped
  Nutmeg

Cut sausage into ½-inch slices and sauté until brown. Put aside. Cut leeks into 1-inch lengths, and split. Cover with boiling salted water and cook until tender.

Drain, reserving 1 cup liquid. Line pie pan with slightly more than half of pastry rolled ⅛ inch thick. Make sauce using butter, flour, liquid, seasonings, and cream. Add leeks, horseradish, and nuts with sausage. Pour into pastry-lined pie pan. Roll out remaining pastry and fit over top of pie; slit to allow for escape of steam. Sprinkle with nutmeg. Bake in preheated hot oven (425°F.) for 30 minutes, or until golden. Makes 6 to 8 servings.

TUNA-VEGETABLE PIE WITH CHEESE PASTRY
¼ cup butter or margarine
¼ cup all-purpose flour
2 cups milk
Seasoned salt and pepper
½ teaspoon monosodium glutamate
2 cups diced cooked potato
1 can (7 ounces) tuna
1 can (8 ounces) peas, drained
Cheese Pastry, unbaked (page 1398)

Melt butter and blend in flour. Gradually add milk and cook, stirring constantly, until smooth and thickened. Add seasoned salt and pepper to taste, and monosodium glutamate. Fold in potato, tuna with the liquid, and the peas. Heat and pour into 1½-quart casserole. Roll out Cheese Pastry ⅛ inch thick, cut into ½-inch strips, and fit over top of pie, lattice fashion. Bake in preheated hot oven (425°F.) for 20 minutes, or until lightly browned. Makes 4 servings.

OLD HOMESTEAD CHICKEN PIE
1 stewing chicken (about 4 pounds), cut up
5 cups water
1 onion
2 celery stalks
2 parsley sprigs
Salt
2 cups (one 1-pound can) onions
1 package (10 ounces) frozen carrots and peas, cooked
6 tablespoons all-purpose flour
Pepper
Standard Pastry for 1-crust 9-inch pie, unbaked (page 1399)
1 egg, slightly beaten

Simmer chicken, covered, in water with onion, celery, parsley, and 1 teaspoon salt for 3 hours, or until tender. Remove chicken; strain and cool broth. Remove meat from bones and cut into large pieces. Put in 2-quart baking dish with onions and carrots and peas. Remove fat from cooled broth. Melt ¼ cup of the fat (add butter if there is not enough) and stir in flour. Add 3 cups of the broth; cook until thickened. Season to taste. Pour over chicken and vegetables, and keep hot. Cover with pastry rolled ⅛ inch thick. Make slits in top crust to let steam escape. Brush with egg. Bake

in preheated hot oven (425°F.) for 30 minutes. Makes 6 servings.

TURKEY PIE
2 cans condensed cream of mushroom soup
2 cups milk
2 cups cooked peas
2 pimientos, sliced
3 cups diced cooked turkey
Meat Pie Pastry, unbaked (page 1399)

In saucepan heat soup, milk, peas, pimiento, and turkey. Put in shallow 2½-quart baking dish. Bake in preheated hot oven (425°F.) for 10 minutes. Reduce heat to moderate (350°F.) and bake for 20 minutes longer. Bake pastry separately at same time; put on top of pie. Makes 6 to 8 servings.

VEGETABLE PIES

These pies are usually made with a single top crust, with the vegetable filling combined with milk, cheese, and/or eggs.

ONION PIE NIÇOISE
Standard Pastry for 1-crust, 8-inch pie, unbaked (page 1399)
3 medium sweet red onions
2 tablespoons butter or margarine
6 ripe olives, pitted and sliced
1 cup milk
½ cup light cream
2 eggs, beaten
Salt and pepper to taste

Line 8-inch pie pan with pastry rolled ⅛ inch thick, and flute edges neatly. Peel and slice onions. Sauté in butter until soft but not brown, for 12 to 15 minutes. Cool. Place onions and olive slices in pie pan. Mix milk, cream, and eggs well. Season with salt and pepper. Pour over onions and olives and bake in preheated moderate oven (375°F.) for 25 to 35 minutes, or until puffed and golden brown. Makes 4 servings as luncheon or supper dish, 6 to 8 servings as appetizer.

ONION CHEESE PIE
6 tablespoons butter or margarine
2 cups crumbs of cheese-flavored crackers
3 large onions, thinly sliced (about 3 cups)
2 eggs
1 cup milk
1 teaspoon salt
¼ teaspoon each of pepper and crumbled dry marjoram
½ cup shredded sharp Cheddar cheese

Melt 4 tablespoons butter and mix with 1½ cups cracker crumbs. Press on bottom and sides of 9-inch pie pan to form a shell. Sauté onions in remaining butter until limp and golden. Spoon into crumb

shell. Beat eggs slightly with milk, salt, pepper, marjoram, and cheese. Turn into skillet and cook over very low heat, stirring, just until cheese melts. Carefully pour sauce over onions; sprinkle reserved crumbs evenly over top. Bake in preheated slow oven (325°F.) for 30 minutes, or until custard is set. Makes 8 servings.

EGG AND POTATO PIE, INDIENNE
½ teaspoon onion salt
6 potatoes, cooked, mashed, and seasoned
6 hard-cooked eggs, cut into chunks
2 tablespoons butter or margarine
1 tablespoon all-purpose flour
½ teaspoon salt
½ teaspoon curry powder
⅛ teaspoon pepper
¾ cup milk
Few parsley sprigs, chopped

Add onion salt to potato and line a shallow 1½-quart baking dish with the mixture. Fill center with the eggs. Melt butter, and blend in flour and seasonings. Gradually add milk and cook, stirring constantly, until thickened. Add parsley and pour over eggs. Bake in preheated moderate oven (375°F.) for about 30 minutes. Makes 6 servings.

RED AND GREEN TOMATO PIE
Standard Pastry for 1-crust 9-inch pie, unbaked (page 1399)
Undiluted evaporated milk
4 cups sliced red and green tomatoes
1½ teaspoons salt
⅛ teaspoon pepper
⅓ cup mayonnaise
⅓ cup grated Parmesan cheese
1 garlic clove, minced

Line pie pan with pastry rolled ⅛ inch thick, crimp edges, and brush shell with evaporated milk. Bake in preheated very hot oven (450°F.) for 5 minutes. Fill shell with tomatoes and sprinkle with the salt and pepper. Mix remaining ingredients and spread on tomatoes. Bake in preheated moderate oven (350°F.) for 40 minutes, or until tomatoes are done. Makes 6 servings.

DESSERT PIES

CAKE PIES
These are rich pies with a cake or candylike filling

CHESS PIE
1 cup firmly packed light brown sugar
½ cup granulated sugar
1 tablespoon all-purpose flour
2 eggs
2 tablespoons milk
1 teaspoon vanilla extract
½ cup butter or margarine, melted
1 cup chopped pecans or California

Cold Veal-and-Ham Pie

walnuts
Standard Pastry for 1-crust 9-inch
pie, unbaked (page 1399)

Mix first 3 ingredients. Beat in eggs, milk, vanilla, and butter. Stir in nuts and pour into pie pan lined with pastry rolled ⅛ inch thick. Bake in preheated moderate oven (375°F.) for 45 minutes. Cool. Makes 6 to 8 servings.

CHOCOLATE BROWNIE PIE

1 can (14 ounces) sweetened
  condensed milk
¼ teaspoon salt
6 ounces semisweet
  chocolate pieces
1 teaspoon vanilla extract
2 tablespoons all-purpose flour
2 eggs, separated
½ cup coarsely chopped nuts
2 tablespoons sugar
  Standard Pastry for 1-crust
  9-inch pie, unbaked (page 1399)
  Vanilla ice cream

Heat condensed milk and salt to boiling, stirring. Remove from heat; beat in chocolate, vanilla, and flour. Add egg yolks, one at a time, beating thoroughly after each addition. Stir in nuts. Beat egg whites until stiff but not dry. Gradually beat in sugar, continuing to beat until very stiff and glossy. Fold into chocolate mixture. Pour into pie pan lined with pastry rolled ⅛ inch thick. Bake in preheated moderate oven (350°F.) for 40 minutes, or until firm. Serve with ice cream. Makes 6 to 8 servings.

CHOCOLATE SPONGECAKE PIE

¾ to 1 cup sugar
2 tablespoons all-purpose flour
¼ teaspoon salt
3 eggs, separated
2 ounces (2 squares) unsweetened
  chocolate, melted
1 cup milk
1 teaspoon vanilla extract
  Standard Pastry for 1-crust
  9-inch pie, unbaked (page 1399)
  Ice cream or whipped cream
  (optional)

Mix first 3 ingredients. Beat egg yolks until thick and lemon colored. Stir into first mixture with chocolate. Add milk and vanilla; beat with rotary beater until blended. Beat egg whites until stiff; fold in. Pour into pie pan lined with pastry rolled ⅛ inch thick. Bake in preheated very hot oven (450°F.) for 10 minutes. Reduce heat to moderate (350°F.) and bake for 30 minutes, or until set. Cool. Makes 6 to 8 servings.

COTTAGE-CHEESE PIE

1½ cups creamed cottage cheese
1 tablespoon all-purpose flour
⅛ teaspoon salt
1 cup heavy cream
⅔ cup granulated sugar
  Grated rind of 1 lemon
  Juice of 1 lemon
3 eggs, separated

⅓ cup dried currants
  Standard Pastry for 1-crust 9-inch
  pie, unbaked (page 1399)
  Confectioners' sugar

Force cheese through a fine sieve or food mill. Blend in flour and salt. Then stir in cream, granulated sugar, lemon rind, and juice. Beat egg whites until stiff but not dry; then beat yolks until thick and lemon colored. Stir egg yolks and currants into cheese mixture. Fold in egg whites and pour into pie pan lined with pastry rolled ⅛ inch thick. Bake in preheated very hot oven (450°F.) for 10 minutes. Reduce heat to moderate (350°F.) and bake for 45 minutes longer, or until pie is firm. Cool; sprinkle with confectioners' sugar. Makes 6 to 8 servings.

LEMON SPONGE PIE

¾ cup sugar
¼ cup butter or margarine, melted
¼ cup all-purpose flour
  Grated rind and juice of 2 lemons
1 cup milk
2 eggs, separated
⅛ teaspoon salt
  Standard Pastry for 1-crust 9-inch
  pie, unbaked (page 1399)

Mix sugar, butter, flour, lemon rind and juice, milk, and egg yolks. Beat egg whites with salt until stiff but not dry. Fold into first mixture. Pour into pie pan lined with pastry rolled ⅛ inch thick. Bake in preheated moderate oven (350°F.) for 40 minutes. Cool. Makes 6 to 8 servings.

SHOOFLY PIE

¾ cup dark molasses
¾ cup boiling water
½ teaspoon baking soda
¼ teaspoon salt
1½ cups sifted all-purpose flour
¼ cup butter or margarine
½ cup firmly packed brown sugar
  Standard Pastry for 1-crust
  9-inch pie, unbaked (page 1399)

Mix first 4 ingredients. With hands, mix next 3 ingredients. Pour about one third of molasses mixture into pie pan lined with pastry rolled ⅛ inch thick. Sprinkle with one third of flour mixture. Continue alternating layers until all ingredients are used, ending with layer of flour. Bake in preheated moderate oven (375°F.) for 35 minutes. Serve warm or cold. Makes 6 to 8 servings.

COCONUT SYRUP PIE

½ cup sugar
1 cup dark corn syrup
¼ teaspoon salt
1 tablespoon all-purpose flour
2 eggs
1 teaspoon vanilla extract
1 tablespoon butter, melted
1¼ to 2 cups flaked coconut
  Standard Pastry for 1-crust
  9-inch pie, unbaked (page 1399)

Beat first 7 ingredients together until well blended. Stir in coconut. Pour into pie pan lined with pastry rolled ⅛ inch thick. Bake in preheated hot oven (400°F.) for 15 minutes. Reduce heat to slow (300°F.) and bake for 30 to 35 minutes longer, or until set. Cool. Makes 6 to 8 servings.

Chocolate Coconut Syrup Pie

Use recipe for Coconut Syrup Pie. Melt 2 ounces (2 squares) unsweetened chocolate with the butter.

Southern Pecan Pie

Use recipe for Coconut Syrup Pie. Substitute 1¼ cups pecan halves for the coconut. Turn up rounded side of some pecan halves after pouring filling into pastry-lined pie pan. Bake in preheated slow oven (300°F.) for about 1 hour.

Chocolate Pecan Pie

Use recipe for Southern Pecan Pie. Melt 2 ounces (2 squares) unsweetened chocolate with the butter.

RAISIN-NUT PIE

3 eggs, separated
1 cup sugar
½ cup butter or margarine
½ cup each of coarsely chopped
  walnuts and pecans
1 cup soft seedless raisins
2 tablespoons vinegar
1 teaspoon ground nutmeg
½ teaspoon ground cinnamon
½ teaspoon ground cloves
¼ teaspoon salt
  Standard Pastry for 1-crust
  9-inch pie, unbaked (page 1399)

Cream together egg yolks, ½ cup sugar, and the butter. Add nuts, raisins, vinegar, and spices. Beat egg whites with salt until almost stiff. Gradually add remaining sugar and beat until stiff. Fold into first mixture and pour into pie pan lined with pastry rolled ⅛ inch thick. Bake in preheated moderate oven (350°F.) for about 40 minutes. Cool. Decorate with unsweetened whipped cream, if desired. Makes 6 to 8 servings.

CRACKER PIE

3 egg whites
¼ teaspoon salt
¾ cup sugar
1 cup chopped pecans
18 plain crackers (unsalted), crushed
1 teaspoon vanilla extract
½ cup heavy cream
¼ cup pineapple topping for ice cream

Beat egg whites with salt until almost stiff. Gradually add sugar and beat until stiff. Fold in nuts, cracker crumbs, and vanilla. Mix well and pour into well-buttered 9-inch pie pan. Bake in preheated slow oven (325°F.) for about 35 minutes. Cool. Whip cream until stiff and fold in pineapple topping. Spread on pie and chill. Makes 6 to 8 servings.

CREAM, CUSTARD, AND MERINGUE PIES

Cream and custard pies are single-crust pies. The fillings for cream pies are smooth and soft, yet firm enough to hold their shape. They are often cooked separately and placed in a previously baked pie shell. Cream pies are often topped with meringue, a mixture of beaten egg whites and sugar. Custard pies, as the name specifies, are made with uncooked milk-and-egg mixtures, poured into an unbaked pie crust and baked.

COFFEE-NUT CREAM PIE

- 1 package (3 ounces) vanilla pudding and pie-filling mix
- 1½ cups milk
- 2 tablespoons instant coffee powder
- ½ cup heavy cream, whipped
  Standard Pastry for 1-crust 8-inch pie, baked (page 1399)
- ¼ cup chopped nuts

Combine pudding mix, milk, and coffee; cook as directed on the package. Cool and fold in cream. Pour into baked pie shell and sprinkle with nuts; chill. Makes 6 servings.

Mocha-Nut Cream Pie

Follow recipe for Coffee-Nut Cream Pie, but use chocolate pudding mix instead of vanilla.

ONE-BOWL PUMPKIN PIE

- 1¾ cups canned pumpkin
- 1 can (14 ounces) sweetened condensed milk
- 2 eggs
- 1 teaspoon ground cinnamon
- ½ teaspoon each of salt and ginger
- ¼ teaspoon ground nutmeg
- ⅛ teaspoon ground cloves
- ½ cup hot water
  Standard Pastry for 1-crust 9-inch pie, unbaked (page 1399)

Put all ingredients except pastry in bowl and beat until blended. Pour into pie pan lined with pastry rolled ⅛ inch thick. Bake in preheated moderate oven (375° F.) for 45 to 50 minutes. Makes 6 to 8 servings.

SWEET POTATO PIE

- 1½ cups mashed cooked sweet potato
- ½ cup firmly packed brown sugar
- 1 teaspoon ground cinnamon
- ½ teaspoon ground allspice
- ¼ teaspoon ground mace
- ¾ teaspoon salt
- 2 eggs, beaten
- 1 can (14½ ounces) undiluted evaporated milk
- 2 tablespoons butter or margarine, melted
  Standard Pastry for 1-crust 9-inch pie, unbaked (page 1399)

Mix all ingredients except pastry. Pour into pie pan lined with pastry rolled ⅛ inch thick. Bake in preheated hot oven (425°F.) for 10 minutes. Reduce heat to moderate (350°F.) and bake for 25 minutes longer, or until set. Cool. Makes 6 to 8 servings.

BUTTERMILK-COCONUT-CREAM PIE

- ¾ cup soft butter or margarine
- 1 cup sugar
- 2 eggs
- 1 tablespoon all-purpose flour
- 1 tablespoon vanilla extract
- 1 cup buttermilk
- ½ cup flaked coconut
  Standard Pastry for 1-crust 9-inch pie, unbaked (page 1399)

Cream butter until light and fluffy. Gradually beat in sugar. Beat in eggs and flour. Add remaining ingredients except pastry and mix well. Mixture will be curdled. Pour into pie pan lined with pastry rolled ⅛ inch thick, and bake in preheated very hot oven (450°F.) for 10 minutes. Reduce heat to slow (300°F.) and bake for 30 minutes longer, or until firm. Serve slightly warm or cold. Makes 6 to 8 servings.

SOUR-CREAM-RAISIN PIE

- 1 cup seedless raisins
- ½ cup plus 3 tablespoons sugar Water
- 1 tablespoon cornstarch
- 1 package (3 ounces) lemon pudding and pie-filling mix
- 2 egg yolks
- 1 cup dairy sour cream
  Standard Pastry for 1-crust 9-inch pie, unbaked (page 1399)

In saucepan mix raisins, 3 tablespoons sugar, and 1 cup water. Bring to boil and simmer for 15 minutes, stirring occasionally. Blend cornstarch with 2 tablespoons water and stir into raisin mixture. Cook, stirring, until thickened. In another saucepan mix lemon pudding mix, remaining sugar, and ¼ cup water. Add 1¾ cups water and the egg yolks, blending thoroughly. Cook, stirring, until mixture comes to a full boil and thickens. Stir into raisin mixture. Cool and fold in sour cream. Pour into baked pie shell and chill until firm. Top with whipped cream or sour cream, if desired. Makes 6 to 8 servings.

CUSTARD PIE

- Standard Pastry for 1-crust 9-inch pie, unbaked (page 1399)
- 4 eggs
- 2¼ cups milk
- ½ cup sugar
- ½ teaspoon salt
  Grating of nutmeg
- ½ teaspoon vanilla extract

Line pie pan with pastry rolled ⅛ inch thick; brush with small amount of slightly beaten white from 1 egg. Add white to remaining eggs; beat slightly. Scald milk; pour over combined eggs, sugar, salt, nutmeg, and vanilla. Mix well and pour into pastry. Bake in preheated hot oven (425°F.) for 25 to 30 minutes. Cool. Makes 6 to 8 servings.

Chocolate-Topped Custard Pie

Bake and cool Custard Pie. Melt ½ cup semisweet chocolate pieces and stir in 2 tablespoons milk. Spread on pie.

Caramel Custard Pie

Follow recipe for Custard Pie. Caramelize the sugar: Heat sugar in heavy skillet over low heat, stirring until brown and syrupy. Gradually stir into hot milk and continue stirring until blended. Proceed as directed.

Coconut Custard Pie

Follow recipe for Custard Pie. Top unbaked pie with ½ cup flaked coconut.

CRISP-CRUST CUSTARD PIE

- 2¼ cups milk
- ½ cup sugar
- ½ teaspoon salt
  Grating of nutmeg
- ½ teaspoon vanilla extract
- 3 eggs
  Standard Pastry for 1-crust 9-inch pie, baked (page 1399)

Scald milk; add sugar, salt, nutmeg, and vanilla. Mix well. Gradually pour over slightly beaten eggs, stirring constantly. Grease a deep 9-inch pie pan with cooking oil; pour in custard mixture. Put pan in larger shallow pan, and pour hot water into outer pan to depth of about 1 inch. Bake in preheated slow oven (300°F.) for 55 minutes, or until set. Remove pan of custard from water; let stand until cold, then chill. Just before serving, carefully loosen custard from bottom; carefully but quickly slide from pan into the baked shell. This is not as difficult as it sounds. Allow custard filling to settle down into the crust for a few minutes before serving. Makes 6 to 8 servings.

VANILLA MERINGUE PIE

- 1 cup sugar
- 6 tablespoons all-purpose flour
  Salt
- 2½ cups milk
- 3 eggs, separated
- 1 tablespoon butter or margarine
- 1 teaspoon vanilla extract
  Standard Pastry for 1-crust 9-inch pie, baked (page 1399)
- ¼ teaspoon cream of tartar

Mix ½ cup sugar, the flour, and ¼ teaspoon salt in top part of double boiler. Add milk and cook over boiling water until thickened, stirring constantly. Cover, and cook for 10 minutes longer, stirring occasionally. Beat egg yolks. Slowly add a small amount of milk mixture to yolks; return to double boiler and cook for 2 minutes, stirring. Remove from heat; add butter and vanilla. Cool and pour into shell. Add a dash of salt and the cream of tartar to egg whites; beat until stiff. Gradually add remaining sugar, continuing to beat until very stiff. Pile lightly on pie and spread to edge. Bake in preheated slow oven (325°F.) for about 18 minutes. Makes 6 to 8 servings.

Chocolate Meringue Pie

Follow recipe for Vanilla Meringue Pie. Add 2 squares (2 ounces) unsweetened chocolate, melted, to the filling with the butter and vanilla. Proceed as directed.

Banana Meringue Pie

Follow recipe for Vanilla Meringue Pie. Slice 2 or 3 ripe bananas into pie shell before pouring in filling. Proceed as directed.

Coconut Meringue Pie

Follow recipe for Vanilla Meringue Pie. Add ½ cup flaked coconut to filling before pouring into shell. Before baking, sprinkle meringue with ¼ cup flaked coconut. Proceed as directed.

OLD-FASHIONED LEMON MERINGUE PIE

    Sugar
⅛ teaspoon salt
6 tablespoons cornstarch
2 cups boiling water
    Grated rind of 1 lemon
¼ cup butter or margarine
3 eggs, separated
½ cup plus 1 teaspoon fresh lemon
    juice
    Standard Pastry for 1-crust
    9-inch pie, baked (page 1399)

Mix 1¼ cups sugar, the salt, and cornstarch. Add water and lemon rind. Cook until thickened, stirring; simmer for 10 minutes. Add butter, but do not stir. Gradually stir into egg yolks mixed with ½ cup lemon juice. Strain into baked pastry shell. Bake in preheated hot oven (400°F.) for 10 minutes. Beat egg whites with remaining lemon juice until stiff. Gradually add 6 tablespoons sugar and beat until very stiff. Pile lightly on pie, and spread to edge. Reduce heat to slow (325°F.) and bake for 18 minutes. Makes 6 to 8 servings.

RHUBARB MERINGUE PIE

1 package (1 pound) frozen
    sweetened rhubarb
2 tablespoons all-purpose flour
½ cup plus 6 tablespoons sugar
    Standard Pastry for 1-crust
    8-inch pie, unbaked (page 1399)
3 eggs, separated
⅛ teaspoon salt
½ cup milk
¼ teaspoon almond extract

Thaw rhubarb just enough to break up solid block. Mix with flour and ½ cup sugar. Put into pie pan lined with pastry

rolled ⅛ inch thick. Beat egg yolks slightly. Add salt, milk, and flavoring. Pour over rhubarb mixture. Bake in preheated very hot oven (450°F.) for 10 minutes. Reduce heat to slow (325°F.) and bake for 30 minutes, or until filling is just set. Cool slightly. Beat egg whites until stiff. Gradually add 6 tablespoons sugar, beating until very stiff. Pile lightly on pie and spread to edge. Bake in preheated hot oven (425°F.) for about 5 minutes. Cool. Makes 6 to 8 servings.

BLACKBERRY-ALMOND MERINGUE PIE

1 quart blackberries
2 tablespoons all-purpose flour
1⅓ cups sugar
½ teaspoon ground cinnamon
2 tablespoons fresh lemon juice
2 tablespoons butter or margarine,
    melted
    Standard Pastry for 1-crust
    9-inch pie, baked until done
    but not browned (page 1399)
3 egg whites
⅛ teaspoon salt
¼ cup ground unblanched almonds

Put berries in a bowl. Mix flour with 1 cup sugar and sift over berries. Add cinnamon, 1 tablespoon lemon juice, and the butter. Stir well and let stand for 10 minutes to draw the juice. Stir again and pour into shell. Bake in preheated very hot oven (450°F.) for 10 minutes. Reduce heat to moderate (350°F.) and bake for 25 to 30 minutes longer, or until berries appear cooked. Remove from oven. Beat egg whites with salt until stiff. Gradually add remaining sugar and beat until very stiff. Fold in remaining lemon juice and pile lightly on pie. Sprinkle with almonds. Put under broiler for 1 or 2 minutes, or until lightly browned; watch closely. Serve slightly warm or cold. Makes 6 servings.

SOUR-CREAM BUTTERSCOTCH MERINGUE PIE

1½ tablespoons all-purpose flour
1½ cups firmly packed light
    brown sugar
½ teaspoon salt
1½ cups dairy sour cream
3 eggs, separated
1½ teaspoons vanilla extract
2 tablespoons butter or margarine,
    melted
    Standard Pastry for 1-crust
    9-inch pie, unbaked (page 1399)
6 tablespoons granulated sugar

Mix first 4 ingredients. Add to beaten egg yolks, vanilla, and butter. Pour into pie pan lined with pastry rolled ⅛ inch thick. Bake in preheated very hot oven (450°F.) for 10 minutes. Reduce heat to moderate (350°F.) and bake for about 30 minutes. Beat egg whites until stiff. Gradually add granulated sugar and beat until very stiff. Pile lightly on pie and

spread to edge. Bake in preheated slow oven (325°F.) for about 18 minutes. Makes 6 to 8 servings.

FRUIT PIES

These are 1- or 2-crust pies or 1-crust pies with lattice tops. Deep-dish pies have a top, rather than a bottom crust. An endless variety of fruits and combinations of fruits, as well as mincemeat, can be used for this popular dessert. Fruit juices, thickened with flour, cornstarch, tapioca, or bread crumbs, may also be used.

FAVORITE APPLE PIE

1¼ cups sugar
¼ cup water
    Pinch of salt
3 pounds tart apples
1 tablespoon all-purpose flour
    Standard Pastry for 2-crust 9-inch
    pie, unbaked (page 1399)
½ teaspoon ground cinnamon
1 tablespoon butter or margarine
    Cream or undiluted evaporated milk

Put sugar, water, and salt in large skillet; cover and heat until sugar begins to dissolve. Peel and core apples; cut into eighths. Drop enough pieces of apple into sugar syrup to cover bottom of skillet; cook gently until just tender, leaving cover on until apples begin to get tender; remove apple pieces carefully to flat pan or tray. Continue until all are done. Thicken syrup with flour mixed with a little water; there should be about ⅓ cup thickened syrup; cool. Roll pastry ⅛ inch thick for 2-crust pie and line deep 9-inch pie pan. Fill with apples; cover with thickened syrup and top with cinnamon and butter. Moisten edge of crust; cover with top crust, which has been slit for steam to escape. Crimp edges firmly. Brush top with cream for glaze. Bake in preheated very hot oven (450°F.) for 15 minutes. Reduce heat to hot (400°F.) and bake for 25 minutes longer, or until apples are well done and crust is golden. Makes 6 to 8 servings.

CARAMEL APPLE PIE

¼ cup dark rum
6 medium apples, peeled, cored, and
    cut into eighths (4 cups)
1 cup sugar
2 tablespoons butter or margarine
½ teaspoon salt
    Standard Pastry for 1-crust 9-inch
    pie, unbaked (page 1399)

Pour rum over apples and turn several times to moisten all pieces. In pie pan heat sugar slowly over low heat, stirring constantly. When sugar is melted and begins to smoke, add butter. Drain apples and pile into pie pan; sprinkle with the salt. Roll pastry to ⅛-inch thickness and cover apples. Prick top of pastry and crimp edges. Bake in preheated hot oven (425°F.) for 15 minutes. Reduce heat to moderate (350°F.) and bake for 20 minutes longer, or until apples are tender. Remove from oven; let stand for 10 minutes. Turn out, crust side down, on large plate. Serve hot or cold. Makes 6 to 8 servings.

GRATED-APPLE PIE WITH CHICKEN-FAT PASTRY
Chicken-Fat Pastry (page 1399)
1 egg white, beaten
Sugar
6 medium apples, peeled
6 tablespoons fresh orange juice
6 tablespoons fresh lemon juice
1½ teaspoons cornstarch
1 tablespoon butter or margarine, melted

Prepare Chicken-Fat Pastry and chill. Roll out a little more than half of dough to ⅛-inch thickness and fit into a 9-inch pie pan. Brush with egg white and sprinkle with a little sugar. Grate apples and mix with fruit juices, ¾ cup sugar, cornstarch, and butter. Put into lined pie pan. Roll out remaining pastry and cut into ½-inch strips. Arrange on pie, lattice fashion. Sprinkle with a little sugar. Bake in preheated very hot oven (450°F.) for 10 minutes. Reduce heat to moderate (350°F.) and bake for 20 minutes longer. Makes 6 to 8 servings.

COLONIAL PEAR PIE
Standard Pastry for 2-crust 9-inch pie, unbaked (page 1399)
4 cups (two 1-pound cans) pear halves
½ cup sugar
2 tablespoons cornstarch
¼ teaspoon each of ground ginger and nutmeg
1 tablespoon fresh lemon juice
1 teaspoon grated lemon rind
1 cup shredded Cheddar cheese

Roll slightly more than half of pastry ⅛ inch thick. Line pie pan. Drain pears, reserving ¼ cup syrup. Cut pear halves into quarters and put into lined pie pan. Mix remaining ingredients except cheese. Cook, stirring constantly, over low heat until clear and thickened. Pour over pears. Roll out remaining pastry, cut into ½-inch strips and arrange over top of pie, lattice fashion. Bake in preheated hot oven (425°F.) for 25 to 30 minutes. Remove from oven and sprinkle with cheese. Return pie to oven for a few minutes to melt cheese. Makes 6 to 8 servings.

BANANA PIE
Standard Pastry for 2-crust 9-inch pie, unbaked (page 1399)
¾ cup firmly packed light brown sugar

2 tablespoons all-purpose flour
⅛ teaspoon salt
6 or 7 ripe medium bananas
3 tablespoons fresh lemon juice
3 tablespoons butter or margarine

Roll slightly more than half of pastry ⅛ inch thick; line pie pan. Mix next 3 ingredients and sprinkle about one fourth into lined pan. Peel bananas and cut into halves crosswise. Split halves lengthwise and arrange one third in pie pan. Sprinkle with one third of sugar mixture and the lemon juice. Dot with 1 tablespoon butter. Repeat until all ingredients are used. Roll out remaining pastry and fit over top of pie. Bake in preheated hot oven (400°F.) for 30 minutes, or until crust is browned and bananas done. Serve warm or cold. Makes 6 to 8 servings.
Note: For a glazed top, brush crust before baking with 1 egg yolk beaten with 1 teaspoon cold water.

BLUEBERRY PIE
Standard Pastry for 2-crust 9-inch pie, unbaked (page 1399)
1 quart blueberries
1½ cups sugar
⅛ teaspoon salt
1½ tablespoons all-purpose flour
1 tablespoon butter or margarine

Roll slightly more than half the pastry ⅛ inch thick. Line pie pan. Wash and drain berries. Mix with sugar, salt, and flour. Put into pastry-lined pie pan. Dot with butter. Roll out remaining pastry and fit over top of pie. Bake in preheated very hot oven (450°F.) for 10 minutes. Reduce heat to moderate (350°F.) and bake for 25 minutes longer. Makes 6 to 8 servings.

SWEET CHERRY PIE
Standard Pastry for 2-crust 9-inch pie, unbaked (page 1399)
5 cups pitted sweet cherries (1½ pounds)
Sugar
1 tablespoon quick-cooking tapioca or
3 tablespoons all-purpose flour
1 teaspoon fresh lemon juice
2 tablespoons butter or margarine

Roll slightly more than half of pastry ⅛ inch thick. Line pie pan. Arrange cherries in pastry, heaping somewhat in center of pie. Sprinkle with mixture of ¾ cup sugar and tapioca, then with lemon juice. Dot with butter. Roll out remaining pastry and fit over top of pie. Cut slits to let steam escape; flute rim. Bake in preheated hot oven (425°F.) for 15 minutes, then reduce heat to moderate (375°F.) and bake for 25 to 30 minutes longer. Remove from oven; sprinkle 2 to 3 tablespoons sugar over top crust. Place under broiler for 2 minutes, or until a delicate brown. Makes 6 to 8 servings.

ORANGE-CRANBERRY-RAISIN PIE
Standard Pastry for 2-crust 9-inch pie, unbaked (page 1399)
1½ cups sugar
¼ cup fresh orange juice
¼ teaspoon salt
Water
3 cups cranberries
1 cup seeded raisins
1 tablespoon cornstarch
1 teaspoon each of grated orange and lemon rind
2 tablespoons butter or margarine

Roll out slightly more than half of pastry ⅛ inch thick. Line pie pan. Bring first 3 ingredients and 2 tablespoons water to boil in saucepan, stirring constantly until sugar is dissolved. Add cranberries and cook, stirring occasionally, until berries pop open. Add raisins. Blend cornstarch and 2 tablespoons water. Add to berry mixture and cook until thickened, stirring constantly. Remove from heat and stir in fruit rinds and butter. Pour into pastry-lined pie pan. Roll out remaining pastry. Moisten edges of filled pie with water and cover with top crust which has been slit to allow steam to escape. Press edges together with tines of fork. Bake in preheated hot oven (425°F.) for about 25 minutes. Makes 6 to 8 servings.

Cranberry Pie
Follow recipe for Orange-Cranberry-Raisin Pie. Omit raisins and increase cranberries to 3½ cups.

LATTICE RHUBARB PIE
Standard Pastry for 2-crust 9-inch pie, unbaked (page 1399)
3 tablespoons all-purpose flour
1 cup sugar
4 cups peeled rhubarb, cut into ½-inch pieces
1 egg
1 tablespoon water
1 tablespoon butter or margarine

Roll out slightly more than half of pastry ⅛ inch thick. Line pie pan. Mix flour and sugar. Put rhubarb in lined pie pan and sprinkle with sugar mixture. Beat egg and water and pour over rhubarb. Dot with butter. Roll out remaining pastry and cut into ½-inch strips. Adjust strips on pie, lattice fashion. Bake in preheated very hot oven (450°F.) for 10 minutes. Reduce heat to moderate (375°F.); bake for about 40 minutes. Makes 6 or 8 servings.
Note: One package (1 pound) frozen rhubarb can be used in recipe above. Decrease sugar to ½ cup.

Pineapple-Rhubarb Pie
Follow recipe for Lattice Rhubarb Pie substituting 1 cup drained pineapple tidbits for 1 cup of the rhubarb. Decrease sugar to ¾ cup.

Nesselrode Chiffon Pie

Lattice Rhubarb Pie

Marbled Chocolate Rum Pie

Banana Meringue Pie

MINCEMEAT PIE WITH CHEESE CRUST

1½ cups all-purpose flour
½ teaspoon salt
⅓ cup shortening
½ cup shredded process
     American cheese
4 cups prepared mincemeat

Sift flour and salt; cut in shortening. Add cheese and toss with fork to blend. Sprinkle with cold water, about 2 tablespoons, and mix with fork until dry ingredients are moistened. Press into a ball. On floured board roll ⅔ of dough to ⅛-inch thickness; press into 9-inch pie pan. Fill with mincemeat. Roll remaining dough and cut into strips ½ inch wide. Arrange on pie, lattice fashion. Trim lattice edges and crimp edges of crust with fingers. Bake in preheated hot oven (400°F.) for 20 minutes, or until lightly browned. Makes 6 to 8 servings.

Brandied Mince Pie

Follow recipe for Mincemeat Pie with Cheese Crust; add ¼ cup brandy to mincemeat.

SWEDISH FRUIT PIE

1 cup seeded raisins
1 cup dried apricots, ground
4 cups pared and sliced apples
2 tablespoons fresh lemon juice
½ teaspoon grated orange rind
¾ cup sugar
1 tablespoon all-purpose flour
¼ teaspoon salt
½ teaspoon ground cinnamon
¼ teaspoon ground nutmeg
     Standard Pastry for 9-inch 2-crust
     pie, unbaked (page 1399)
1 tablespoon butter or margarine

Combine first 5 ingredients. Mix sugar, flour, salt, and spices; stir into first mixture. Roll out half of pastry ⅛ inch thick and use to line deep pie pan. Fill with fruit mixture and dot with butter. Roll out rest of pastry, cover pie, and crimp edge. Make several slits near center to allow steam to escape. Bake in preheated hot oven (425°F.) for 10 minutes; reduce heat to moderate (375°F.) and bake for about 40 minutes longer. Makes 6 to 8 servings.

DEEP-DISH FRESH APPLE PIE

3 tablespoons quick-cooking tapioca
¾ cup granulated sugar
⅓ cup firmly packed brown sugar
¼ teaspoon salt
1 teaspoon ground cinnamon
     Ground nutmeg
5 cups sliced peeled tart apples
     Standard Pastry for 1-crust 8-inch
     pie, unbaked (page 1399)
     Whipped cream

Mix tapioca with sugars, salt, cinnamon, and ½ teaspoon nutmeg. Fold in apple slices. Pour mixture into a deep 8-inch square baking dish. Roll pastry into an 8-inch square. Cut several slits near center of pastry and arrange pastry on apples. Bake in preheated hot oven (425°F.) for about 35 minutes. Serve with whipped cream spiced with nutmeg. Makes 6 servings.

DEEP-DISH PANTRY APPLE PIE

1 tablespoon all-purpose flour
½ cup firmly packed dark brown sugar
1 cup granulated sugar
1 teaspoon ground nutmeg
5 cups (two 1-pound, 4-ounce cans)
     drained apple slices
2 teaspoons fresh lemon juice
2 tablespoons butter or margarine
     Standard Pastry for 1-crust 9-inch
     pie, unbaked (page 1399)

Mix first 4 ingredients and put one third of mixture in well-buttered deep baking dish. Cover with half the apples. Sprinkle with 1 teaspoon lemon juice and half of remaining sugar mixture. Cover with remaining apples, lemon juice, and sugar mixture. Dot with butter and cover with pastry rolled to fit baking dish, pressing pastry firmly against edge of dish to seal. Make a few slits to allow steam to escape. Bake in preheated hot oven (425°F.) for 40 to 50 minutes. Serve warm. Makes 6 to 8 servings.

INDIVIDUAL DEEP-DISH PIES

The secret of deep-dish pies is to cook the crusts and the fillings separately. The crusts are baked on a cookie sheet, or in ovenproof dishes. The fillings cook on top of the stove, just long enough to thicken without losing the fragrance and flavor. To serve, put the filling and crusts together and bring them to the table warm: not hot, not cold. Since these are individual pies, adding ice cream, hard sauce, whipped cream, a wedge of cheese, or a lavish pouring of rich sweet cream is a matter of individual preference. The crusts can be baked ahead of time. Store them in an airtight container, or wrap them in foil or plastic wrap. They'll keep for 1 or 2 weeks in the refrigerator, or for several months in the freezer. Before serving, put on cookie sheet or on top of fillings; reheat in oven.

Blueberry Pies

4 cups (two 15-ounce cans) blueberries
     in heavy syrup
2 tablespoons sugar
¼ teaspoon salt
2 to 3 tablespoons quick-cooking
     tapioca
     Dash of fresh lemon juice
     Pastry for Individual Deep-Dish Pies,
     page 1399)

Combine all ingredients except pastry in saucepan. Bring to boil, stirring constantly, and simmer about 5 minutes, until slightly thickened and clear. Spoon into 4 individual dishes, cool slightly. Top with crusts and serve. Makes 4 servings.

Sour-Cherry Pies

4 cups (two 1-pound cans) water-packed
     pitted red sour cherries
1 cup sugar
2½ to 3 tablespoons quick-cooking
     tapioca
⅛ teaspoon salt
1 tablespoon butter or margarine
     Pastry for Individual Deep-Dish Pies,
     page 1399)

Drain cherries; reserve juice. Combine cherries, ½ cup juice, and remaining ingredients in saucepan. Bring to boil, stirring constantly; simmer for about 5 minutes, until slightly thickened and clear. Spoon into 4 individual dishes; cool slightly. Top with crusts and serve. Makes 4 servings.

Apricot-Pineapple Pies

1 box (11 ounces) dried apricots
2 cups water
1 cup (one 9-ounce can) crushed
     pineapple
⅛ teaspoon salt
1 cup sugar
2 tablespoons cornstarch
     Pastry for Individual Deep-Dish Pies,
     page 1399)

Put apricots in saucepan and add water. Bring to boil, cover, and simmer for 25 minutes, or until almost tender. Add pineapple, then dry ingredients mixed together. Simmer for 10 minutes longer, or until slightly thickened and clear, stirring frequently. Spoon into 4 individual dishes, cool slightly. Top with crusts and serve. Makes 4 servings.

CHIFFON, JELLIED, AND FROZEN PIES

Chiffon pies are rich and delicate, made with a cooked custard, flavoring, gelatin, and beaten egg whites or whipped cream. The filling is placed in a baked pie shell and chilled. Jellied pies are very similar to the chiffon, but are usually made without egg whites and have a creamier consistency. Frozen pies are an ice-creamlike mixture put into baked shells and frozen.

Velvety Chiffon Pies

1 cup milk
1 envelope unflavored gelatin
¾ cup sugar
¼ teaspoon salt
4 eggs, separated
1 teaspoon vanilla extract
     Crumb Crust, baked (page 1399)

Put milk in top part of small double

boiler. Soften gelatin in milk. Add ¼ cup sugar, the salt, and egg yolks. Beat slightly to blend. Put over simmering water and cook, stirring constantly, until mixture is thickened and coats a metal spoon. Remove from heat and add vanilla. Chill until thickened but not firm. Beat egg whites until foamy; gradually add remaining sugar, beating until stiff but not dry. Fold this meringue into gelatin mixture. Pile lightly into cold Crumb Crust; chill until firm. Serve plain, or spread with sweetened whipped cream. Makes 6 to 8 servings.

Banana Chiffon Pie

Follow recipe for Velvety Chiffon Pie. Fold 1 diced large ripe banana into gelatin mixture with the meringue. Spread firm pie with whipped cream. Just before serving, garnish with banana slices.

Caramel Chiffon Pie

Follow recipe for Velvety Chiffon Pie. First heat ¼ cup sugar in small skillet until golden brown. Add to egg-yolk mixture before cooking. Use ¼ cup each of brown and granulated sugar in meringue. Add ¼ cup chopped nuts.

Coffee Chiffon Pie

Follow recipe for Velvety Chiffon Pie, adding 2 tablespoons instant-coffee powder to hot mixture.

Nesselrode Chiffon Pie

Follow recipe for Velvety Chiffon Pie, substituting 2 tablespoons brandy for the vanilla extract. Fold ¼ cup diced mixed candied fruits into filling with the meringue. Pour into crumb crust and chill. Garnish firm pie with whipped cream, candied cherries, and angelica.

Peanut Crunch Chiffon Pie

Follow recipe for Velvety Chiffon Pie. Beat ⅓ cup peanut butter into hot mixture with rotary beater. Spread firm pie with whipped cream and top with ¼ cup crushed peanut brittle.

Candy Chiffon Pie

Follow recipe for Velvety Chiffon Pie, but use ½ teaspoon each of vanilla and peppermint extracts. Tint pink with red food coloring. Pour into crumb crust made with vanilla wafers and chill. Garnish firm pie with whipped cream and crushed hard peppermint candy.

CANTALOUPE CHIFFON PIE

1 medium cantaloupe, peeled
1 envelope unflavored gelatin
3 eggs, separated
¾ cup sugar
½ teaspoon salt
¼ cup fresh lemon juice
1 cup heavy cream, whipped
   Crumb Crust made with graham
   crackers, baked (page 1399)

Shred fine or purée in blender half of cantaloupe, or enough to make 1 cup pulp. Put in top part of small double boiler. Soften gelatin in the pulp. Add slightly beaten egg yolks, ¼ cup sugar, and the salt. Cook over boiling water, stirring, until thickened. Add lemon juice and cool. Cut remaining cantaloupe into small cubes and add to cooled mixture. Beat egg whites until foamy; gradually beat in ½ cup sugar and beat until stiff but not dry. Fold meringue and half of cream into cantaloupe mixture. Pour into cold crust; decorate top with remaining whipped cream and chill until firm. Makes 6 to 8 servings.

LEMON CHIFFON PIE IN PASTRY SHELL

1 envelope unflavored gelatin
1 cup sugar
¼ teaspoon salt
¼ cup fresh lemon juice
½ cup water
4 eggs, separated
2 teaspoons grated lemon rind
   Standard Pastry for 1-crust 9-inch
   pie, baked (page 1399)
   Whipped cream

In top part of small double boiler mix gelatin, ½ cup of the sugar, and the salt. Beat in liquids and egg yolks. Put over simmering water and cook, stirring, until mixture thickens and coats a metal spoon. Remove from heat and add lemon rind. Chill until thickened but not firm. Beat egg whites until foamy; gradually add remaining sugar, beating until stiff. Fold into gelatin mixture. Pile in cold pie shell. Chill until firm. Decorate with whipped cream. Makes 6 to 8 servings.

Lime Chiffon Pie

Follow recipe for Lemon Chiffon Pie, substituting lime juice and rind for lemon. Add a few drops each of green and blue food coloring.

PEPPERMINT CHOCOLATE CHIFFON PIE

1 envelope unflavored gelatin
¼ cup cold water
½ cup strong coffee
6 ounces semisweet chocolate pieces
4 eggs, separated
½ cup sugar
¼ teaspoon salt
1 teaspoon vanilla extract
   Chocolate Pie shell, baked
   (page 1399)
   Whipped cream
   Peppermint-stick candy

Sprinkle gelatin on ¼ cup cold water to soften. Heat coffee and chocolate together until chocolate is melted, stirring constantly. Remove from heat; add softened gelatin and stir until dissolved. Beat egg yolks thoroughly. Add yolks, ¼ cup

sugar, salt, and vanilla to chocolate mixture; mix well. Chill until slightly thickened. Beat egg whites until foamy. Gradually add remaining sugar and beat until stiff. Fold egg whites into chocolate mixture; pile lightly into cold Chocolate Pie Shell. Chill until firm. Garnish with whipped cream and bits of peppermint-stick candy, if desired. Makes 6 to 8 servings.

PUMPKIN CHIFFON PIE

1 envelope unflavored gelatin
⅔ cup sugar
½ teaspoon salt
½ teaspoon ground ginger
¼ cup water
3 eggs, separated
½ cup Triple Sec or Cointreau
1¼ cups canned pumpkin
½ cup heavy cream, whipped
   Crumb Crust made with gingersnaps,
   baked (page 1399)

In top part of small double boiler mix gelatin, ⅓ cup sugar, the salt, and ginger. Stir in water. Then beat in egg yolks, one at a time. Add Triple Sec and cook over simmering water, stirring constantly, until gelatin is dissolved and mixture is slightly thickened. Remove from heat and stir in pumpkin. Cool. Beat egg whites until stiff but not dry. Gradually add remaining ⅓ cup sugar and beat until very stiff. Fold in gelatin mixture and whipped cream. Pile lightly into cold Crumb Crust and chill until firm. Decorate with more whipped cream and with candied ginger if desired. Makes 6 to 8 servings.

LEMON AMBROSIA PIE WITH COCONUT CRUST

½ teaspoon salt
1½ cups sugar
6 tablespoons cornstarch
1½ cups boiling water
2 eggs, separated
2 tablespoons butter or margarine
1 teaspoon grated lemon rind
⅓ cup fresh lemon juice
1 teaspoon vanilla extract
1 envelope unflavored gelatin
¼ cup cold water
1 cup light cream
   Coconut Crust, baked (page 1399)
½ cup flaked coconut, toasted
   and cooled

In top part of double boiler mix salt, sugar, and cornstarch. Gradually stir in boiling water. Cook over direct heat, stirring, until smooth and thickened. Put over boiling water and cook, covered, for 10 minutes. Stir small amount into beaten egg yolks, then combine the two mixtures in double boiler and cook, stirring, for 2 minutes. Add butter, rind, juice, and vanilla. Take out 1 cup filling and set aside. Soften gelatin in cold water and stir into remaining filling. When dissolved, stir in cream. Chill until thickened; fold in stiffly beaten egg whites. Pour into cooled Coconut Crust shell; chill until firm. Spread reserved filling on pie; top with coconut. Chill. Makes 6 to 8 servings.

BLACK-BOTTOM PIE WITH CHOCOLATE CRUST

1 envelope unflavored gelatin
¾ cup sugar
¼ teaspoon salt
1½ cups milk
4 eggs, separated
1 tablespoon cornstarch
2 tablespoons rum
1½ squares (1½ ounces) unsweetened chocolate
Crumb Crust made with chocolate-cookie crumbs, baked (page 1399)
Whipped cream
Shaved semisweet chocolate

Mix gelatin, ¼ cup sugar, and the salt in top of small double boiler. Add milk, egg yolks and cornstarch; beat to blend. Put over simmering water and cook, stirring constantly, until mixture thickens and coats a metal spoon. Remove from heat and add rum. Measure out ½ cup of the mixture and blend in chocolate. Spread in bottom of cold Crumb Crust. Chill remaining mixture until thickened but not firm. Beat egg whites until foamy; gradually add remaining sugar, beating until stiff but not dry. Fold into gelatin mixture. Pile lightly on chocolate mixture. Chill until firm. Top with whipped cream and shaved chocolate. Makes 6 to 8 servings.

CHERRY BAVARIAN PIE

1 cup undiluted evaporated milk
2 cups (one 1-pound can) pitted red sour cherries
¾ cup sugar
1 envelope unflavored gelatin
3 tablespoons fresh lemon juice
Red food coloring
Standard Pastry for 1-crust 9-inch pie, baked (page 1399)

Chill evaporated milk in freezer tray until ice crystals form around edge. Drain cherries, reserving liquid. In saucepan mix sugar and gelatin; gradually add liquid and heat, stirring constantly, until sugar and gelatin are dissolved. Remove from heat and add lemon juice and cherries. Chill until thickened but not firm. Add a few drops of red food coloring. Whip milk until stiff and fold into first mixture. Pile into cold shell and chill until firm. Makes 6 to 8 servings.
Note: Try a sprinkle of nutmeg over this.

PEACH PARFAIT PIE

1 box (3 ounces) peach- or lemon-flavored gelatin dessert
1¼ cups hot water
1 pint peach or vanilla ice cream
2 fresh peaches, peeled and diced (1 cup)
¼ cup sugar

Standard Pastry for 1-crust 9-inch pie, baked (page 1399)
½ cup heavy cream

Dissolve gelatin in hot water. At once add ½ cup ice cream and stir until blended. Repeat until all of ice cream is added. Chill until almost firm. Mix peaches with sugar and fold into mixture. Pour into cold shell and chill until firm. Whip cream and spread on pie. Makes 6 or 8 servings.

MARBLED CHOCOLATE RUM PIE

1 envelope unflavored gelatin
1 cup sugar
⅛ teaspoon salt
2 eggs, separated
1 cup milk
¼ cup rum
12 ounces semisweet chocolate chips
1 cup heavy cream
1 teaspoon vanilla extract
Standard Pastry for 1-crust 9-inch pie, baked (page 1399)

In top part of double boiler mix gelatin, ¼ cup sugar, and the salt. Beat in egg yolks, milk, and rum. Cook over boiling water, stirring constantly, until slightly thickened. Remove from heat and stir in chocolate until thoroughly blended. Chill until thickened but not set. Beat egg whites until they are foamy; gradually add ½ cup sugar and beat until very stiff. Fold into chocolate mixture. Whip cream with remaining sugar and vanilla until stiff. Alternate two mixtures in cold pie shell; swirl with spoon. Chill until firm. Makes 6 to 8 servings.

PEACH MERINGUE PIE

8 egg whites
½ teaspoon cream of tartar
½ teaspoon salt
1⅓ cups granulated sugar
1⅓ cups sifted confectioners' sugar
1 teaspoon vanilla extract
1 package (3¼ ounces) vanilla-pudding and pie-filling mix
¼ teaspoon almond extract
About 1½ cups sliced peaches
¼ cup blueberries

Have egg whites at room temperature. Beat at moderate speed until foamy. Add cream of tartar and salt and beat to distribute. Turn mixer to moderately high speed and add granulated sugar very gradually. Then add confectioners' sugar gradually. Stop mixer and scrape bowl so that no undissolved sugar remains around the edge of bowl. Add vanilla. Continue beating until mixture is thick and satiny and stands in stiff peaks, about 20 minutes. Mark a 9-inch circle on unglazed brown paper; put on cookie sheet. Spread some of meringue on brown paper within circle to form a base about ¾ inch thick. Put remaining meringue around edge of circle with a pastry bag and tube or with

a spoon. Bake in preheated slow oven (275°F.) for 1¼ hours. Turn off heat and leave in oven for 1 hour longer. Remove paper and cool on rack. Prepare pudding according to package directions, flavor with almond extract, and chill. Use to fill meringue. Top with peaches and sprinkle with blueberries. Makes 10 to 12 servings.

FROZEN MARBLE PIE

1¼ cups chocolate-cookie crumbs
1 tablespoon granulated sugar
¼ cup butter
1 egg white
⅛ teaspoon salt
½ cup confectioners' sugar
2 cups heavy cream, whipped
2 tablespoons sherry
1 ounce (1 square) unsweetened chocolate, melted and slightly cooled
1 teaspoon vanilla extract

Turn refrigerator control to coldest setting. Mix crumbs, granulated sugar, and butter. Press mixture onto bottom and sides of greased 9-inch pie pan. Bake in preheated moderate oven (350°F.) for 10 minutes. Chill. Beat egg white and salt until frothy; gradually add confectioners' sugar and continue beating until stiff but still glossy. Fold in cream. Divide mixture into halves. Add sherry to one part. Fold chocolate and vanilla into remainder. Spoon mixtures alternately into chilled crust. Freeze. Makes 6 to 8 servings.

FROZEN LEMON PIE

4 eggs, separated
Grated rind of 1 lemon
⅓ cup fresh lemon juice
⅔ cup sugar
1 cup heavy cream, whipped
⅛ teaspoon salt
⅓ cup fine graham cracker crumbs

In top part of double boiler mix egg yolks, lemon rind and juice, and sugar. Cook over hot water, stirring constantly, until mixture thickens and coats a metal spoon. Cool. Beat egg whites with salt until stiff. Fold with cream into first mixture. Butter a 9-inch pie pan and sprinkle with half the crumbs. Pour in lemon mixture and sprinkle with remaining crumbs. Freeze until firm. Makes 6 to 8 servings.

PASTRY RECIPES

CHEESE PASTRY
For 8- or 9-inch pies, with 1 crust or 1 lattice top

Mix 1 cup all-purpose flour and ¼ teaspoon salt. Cut in ⅓ cup shortening. Add ¼ cup grated sharp stale cheese. Add 2 tablespoons ice water or just enough to moisten dough, mixing lightly with a fork. Press into a ball.

CHICKEN-FAT PASTRY
For 8- or 9-inch pies,
with 2 crusts or 1 crust with lattice top
2¼ cups sifted all-purpose flour
¾ teaspoon salt
¾ cup chilled chicken fat
6 tablespoons milk

Put flour and salt in bowl and cut in fat. Gradually add milk and mix lightly with fork until dry ingredients are moistened. Squeeze into a ball.

CHOCOLATE PIE SHELL
For 8- or 9-inch pies, with 1 crust.
1½ cups sifted all-purpose flour
½ teaspoon salt
2 tablespoons cocoa
½ cup shortening

Mix dry ingredients well. Cut in shortening until pieces are the size of peas. Sprinkle 3 tablespoons cold water over flour mixture, mixing until dough forms a ball when pressed together. Roll out between 2 sheets of wax paper. Remove top sheet of paper; invert pastry on pie pan. Remove second paper and fit pastry into pan. Flute edge. Prick with fork and bake in preheated very hot oven (450° F.) for 10 to 12 minutes.

COCONUT CRUST
For 8- or 9-inch pies, with 1 crust.
½ teaspoon salt
1 cup all-purpose flour
⅓ cup shortening
½ cup flaked coconut, toasted and cooled
3 tablespoons milk (about)

Mix salt and flour. Cut in shortening. Stir in coconut. Blend in 3 tablespoons milk, or enough to make a dough that will form a ball. Roll out between 2 sheets of wax paper to fit pie pan. Crimp edges and bake in preheated hot oven (400°F.) for 10 to 12 minutes. Cool.

CRUMB CRUST
For 8- or 9-inch pies, with 1 crust.
Mix 1½ cups fine graham-cracker, vanilla-wafer, corn-flake, gingersnap, or chocolate-cookie crumbs and ¼ cup soft butter. With graham crackers, add ¼ cup sugar; with corn flakes, add 2 tablespoons sugar; with chocolate cookies, 1 tablespoon. Omit sugar if vanilla wafers or gingersnaps are used. Mix well and press into pie pan. Bake in preheated moderate oven (375°F.) for about 8 minutes.

MEAT PIE PASTRY
Top crust for 8- or 9-inch pies
Mix 2 cups sifted all-purpose flour and 1 teaspoon salt. Cut in ⅔ cup shortening. Mix 1 egg yolk with 3 tablespoons water. Mix lightly into flour mixture. Roll to ½-inch thickness and cut into diamonds or other desired shapes. Put on ungreased baking sheet. Prick tops with fork and

brush with slightly beaten egg white. Bake in preheated moderate oven (375°F.) for about 25 minutes; or bake while baking pie.

PASTRY FOR INDIVIDUAL DEEP-DISH PIES
For 4 individual crusts
Mix 1 cup sifted all-purpose flour and ½ teaspoon salt. With pastry blender or finger tips, work in ½ cup shortening until bits of fat are size of peas. Sprinkle with about 2½ tablespoons water, a little at a time, until entire mixture gets moistened. Press into ball; handle as little as possible; chill for 10 minutes. Makes at least 4 individual crusts.

■ **To Shape Crusts—Wreath:** Before chilling, press pastry into a 1-inch roll. Refrigerate for several hours. Cut into thin slices and arrange slices on cookie sheet in 4 circles, overlapping slices.

Star or Wedges: Roll out pastry on floured board. Cut 4 stars with star cookie cutter. To make wedges, cut 4 rounds with scalloped cutter, then quarter each with pastry wheel. Put on cookie sheet to bake.

Lattice: Roll out pastry on floured board; cut strips. Crumble foil in bottom of 4 individual ovenproof baking dishes; cover with small sheets of foil; press in smoothly ½ inch below tops of dishes. Weave lattice on foil; trim around edges. Moisten ends of lattice and put long strips of pastry around rims of dishes, pressing against ends of lattice. Put dishes on cookie sheet to bake.

Cutout: Roll out pastry on floured board; cut 4 circles 1 inch larger in diameter than tops of ovenproof baking dishes; cut star or other design from center. Fold under outside edges of pastry, and flute with fingers. Prepare 4 individual ovenproof baking dishes with foil as for Lattice. Put pastry on foil, and set dishes on cookie sheet to bake.

■ **To Bake Crusts—**For golden crusts brush unbaked pastry with cream, melted butter, beaten egg, or undiluted evaporated milk. Bake for about 12 minutes in preheated hot oven (425°F.) until nicely browned. Cool slightly. For Lattice or Cutout Crusts, transfer baked crusts from foil to a rack.

STANDARD PASTRY
For 8- or 9-inch pies, with 1 or 2 crusts,
or 1 crust with lattice top
Note: Double amount of ingredients when making lattice-top and 2-crust pies.
Mix 1 cup sifted all-purpose flour and ½ teaspoon salt. Cut in ⅓ cup plus 1 tablespoon lard or hydrogenated shortening. Sprinkle with 2 tablespoons water, a few

drops at a time, and mix lightly with a fork until all dry ingredients are moistened. Press firmly into a ball. Roll as directed in individual recipe. If a baked shell is required, roll pastry ⅛ inch thick. Fit into pie pan, flute edges and prick with fork. Bake crust in preheated very hot oven (450°F.) for 10 to 12 minutes.

PIG—The word can be used as a synonym for swine, an omnivorous hoofed mammal with a stout bristle-covered body, short legs, and a long snout; however, in the United States a pig is generally considered to be a young swine, with the word "hog" used to describe the adult animal.

Charles Lamb, who may be considered the literary authority on pigs, is specific as to what a pig should be: "I speak not of your grown porkers—things between pig and pork—those hobbydehoys —but a young and tender suckling—under a moon old . . ."

The suckling pig is a young animal that has not been weaned from its mother. Thus, as in young milk-fed veal, it is especially tender and succulent. Suckling pig, served roasted whole with an apple in its mouth, is a traditional English Christmas dish, and in fact suitable for any festive occasion. In this country fresh suckling pigs are available only from Thanksgiving through New Year's.

ROAST STUFFED SUCKLING PIG
1 suckling pig (about 12 pounds dressed)
Salt
1 tablespoon caraway seeds
½ cup butter or margarine
2 pounds sauerkraut
1 onion, chopped
4 unpeeled tart apples, cored and chopped
½ pound bacon in one piece
1½ cups beer
Watercress
Glazed lady apples

Wash and dry pig well. Rub inside with salt and caraway seeds. Heat butter and sauté sauerkraut and onion for about 10 minutes. Add apples. Stuff pig loosely with this mixture (too tight a stuffing will make it burst open during the roasting) and fasten with skewers. Lace or sew the opening with heavy kitchen string. Truss hind legs and forelegs close under the body, facing forward. Lay pig on rack in large roasting pan, or use 2 wooden spoons as a rack. Place a wooden plug or block in its mouth and cover the ears and tail with little envelopes of unglazed brown paper, buttered, to prevent scorching. Soak the bacon in the beer and keep warm on stove. Roast the pig in preheated moderate oven (350°F.) for 4 to 5 hours, depending on size, or until it is golden brown. To test for doneness, insert skewer into thickest part of meat. If watery liquid comes out, the meat is still raw; if it spurts fat, the meat is ready.

Now this is important: Baste the meat frequently, every 10 minutes at first, and every 5 minutes for the last hour, by rubbing the beer-soaked bacon over the surface, and by using the pan drippings. Otherwise the skin won't crackle, and a good crackling skin is one of the highlights of roast pig.

When the pig is done, uncover the ears and tail, and replace the plug in its mouth with a red apple. Serve on a bed of watercress and garnish with glazed lady apples. Makes about 25 servings.

HOW TO CARVE A SUCKLING PIG

A suckling pig should rest on a platter of sufficient size to give the carver ample room to work. The platter should be placed so that the pig faces away from the carver, at a 45-degree angle with the edge of the table. First, insert the carving fork between the two shoulders, straddling the backbone, and sever the head from the main part of the shoulder. This is done by cutting between either pair of the four middle neck vertebrae. The second step is to remove the front legs in a circular cut. The third step is to remove the two small hams.

Now remove the fork from its original position and place it securely in the left flank at about the center of the pig. Next, starting at the rear end, split the entire backbone lengthwise, dividing the pig into two long halves, each half consisting of a forequarter and hindquarter.

After this, each half is divided into the number of chops necessary for service. The chops being small, it is advisable to make each chop of double thickness.

This method of carving suckling pig sounds more difficult than it actually is. Only very young pigs can be served as suckling pigs, and it will be noted, particularly when splitting the backbone, that although accuracy is essential the task is much simplified by the fact that the bones are very soft and can be cut quite readily.

According to the size of the suckling pig, the small hams and front legs can be served whole or carved into two servings by cutting each along the bone and thus dividing it.

PIGEON—The words pigeon and dove are used interchangeably and refer to any bird of the very large and widely distributed family *Columbidae* which contains almost 300 species. All domestic pigeons are descendants of one wild

species, the Rock pigeon, *Columba livia*. Full-grown, these birds are almost too tough to be edible, and in this country only the young, known as squabs, are eaten.

PIKE—An important family of American fresh-water food and game fish which includes the pike, the smaller pickerel, and the larger muskellunge. All have long bodies, heads with sharp points, jaws that look like a duck's bill, and vicious teeth. The common, or Great Lakes, pike (and the only variety also known in Europe) is grayish-blue or green in color with many whitish or yellowish spots. It is found throughout the northern section of the United States east of the Rockies, in Canada, and in Alaska. Specimens exceeding forty pounds in weight and four feet in length have been taken, but the pike in markets seldom weighs over ten pounds.

Pickerels, among which are the eastern green or jack pike, the banded and the western pickerel, can grow to weigh as much as eight pounds, but the average is two to three.

The muskellunge, largest member of the pike family and a famous game fish because of its fighting qualities, averages five to six feet in length and often weighs over sixty pounds.

Pike have a good texture and flavor and care should be taken in cooking them. Pike and pickerel can be used interchangeably in recipes.

Availability—Fresh pike is available year round, whole or in fillets. Pike and pickerel fillets are available frozen. Muskellunge is not generally found in fish markets.

Purchasing Guide—See Perch, page 1362.

Storage—See Perch, page 1362.

Nutritive Food Values—Good source of protein.

☐ Muskellunge, 3½ ounces, raw = 109 calories

☐ Pickerel, 3½ ounces, raw = 84 calories

☐ Pike, 3½ ounces, raw = 90 calories

Basic Preparation—These are lean fish and are best steamed, poached, panfried, or baked. See Perch, page 1363.

CHILLED PIKE APPETIZER WITH COCKTAIL SAUCE

1½ pounds fresh or thawed frozen pike fillets
2 cups water

1½ teaspoons salt
1 garlic clove, minced
⅔ cup chili sauce
¼ cup sweet pickle relish
Juice of 1 lemon
2 tablespoons prepared horseradish
⅓ cup minced celery
1 teaspoon grated onion

Wipe fish with damp cloth or paper towel. Bring water, salt, and garlic to boil. Reduce heat and add fish. Cover and simmer gently for about 8 minutes, or until fish flakes easily when tested with a fork. Cool in liquid. Drain and flake fish. Chill thoroughly. Meanwhile, combine remaining ingredients and chill. Serve on fish flakes as appetizer. To serve as salad, arrange fish on lettuce or other greens and top with the sauce. Makes 4 servings.

CREAMED BROILED PIKE

4 cups water
3 tablespoons white vinegar
1 tablespoon salt
Four ½-pound to 1-pound whole pike
Salt and pepper to taste
1 cup heavy cream

Combine water, vinegar, and salt. Wash fish in it; this will firm the fish. Dry fish and split into halves. Put skin side down in greased shallow baking dish. Season with salt and pepper. Pour cream over fish. Broil 6 inches from source of heat for 8 to 10 minutes. Do not turn. Makes 4 servings.

LEMON-BROILED PIKE FILLETS

¼ cup fresh lemon juice
1 teaspoon grated lemon rind
½ cup butter, melted
2 pounds pike fillets

Combine lemon juice, rind, and melted butter. Dip fish fillets into sauce. Reserve remaining sauce. Panbroil fillets until one side is browned. Turn and baste with remaining sauce. Cook until browned and flaky. Do not overcook. Serve on hot dish, with lemon twists. Make 4 to 6 servings.

BAKED FILLETS OF PIKE MORNAY

1 pound pike fillets
Salt and pepper to taste
Butter
Mornay Sauce (about 1¼ cups)

Wash fish. Drain, and place in buttered shallow baking dish. Sprinkle with salt and pepper. Dot with butter. Bake in preheated moderate oven (350°F.) until fish flakes, about 20 minutes. Pour hot Mornay Sauce over fish. Place under broiler. Cook until golden brown and bubbly. Makes 4 servings.

Mornay Sauce

2 tablespoons butter or margarine
2 tablespoons all-purpose flour
1 cup milk, or milk and light cream
1 egg yolk, slightly beaten
2 tablespoons each of grated Swiss and Parmesan cheese
Salt and pepper

Melt butter and blend in flour. Gradually add milk and cook, stirring constantly, until thickened. Beat in egg yolk and cheese, and salt and pepper to taste. Makes about 1¼ cups.

PIKE, AMERICAN INDIAN STYLE

2 pounds whole pike
1 teaspoon salt
⅛ teaspoon pepper
¼ cup all-purpose flour
¼ cup cornmeal
3 tablespoons bacon fat or vegetable oil

Remove heads and tails from fish; wipe fish with damp cloth. Mix remaining ingredients except bacon fat. Roll fish in the mixture, and brown in bacon fat for about 4 minutes on each side. Makes 6 servings.

PIKE BAKED IN ALMOND SAUCE

2 pounds pike fillets
1 onion, sliced
1 bay leaf
6 peppercorns
   Dash of thyme
2 tablespoons butter or margarine
½ cup chopped almonds
   Few parsley sprigs, minced
1 chicken bouillon cube
2 tablespoons boiling water
1 tablespoon fresh lemon juice

Wipe fillets with a damp cloth. Arrange onion, bay leaf, peppercorns, and thyme in shallow baking dish. Put fillets on top. Melt butter in skillet; add almonds, and brown lightly. Add parsley, bouillon cube dissolved in the water, and lemon juice. Pour over fish. Bake in preheated moderate oven (350°F.) for about 30 minutes. Makes 6 servings.

PIKE WITH EGG SAUCE

1½ pounds pike fillets
1 garlic clove, minced
   Salt and pepper
½ cup boiling water
¼ cup butter or margarine
3 tablespoons flour
½ teaspoon Worcestershire
1 teaspoon prepared mustard
1½ cups milk
3 hard-cooked eggs, diced
3 tablespoons dry white wine
   Paprika

Cut fish into serving pieces and arrange on greased rack in large skillet. Sprinkle fish with garlic, salt, and pepper. Put boiling water in bottom of skillet. Cover; simmer for 15 minutes. Meanwhile, melt butter in saucepan. Blend in flour and seasonings. Add milk and cook until thickened, stirring constantly. Add eggs and wine; season with salt and pepper. Cover fish with sauce and sprinkle with paprika. Makes 4 servings.

MARINATED PICKEREL

1½ pounds pickerel
   Cornmeal or fine dry bread crumbs
2 garlic cloves
¼ cup olive oil
1 tablespoon chopped fresh rosemary
   or 1 teaspoon dried rosemary
1 cup wine vinegar

Salt and pepper
   Watercress

Dip fish into cornmeal. Brown 1 garlic clove in oil; remove garlic; add fish and cook until done. Sprinkle flat dish with rosemary; put fish on top and sprinkle with more rosemary. To oil remaining in skillet, add second garlic clove and brown lightly. Remove garlic and add vinegar; heat gently. Pour over fish. Season. When cold, cover; chill overnight. Garnish with cress. Makes 4 to 6 servings.

MUSKELLUNGE BAKED IN SPANISH SAUCE

1 muskellunge (about 12 pounds)
   Salt
8 slices of bacon, diced
1 garlic clove, minced
1 large onion, minced
2 bay leaves
2 cans (29 ounces each) tomatoes
¼ teaspoon pepper

Wipe fish with damp cloth or paper towel, and put in shallow baking dish. Sprinkle lightly with salt. Cook bacon until golden brown. Add garlic and onion, and cook a few minutes longer. Add bay leaves, tomatoes, pepper, and salt to taste. Bring to boil and simmer for 10 minutes. Pour over fish. Bake in preheated moderate oven (375°F.) for 1¼ hours, or until fish flakes easily with a fork. Serve with hot cooked rice if desired. Makes 12 to 16 servings.

PILAF—A rice dish basic to the cuisines of Greece and the entire Near East, and found throughout southern Asia. Depending on the country, alternate spellings of the word are *pilau, pilaff, pilaw, pilav,* and *pello*. The dish is usually made of well-seasoned long-grained rice sautéed in oil or butter, then boiled in bouillon or broth. A pilaf can contain meats, fish, seafood, vegetables, and any herbs or spices. In pilaf the grains emerge well cooked and separate, never mushy. The slow cooking of the rice in well-seasoned liquid imparts flavor to the grain.

There are as many kinds of pilaf as there are people who make them. Indian pilaf can be hot with curry; some Turkish pilafs are very bland. The advantage of pilaf, to the American as well as to the Asian cook, is that an extremely tasty main dish can be made with whatever is at hand, once the basic method of cooking the rice is mastered.

Pilafs can also be made with other grains, such as barley, or cracked wheat. Plain, or with additional ingredients, all pilafs are welcome alternates to potatoes and pasta.

When making a pilaf it must be remembered that there is a definite relation between the amount of rice or other grain and the liquid used, and the dish

must be cooked slowly, over very low heat. Depending on the kind of rice, or grain, the amount of liquid may vary somewhat, since grains have a different rate of absorption.

PLAIN PILAF

¼ cup butter or other fat
2 cups uncooked rice
2 cups boiling chicken or other bouillon
   Salt and pepper

In heavy saucepan melt butter. Sauté rice in it over medium heat for 3 to 5 minutes, until golden and transparent. Stir constantly. Pour in chicken bouillon; the rice will sizzle in an alarming manner. Cover tightly (the Middle Easterners cover the pan with a cloth before putting on the lid) and cook over lowest possible heat for 20 to 25 minutes, or until the rice is just tender and all the liquid absorbed. Season with salt and pepper to taste. Keep rice hot for 5 to 10 minutes before serving. This is not absolutely necessary, but it improves the pilaf. It can be done by standing the rice on the warm stove, or wrapping a cloth around the pan, or keeping it in a warm oven. Makes 6 to 8 servings.

GREEK RICE AND PORK PILAF

¼ pound lean pork, diced
3 slices of bacon, diced
1 onion, chopped
1 cup uncooked rice
   Salt and pepper
2 cups hot water
2 small sweet red peppers, cut into 1-inch pieces
½ cup green peas, cooked

In a skillet, cook first 3 ingredients until pork is browned. Add rice, salt, and pepper; cook for a few minutes. Pour off excess fat. Add hot water and peppers. Bring to boil. Simmer, covered, for 20 to 25 minutes, or until rice is done. Add peas. Makes 4 servings.

MADRAS CHICKEN PILAU

1 stewing chicken (about 5 pounds)
5 cups water
1 large onion, chopped
3 teaspoons salt
6 peppercorns
1 cup uncooked long-grained rice
2 tablespoons butter or margarine
3 teaspoons curry powder
2 cups chicken bouillon
¼ cup seedless raisins
¼ cup slivered toasted blanched almonds

Wash chicken and cut into serving pieces. Place in a 2-quart saucepan with 3 cups water, onion, 2 teaspoons of the salt, and the peppercorns. Cover and cook slowly for 1 hour, or until chicken is tender. Soak rice in 2 cups water for 30 minutes. Drain. Stir and cook in butter or margarine along with curry powder for 3 minutes. Add bouillon and remaining salt. Cover and cook for 15 minutes, or until rice is tender and all water is absorbed. Carefully stir in raisins and almonds. To serve, place a layer of rice on a serving dish; arrange over it the cooked chicken, boned if desired; cover with remaining rice. Makes 6 servings.

CRACKED-WHEAT PILAF

3 tablespoons butter or margarine
1 cup cracked wheat
¼ cup chopped onion
3 to 4 cups boiling consommé
1½ teaspoons salt
¼ teaspoon pepper

Melt butter in heavy saucepan. Stir cracked wheat and onion into it. Cook, stirring constantly, for 3 minutes. When cracked wheat is golden, add 3 cups of the consommé and salt and pepper. Simmer, covered, over low heat for about 30 minutes, or until tender. After 20 minutes, check for moisture; if necessary, add remaining consommé (start with ½ cup) to prevent scorching. Serve instead of potatoes or rice. Makes 4 to 6 servings.

VEGETABLE PILAF

1 tablespoon milk
6 to 7 saffron shreds or pinch of powdered saffron
1 tablespoon butter
Pinch of ground cinnamon
5 whole cloves
Pinch of garlic salt (optional)
1 tablespoon minced onion
½ cup raw peas
1 cup uncooked rice
2 teaspoons curry powder
2½ cups water
Pinch of salt
1 tablespoon chopped cashew nuts (optional)
1 tablespoon chopped raisins (optional)
1 tablespoon shredded coconut, unsweetened

Warm milk; add saffron 30 minutes before cooking. Melt butter in a saucepan. Add cinnamon, cloves, garlic salt (if desired), and onion. When onion is tender and pink in color, add peas and rice. Add curry powder and stir. Add milk and saffron, then water and salt. Add cashew nuts and raisins. Cover and cook until rice is tender, about 25 minutes, or until water is absorbed, stirring occasionally. Put in serving dish, sprinkle with unsweetened shredded coconut, and serve hot. Makes 4 servings.

PIMIENTO—A large-fruited, sweet, heart-shape pepper. See PEPPER (Capsicum), page 1358.

PINCH—As used in recipes, pinch refers to a small amount of a dry ingredient such as a ground spice, about as much as may be picked up between the tip of the index finger and the thumb.

PINEAPPLE—This hardy perennial herbaceous plant is a native of northern South America. The plant grows about knee-high, has a short stem and a round head of stiff grayish striped leaves that are about three feet in length and have spiny tips and prickly edges. The lavender-blue flowers grow in these heads, and the golden yellow fruit emerges from the leaves. Pineapples weigh from one to twenty pounds; the average weight is between three and six.

The English called the fruit pineapple because of its resemblance to a pine cone. In French, German, Italian, and other European languages its name is *ananas,* from the Paraguayan Guarani Indian *naná,* which means "excellent fruit." The pre-Incans and the Incans of Peru cultivated the fruit as we know it, for it is represented on old pottery vessels. From its native South American home it traveled to the West Indies where Columbus saw it in 1493. The Indians had huts with pineapples or pineapple tops near the entrance. This meant that stangers were welcome. The Spanish who came to the Islands took the custom of pineapples as signs of hospitality back to Spain, and they, too, gave it a name reflecting its resemblance to the pine cone, *piña.* From there the custom was passed to England, and the English colonists who settled in America built their houses with carved pineapples over the doorways and on the gateposts.

When the pineapple fruit was transported to Spain and Portugal, there was great loss due to spoilage. Out of a whole shipment to Portugal, only one pineapple arrived unspoiled. But this one, said a member of the court, "in softness is the melon's equal; in flavor it surpasses all garden fruits." An 18th-century gardener called it "as handsome as the watermelon, as delicious as the strawberry, as freshly aromatic as the cucumber, as heady as wine." A Frenchman in 1658 waxed even more lyrical when describing this fruit of the "Caribby Island." He said: "The Ananas or Pine apple is accounted the most delicious fruit not only of these islands, but of all America. It is so delightful to the eye and of so sweet a scent that Nature may be said to have been extremely prodigal of what was most rare and precious in her Treasury to this plant." Northern European gardeners refused to be deprived of the joys of pineapples and experimented with growing it under glass.

The pineapple was introduced to Hawaii in 1790 by a Spanish adventurer, Don Francisco de Paula y Marin. And although today Hawaii produces most of the world's supply, for almost 100 years the pineapple was considered a weedy pest. It was not widely cultivated until the 1880's when an English horticulturist, Captain John Kidwell, scientifically developed the commercial growing of the fruit. The first cannery, which he opened in 1892, processed only 1,000 plants, but the industry prospered immensely and by the 1960's well over three quarters of a billion pounds of canned pineapple and juice was being exported annually. Some fresh pineapple is also exported by Hawaii, but most of the fresh pineapple available in the continental United States comes from Puerto Rico and Mexico.

Availability—Fresh pineapple is available year round, with peak season from March through June.

Canned pineapple, in syrup pack, is available in slices, chunks, tidbits, spears, and crushed. Slices, tidbits, and juice are available in dietetic pack.

Canned and frozen pineapple juice and pineapple juice in combination with other juices are available, as are frozen pineapple chunks. Pineapple slices and pieces are available candied and preserved.

Purchasing Guide—Select fresh pineapples that are heavy for their size, slightly soft to touch, golden yellow in color, with a piny aroma. Avoid fruit that is too green. Overmaturity is indicated by slight decay at the base or dark soft watery spots.

Storage—Cover ripe pineapples, refrigerate, and use as soon as possible. Allow unripe pineapples to ripen at room temperature, but not in sunlight.

☐ Fresh, refrigerator shelf: 2 to 3 days
☐ Fresh, prepared for freezing; and frozen, refrigerator frozen-food compartment: 3 months
☐ Fresh, prepared for freezing; and frozen, freezer: 1 year
☐ Canned, kitchen shelf: 1 year
☐ Canned, refrigerator shelf, opened: 4 to 5 days

Nutritive Food Values—Pineapple is a fair source of vitamin C, and has small amounts of vitamin A.
- [ ] Raw, 3½ ounces = 52 calories
- [ ] Canned, water pack, 3½ ounces, solids and liquid = 39 calories
- [ ] Canned, light syrup pack, 3½ ounces, solids and liquid = 59 calories
- [ ] Canned, heavy syrup pack, 3½ ounces, solids and liquid = 74 calories
- [ ] Canned, extra heavy syrup pack, 3½ ounces, solids and liquid = 90 calories
- [ ] Frozen chunks, 3½ ounces = 85 calories
- [ ] Canned juice, 3½ ounces, unsweetened = 55 calories
- [ ] Frozen concentrate, 3½ ounces, unsweetened and undiluted = 179 calories
- [ ] Frozen concentrate, 3½ ounces, unsweetened and diluted with 3 parts water = 52 calories
- [ ] Candied, 3½ ounces = 316 calories

Basic Preparation—There are many ways in which fresh pineapple can be cut for serving:

1. Remove leaves. Cut fruit into 1-inch rings. Pare and core. Leave as rings or cut into smaller pieces.

2. Cut into halves through fruit and leaves. Remove flesh from shell using sharp knife or a grapefruit knife. Cut flesh into small pieces, mix together with other fruits, and refill shells.

3. Do not remove leaves. Quarter pineapple. (Very large pineapples should be cut into eighths.) Remove flesh with sharp knife. Cut flesh into halves lengthwise and into small sections crosswise. Replace on shell. Serve as appetizer, using toothpicks to eat the fruit.

- [ ] **To Freeze**—Use fully ripe firm pineapples. Pare and remove core and eyes. Cut into cubes, wedges, spears, or slices, as desired. Pack fruit into freezer containers and cover with cold syrup, made by boiling 4 cups water with 7 cups sugar until clear. Leave ½-inch headspace. Seal.

Note: Pineapple juice may be used instead of all or part of the water used to prepare syrup.

PINEAPPLE COOK BOOK

APPETIZERS AND SPREADS

PINEAPPLE FRUIT CUP SERVED IN THE HALF SHELL
- 1 small pineapple
- 1 bright red apple
- Juice of ½ lemon
- 1 fresh peach
- 1 pint strawberries
- 2 tablespoons kirsch
- ¼ cup sugar
- Few mint sprigs

Halve pineapple lengthwise keeping the leaves intact and cutting right through them. With a sharp knife, cut along the underside of the core and around the skin to loosen the edible part of the fruit, being *very careful* not to puncture the shell. Scoop out the pulp; core and dice it. Dice and core, but do not peel, the apple. Quickly brush with lemon juice so that it doesn't turn brown. Cut peach into thin slices. Wash and stem most of strawberries, leaving out a few plump ones, unstemmed, for garnish. Combine fruits, again sprinkling with lemon juice. Add kirsch and sweeten to taste. Spoon into pineapple shells; chill. Garnish with unstemmed strawberries and fresh mint sprigs. Makes 2 servings.

MINTED PINEAPPLE CUP
Drain 2¼ to 2½ cups (one 1-pound, 4-ounce can) pineapple chunks, reserving syrup. Put pineapple in bowl. Measure ¾ cup syrup into small saucepan; add ¼ cup each of fresh orange and lemon juice and ¾ cup after-dinner mints. Bring to boil and stir until mints are dissolved. Pour over pineapple; chill. Makes 4 servings.

PINEAPPLE-PEANUT SPREAD
Mix well ¼ cup soft butter, ⅔ cup smooth or crunchy peanut butter, and ⅔ cup well-drained crushed pineapple. Makes about 1⅓ cups.

PINEAPPLE, TONGUE, AND CHEESE SPREAD
Mash 4 ounces of cream cheese. Stir in 1 cup ground or chopped smoked beef tongue and ½ cup drained crushed pineapple. Moisten, if necessary, with a little pineapple juice. Makes about 1¾ cups.

PINEAPPLE-AVOCADO SPREAD
Peel and mash 1 small ripe avocado. Add ½ cup drained crushed pineapple, 2 teaspoons fresh lemon juice, and 2 tablespoons mayonnaise; season with salt to taste. Makes about 1 cup.

SPRING-FRUIT JAM
- 3 cups shredded fresh pineapple
- 2 cups cut rhubarb
- 4 cups hulled strawberries
- Dash of salt
- 4½ cups sugar

Put pineapple in large preserving kettle without added liquid and cook for 10 minutes. Add rhubarb, strawberries, and salt; cook for 20 minutes. Add sugar; bring to boil and boil rapidly, stirring frequently, until thick, 25 to 30 minutes. Skim and pour into hot sterilized jars. Seal. Makes six ½-pint jars.

MAIN DISHES

ANANAS (PINEAPPLE) PILAU
- 6 pork chops
- 1 onion, sliced thin
- 2 tablespoons butter or margarine
- 8 cloves
- ½ teaspoon salt
- 1 teaspoon crushed coriander seeds
- 1 medium pineapple
- 1 cup sugar
- ½ cup fresh lemon juice
- ½ teaspoon ground ginger
- 1 cup uncooked rice
- ½ teaspoon ground cinnamon

Brown chops on both sides; remove from skillet. Cook onion in butter with cloves, salt, and coriander. Add chops and 1½ cups water; simmer for 20 minutes. Remove chops; strain gravy, adding water if necessary to make 1 cup. Cut peeled pineapple into ½-inch slices. Boil sugar, lemon juice, and ginger for 5 minutes. Add pineapple and cook until just tender, adding water if necessary to keep it from sticking. Cook and drain rice. Cut half of pineapple into pieces and add to rice. Put rice in casserole, arrange chops over it, and top with pineapple slices. Sprinkle with cinnamon and pour gravy over all. Cover; bake in preheated slow oven (300°F.) for 35 to 40 minutes. Makes 6 servings.

1—Pineapple, Tuna, and Rice Salad
2—Jellied Pineapple Cheese Cake
3—Cherry-Almond-Pineapple Jam
4—Spiced Pineapple Relish
5—Two-Tone Pineapple Salad
6—Pineapple Spareribs

PINEAPPLE SWEET-AND-SOUR PORK

1 pound lean pork, cut into ½-inch
  pieces
2 tablespoons cooking oil
  Salt and pepper to taste
1 cup beef bouillon
1 large green pepper, slivered
1 small onion, thinly sliced
2½ cups (one 1-pound, 4½-ounce can)
  pineapple chunks, drained
¼ cup sugar
½ cup pineapple syrup
¼ cup vinegar
3 tablespoons cornstarch
2 teaspoons soy sauce
  Hot cooked rice

Brown pork in hot oil. Season. Add
bouillon. Simmer, covered, for 30 minutes. Add vegetables and pineapple.
Blend together next 5 ingredients and add
to mixture. Cook, stirring frequently, for
10 minutes. Serve on rice. Makes 4 servings.

PINEAPPLE SPARERIBS

2½ to 3 pounds meaty pork spareribs
  Salt and pepper to taste
1 small onion, chopped
½ green pepper, cut into ½-inch pieces
1 celery stalk, thinly sliced
2 tablespoons pork fat
1 tablespoon cornstarch
2 cups (two 9-ounce cans) pineapple
  tidbits
¼ cup vinegar
3 tablespoons soy sauce

Cut ribs into serving pieces and put in
shallow roasting pan. Season. Bake in
preheated moderate oven (350°F.) for
2 hours, turning pieces and pouring off
fat 2 or 3 times. Cook onion, green
pepper, and celery in pork fat for 5
minutes. Blend in cornstarch. Add remaining ingredients and cook, stirring,
until thickened. Pour over ribs and bake
for 45 minutes longer. Makes 4 to 6
servings.

PINEAPPLE AND PORK CASSEROLE

2 cups diced roast pork
2 cups diced canned sweet potatoes
1 cup (one 9-ounce can) pineapple
  spears
½ teaspoon prepared mustard
  Salt and pepper to taste
2 tablespoons brown sugar
2 tablespoons butter or margarine

Put meat and sweet potatoes in a shallow
casserole. Drain pineapple and add
enough water to syrup to make ½ cup.
Mix liquid with mustard and pour over
meat mixture. Season. Top with pineapple. Sprinkle with sugar and dot with
butter. Bake in preheated moderate oven
(350°F.) for about 30 minutes. Baste
occasionally with pan liquid. Makes 4
servings.

PINEAPPLE-HAM LOAF

¼ cup firmly packed light brown sugar
1 to 1½ cups drained pineapple chunks
  Whole cloves
2 eggs
1 can (10½ ounces) cream-of-mushroom
  soup
¼ cup each of ketchup and water

1 pound ready-to-eat ham, ground
1 pound veal, ground
1 cup fine dry bread crumbs
½ teaspoon salt
¼ teaspoon pepper
1 small onion, minced
3 tablespoons chopped green pepper

Grease a loaf pan (9 x 5 x 3 inches)
and sprinkle with sugar. Stick pineapple
chunks with cloves and arrange, clove
side down, in pan. Beat eggs slightly and
stir in soup, ketchup, and water. Add
remaining ingredients and mix well. Pack
on pineapple in pan. Bake in preheated
moderate oven (350°F.) for about 1
hour. Makes 8 servings.

PINEAPPLE, YAM, AND HAM CASSEROLE

2 cans (1 pound each) yams in syrup
¼ cup melted butter or margarine
¼ cup firmly packed brown sugar
⅛ teaspoon ground cinnamon
¾ teaspoon salt
1½ cups diced cooked ham
1 cup drained pineapple tidbits
½ cup flaked coconut

Drain yams and mash. Beat in 3 tablespoons of the butter and the sugar, cinnamon, and salt. Fold in ham and ¾
cup pineapple. Put in 1½-quart casserole.
Mix remaining butter and pineapple and
the coconut. Spread on top of mixture.
Bake in preheated moderate oven (350°
F.) for about 45 minutes. Makes 4
servings.

LAMB SERENDIPITY

6- pound leg of lamb, weighed after
  boning
½ garlic clove
1 tablespoon scraped onion pulp
6 tablespoons melted butter or
  margarine
1 teaspoon ground ginger
  Salt and pepper
1 cup pineapple pulp
1 tablesoon brown sugar
2 tablespoons finely chopped parsley
2 cups toasted small bread crumbs
1 cup pineapple juice

Have leg of lamb boned but not rolled.
Crush garlic and mix with onion. Turn
into pan with 2 tablespoons butter, ½
teaspoon ginger, and salt and pepper to
taste. Add pineapple, sugar, and parsley.
Sauté for 3 minutes. Remove from stove
and mix with bread. Stuff lamb and sew
up cavity. Dust lamb with remaining
ginger and salt and pepper. Coat with
remaining butter. Sear in preheated hot
oven (425°F.) for 5 minutes. Reduce
heat to moderate (350°F.). Cover and
bake for 2½ hours, basting occasionally
with juice. Makes 8 to 10 servings.

PINEAPPLE TERIYAKI

3 to 4 pounds beef tenderloin or sirloin,
  about 1 inch thick
2½ cups (one 1-pound, 4½-ounce can)
  pineapple chunks
⅓ cup soy sauce
1 teaspoon ground ginger
1 teaspoon sugar
½ teaspoon garlic salt

Cut meat into 1-inch cubes. Drain syrup
from pineapple into a bowl. Add next
4 ingredients and mix well. Put beef in
shallow pan and cover with soy mixture.
Let stand for about 1 hour, turning several times. Drain meat and thread on
skewers alternating with pineapple cubes.
Broil, or cook over coals, turning frequently, until meat is browned and done.
Makes 6 to 8 servings.

HAWAIIAN PINEAPPLE AND CHICKEN

½ cup each of sliced water chestnuts,
  bamboo shoots, and celery
¼ cup sliced Chinese cabbage
2 tablespoons cooking oil
2 cups diced cooked chicken
1 tablespoon brown sugar
1 tablespoon vinegar
1 teaspoon monosodium glutamate
3 tablespoons soy sauce
2 cups chicken bouillon
1 cup drained pineapple cubes
3 tablespoons cornstarch
3 tablespoons cold water
¼ cup chopped green onion
  Chow-mein noodles

Cook vegetables in oil for 5 minutes,
stirring. Add next 7 ingredients and bring
to boil. Stir in cornstarch blended with
water. Cook, stirring constantly until
thickened. Sprinkle with onion and serve
on noodles. Makes 4 servings.

PINEAPPLE AND SHRIMPS, CHINESE STYLE

¼ cup firmly packed brown sugar
1½ tablespoons cornstarch
½ teaspoon salt
¼ cup vinegar
1 tablespoon soy sauce
½ teaspoon ground ginger
2½ cups (1-pound, 4½-ounce can) pineapple chunks
1 green pepper, cut into strips
1 medium onion, cut into rings
1 pound cleaned shelled cooked shrimps
  Hot cooked rice

Blend sugar, cornstarch, and salt in large
saucepan or skillet. Add vinegar, soy
sauce, ginger, and syrup from pineapple.
Cook, stirring constantly, until thickened.
Add pineapple, pepper, and onion; cook
for 2 or 3 minutes. Add shrimps and
bring to boil, stirring. Serve on hot rice.
Makes 4 to 6 servings.

ORIENTAL PINEAPPLE AND TUNA

1⅔ cups (one 13½-ounce can) pineapple
  chunks
¼ cup vinegar
¼ cup sugar
2 teaspoons soy sauce
½ teaspoon monosodium glutamate
½ cup water
2 tablespoons cornstarch
1 onion, cut into thin wedges
1 medium green pepper, cut into strips
1 can (7 ounces) tuna chunks, drained
1 tomato, canned or peeled fresh
  Hot cooked rice

Drain syrup from pineapple into large
saucepan or skillet. Add vinegar, sugar,
soy sauce, and monosodium glutamate.
Stir in water and cornstarch blended.
Cook, stirring, until thickened. Add pine-

apple and remaining ingredients except rice; cook, covered, until ingredients are just heated. Serve on rice. Makes 4 servings.

MEAT ACCOMPANIMENTS

PIQUANT PINEAPPLE AND BEETS
½ cup crushed pineapple
2 tablespoons vinegar
2 tablespoons each of sugar and cornstarch
2 cups (one 1-pound can) sliced or diced beets, drained
2 tablespoons butter or margarine
Salt and pepper

Bring pineapple and vinegar to boil. Combine sugar and cornstarch and stir into mixture. Cook, stirring constantly, until smooth and thickened. Add beets and butter. Heat well and season to taste. Serve hot as a relish. Makes 4 servings.

PINEAPPLE RICE
1¼ cups raw rice
3 tablespoons butter
1⅔ cups, about (one 13½-ounce can), crushed pineapple
1 teaspoon salt
1¾ cups water
⅓ cup firmly packed light brown sugar
2 teaspoons grated lemon rind
¼ teaspoon ground nutmeg

Cook rice in butter in a saucepan until opaque. Drain pineapple, reserving ¼ cup syrup. Combine syrup, salt, and water with rice. Bring to boil and simmer, covered, for 15 minutes, or until rice is tender and water is absorbed. Mix in pineapple, sugar, lemon rind, and nutmeg. Put in 1½-quart casserole and bake, covered, in preheated hot oven (400°F.) for about 20 minutes. Serve with cold meats. Makes 4 to 6 servings.

PINEAPPLE BAKED BEANS
3½ cups (two 1-pound cans) Boston-style baked beans
1 cup pineapple chunks or tidbits
Salt, pepper, and powdered mustard
¼ cup firmly packed brown sugar
Vinegar
9 slices of bacon, halved

Put half of beans in shallow baking dish. Add half of pineapple and mix lightly. Sprinkle with salt, pepper, and mustard, then with half of sugar. Sprinkle with vinegar. Repeat with remaining ingredients except bacon. Cook bacon lightly. Put on beans. Bake in preheated moderate oven (375°F.) for 30 minutes. Makes 6 servings.

BROILED PINEAPPLE SLICES
Brush pineapple slices with melted butter or margarine and sprinkle with brown or granulated sugar. Broil without turning for 5 to 8 minutes, or until hot and lightly browned. Serve with hamburgers, chops, or ham.

Lebanese Pineapple

Pineapple and Shrimps, Chinese Style

SPICED PINEAPPLE RELISH

2½ cups (one 1-pound, 4½-ounce can)
    pineapple chunks
⅔ cup cider vinegar
1 cup sugar
    Dash of salt
6 to 8 whole cloves
1 cinnamon stick

Drain pineapple, reserving syrup. Bring ⅔ cup pineapple syrup and remaining ingredients to boil and simmer for 10 minutes. Add pineapple and bring to a boil. Cool and store in refrigerator. Good with chops. Makes 4 to 6 servings.

SALADS

PINEAPPLE-HAM SALAD

1½ cups well-drained crushed pineapple
2 cups diced cooked ham
3 cups shredded cabbage
½ cup mayonnaise
¼ cup pineapple syrup
    Salt

Mix pineapple, ham, and cabbage. Blend mayonnaise and syrup. Add to first mixture. Add salt to taste. Makes 6 servings.

PINEAPPLE, TUNA, AND RICE SALAD

1 can (6½ ounces) white-meat tuna
    fish, flaked
1 cup (one 9-ounce can) pineapple
    tidbits, drained
2 cups cold cooked rice
¾ cup thinly sliced celery
⅓ cup sliced stuffed olives
¼ cup minced green pepper
    Salt
½ cup mayonnaise
    Salad greens

Combine tuna, pineapple, rice, celery, olives, and green pepper. Chill. Add salt to taste and mayonnaise; mix lightly. Serve on greens. Makes 4 servings.

PINEAPPLE SLAW

¼ cup finely diced green pepper
¾ cup diced unpeeled apples
3 cups shredded cabbage
1¼ cups each of shredded carrot and
    fresh pineapple
1 teaspoon sugar
¼ teaspoon salt
1 tablespoon fresh lemon juice
2 tablespoons mayonnaise

Toss together green pepper, apples, cabbage, and 1 cup each of carrot and pineapple. Combine sugar, salt, lemon juice, and mayonnaise and add. Toss. Garnish with remaining shredded carrot and pineapple. Makes 4½ cups.

TWO-TONE PINEAPPLE SALAD

1½ cups boiling water
2 boxes (3 ounces each) lime-flavored
    gelatin
1 cup drained crushed pineapple
1 cup pineapple syrup
1 cup creamed cottage cheese, sieved
1 cup heavy cream, whipped
4 pineapple slices, halved
    Watercress

Pour water over contents of 1 box of gelatin and stir until dissolved. Chill until slightly thickened and fold in pineapple. Pour into 1½-quart mold and chill until firm. Heat syrup to boiling and pour over contents of second box of gelatin; stir until dissolved. Chill until slightly thickened. Fold in cheese and cream. Pour over first mixture. Chill until firm. Unmold on serving plate and garnish with pineapple and watercress. Makes 6 servings.

PINEAPPLE-ORANGE SALAD

Mix 1 cup each of dairy sour cream, flaked coconut, drained mandarin-orange sections and pineapple chunks, and miniature marshmallows. Let stand in refrigerator for several hours. Put on greens and garnish with toasted walnuts. To toast walnuts, put in preheated slow oven (300°F.) for 10 minutes. Makes 4 to 6 servings.

PINEAPPLE-CUCUMBER SALAD

1⅔ cups (one 13½-ounce can) crushed
    pineapple, drained
2 cups diced peeled cucumbers
    Salad greens
1 cup dairy sour cream
1 tablespoon honey
1 tablespoon grated lemon rind
4 slices of pineapple, halved

Mix crushed pineapple and cucumbers. Line a bowl with greens and put pineapple-cucumber mixture in a mound in center. Mix next 3 ingredients and spoon around edge of mound. Garnish with pineapple slices. Makes 4 servings.

FRESH PINEAPPLE AND AVOCADO SALAD

1 ripe medium avocado
4 slices of fresh pineapple
2 tablespoons olive or salad oil
2 teaspoons fresh lime or lemon juice
¼ teaspoon salt
½ teaspoon sugar
    Lettuce or other salad greens

Chill avocado and pineapple. Remove peel and pit from avocado. Cut into ½-inch cubes. There should be 1¾ cups. Peel pineapple and cut into wedges. There should be 2½ cups. Add to avocado. Combine oil, lime juice, salt, and sugar. Add to fruit. Toss lightly. Serve on lettuce or other salad greens. Makes 6 servings.

DESSERTS AND BEVERAGES

PINEAPPLE-NUT PUDDING

1 cup biscuit mix
½ cup drained pineapple tidbits
¼ cup chopped nuts
¼ cup milk
1 cup pineapple syrup or juice
½ cup firmly packed brown sugar
2 tablespoons butter or margarine
    Dash of ground nutmeg or cinnamon
    Cream

Combine biscuit mix, pineapple, and nuts. Spread thin in bottom of greased baking dish (10 x 6 x 2 inches). Bring next 4 ingredients to boil and pour over dough. Bake in preheated moderate oven (375°F.) for 30 minutes. Sprinkle with nutmeg and serve with cream. Makes 6 servings.

LEBANESE PINEAPPLE

1 small pineapple
1 orange
½ pound seedless green grapes
    Juice of ½ lemon
1½ tablespoons chopped crystallized
    gingerroot or chopped citron
¼ cup sugar (about)
3 egg whites
¼ cup honey
3 tablespoons toasted shredded almonds
2 strawberries
2 grape leaves and a few fresh flowers

Prepare the pineapple and pulp, following recipe for Pineapple Fruit Cup Served in the Half Shell (page 1403). Combine diced pineapple with the orange, peeled, diced, and stripped of all white membrane; grapes, washed and stemmed; lemon juice; and 1 tablespoon gingerroot. Blend this mixture and sweeten to taste. Spoon mixture into pineapple shells.

Beat 3 egg whites until they stand in stiff peaks. Blend in the honey by stirring gently. Mound this mixture on top of the fruit-filled shells, making sure to spread meringue to the sides of the shells to keep it from shrinking. Sprinkle meringue with almonds and remaining gingerroot. Bake in preheated hot oven (400°F.) for 5 minutes. Watch meringue so it doesn't get overbrown. Let shells cool, then chill them in the refrigerator. Serve each half shell with a whole strawberry perched on top. For a truly handsome dish, bed the shells on grape leaves and decorate with a few fresh flowers. Makes 2 servings.

PINEAPPLE AND CREAM-CHEESE PIE

1 box (10 ounces) piecrust mix
½ cup well-drained crushed pineapple
¾ cup sugar
1 tablespoon all-purpose flour
⅛ teaspoon salt
12 ounces cream cheese
4 eggs
¼ cup each of heavy cream and milk
1 teaspoon vanilla extract

Prepare piecrust mix as directed on the label. Line 10-inch pie pan with pastry and bake in preheated very hot oven (450°F.) for 10 minutes, or until lightly browned. Spread pineapple in bottom of shell. Mix sugar, flour, and salt. Mash cheese and beat into sugar mixture. Beat eggs slightly; add cream, milk, and vanilla. Stir into cheese mixture. Pour into crust. Bake in preheated moderate oven (350°F.) for 30 minutes, or until firm. Cool; chill. Makes 6 to 8 servings.

TWO-CRUST PINEAPPLE PIE

2½ cups (one 1-pound, 4½-ounce can) crushed pineapple
¼ cup sugar
2 tablespoons cornstarch
¼ tesapoon salt
1 tablespoon butter
1 tablespoon fresh lemon juice
  Standard Pastry for 2-crust 8-inch pie, unbaked (page 1399)

Put pineapple in saucepan. Mix next 3 ingredients and stir into pineapple. Bring to boil and cook, stirring, for 2 minutes, or until thick and clear. Remove from heat and stir in butter and lemon juice. Line pie pan with pastry, pour in filling, and adjust top crust. Or top with lattice strips. Bake in preheated hot oven (425° F.) for 25 to 30 minutes. Makes 6 servings.

PINEAPPLE-APRICOT UPSIDE-DOWN CAKE

¼ cup butter or margarine
½ cup firmly packed dark brown sugar
4 slices of pineapple, cut into halves
14 dried apricot halves, soaked in hot water
¼ cup shortening
⅔ cup sugar
1 egg
2¼ cups sifted all-purpose flour
1 tablespoon baking powder
½ teaspoon salt
1 cup milk

Cream butter and stir in brown sugar. Spread mixture in the bottom of an 8-inch square pan. Top with pineapple and apricots. Cream shortening until light and fluffy. Gradually beat in sugar. Stir in egg. Sift flour with baking powder and salt. Add dry ingredients alternately with milk, beginning and ending with flour. Pour batter over fruit in pan. Bake in preheated moderate oven (375°F.) for about 35 minutes. Turn upside down onto serving plate.

PINEAPPLE MERINGUE CAKE

¼ cup margarine
  Sugar (about 1 cup)
2 egg yolks
1 cup sifted cake flour
1 teaspoon baking powder
⅛ teaspoon salt
⅓ cup milk
½ teaspoon vanilla extract
2 egg whites
½ cup well-drained crushed pineapple
½ cup heavy cream, whipped

Cream margarine until light and fluffy. Beat in ½ cup sugar. Beat in egg yolks. Sift together cake flour, baking powder, and salt. Add this alternately with milk and vanilla to creamed mixture, beating until smooth. Pour into greased and floured 8-inch square baking pan. Beat egg whites until stiff. Gradually beat in ½ cup sugar, 1 tablespoon at a time; beat until stiff and glossy. Spread meringue on cake. Bake for about 25 minutes, or until done. Remove from oven; cool in pan on rack. Cut into squares and

serve topped with crushed pineapple combined with heavy cream that has been whipped and sweetened with 1 tablespoon sugar.

JELLIED PINEAPPLE CHEESECAKE

20 graham crackers
  Sugar (about 1 cup)
⅛ teaspoon ground cinnamon
¼ cup soft butter or margarine
1 envelope unflavored gelatin
2 cups water
1 box lemon-pie mix
⅛ teaspoon salt
1 egg yolk
8 ounces cream cheese
1 cup drained crushed pineapple
3 egg whites
⅓ cup pineapple preserves

Crush crackers fine with rolling pin, or crush in blender. Mix crumbs with 3 tablespoons sugar, the cinnamon, and butter. Press firmly onto bottom and ⅔ of the way up sides of buttered 9-inch springform cake pan, reserving 2 or 3 tablespoons crumbs for top. Soften gelatin in ¼ cup cold water. In saucepan combine pie mix, ½ cup sugar, the salt, 1¾ cups water, and the egg yolk. Mix well. Cook until thickened, stirring. Add gelatin and stir until dissolved. Mash cheese and stir in lemon mixture. Beat with rotary beater until smooth. Fold in pineapple. Beat egg whites until foamy; add 3 tablespoons sugar and beat until stiff. Fold into cheese mixture. Pour into pan; sprinkle remaining crumbs around edge. Chill until firm; spread center with preserves. Makes 8 to 10 servings.

PINEAPPLE-OATMEAL COOKIES

½ cup soft butter or margarine
½ cup granulated sugar
½ cup firmly packed brown sugar
1 egg
1 cup (one 9-ounce can) crushed pineapple
1½ cups rolled oats
1 cup sifted all-purpose flour
½ teaspoon each of baking soda, salt, and ground cinnamon
  Dash of ground nutmeg
½ cup chopped walnuts

Cream butter. Add sugars and beat until light. Add egg and beat well. Add pineapple, oats, sifted dry ingredients, and nuts; mix well. Drop by teaspoonfuls onto ungreased cookie sheets. Bake in preheated moderate oven (375°F.) for about 15 minutes. Makes about 4 dozen.

SWEET RICE AND PINEAPPLE DESSERT

Rice:
1 cup packaged precooked rice
1 envelope unflavored gelatin
3 tablespoons water
2 tablespoons sugar
¼ teaspoon salt
1 teaspoon vanilla extract
1 cup heavy cream, whipped

Prepare rice according to package directions. Set aside. Soak gelatin in cold water for 5 minutes. Add this to dry *hot*

rice, then add sugar, salt, and vanilla. Mix all together thoroughly and cool. When cold, fold in cream; pack into mold rinsed in cold water and chill until firm.

Pineapple:
1 medium pineapple, peeled and sliced
½ cup sugar

Sweeten pineapple slices and chill.

Sauce:
¼ cup sugar
1 tablespoon cornstarch
½ teaspoon ground ginger
¾ cup boiling water
7¾-ounce jar apricot-applesauce (junior food)
2 tablespoons fresh lemon juice

Mix sugar, cornstarch, and ginger; stir in boiling water. Let boil for 5 minutes. Cool. Add sauce and lemon juice. Chill.

Garnish:
8 maraschino cherries
  Angelica
½ cup toasted shredded blanched almonds

Cut cherries into halves. Snip angelica into little diamond shapes. Reserve.

Unmold rice on a platter. Decorate top and sides with angelica and cherries. Swirl pineapple slices around base; sprinkle with nuts. Serve with sauce. Makes 6 servings.

HEAVENLY PINEAPPLE MOUSSE

1 large pineapple
  Juice of ½ lemon
3 egg yolks
½ cup sugar
⅛ teaspoon salt
1½ envelopes unflavored gelatin
½ cup cold milk
1 cup heavy cream, whipped
2 tablespoons kirsch, Madeira, rum, or Cointreau
  Green leaves and ¼ pound fresh black cherries with stems

Select a large pineapple with a regal topknot of leaves. Cut off top about 2 inches below the stem and save. With a very sharp knife remove the edible part of the fruit. Do not puncture the shell. Cut away from pulp as much of the tough core as possible. Reserve pulp to use in the filling. Chill the shell and its leafy "lid," because they will be used later as a container. Grate pineapple pulp to make 1 cup and add lemon juice. Set aside. Beat egg yolks, sugar, and salt until thick and lemon-colored. Add pineapple and mix well. Set aside. Sprinkle gelatin on milk to soak for 5 minutes. Cook egg-pineapple mixture in top part of a double boiler, stirring, until mixture coats a metal spoon. Add gelatin and stir until dissolved. Chill until mixture begins to thicken, then fold in cream to which you've added the liqueur. Fill chilled pineapple shell; chill until firm. Replace pineapple top and serve bedded on leaves with a wreath of cherries. Makes 4 servings.

CREAMY PINEAPPLE SHERBET
1 pineapple
½ cup sugar
1 cup water
1 cup heavy cream, whipped
1 tablespoon rum
Crushed ice

Cut top from pineapple; cut around inside to loosen pulp; scoop out and reserve. Combine sugar and water; boil for 5 minutes; cool. Whirl pineapple pulp to a purée in blender, or rub through a sieve. Measure 1 cup. Mix with cooled syrup and freeze in trays until mushy. Fold in whipped cream into which rum has been stirred. Pack into pineapple shell. Replace pineapple lid and serve in a bowl of crushed ice. Since speed is essential, have bowl of ice ready before you mix cream and rum with pineapple. Let guests spoon out their own portions. Makes 4 servings.

LOW-CALORIE PINEAPPLE SHERBET
2½ cups (one 1-pound 4-ounce can) unsweetened pineapple juice
1 teaspoon unflavored gelatin
2 teaspoons noncaloric liquid sweetener
Juice of 1 lemon
Dash of salt
1 egg white

Turn refrigerator control to coldest setting. Put 2 tablespoons juice in small saucepan, sprinkle with gelatin, and let stand for 5 minutes. Dissolve over hot water or very low heat. Add to remaining juice. Stir in sweetener and lemon juice. Pour into refrigerator tray and freeze until mushy. Beat with rotary beater or electric mixer until fluffy. Fold in stiffly beaten salted egg white, return to refrigerator tray, and freeze until firm. Makes 6 servings.

PINEAPPLE ICE

Mix 1 cup sugar and 2 cups water in saucepan. Bring to boil and boil for 5 minutes. Cool. Add 2½ cups (one 1-pound, 4½-ounce can) crushed pineapple, ½ cup fresh lemon juice, and dash of salt. Freeze until firm in crank freezer, following manufacturer's directions for freezing. Let stand in ice and salt or in freezer for several hours to mellow before serving. Makes about 1½ quarts.

Pineapple Ice with Crème de Menthe
Pile ice in serving dishes and make a deep depression in center of each serving. Fill hollow with green crème de menthe.

GINGERED LEMON PINEAPPLE
1 quart lemon ice cream or sherbet
⅓ cup finely chopped candied gingerroot or drained preserved gingerroot
Fresh pineapple, cut into bites or slices
Lemon slices or mint leaves for garnish

Allow ice cream to soften slightly; fold in ginger. Refreeze. Serve scoops of ice cream over chilled pineapple. Garnish each serving with lemon leaves. Makes 6 servings.

PINEAPPLE-PAPAYA CONSERVE
2 cups shredded fresh pineapple
2 cups diced fresh papaya
4 cups sugar
4 teaspoons finely grated fresh gingerroot

Peel pineapple and shred by scraping with tines of a silver fork. Discard core. Combine all ingredients in a large kettle. Bring to a boil, reduce heat, and simmer until thick. Pack in sterilized jars and seal. Makes about six ½-pint jars.

CHERRY-ALMOND-PINEAPPLE JAM
3½ cups sugar
2½ cups (one 1-pound, 4½-ounce can) crushed pineapple
⅓ cup halved candied cherries
¾ cup water
1 box powdered fruit pectin
½ teaspoon almond extract

Measure sugar and set aside. In large saucepan mix pineapple, cherries, and water. Add pectin and mix well. Bring to a hard boil. At once stir in sugar. Stirring constantly, bring to a full rolling boil and boil hard for 1 minute. Remove from heat and skim off foam. Add flavoring. Then stir and skim by turns for 5 minutes to prevent floating fruit. Ladle quickly into hot sterilized jars and seal. Makes about 5 half-pint jars.

FRESH PINEAPPLE PUNCH
Peelings from 1 medium pineapple
Peelings from 1 fresh orange
8 whole cloves
½ cup sugar
4 cups boiling water
½ cup fresh orange juice
½ cup fresh lemon juice

Wash pineapple peelings thoroughly. Place in a container with orange peel, cloves, and sugar. Add boiling water. Cover; let stand overnight. Strain; add orange and lemon juice. Serve over ice. Makes 5 cups.

ISLAND DREAM
1½ cups pineapple juice
½ cup fresh orange juice
½ cup nonfat dry-milk crystals
1 ripe banana, sliced
2 scoops of pineapple sherbet

Combine fruit juices, dry-milk crystals, and banana in blender container. Cover and whirl at high speed. Uncover (only if blender has a lid with no opening in the center) and with motor on, add pineapple sherbet. Pour into tall glasses. Makes 2 drinks.

PINE NUT—The edible seed of several varieties of pines; the seed develops in the pine cone which is heated in order to spread its scales and make the seed easy to dislodge. Some pine nuts come from native American trees in the Rocky Mountains and on the Pacific coast, where they are known as Indian nuts, pignons, or piñons. Others come from the Mediterranean stone pine, a large tree resembling an open umbrella. These pine nuts are often imported into the United States as pignolias or pinolias, both corruptions of the Italian name for the nut, *pinocchio*.

Pine nuts are the size of a small bean, with a thin, light brown shell. The meat is white or cream-colored. The texture is soft and the flavor mild. The southern European variety is longer and yellower than our native pine nuts, but both are delicious.

They are widely used in Mediterranean and Near Eastern cookery, where they are added to meat, rice, and vegetable dishes for additional taste and nourishment. The cookery of the Arab world relies on them heavily.

Availability—Both imported and domestic pine nuts are available, the imported being the variety most commonly found, shelled, in food stores and nut shops. The domestic, generally called Indian nuts are found in nut shops, shelled and in-the-shell.

Storage—Keep in jar, tightly covered, in refrigerator. Can be frozen shelled; will then keep for about 1 year.

Nutritive Food Values—Pine nuts contain some protein, and are high in fat.
☐ Imported, 3½ ounces = 552 calories
☐ Domestic, 3½ ounces = 635 calories

MEAT ROLLS WITH PINE NUTS
¼ cup pine nuts
1 tablespoon butter
1 pound ground lamb or beef

¼ cup chopped parsley
1 medium onion, minced
    Salt and pepper
1 can (8 ounces) tomato sauce

Brown pine nuts in butter. Mix together lamb, parsley, onion, and salt and pepper to taste. Shape into 4 rounds. With hands, flatten rounds and fill each with 1 tablespoon of pine nuts. Cover pine nuts with meat. Place in shallow baking dish and pour tomato sauce over meat rolls. Bake in preheated moderate oven (350°F.) for 30 minutes. Makes 4 servings.

PINE-NUT COOKIES

4 eggs
1½ cups granulated sugar
½ teaspoon grated lemon rind
    Few drops of oil of anise
2¼ cups sifted all-purpose flour
¼ teaspoon salt
    Confectioners' sugar
    Pine nuts

Put eggs and granulated sugar in top part of double boiler over hot water. Beat with rotary beater until mixture is lukewarm. Remove from water; beat until foaming and cool. Add flavorings and fold in flour and salt. Drop by teaspoonfuls onto greased and floured cookie sheets. Sprinkle with confectioners' sugar and nuts. Let stand for 10 minutes; bake in preheated moderate oven (375°F.) for about 10 minutes. Makes about 5 dozen.

PIPÉRADE—A combination of tomatoes, sweet peppers, and onions, or any two of them, which is cooked until very tender. To this combination eggs are added. The dish probably originated in the Basque area of France. There are numerous variations, but at least one variety is described as a frothy purée in which it is impossible to tell what is egg and what is vegetable.

PIPÉRADE

2 large sweet peppers, sliced
2 tablespoons olive oil
2 large tomatoes, peeled and diced
    Salt and pepper
½ small garlic clove, crushed
4 eggs

Cook peppers in the oil until soft. Add tomatoes and cook to a purée. Season with salt and pepper to taste and the garlic. Add eggs one at a time. Stir, and cook quickly to a soft scramble. Makes 4 servings.

PISTACHIO—The edible seed of a small evergreen tree, *Pistacia vera*. Cashew and sumac trees are members of the same family. Although some members of the genus have been found growing wild in the Canary Islands, Mexico, and Cali-

fornia, the species of pistachio tree cultivated for its nut is native to Asia Minor, and was first brought into Europe in the 1st century A.D. by Vitellius, a Roman governor of Syria.

A dry-climate tree, it was introduced into the middle and southern sections of the United States in the middle of the 18th century, and independently into California in the 1870's. The fruits of the pistachio tree grow in clusters. Each fruit is about the size of an olive, about one half to one inch long with a thin, hard, brownish-red shell. Within it is found a seed, the pistachio nut, which is pale green to creamy white in color, a single solid piece. It has a fine texture and mild pleasing flavor. The nutmeats are used for coloring and flavoring ice cream, cakes, and confectionery. They are also eaten out of the shell as is, or salted. The color of the nut is so distinctive that its name has been given to a special shade of light green.

Availability and Purchasing Guide—Pistachios are available year-round, sold in-the-shell, shelled, and salted.

☐ 2 pounds in-the-shell = 1 pound shelled = 3 cups

Storage—Store, covered, in refrigerator.

☐ Refrigerator shelf: 3 months
☐ Refrigerator frozen-food compartment, wrapped for freezing: 6 months
☐ Freezer, wrapped for freezing: 1 year

Nutritive Food Values—Pistachios contain some protein and niacin and are rich in calcium, phosphorus, iron, vitamin A, and thiamine.

☐ 3½ ounces, shelled = 594 calories

PISTACHIO FRUIT CUP

2 cups tangerine segments
1 cup grapefruit segments
1 cup diced pears
1 cup seedless grapes
2 tablespoons fresh lemon juice
    Sugar
    Cranberry or raspberry sherbet
½ cup chopped pistachio nuts

Combine fruits and sprinkle with lemon juice. Add sugar to taste. Chill. Put in 6 sherbet glasses. Top each serving with a small scoop of sherbet and sprinkle with nuts. Makes 6 servings.

FROZEN PISTACHIO CUSTARD

2 cups milk
3 eggs, beaten
¾ cup sugar
⅛ teaspoon salt
1 cup heavy cream, whipped
1½ teaspoons vanilla extract
1½ teaspoons almond extract
    Green food coloring
½ cup chopped pistachio nuts

Heat milk in top part of double boiler over boiling water. Mix eggs, sugar, and salt. Gradually stir in hot milk. Put mixture back in double boiler and cook over

simmering water, stirring constantly, until mixture thickens and coats a metal spoon. Remove from heat and cool. Fold in whipped cream, flavorings and enough food coloring to tint mixture a delicate green. Add nuts and pour into refrigerator tray. Freeze until firm. Makes 6 servings.

PIZZA—A savory open pie of Italian origin, which since World War II, when the GI's discovered it in Italy, has become a popular American dish. The word *pizza* in Italian means "pie," any kind of pie, and the particular pie that we have come to call pizza is a *pizza alla Napoletana*, a dish typical of Naples.

A pizza consists of a thin layer of yeast dough, rolled or patted to fit a large cookie sheet or special pizza pan, topped with tomatoes and herbs and slices of Mozzarella cheese. The variations are endless—anchovies, sausages, vegetables, olives—in fact anything goes into the sauce. The pizza is then baked until the cheese is bubbly and the crust edge is golden brown.

While the pizza is hot, it is cut into pie-shape wedges. The style of eating is also highly individual. The wedge may be eaten from the point to the crust, it may be folded lengthwise, it may be rolled, but it is not supposed to be eaten with a knife and fork.

Frozen pizzas complete and ready to bake are available, as are packaged pizza mixes containing mix for the dough, sauce, cheese, and/or sausage.

Caloric Values

☐ Home recipe, 3½ ounces, cheese topping, baked = 236 calories
☐ Frozen, 3½ ounces, baked = 245 calories

PIZZA

1 package active dry yeast or
    2 cakes compressed yeast
¼ cup lukewarm water*
1½ teaspoons sugar
2½ teaspoons salt
½ cup shortening
1¾ cups boiling water
6 cups sifted all-purpose flour
2 cans (2 ounces each) flat anchovy fillets
2 or 3 garlic cloves, minced
6½ cups (two 1-pound, 12-ounce cans) Italian-style tomatoes, drained
    Pepper, cayenne, salt
1 pound Mozzarella cheese, thinly sliced
⅔ cup grated Parmesan cheese
    Crumbled, dried oregano

Sprinkle dry yeast or crumble cake yeast into warm water. *Use very warm water (105°F. to 115°F.) for dry yeast; use lukewarm water (80°F. to 90°F.) for compressed. Let stand for a few minutes, then stir until dissolved. Put sugar, salt, and shortening in bowl; add boiling water and stir until shortening is melted. Cool to lukewarm. Stir in yeast mixture. Add half of flour; beat until smooth. Gradually stir in remaining flour. Divide dough into 4 portions. Roll each on floured board to about 13 inches in diameter. Shape on bottom and sides of lightly greased 12-inch pizza pans. Let rise in warm place until light. Drain anchovies; mix anchovy oil with garlic and brush on dough. Cover with tomatoes; season. Arrange Mozzarella and anchovies on top. Sprinkle with Parmesan and oregano. Bake in preheated hot oven (425°F.) for 15 to 20 minutes. Cut into wedges and serve at once. Makes four 12-inch pizzas.

■ Variations—1. Omit Mozzarella and anchovies. Substitute thinly sliced Italian sausage, cooked sausage links, salami, frankfurters, or smoked tongue. Sprinkle with cheese and bake as directed.

2. Omit tomatoes; substitute canned spaghetti sauce. Omit anchovies if meat sauce is used. Proceed as directed.

LITTLE PIZZA

Split English muffins; toast; spread with olive oil. Sprinkle with garlic salt; spread with canned spaghetti sauce. Sprinkle with dried oregano. On each half, put 2 strips of sliced Mozzarella cheese. Top each slice with a flat anchovy fillet. Bake in preheated moderate oven (375°F.) for 10 minutes, or until muffin is hot and cheese melted. If desired, garnish with a bit of chicory, waffled carrot slices, and a ripe olive.

PICNIC PIZZA

To serve 4, allowing 2 rolls for each, cut deep slits in top of 8 oblong hard rolls. Fry 1 pound hamburger until brown; add ⅔ cup tomato sauce, ¾ teaspoon salt, ¼ teaspoon garlic salt, ¼ cup sliced stuffed olives, and 1 cup diced Muenster or Mozzarella cheese. Fill rolls; sprinkle with dried oregano. Wrap in foil. Cook on rack over hot coals for about 15 minutes, turning often.

HOT PIZZA ROLLS

4 sandwich rolls
  Margarine
4 slices of Mozzarella cheese
2 cups spaghetti meat sauce
¼ pound salami or pepperone, diced
½ cup canned chopped mushrooms
  Grated Parmesan cheese

Split rolls and spread with margarine. Place 1 slice of cheese on each open-faced roll. Cover with ⅔ of meat sauce. Sprinkle with diced meat and chopped mushrooms. Top with remaining sauce and sprinkle with Parmesan cheese. Place under broiler until rolls are lightly browned and cheese is melted. Makes 4 servings.

A Variety of Pizzas:
Anchovy; Italian Sausage; Pepperone

PLANK, TO—A method of cooking and serving on a plank or board. Special planks are necessary for this procedure and should be one inch thick, made of oak, hickory, or pine. Before they are first used, they should be seasoned by being soaked overnight in cold water, brushed well with oil, and warmed for an hour in a slow oven. Steaks or fish can be planked. A thick steak should be broiled or panbroiled first for 5 minutes on each side, then put on the plank, and surrounded with Duchess potatoes, if desired. The food is baked in preheated moderate oven (375°F.) for about 15 minutes, or until the steak is done and the potatoes are brown. A plank can be garnished with sautéed mushrooms, buttered peas, broiled tomatoes, carrots, onions, etc. If preferred, the steak can be broiled until done, put on a heated plank, garnished with vegetables, and put in the oven or under the broiler to heat or brown lightly. A whole fish can be baked on an oiled plank and garnished with hot cooked vegetables.

PLANTAIN—The fruit of a large tree-like tropical herb, *Musa paradisiaca.* The plantain belongs to the same family as the common eating banana. Plantains, however, are larger, starchier, and less sweet; they must be cooked to be palatable. When boiled, baked, fried, or made into flour they are excellent and very digestible.

Plantain is an extremely old plant, probably native to southern Asia, but now grown in most tropical countries. More than seventy-five varieties are known. Plantain is an important food plant in the tropics, occupying the same position of an essential staple as does the potato in the temperate zones.

Availability—Plantains can be bought year round in markets catering to people of Spanish, West Indian, and Latin American descent.

Storage—When green or slightly green, store at room temperature. Refrigerate very ripe plantains.

☐ Kitchen shelf: 5 days
☐ Refrigerator shelf: 1 to 2 days

Nutritive Food Values—High in carbohydrates and a fair source of vitamins A and B.

☐ 3½ ounces, raw = 119 calories

PLANTAIN BALLS SOUP
2 green plantains, peeled
8 cups chicken broth
3 medium potatoes, peeled and diced
1 tablespoon chopped parsley
2 ripe plantains, peeled
   Salt to taste

Cover green plantains with salted water

and cook for 5 minutes. Add plantains to broth with potatoes and parsley. Cook until plantains are tender. Remove plantains and mash. Shape mashed plantains into small balls. Add to broth. Boil ripe plantains in salted water to cover until tender. Drain and mash plantains. Shape ripe mashed plantains into balls and add them to the broth. Season to taste with salt. Serve immediately. Makes 6 servings.

PLANTAIN WITH PORK CRACKLINGS
Cut each of 3 half-ripe plantains into 4 crosswise pieces and soak in salted water for 15 minutes. Drain and wipe dry. Sauté in hot lard or olive oil until light brown. Mash together sautéed plantains and ½ pound very crisp pork cracklings. Add a little salt and serve hot. Makes 4 servings.

BAKED PLANTAINS
Wash and dry very ripe plantains with black skin. Do not peel. Make a deep gash lengthwise in skin. Put on a baking sheet. Bake in preheated moderate oven (350°F.) for 45 minutes, or until plantain is easily pierced. Serve.

PLANTAIN CHIPS
4 green plantains
2 teaspoons salt
   Water
   Shortening for frying

Peel plantains. Cut into crosswise slices about ½ inch thick. Cut slices on a slant so they will have an oval shape. Add salt to water and soak slices for 1 hour. Drain and dry. Fry plantain in shallow shortening until slices are tender but not yet crisp. Remove from fat and flatten by pressing between sheets of absorbent paper. Drop into shortening again and fry until crisp. Drain on absorbent paper. Makes 20.

JAMAICAN PLANTAIN TURNOVERS
   Standard Pastry for 8-inch 2-crust pie, unbaked (page 1399)
1 cup finely mashed very ripe plantain
¼ cup sugar
1 tablespoon butter or margarine
1 teaspoon vanilla extract
½ teaspoon nutmeg
   Red food coloring
   Milk

Roll pastry to ⅛ inch thickness and cut into 4-inch rounds. Chill. Mix plantain, sugar, and butter in saucepan. Cook, stirring, until heated and blended. Cool. Add vanilla, nutmeg, and a few drops of coloring. Put a spoonful of the mixture on one half of each round. Moisten edge of pastry and fold over. Seal edges and prick tops of turnovers. Brush tops with milk. Bake in preheated very hot oven (450° F.) for 10 minutes. Reduce heat to moderate (350°F.) and bake for 10 to 15 minutes longer, or until browned. Makes 12 turnovers.

PLUM—The tree and edible fruit of many species of the genus *Prunus,* a large family which also includes almonds, apricots, cherries, and peaches. The plum tree is often grown for its ornamental foliage and charming white flowers. The fruits grow in clusters, have a smooth skin, and a flattened pit. Plums may be round or oval; with a skin in various shades of red, purple, blue, yellow, or green. The flesh is thick and juicy and it may be sweet or tart. They are delicious in their natural state, or stewed, made into a sauce, and in any number of desserts.

Most important among the many plum varieties are the common, or European, plum, *Prunus domestica;* the oriental, or Japanese, plum, *P. salicina;* the native American wild plums of the north, which include *P. americana, P. nigra,* and *P. mexicana;* and the beach plum, *P. maritima.*

The European plum is the plum of history and literature. European plums may be yellow, red, blue, or purple. Thought to be native to western Asia, they have been cultivated for over 2,000 years. Among the best-known types of European plum are the Italian, or prune-plum, generally blue-purple in color with sweet firm flesh, excellent for eating out of hand and for coloring; the damson plum, a very small and firm fruit, generally purple, although the well-known Mirabelle is a yellow variety; and the greengage plum, small, round, and greenish-yellow in color, with a tangy, yet sweet taste.

The Japanese plums have a yellow ground color overlaid with various shades of red. They are pointed or heart-shape, juicy, sweet, and firm. Probably native to China they were first introduced to the United States in 1870.

The native American plums are small and tend to be watery, with yellow or reddish-yellow skin and flesh. They can be cultivated farther north than can the imported varieties. Beach plums grow wild and are found along the Atlantic coast from Canada to Virginia. Seldom cultivated, they grow chiefly in sandy soil. The fruit is small and dark blue-purple when ripe. Too sour to eat raw, they are delicious cooked.

Availability and Purchasing Guide—Fresh plums can be found from June through October, with a few, imported from Latin America, available from January through March.

Canned prune-plums, greengage, and Mirabelles are available, whole with pit in, in syrup or water pack.

Other plum products available include plum preserves, plum butter, and wild-beach-plum jelly.

Select fresh, plump, smooth plums that are firm but not hard. Color is not a reliable guide as species vary widely. Avoid cracked, shriveled, or softened fruit. Plums with a brownish color have been sunburned and are usually of poor quality.

Storage—Ripe fruit should be covered and refrigerated. Allow unripe fruit to ripen at room temperature.

- ☐ Canned, kitchen shelf: 1 year
- ☐ Fresh, refrigerator shelf: 1 week
- ☐ Fresh, cooked; or canned, opened, refrigerator shelf: 4 to 5 days
- ☐ Fresh, refrigerator frozen-food compartment, prepared for freezing: 2 to 3 months
- ☐ Fresh, freezer, prepared for freezing: 1 year

Caloric Values

- ☐ Fresh prune-plums, 3½ ounces, raw = 75 calories
- ☐ Fresh damson, 3½ ounces, raw = 66 calories
- ☐ Fresh Japanese and hybrid, 3½ ounces, raw = 48 calories
- ☐ Canned prune-plums, 3½ ounces, solids and liquid, water pack = 46 calories
- ☐ Canned prune-plums, 3½ ounces, solids and liquid, light syrup pack = 64 calories
- ☐ Canned prune-plums, 3½ ounces, solids and liquid, heavy syrup pack = 83 calories
- ☐ Canned prune-plums, 3½ ounces, solids and liquid, extra heavy syrup pack = 102 calories
- ☐ Canned greengage, 3½ ounces, solids and liquid, water pack = 33 calories

Basic Preparation

☐ **To Freeze**—Use ripe fruit, firm, with no blemishes. Cut into halves or quarters, removing pits. Put fruit into freezer containers. Cook 4 cups water with 5 cups sugar until syrup is clear and sugar dissolved. Cool. Cover fruit with syrup, leaving ½-inch headspace. Seal.

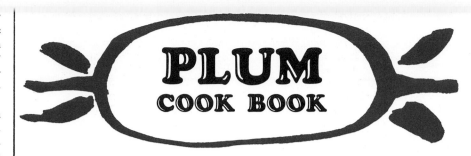

PLUM COOK BOOK

PRUNE-PLUM AND GRAPE SALAD

- 10 fresh pitted prune-plums
- 8 ounces cottage cheese
  Fresh seedless grapes
- ½ head lettuce
  Mayonnaise

Wash plums and split into halves. Pile cottage cheese on 10 halves; top with the remaining halves. Arrange on lettuce with fresh grapes. Serve with mayonnaise. Makes 5 servings.

STEWED FRESH PLUMS

- ½ cup sugar
- 1 cup water
- 1/16 teaspoon salt
- 1 tablespoon fresh lemon juice
- 1 cinnamon stick
- 1 pound fresh ripe plums

Combine sugar, water, salt, and lemon juice in saucepan. Add cinnamon stick and bring to boiling point, stirring constantly. Wash plums, cut into halves, and place in boiling syrup. Boil for 3 to 5 minutes, or until tender. Remove from heat and chill. Serve as a dessert or meat accompaniment. Makes 4 servings.

FRESH PLUM SAUCE

- 1 pound (about 12 large) ripe fresh plums
- ½ cup sugar
- 1 tablespoon fresh lemon juice
- ¼ teaspoon almond extract

Slice plums, mash, and put through a sieve. Stir in sugar, lemon juice, and almond extract. Serve over ice cream, gingerbread, or cake. Makes 1½ cups.

PLUM GARLIC SAUCE

- ½ pound prune-plums (about 2 cups), pitted
- 2 to 3 garlic cloves, minced
  Salt and pepper
- 1 tablespoon minced parsley

Cook plums in water to cover. Drain, and reserve liquid. Force plums through a sieve or whirl in blender. Stir sufficient plum liquid into the purée to achieve the consistency of thick cream. Add garlic, and season with salt and pepper to taste. Bring to a boil. Reduce heat and simmer for 5 minutes. Add parsley. Makes 1 cup.
Note: This sauce is very good for brushing roast chicken and shish kabob.

DAMSON-PLUM BUTTER

- 5 to 6 pounds damson plums (about 4 cups)

- 4 cups water
- 2 cups sugar
- ½ teaspoon almond extract

Wash plums and cut into halves. Add water and bring to a boil. When plums are tender, press pulp through a sieve. Add sugar to the pulp and cook, stirring constantly, until thickened. After 15 minutes spoon a little of the mixture into a plate to see if it sets. When it does, add flavoring and pour into sterilized glasses. Seal, cool, and store. Makes 3 to 4 pints.

FRESH PRUNE-PLUM PUDDING

- 1 cup sifted all-purpose flour
- 1½ cups sugar
- ½ teaspoon salt
- 1½ teaspoons baking powder
- ½ cup milk
- 3 tablespoons shortening, melted
- 2 cups sliced fresh prune-plums
- 1 cup boiling water

Sift flour, ½ cup of the sugar, the salt, and baking powder together into a mixing bowl. Add milk and melted shortening. Beat until well blended. Turn into a greased baking pan (8 x 8 x 2 inches). Cover with sliced plums and sprinkle with the remaining sugar. Pour boiling water over all. Bake in preheated moderate oven (375°F.) for 45 minutes, or until done. Serve warm, with cream if desired. Makes 6 servings.

REFRIGERATOR PLUM BREAD PUDDING

- 3 cups (1½ pounds) sliced fresh plums
- ¾ to 1 cup sugar
  Ground cinnamon
- 1 tablespoon fresh lemon juice
- 2 teaspoons cornstarch
- 1 tablespoon cold water
- ¼ teaspoon vanilla extract
- 6 or 7 slices of bread
  Butter or margarine
  Whipped cream (optional)

Place plums, sugar, ¼ teaspoon cinnamon, and lemon juice in a saucepan. Cover and cook for 10 minutes. Mix cornstarch with water and add. Cook, stirring constantly, for 1 minute, or until thickened. Remove from heat and cool slightly. Stir in vanilla. Butter bread and sprinkle with cinnamon. Arrange bread and plums in alternate layers in a loaf pan (9 x 5 x 3 inches). Chill for several hours or overnight. Spoon into individual serving dishes. Top with whipped cream if desired. Makes 6 to 8 servings.

Jellied Fresh Plums   *Prune-Plum and Grape Salad*

VANILLA FRESH-PLUM COMPOTE
¼ cup sugar
1 cup water
1 tablespoon fresh lime juice
½ teaspoon vanilla extract
1½ pounds fresh plums, sliced

Combine sugar, water, and lime juice in saucepan. Stir until sugar is dissolved. Heat to boiling point. Boil for 2 or 3 minutes. Cool. Add vanilla extract and plums. Chill and serve. Makes 5 servings.

FRESH PLUM WHIP
¾ pound fresh plums
¼ cup water
½ teaspoon grated lemon rind
½ cup sugar
2 egg whites

Wash plums. Place in saucepan with the water. Cover and cook gently for 20 to 25 minutes, or until tender. Push through a sieve or whirl in blender. Measure 1 cup purée. Cool. Stir in lemon rind and ¼ cup of the sugar. Beat egg whites until they stand in soft peaks. Gradually beat in remaining sugar and carefully fold into plum purée. Pile lightly in sherbet glasses. Top with a slice of fresh plum, if desired. Makes 4 servings.

Fresh Plum Whip with Soft Custard
Place 2 tablespoons soft custard in each sherbet glass. Finish filling with Plum Whip.

JELLIED FRESH PLUMS WITH GOLDEN FRESH-LEMON SAUCE
2 envelopes unflavored gelatin
½ cup cold water
1¼ cups hot water
¾ cup sugar
⅓ cup fresh lemon juice
½ cup fresh orange juice
2 cups sliced fresh plums
   Golden Fresh-Lemon Sauce

Soften gelatin in cold water. Add hot water and stir until gelatin is dissolved. Stir in sugar and juices. Chill until mixture is about as thick as fresh egg whites. Fold in sliced plums. Turn into a 5-cup mold. Chill until firm and ready to serve. To serve, turn out onto a serving plate and serve with Golden Fresh-Lemon

Sauce. Makes 6 to 8 servings.

Golden Fresh-Lemon Sauce

2 eggs, separated
1½ tablespoons fresh lemon juice
⅔ cup sifted confectioners' sugar
 Dash of salt
½ teaspoon vanilla extract
¼ teaspoon grated lemon rind

Beat egg yolks with lemon juice until light and creamy. Gradually beat in ⅓ cup of the sugar. Add salt to egg whites and beat until they stand in soft peaks. Gradually beat into egg whites the remaining sugar, the vanilla, and grated rind. Fold into egg-yolk mixture. Serve over Jellied Fresh Plums. Serve this sauce the same day it is made. Makes 2 cups.

Jellied Fresh-Plum Salad

Serve on head lettuce with mayonnaise and cottage cheese. Omit Golden Fresh-Lemon Sauce.

DEEP-DISH PLUM PIE

2 pounds prune-plums
½ cup firmly packed brown sugar
½ cup granulated sugar
⅛ teaspoon ground cloves
¼ teaspoon ground nutmeg
 Pinch of salt
2 tablespoons quick-cooking tapioca
2 teaspoons fresh lemon juice
1 tablespoon butter
 Standard pastry for 1-crust 9-inch pie, unbaked (page 1399)

Cut washed plums into halves; remove pits. Arrange cut fruit in baking pan (9 x 9 x 2 inches) with cut side down. Combine sugars, spices, salt, and tapioca, and sprinkle over the fruit. Shake dish slightly so that sugar will sift down through the fruit. Sprinkle with lemon juice and dot with butter. Bake in preheated moderate oven (375°F.) for 20 minutes to start the fruit cooking. Roll pastry; cut nine 3-inch circles. Remove pie from oven and place pastry circles over fruit. Return to oven and continue baking for about 20 minutes, or until fruit is tender and pastry is brown. Serve warm or cold. Makes about 8 servings.

PLUM-ORANGE TWISTS

¼ cup soft butter or margarine
2 cups biscuit mix
2 tablespoons granulated sugar
1 tablespoon grated orange rind
1 egg
⅓ cup heavy cream
½ cup damson-plum preserves
 Confectioners' sugar

Cut butter into biscuit mix. Stir in granulated sugar and rind. Beat egg and cream until blended; with fork, stir into first mixture. Put on floured board and knead a few times. Roll out to form a rectangle 15 x 3 inches. Spread with preserves, and fold twice lengthwise to form a rectangle 1 x 15 inches. Cut crosswise into 1-inch strips. Twist each strip twice to form a spiral. Put on foil-covered cookie sheet and bake in pre-

heated very hot oven (450°F.) for 10 to 12 minutes. Sift confectioners' sugar over warm twists. Makes 15.

PLUM MINCEMEAT

4 pounds prune-plums
5 medium apples
½ cup cider vinegar
 Juice and grated rind of 1 orange
 Juice and grated rind of 1 lemon
2 pounds (4½ cups) light brown sugar
½ pound dried currants, rinsed and drained
½ pound raisins
1 pound ready-cut mixed peels
1½ teaspoons salt
½ teaspoon ground allspice
1 teaspoon each of ground nutmeg and cloves

Wash prune-plums, pit, and cut into coarse pieces. Peel and grate apples; add to prune-plums along with vinegar, juices, and grated rinds of orange and lemon. Bring to boil, then simmer, stirring occasionally, until fruit is just tender, about 30 minutes. Add remaining ingredients and cook slowly until fairly thick, about 1 hour. Stir frequently to prevent scorching. Pour into hot sterilized jars; seal at once. Store in cool dry place. Makes about 6 pints.

FRESH-PLUM JAM

4 pounds fresh plums
½ cup water
1 box powdered pectin
8 cups sugar

Wash plums, remove pits, and chop pulp. Place in deep 6-quart kettle with water. Simmer, covered, for 5 minutes. Remove cover, add powdered pectin, and bring to a rapid boil, stirring rapidly all the while. Add sugar and bring to a full rolling boil, stirring constantly. Boil for 1 minute. Remove from heat. Skim off foam and continue to stir and skim by turns for 5 minutes, to cool slightly. Ladle into hot sterilized jars. Seal. Makes twelve ½-pint jars.

PLUM DUMPLINGS

12 fresh plums
12 sugar cubes
3 tablespoons butter
2 cups sifted all-purpose flour
2 cups riced cold cooked potatoes
1 teaspoon salt
2 eggs, well beaten
¾ cup dry bread crumbs mixed with 3 tablespoons melted butter

Remove pits from plums carefully without breaking them apart. Replace pit with a cube of sugar. Cut butter into flour until mixture resembles coarse cornmeal. Add potatoes and salt. Stir in eggs and knead dough on a lightly floured board until smooth. Roll out dough ¼ inch thick. Cut dough into 3-inch squares. Place 1 plum on each square of dough. Moisten edges of dough with water and pinch dough to enclose the plum completely. Roll the dumpling between floured

hands until it is ball shaped. Carefully drop dumplings into simmering water, only a few at a time. Cook, uncovered, for 15 minutes. Drain carefully and roll each dumpling in buttered crumbs. Makes 6 servings.

PLUM CAKE COBBLER

3½ cups (one 30-ounce can) prune-plums, packed in syrup
 Sugar
2 tablespoons cornstarch
¼ cup butter or margarine
1 egg, slightly beaten
2 cups sifted all-purpose flour
3 teaspoons baking powder
¼ teaspoon salt
1 cup milk

Drain plums, reserving syrup. Pit plums and arrange, skin side down, in baking dish (12 x 8 x 2 inches). Mix ¾ cup sugar and cornstarch in saucepan. Add syrup and cook, stirring constantly, until clear and thickened. Pour over plums. Cream butter. Add ⅔ cup sugar and beat until light. Add egg and beat well. Add sifted dry ingredients alternately with milk, beating until smooth. Spread on plums. Bake in preheated moderate oven (375° F.) for about 30 minutes, or until done. Serve with whipped cream, if desired. Makes 6 servings.

PLUMS WITH MOCK DEVONSHIRE CREAM

Chill 3½ cups (one 30-ounce can) prune-plums. Beat 1 package (3 ounces) soft cream cheese, ⅓ cup heavy cream, dash of salt, and ¼ teaspoon almond extract until smooth and fluffy. Chill and serve with plums. Makes 4 servings.

PLUM SNOW PUDDING

1 envelope unflavored gelatin
¾ cup sugar
¼ teaspoon salt
 Grated rind and juice of 1 lemon
2 egg whites
8 plums
¾ cup light corn syrup

In top part of double boiler soften gelatin in ½ cup cold water for 5 minutes. Put over boiling water and stir until dissolved. Remove from heat. Add sugar, salt, lemon rind and juice, and ¾ cup cold water; stir until dissolved. To chill quickly, put top part of double boiler over ice water and stir frequently until mixture begins to set. Add egg whites and beat with rotary beater until light and fluffy. Turn into 1½ quart mold. Chill until firm. Cook 2 plums in corn syrup until tender. Force syrup and plums through strainer or purée in blender. Slice 6 remaining plums and add to strained plums. Serve as sauce over pudding. Makes 4 servings.

INDIVIDUAL PLUM SHORTCAKES

1½ cups sifted all-purpose flour
2¼ teaspoons baking powder
 Salt

¼ cup plus 3 tablespoons sugar
6 tablespoons shortening
1 egg, beaten
⅓ cup light cream or milk
1 tablespoon butter or margarine, melted
3½ cups (one 30-ounce can) prune-plums, packed in syrup
1½ tablespoons cornstarch
¼ teaspoon almond extract

Sift flour, baking powder, ½ teaspoon salt, and 3 tablespoons sugar into bowl. Cut in shortening. Mix egg and cream, and add to dry ingredients. Mix to form a soft dough. Roll out on floured board to ¼-inch thickness. Cut into 8 rounds with 2½-inch cutter. Put 4 rounds on baking sheet and brush with melted butter. Top with remaining rounds. Bake in preheated very hot oven (450°F.) for 10 to 15 minutes. Mix remaining sugar, cornstarch, and a dash of salt in saucepan. Drain plums and add syrup to saucepan. Cook, stirring constantly, until clear and thickened. Pit plums and cut into halves. Add to hot mixture with flavoring. Serve between and on top of split shortcakes. Makes 4 servings.

PLUM CONSERVE

3½ cups (one 30-ounce can) prune-plums packed in syrup
½ cup seedless raisins
1 cup sugar
1 medium orange, thinly sliced
1 tablespoon fresh lemon juice
1 cup chopped walnuts

In large saucepan mix plums, raisins, sugar, and orange. Bring to boil and simmer for 40 minutes, or until thick. Remove pits. Add lemon juice and nuts. Mix well and pour into hot sterilized jars; seal. Makes about four ½-pint jars.

DAMSON-PLUM PRESERVES

3 pounds damson plums
4½ cups sugar
1½ cups water
⅛ teaspoon salt

Wash plums and remove stem and blossom ends. Prick each plum several times with sharp fork. Combine sugar, water, and salt; bring to boil. Add plums; simmer until fruit is clear and tender and syrup sheets from spoon. Pack into hot sterilized jars and seal. Makes about 4 pints.

PLUM PUDDING—A suet pudding which like plum cake never contains plums but is made with currants, raisins, citrus peels, and spices, and is either steamed or boiled. It is served for dessert with hard sauce, foamy sauce or other preferred sauce.

PLUM PUDDING

1⅓ cups sifted all-purpose flour
1¼ teaspoons salt
¼ teaspoon baking soda

¼ teaspoon each of ground allspice, cinnamon, cloves, and nutmeg
⅛ teaspoon ground mace
¾ cup firmly packed brown sugar
1⅓ cups ground beef suet
1 cup seeded raisins
¾ cup seedless raisins
1 cup golden raisins
¾ cup dried currants
¾ cup chopped candied mixed fruit peel
2 eggs, beaten
⅓ cup fresh orange juice

Sift dry ingredients except sugar. Add sugar and remaining ingredients. Mix well and pour into greased 1½-quart pudding mold. Cover, put on rack in kettle, and add boiling water to come halfway up sides of mold. Put lid on kettle and steam for about 4 hours. Serve hot with a hard sauce or foamy sauce. Makes 12 servings.

POACH, TO—A method of cooking used to preserve the delicate texture and prevent the toughening of such foods as fish, chicken, and eggs.

The food is immersed more or less completely in water or other liquid. The water may be either at or below the boiling point, depending on the type of food being cooked. It is important to maintain a low temperature to preserve the shape and texture of the food. Vinegar or lemon juice can be added to the liquid for flavor and to assist in maintaining the shape. Vegetables and seasonings such as salt and herbs can be added for flavor.

POI—A staple food of the Pacific, and particularly Hawaii, made from the edible root of the taro. The taro is a plant of the subtropics and tropics, grown for its large underground tuber which has a high starch content and is extremely digestible. It is interesting that the Kanaka, the Polynesian inhabitants of the Hawaiian Islands, who live largely on taro, do not have a word for "indigestion."

The taro root is too acrid to eat raw. To make poi, the root is cooked, pounded, and kneaded until smooth, then mixed with water. It is either strained and served immediately, or more commonly, allowed to ferment for a few days. The amount of water added varies according to the way the poi will be eaten. Poi is always eaten with the fingers. One-finger poi is the thickest, allowing it to be eaten with one finger. Two-finger poi is thinner in consistency, and three-finger poi is the thinnest. It is eaten by itself, as an accompaniment for meat or fish, or mixed with milk and/or sugar as a porridge.

To the uninitiated, the grayish-white poi has a bland uninteresting flavor.

When allowed to ferment, it develops an acid flavor.

Canned poi is available in Hawaii and in some specialty food stores in the continental United States.

POLENTA—The Italian word for cornmeal, for cornmeal mush, and for dishes made with cornmeal mush. Polenta is a staple dish of northern Italy, where it is often eaten in place of bread.

Traditionally, polenta was cooked in a big copper kettle called *paiuolo*, which was hung over the open hearth on which the farm cooking was done, much as in our colonial days. Now the *paiuolo* may be made of aluminum and stand on a gas or electric stove or a coal or wood stove. The principle of making good polenta is still the same; the cornmeal must be constantly stirred with a wooden paddle or spoon until a thin crust forms around the edge of the pan.

POLENTA

2 quarts boiling water
3 teaspoons salt
4 cups yellow cornmeal

In a 4-quart heavy-clad kettle, bring the salted water to a rapid boil. Slowly add cornmeal, stirring constantly with a long wooden spoon. Do not let the meal lump. Reduce heat. Stir the polenta slowly but constantly as though you were folding egg whites into a waffle batter. Cook for about 45 minutes, until a thin crust begins to line the pan and the polenta is well set. Shake the kettle to loosen the cornmeal cake at the sides before turning it out onto a large round platter. Cut the pieces with a knife as you would slice bread. Serve with a meat or tomato sauce. Makes 8 to 10 servings.

POLENTA WITH EGG SAUCE

1 cup butter or margarine
1 quart tomatoes
6 eggs, well beaten
Salt and pepper
1 recipe Polenta (above)
Grated Parmesan cheese

Melt butter in a large heavy skillet. Add tomatoes and simmer for 15 to 20 minutes. Add eggs and cook for another 5 minutes, stirring constantly with a wooden spoon. Season with salt and pepper to taste. Cut polenta with a firmly gripped string. Serve topped with egg sauce and grated cheese. Makes 8 to 10 servings.

POLENTA WITH ITALIAN SAUSAGE

2 cups water
1 cup yellow cornmeal
1 teaspoon salt
1 pound Italian sausage
1 garlic clove, minced
2 tablespoons chopped parsley
2⅓ cups (one 1-pound, 4-ounce can) tomatoes

Salt and pepper
¼ cup grated Parmesan cheese

Add water to cornmeal and salt in top part of double boiler. Bring to boil over direct heat, stirring constantly. Cover and cook over boiling water for about 1¼ hours, stirring occasionally. Cut sausage into thick slices and brown slowly in skillet. Add garlic and cook until lightly browned. Add parsley and tomatoes, cover, and simmer for about 1 hour. Season to taste with salt and pepper. When ready to serve, spread half of cornmeal mush on hot serving platter, cover with half of sauce; repeat. Sprinkle with cheese and garnish with parsley if desired.

Note: Sausage meat may be used instead of Italian sausage. Shape meat into about 16 patties and brown slowly; pour off fat and continue as above.

BAKED POLENTA WITH SALAMI AND TOMATOES

1 cup cornmeal
4 cups water
¼ pound salami, chopped
2 teaspoons salt
3 tomatoes
½ teaspoon chili powder
¼ cup grated Parmesan cheese

Mix cornmeal and water in top part of double boiler; bring to boil over direct heat, stirring constantly. Add meat and 1½ teaspoons salt; cover and cook over boiling water for 30 minutes. Pour into shallow pan and cool. Cut into squares and arrange in greased baking dish; cover with chopped peeled tomatoes; sprinkle with chili powder, cheese, and remaining salt. Bake in preheated moderate oven (375°F.) for about 25 minutes. Makes 4 servings.

POLENTA CASSEROLE

¾ cup yellow cornmeal
2 cups milk or water
1 egg
1 cup grated Romano cheese
1½ teaspoons salt
⅛ teaspoon white pepper
½ cup olive or cooking oil
1 onion, minced
1 can (6 ounces) tomato paste
2⅓ cups (one 1-pound 3-ounce can) tomatoes
2 sweet or hot Italian sausages, cut into chunks

Combine cornmeal and milk in saucepan. Bring to a boil; cook, stirring, until thickened. Reduce heat and cook for 5 minutes longer. Beat in egg, ½ cup cheese, and next 4 ingredients. Pour into pan (9 x 9 x 2 inches), and chill for several hours, or overnight. Cut into squares and arrange in greased shallow casserole. Mix tomato paste and tomatoes, and pour over squares. Sprinkle with ½ cup cheese. Lightly brown sausage in skillet and put on top of cheese. Bake, uncovered, in hot oven (400°F.) for about 30 minutes. Makes 4 servings.

POLISH COOKERY

by Jean Karsavina

The history of the thousand-year-old Polish state is stormy; however, regimes may come and regimes may go, but the Poles consistently take their food seriously. And nothing pleases them more than to have it shared, and appreciated. Polish hospitality is legendary: it has been celebrated in classic poetry, in folk say and folk song. "Happy the squire when his guests are many/ On bended knee he begs them to have seconds. . . ."

A close relative who recently spent a month visiting and touring the countryside tells me the tradition is as strong as ever. In first-class hotels, waiters still go into a huddle with you to see that you dine in gourmet style. The more modest workaday restaurants and bars (a "bar" in Poland is not a place to drink, but to eat standing up at a counter) may not have extensive menus, but they serve traditional dishes cooked, as my relative puts it, "so they are worth eating." More importantly, invitations to lunch, tea, dinner, and supper are extended at the slightest provocation not only to friends but to casual acquaintances as well. The Poles are great believers in their old proverb, "When a guest's in the house, the Good Lord is there too."

Because Polish cookery is so little known in this country, people have some odd misconceptions about it. "There is *no* typically Polish cooking," I am sometimes told in a tone of authority. "It's all French" . . . (or Russian, or German, or Hungarian, as the case may be, depending on where the misinformation was gathered). "No," I explain patiently, "it has a character all its own." And indeed it has, having evolved over the centuries, inevitably influenced, in a country situated at the crossroads of East and West, by various foreign tastes superimposed on native preferences.

Consider, for instance, that from medieval times until well into the 19th century the royal and princely houses were forever making alliances with foreign potentates. In fact, a number of Poland's kings and queens were French, Czech, Saxon, Hungarian. It was the beautiful Sforza princess, arriving with her retinue to become Queen Bona, who introduced greens and the tomato to the country's produce gardens. The scullery maids then quickly learned from the palace chefs what to do with the newfangled foods, which presently caught the people's fancy, and soon a new word was coined: Today the Polish word for green vegetables is *wloszczyzna,* which literally translated means "things Italian."

o·o·o·o·o·o·o·o·o·o·o·o·o

Crusaders and merchants of the Hanseatic League returning from the East popularized spices, dried and smoked fish, eggplant, rice, Jerusalem artichokes, and of course tea from China. Tea remains the most popular nonalcoholic beverage, although in the cities, where coffeehouses are the place to meet one's friends or to scan the daily papers, a great deal of coffee is drunk at all hours of the day and night. People generally order it very strong and very black, often with a small dish of ice cream on the side or, in Warsaw, with the little cream-filled pastry tarts so famous throughout Europe that prior to World War II a shipment of them used to be flown daily to France.

Poland's hereditary aristocracy, living in feudal splendor on their vast estates, was largely French-oriented and considered it *de rigueur* to import not merely Paris wardrobes but Parisian cooks as well. However, they shared with the man in the street a fiercely embattled nationalism which extended into the kitchen. Thus a happy gastronomic duality came into being: A hundred guests, invited for a boar hunt, might be served an alfresco luncheon in the fields, starting with Danzig vodka, ending with 150-year-old Polish mead, and in between huge servings of *bigos,* hunter's stew, which in its pristine form takes a week to prepare; that same night they might sit down in the great hall to feast on imported lobster, a poached whole lake salmon or two, roast suckling pig, and turkey garnished with several dozen ortolans. This kind of magnificence is now past, but the *bigos* in simplified form is still eaten everywhere.

Quite possibly the fact that Poland was long a country of contrasts, the rich very rich, the poor often very poor, is another reason for the enormous variety of its fare. Country folks long ago learned to utilize whatever was at hand: wild honey, wild berries and mushrooms, the fish in stream and lake, the crayfish in the swamp, game and game birds to be trapped in the vast forests. Mushroom picking, in fact, remains a favorite summer pastime, and since by some happy freak of nature the edible and the poisonous varieties in Poland are distinctly different in appearance, even children are unlikely to make mistakes. And many a romance starts during these expeditions.

Some of the mainstays of everyday diet are cabbage and potatoes stored for use the year round, *kasza* (which may mean buckwheat groats, pearl barley, or cereal meal), the herring so abundant in the Baltic, and clabber. The clabber is allowed to set in large crocks which, in the country, are then kept cool in the spring house; the clabber is served with steaming boiled potatoes and cracklings, an effortless, nourishing meal. Herring, salted, smoked, pickled, and fresh, combines with potatoes or egg dishes. Cabbage generally turns up as thick cabbage soup, *kapuśniak,* enriched with a marrow bone, dried mushrooms, and sour cream. Barley has given its name to barley soup, *krupnik.* Since meat may be expensive and rather scarce, a great many recipes make a virtue of necessity and use the cheapest cuts. Tripe, for instance, is something of a national dish. As for the sour cream and mushrooms, they are the basis of a hundred sauces, a great many of them quick and extremely simple to prepare.

The Poles cannot do without their soup. In addition to the ones just mentioned, which are practically one-dish meals in themselves, a perennial favorite is *barszcz czysty,* a clear beet soup made with rich beef stock and served with tiny mouth-watering meat pastries. It turns up as the first course at an ordinary family meal, at an elegant dinner party—in which case it is served in cups—and in all restaurants. Fruit soups, too, are popular, served hot in winter and cold in summer.

When I was a child, the one cook book in both my mother's and my grandmother's home was *Uniwersalna Ksiazka Kucharska* (The Universal Cook Book) by Mme. Marja Ochorowicz-Monatowa, who was truly the Escoffier of Polish cookery. I still have my mother's copy of it, the pages so brittle that whenever I look into it, the floor must be swept. It was the kind of "kitchen Bible" meant for accomplished cooks, not those just beginning to learn: directions are apt to be of the use-your-judgment variety and proportions vague. Mme. Marja, an upper-class lady, was something of a snob. "I am writing this in order to give young women in general, and brides in particular, some knowledge of how to manage their kitchen help and their accounts, since everyone knows how the servants will steal one blind and dumb unless there is some supervision," she says in her preface. Then she adds rather pettishly that the young marrieds should find "at least a half-hour a day for household matters, rather than become totally absorbed with singing lessons, piano lessons and fine embroidery."

She also delights in mentioning special recipes she picked up while a guest at the estate of this prince and that count: consequently, some of these are so extravagant, complicated, and time-consuming as to be totally useless in our modern way of life. On the other hand, a recipe which begins quite grandly with the statement, "I learned it at the court of Emperor Franz-Joseph of Austria, for whom no meal was complete without it," turns out to be an excellent but very simple one for boiled beef. Mme. Monatowa has long since been superceded by more modern and scientifically oriented experts, but her influence remains, and echoes of her style can be heard in every cook book out of Poland.

The recipes which follow are a cross-section of typical meals, ranging from the very modest to special-occasion, gala ones. All of them have been adapted as much as possible to our modern kitchen and our American way of eating. Since I myself am no believer in spending the best hours of my life over a hot stove, I have long since worked out all kinds of shortcuts, including a recipe for *bigos* which need *not* be started a week ahead of the dinner party! Many mouth-watering recipes which just cannot be simplified are ignored in my house. And judging by the response of dinner guests, especially the male ones, no one is the worse for it!

SOUPS

KAPUŚNIAK
(Cabbage Soup)

1 ham bone, joint (1 pound), cracked
2 or 3 dried mushrooms,
   simmered until tender,
   cut into strips
½ pound diced
   mixed vegetables
2½ cups sauerkraut,
   with juice drained off
   (Reserve the juice)
1 medium onion, chopped
1 tablespoon caraway seeds
½ medium onion, minced
3 to 4 tablespoons all-purpose flour
3 tablespoons bacon fat
   Salt and pepper to taste

Combine ham bone, the mushrooms together with liquid in which they cooked, vegetables, sauerkraut, chopped onion, and caraway seeds. Add 8 cups water and simmer until any leftover meat falls off the bone, about 1 hour. By then about 2 cups of the liquid should have evaporated.

Brown the minced onion and flour in the bacon fat, add a little of the soup liquid, stirring constantly, and thicken the soup with the mixture.

Remove soup bone, adjust seasoning, and if necessary add a little sauerkraut juice to taste. Serve with boiled potatoes and black bread. Makes about 6 servings.

BARSZCZ CZYSTY
(Clear Beet Soup)

5 medium beets
1 pound beef soup meat
   (plate, shank, or brisket)
   Soup bone (joint) cracked
8 to 9 cups cold water
½ pound mixed diced vegetables

1 onion, sliced and
  browned lightly
1 bay leaf
  Ground allspice to taste
1 garlic clove, minced (optional)
  Salt, pepper, and sugar to taste
1 cup canned sour beet juice

Peel and shred the beets and cook in water until tender. Strain and reserve the liquid. Use the beets in a salad, or discard them. Put soup meat and bone in a kettle and add water to cover. It is better to start with more water and let it cook away than to add water later on. Bring to a boil, reduce heat, and continue cooking, skimming occasionally, until meat is half done. Add vegetables and onion, spices, and seasoning, and continue simmering until meat is tender.

Strain, reserving boiled meat. Combine with sour beet juice and 1 cup reserved beet liquid. Season to taste, skim off fat, and bring to a boil. Serve in plates with cut boiled potatoes or dumplings stuffed with meat (see note), or in cups, with croutons. Makes about 6 servings.

Note: Meat dumplings can be prepared according to any standard recipe for ravioli, but with dough rolled out thinner, or as for the Chinese meat dumplings in won ton soup.

BARSZCZ ZIMNY
(Cold Borsch with Beet Greens)
1 pound veal with bone
8 cups cold water, about
¾ cup diced mixed vegetables
1 garlic clove
1 bay leaf (optional)
6 crayfish or 6 large or 12 small
  shrimps
½ pound young beets with greens
1 cup canned sour beet juice
  or pickle juice
2 or 3 hard-cooked eggs, sliced or
  quartered
1 tablespoon fresh dill, chopped
1 small fresh cucumber or dill pickle,
  diced
2 tablespoons all-purpose flour
1 cup dairy sour cream
  Salt, pepper, and sugar to taste

Put meat in kettle and add water to cover. It is better to start with more water and let it cook away than to add water later on. Bring to a boil, reduce heat, and continue cooking, skimming occasionally, until meat is half done. Add diced vegetables, garlic, bay leaf, and simmer until meat is tender. While stock cooks, scrub the crayfish clean and add to soup pot. Whether crayfish or shrimps are used, cook only during the last 15 minutes. Stock is done when meat is tender. Wash and scrape beets with greens, shred, and cook in small amount of water with some of the sour juice added, until tender. Peel crayfish or shrimps, cut into pieces, and place in tureen along with beets and beet greens, eggs, dill, and cucumber or pickle.

Strain the soup stock and skim the fat. Combine flour and sour cream and add to

stock, add the rest of the beet juice, and bring to a boil. Pour into tureen over other ingredients. Adjust seasoning, adding salt and sugar to taste. Allow to cool. Makes 6 servings.

Note: A somewhat simpler variation is to omit the crayfish or shrimps and use the veal from the stock, which in that case should be diced.

KRUPNIK
(Barley Soup)
½ pound soup bone (joint) with
  some meat, cracked
½ pound diced mixed vegetables
2 dried mushrooms
3 or 4 medium potatoes, pared and
  diced
½ cup pearl barley, cooked in 4 parts
  water or according to directions
  on box
3 tablespoons butter
1 cup dairy sour cream
  Salt and pepper to taste
1 or 2 raw egg yolks
1 tablespoon chopped parsley, dill,
  or combination of both

Prepare stock as for *Barszcz Zimny* with soup bone, mixed vegetables, and mushrooms, using about 8 cups water. When meat is half done, add the potatoes and continue cooking until done. Cook the pearl barley separately, adding half the butter. When meat and potatoes are done, remove bones and meat and add vegetables and stock to the barley. Cut mushrooms into strips and return to soup. Bring to a boil. Add sour cream, check the seasoning, and stir in egg yolks, a little at a time, taking care not to let them curdle. Pour into a tureen; add the remaining butter and the parsley. Makes 6 servings.

Note: For a less filling soup, omit the sour cream and the egg yolks.

FRUIT SOUPS
Clear fruit soup may be made out of fresh apples, plums, cherries, blueberries, or currants. It is also excellent made of dried apricots, in which case the fruit should be soaked for 24 hours, or until it has swelled up. Fruit soup may be served hot or cold. The basic recipe is the same for all fruit, with the exception of strawberries and raspberries (see recipe).

CLEAR FRUIT SOUP
4 cups cut unpeeled fruit or berries,
  rinsed
6 cups water
2 or 3 cloves
½ cinnamon stick
  Lemon peel to taste
2 tablespoons potato starch or
  cornstarch
½ cup sugar, or to taste

Combine fruit, water, cloves, cinnamon, and lemon peel and simmer until fruit begins to fall apart. Press fruit and liquid through a sieve, discarding only the skins and pits. Dissolve starch in a little cold water, stir into liquid, and bring to a

boil. Add sugar to taste. Chill if desired. Serve with croutons. Makes 6 or 7 servings.

FRUIT SOUPS WITH SOUR CREAM
Prepare as above, but omit potato starch and substitute 3 tablespoons all-purpose flour beaten into 1 cup dairy sour cream. Add not more than 3 tablespoons sugar instead of the ½ cup.

WILD STRAWBERRY OR RASPBERRY SOUP
1½ quarts wild strawberries or raspberries
5 to 6 cups cold boiled water
1 cup light white wine
  Juice of ½ lemon
1 cup dairy sour cream
  Sugar

Pick over the berries, reserving 1 cup of the best ones for garnish. Press the rest through a sieve, using the water to get as much of the fruit through as possible. Add wine and lemon juice, then sour cream, and mix thoroughly. If too tart, sweeten sparingly with sugar. Add the remaining whole berries and chill before serving. Serve with wedges of toast or sweet crackers. Makes 8 to 10 servings.

FISH

Fish are abundant in Poland's streams and natural and man-made lakes, and fresh-water fish are more popular in Polish cookery than those from the sea. Poaching is a favorite method. Another is to bake a whole fish wrapped in white paper saturated with butter, with more butter used for basting; the paper is removed when the fish is done and the fish allowed to brown lightly for another few minutes. Aluminum foil may be substituted, but it should be perforated or left slightly open at the top, otherwise the fish will steam instead of baking.

Horseradish Sauce (page 1422) is a frequent addition.

For a quick garnish to dress up any poached, steamed, or even panbroiled fish, try Egg Sauce for Fish (page 1422).

COURT BOUILLON
FOR POACHING FISH
1 large onion
1 or 2 carrots
1 parsley root
½ celery root
½ parsnip or kohlrabi
2 celery stalks, with leaves
1 leek
¼ bunch each of dill
  and parsley
1 bay leaf
12 peppercorns
  Salt
  Wedge of lemon with rind
  (optional)

Cut up all vegetables and tie the dill and parsley with string. Put all the ingredients in a large saucepan with about 5 cups water and bring to a boil. Let simmer until the vegetables are tender, allowing some of the water to evaporate. For boiling fish, use enough court bouillon to cover. For poaching, use just enough so that the fish will steam.

SZCZUPAK CZY KARP PO POLSKU
(Pike or Carp à la Polonaise)

1 pike or carp (3 pounds),
  cleaned, head left on
4 cups Court Bouillon (see recipe
  above)
1 pound potato balls
  or very small young potatoes
  Horseradish Sauce
3 tablespoons butter
  for garnish
  Few parsley sprigs
  for garnish

Arrange the fish, preferably on a rack, in a long dish with cover. Pour in the boiling Court Bouillon and simmer, well covered, for 15 minutes. In the meantime, boil the potatoes and prepare the Horseradish Sauce.

When fish is ready, remove with rack and drain. Transfer fish to hot ovenproof platter. Cover with Horseradish Sauce and dot with part of the butter. Return to oven for 20 minutes, or until sauce is lightly browned. Arrange the potatoes around the fish and pour remaining butter, melted, over it. Garnish with parsley sprigs and serve at once. Makes 5 servings.

Sos Chrzanowy
(Horseradish Sauce)

2 tablespoons all-purpose flour
1 cup dairy sour cream
1 cup beef or chicken bouillon,
  boiling hot
2 to 3 tablespoons grated horseradish
  Salt to taste
1 tablespoon vinegar
  Sugar to taste
2 tablespoons butter
2 egg yolks

Combine flour, sour cream, and bouillon, stirring constantly until smooth. Add the horseradish, salt, vinegar, and sugar. Cream butter and egg yolks and slowly add the hot sauce, a spoonful at a time, stirring constantly to prevent curdling. Pour over the fish.

Note: This sauce is also excellent with boiled beef and with other fish. For meat dishes, serve separately in a sauceboat.

A variation of the same sauce calls for half the amount of bouillon and a *roux* of 3 tablespoons each of butter and flour. For some reason, this sauce can be reheated, while the first one cannot.

ŁOSOŚ DO SOSÓW GORĄCYCH I ZIMNYCH
(Poached Salmon)

A whole young salmon makes an elegant party dish, served hot for dinner or cold at a buffet supper. Fresh-water salmon is preferred to the salt-water variety in Poland, and is also easier to come by, but salt-water salmon, more widely available in the United States, is satisfactory. Also, this recipe has been adapted to the needs of the modern home, which means that the amounts are enough for 6 to 8 portions, not a small army.

3 to 4 pounds salmon, cut in one piece,
  skin left on
  Court Bouillon to cover (page 1421)
3 tablespoons melted butter
  Parsley for garnish
  Lemon wedges

Arrange the fish in a pot just large enough to hold it and add the boiling Court Bouillon. Reduce heat and simmer, covered, for 25 to 30 minutes, or until done. Drain, remove the skin, and arrange on hot platter. Sprinkle with melted butter and garnish with parsley and lemon wedges. Serve hot with hollandaise or caper sauce, or cold with a good homemade mayonnaise, rémoulade, mustard, or tartare sauce. Makes 6 to 8 servings.

Note: This recipe may also be adapted for individual salmon steaks.

RAKI GOTOWANE
(Boiled Crayfish)

30 live crayfish
  Salt (enough to make water
  taste like seawater)
½ bunch of dill
1¼ cups drawn butter
1 to 2 tablespoons chopped dill

Take each crayfish by the shell from the top and clean with a stiff brush under running water. Plunge into boiling water; when the water has again come to a boil, drain and scrub a second time. (Remember, crayfish live in mud!) Place in fresh salted boiling water, just enough to cover, add the bunch of dill, and simmer until crayfish turn red. Do not overcook. Discard the dill.

Serve in a tureen, in the liquid in which they have cooked. Combine the drawn butter and chopped dill and serve in individual dishes for each person to dip his own. Makes 5 servings.

Note: This recipe may be used for shrimps.

SOUFFLÉ ZE ŚLEDZIA
(Herring Soufflé)

2 or 3 milch herrings,
  depending on size
  Milk for soaking
1 large onion, minced and
  cooked only until transparent
2 pounds potatoes, cooked
½ cup bread crumbs
2 tablespoons butter
2 eggs, separated
  Salt and pepper to taste
  Butter and bread crumbs

Soak the herrings in milk overnight, preferably for a full 24 hours. Bone. Combine with onion and potatoes and put through food grinder or whirl in a blender. Add bread crumbs, butter, and egg yolks and mix thoroughly. For a moister consistency, use less bread crumbs. Season to taste. Beat egg whites until stiff and fold into mixture. Line a 2-quart casserole with butter and bread crumbs and pour in the mixture. Dot with more butter and bread crumbs, and bake in preheated hot oven (400°F.) for about 20 minutes. Serve with a green salad or Mizerja, I or II (page 1430). Makes about 4 servings.

SOS Z JAJ DO RYBY
(Egg Sauce for Fish)

3 to 4 tablespoons sweet butter
2 hard-cooked eggs, chopped
  Salt and pepper to taste
  Dash of lemon juice (optional)
  Parsley for garnish

Melt the butter and let brown lightly, add hard-cooked eggs and seasoning, and continue cooking for 2 to 3 minutes, or until eggs just begin to brown. Do not overcook. Pour over fish and serve at once.

MEAT AND GAME

ROZBRATLE Z CEBULĄ
(Beef Steaks with Onion)

  Vinegar Marinade
4 short-cut steaks (8 ounces each;
  use good quality meat)
3 tablespoons butter, margarine, or
  fat for frying
1 medium onion, sliced
2 tablespoons melted butter

Marinate the steaks overnight in refrigerator, preferably for a full 24 hours. Remove from Vinegar Marinade and wipe dry. In a skillet, heat butter or fat until brown, then quickly brown the steaks on both sides, leaving the center pink or red, depending on preferred degree of doneness. Remove to hot platter and keep hot.

In the same skillet, quickly brown or braise the onion, depending on personal preference. Arrange onion on top of the steaks and sprinkle with the melted butter. Serve immediately with panfried or French-fried potatoes, a cucumber-and-tomato salad, and a green or yellow vegetable. Makes 4 servings.

Vinegar Marinade for Meat

Proportions are for 3 pounds meat and should be changed according to need:

3 cups water
1 large onion, sliced
9 allspice berries
9 peppercorns
6 tablespoons cider vinegar
4 or 5 bay leaves

Combine water and onion with allspice and peppercorns, and cook until onion is soft. Add vinegar and allow to cool. Place meat in a crockery bowl, pour liquid over it, and arrange the onion and bay leaves on top. Let stand in refriger-

Bigos Polski

Czarna Kasza with Mushroom Sauce

Barszcz Czysty with boiled potatoes

ator for 3 to 5 days or as specified in recipe. Turn the meat occasionally.

Note: This marinade is good for beef, lamb, duck, goose, and game.

SZTUFADA
(Braised Beef)

3 pounds beef rump, round,
  or top sirloin
2 teaspoons crumbled
  dried marjoram
  Vinegar Marinade (above)
2 ounces salt pork
  or 2 or 3 strips bacon
  Salt
3 tablespoons butter
  or bacon fat for frying
3 tablespoons tomato paste
1 beef bouillon cube dissolved in
  very little water
⅓ cup dry red wine
1 garlic clove
  Salt, pepper, and paprika to taste

Choose a compact piece of meat without much fat. Rub well with marjoram and marinate in the refrigerator for 1 to 2 days. Slice salt pork into pieces 1¼ x ¼ inch thick and sprinkle with salt and more marjoram. Remove meat from marinade, wipe dry, and lard with salt-pork strips in even rows.

In a skillet heat butter to very hot and quickly brown meat on all sides. Transfer to casserole, add fat from the skillet, all the vegetables from the marinade, the tomato paste, bouillon cube and water, any remaining marjoram, the wine, garlic, and seasonings. Simmer, tightly covered, for about 2 hours, or until tender. Slice fairly thin. Serve with baked, boiled, or mashed potatoes, and with red cabbage or any vegetable of choice. Makes 6 or 7 servings.

POLĘDWICA PIECZONA
(Roast Beef Tenderloin)

Beef tenderloin, roasted on a spit or in the oven and served whole, with or without a piquant sauce, is an excellent choice for a special-occasion dinner. Although admittedly in the luxury class, it is not as extravagant a dish as it might at first seem, since there is no waste and, because cooking time is short, very little shrinkage.

1 whole beef tenderloin,
  about 3 pounds
2 ounces salt pork or a few
  strips of bacon for larding
  Olive oil and fresh lemon juice
  Salt
  Melted butter

Remove all fat from meat; using a larding needle, lard evenly with salt pork. Rub with olive oil, sprinkle with lemon juice, and refrigerate overnight. Directly before cooking, sprinkle lightly with salt. Roast on rotisserie spit if one is available, using high heat and brushing frequently with melted butter so that meat is brown on the outside and red, or pink, inside.

In the absence of a rotisserie, preheat oven to very hot (475°F.), brown quickly

on all sides in butter in a shallow baking dish, and roast in oven for another 20 minutes, basting frequently. Transfer to hot platter, slice thin, and serve with tiny potato balls and several kinds of vegetables, according to preference. Makes 6 to 8 servings.

POLĘDWICA Z MADERĄ I TRUFLAMI
(Tenderloin with Madeira Sauce and Truffles)

Prepare meat as for Roast Beef Tenderloin, above, and serve with a sauce made as follows:

2 tablespoons butter
2 tablespoons all-purpose flour
  (less if preferred)
1 cup beef bouillon plus 1 bouillon
  cube
½ cup Madeira or sherry
1 or 2 truffles (one 1½-ounce can),
  diced fine (or substitute 1 cup
  mushroom caps, sliced and simmered
  in 2 tablespoons butter)

Melt butter but do not brown. Add flour, stirring until smooth. Slowly add the bouillon, taking care that sauce thickens without lumping. Add the Madeira and truffles and simmer, covered, until truffles are tender and sauce is medium-thick and bubbly. Pour over sliced tenderloin on platter.

POLĘDWICA W ŚMIETANIE
(Beef Fillet in Sour Cream)

Prepare as for Roast Beef Tenderloin at left, omitting the lemon juice. Brown quickly on all sides in butter in a shallow baking dish. Dredge with flour. Combine ¼ cup strong beef bouillon and ½ cup dairy sour cream and pour over the meat. Cover and simmer over low heat basting frequently with pan gravy, until meat is tender but not dry. Serve with buttered beets and mashed potatoes. Makes 6 to 8 servings.

FILETY Z POLĘDWICY
(Filet Mignon with Mushrooms)

1½ pounds filet mignon,
  cut into 5 portions
  Salt and pepper to taste
3 tablespoons butter, margarine,
  or other fat for frying
5 toast rounds, sautéed in butter
  until crisp
3 ounces liver paté
¼ pound mushroom caps
2 tablespoons butter
  Madeira Sauce (below)

Sprinkle meat with salt and pepper directly before cooking. Panbroil quickly on both sides in very hot butter, so that each piece is brown outside and red or pink in the center. Transfer to hot toast rounds. Spread each piece with some of the paté.

In the meantime wash, drain, and slice the mushrooms for garnish. Add remaining butter, sprinkle with a little water, cover, and braise for a few minutes. Season with salt and pepper to taste.

When lightly brown, turn carefully, and brown on the other side. Arrange mushrooms over the paté on meat rounds and place on a platter in hot oven for another minute, taking care that the meat remains rare. Serve immediately with Madeira Sauce. Makes 5 servings.

Madeira Sauce

Combine 2 tablespoons, 1 can (10¾ ounces) beef gravy, and ⅓ cup Madeira. Bring to a boil and simmer for 3 minutes. Season to taste with salt and pepper.

KOTLECIKI Z MÓZGU
(Brain Cutlets)

1½ pounds calf's brains
  Court Bouillon for Parboiling Brains
  Salt and pepper to taste
1 medium onion, minced (optional)
  All-purpose flour for dredging
1 egg, lightly beaten (optional)
  Bread crumbs for rolling
¼ cup butter
  Lemon wedges

Parboil brains in Court Bouillon and let them cool and dry off. Remove membranes, cut brains into slices, and season. Mix gently with minced onion. Dredge with flour, dip into egg, then into bread crumbs. Fry in hot butter until golden brown. Serve with lemon wedges. Makes 5 servings.

Note: Beef brains or pork brains may be substituted, in proportionate amounts, but calf's brains have the most delicate taste. No matter how they are later prepared, they should first be parboiled in the Court Bouillon below.

BRAINS PARBOILED IN
COURT BOUILLON

Combine 1 medium onion, quartered; 1 carrot, sliced; 1 bay leaf, a few peppercorns, ½ lemon with the rind left on and 4 cups boiling water. Add brains and bring to boil; simmer until the membranes darken, for 8 to 10 minutes.

FLACZKI PO WARSZAWSKU
(Tripe à la Warsaw)

2 pounds beef tripe
1 pound beef bones, half joint,
  half marrow bone, split
4 cups strong beef bouillon,
  or a little less
¾ cup shredded mixed vegetables
  (onion, carrot, celery, celery root,
  parsley root, leek, etc.)
¼ cup butter
3 tablespoons all-purpose flour
  Ground nutmeg, ginger, and allspice
  to taste
½ teaspoon ground marjoram, or more,
  depending on preference
  Salt and pepper to taste
3 tablespoons grated Parmesan cheese
3 tablespoons bread crumbs
4 tablespoons butter
1 heaping tablespoon chopped
  fresh parsley

Clean tripe thoroughly, scraping with a knife and scrubbing with vegetable brush. Rinse several times in warm water. Parboil, starting in boiling water; drain, and rinse again. Allow to drain. Bring 2 quarts water to a brisk boil, add the tripe and the bones, and simmer until tender, about 4 hours, skimming occasionally. By this time water should have almost boiled away. In the meantime, heat the beef bouillon. Add 3 cups to tripe. Simmer vegetables in remaining bouillon until soft. Remove vegetables from heat. Remove tripe from bouillon, reserving the bouillon, and cut tripe into strips about 1½ inches long. Remove marrow from bones and chop fine. Discard bones.

Make a brown *roux* of 3 tablespoons butter and the flour; add some of the reserved bouillon, stirring constantly until smooth. Add the tripe, marrow, and vegetables, and season. Mix well and bring to a boil. Simmer over low heat until the sauce bubbles. If sauce is too scant, add more bouillon. Arrange mixture in a deep flameproof dish, sprinkle with grated cheese, then with bread crumbs browned in remaining butter. Bake in preheated hot oven (425°F.) for 15 minutes, or until top is brown. Sprinkle with parsley and serve at once. Makes 4 servings.

Note: Tripe is traditionally served with suet balls made with marrow, or with potato dumplings flavored with marjoram. Boiled potatoes garnished with brown butter are a good addition.

Lamb is the least popular meat in Poland. In fact, there are practically no native lamb dishes; most of the recipes for lamb given in Polish cook books give credit to foreign sources: English chops, French gigot, Russian shashlik, lamb-and-eggplant dishes from Asia Minor, and so on. For that reason no lamb recipes are included here.

Veal, on the other hand, is a very popular meat and is of high quality, the very pale off-white variety rather than the reddish-pink which, of course, comes from older animals. Much of it is prepared in classical ways: veal cutlet, natural or breaded; roasts, and chops. The cardinal rule in preparing veal for roasting is to blanch it: pour boiling water over it, then sprinkle with lemon juice 1 or 2 hours before using. This tenderizes the meat and also acts as searing does for beef: it seals in the meat juices and keeps the roast from drying out. Larding is also recommended.

The recipes given below are great favorites, and have the additional virtue of being economical, since stuffing or a rich sauce makes the meat go a lot further than it ordinarily would. The stuffing, especially, is typical.

NERKÓWKA LUB MOSTEK NADZIEWANE PO POLSKU
(Stuffed Breast or Shoulder of Veal à la Polonaise)

3 pounds veal loin, preferably with kidney left in, or 3 to 4 pounds breast or shoulder of veal
Juice of ½ lemon
2 eggs, separated
½ cup butter
1 cup bread crumbs
¼ cup chopped fresh dill or dill and parsley combined
Salt, pepper, and freshly grated nutmeg to taste

Have the butcher make a pocket in the meat for stuffing, taking care that the incision goes in deep, in order to have the stuffing evenly distributed. If using a loin with the kidney in, remove excess fat from around the kidney, then secure it with toothpicks or cotton thread. Blanch the roast and sprinkle with lemon juice.

Prepare stuffing. Cream the egg yolks with half of the butter, combine with bread crumbs, add the dill, and season to taste, using quite a bit of nutmeg. Beat the egg whites until stiff and fold into the mixture. Fill the pocket with the stuffing, being careful to use a light touch, since too tight stuffing will make the mass heavy. Skewer, sew, or secure with toothpicks. Rub the outside with salt and butter.

Start the roast in preheated very hot oven (450°F.), basting first with the rest of the butter, and later with pan juices. Reduce the heat to 325°F. after first 15 minutes, or as soon as the skin begins to brown. Occasionally baste with cold water, as this breaks down the fibers and makes the meat more tender. Roast for about 25 minutes to the pound, or use meat thermometer. When meat is done, remove from pan and keep warm. Scrape sides and bottom of roasting pan, add a very little water, and allow to bubble up. No thickening is needed for the gravy. Makes about 6 servings.

Note: This kind of roast is excellent served with potatoes roasted in the pan along with the meat. Cucumber Salad with Sour-Cream (*Mizerja II*), page 1430, is also recommended.

PIECZEŃ CIELĘCA Z SARDELAMI
(Veal Roast with Anchovies)

3 to 4 pounds veal for roasting, boned
3 ounces salt pork for larding
1 small can (2 ounces) flat anchovies
2 tablespoons anchovy paste
Salt and pepper to taste
Butter
1 cup dairy sour cream
½ tablespoon flour
1 tablespoon capers

Have the butcher bone the meat and cut it down the middle lengthwise for stuffing, but without cutting into 2 separate halves. Blanch for 1 hour before using.

Cut the salt pork into thin strips. Cut the anchovies into strips. Using a larding needle, lard the meat, alternating the salt pork and anchovies. Spread with anchovy paste inside and out, close the opening and secure roast by tying firmly with string. Season sparingly, since both the anchovies and capers will give the meat their own salty flavor. Dot with butter and roast in preheated very hot oven (450°F.) for 10 to 15 minutes, so that meat browns quickly. Reduce heat and continue roasting, basting frequently, for about an hour more.

Combine sour cream, flour, and capers, and spread over the meat. Continue cooking until the sauce browns a little, another 10 to 15 minutes. Serve with roast potatoes and a green salad, or with a potato-and-celery-root salad. Makes 6 to 8 servings.

ZRAZY CIELĘCE ZAWIJANE
(Stuffed Veal Birds)

1 pound veal cutlet, cut very thin
¼ pound mushrooms, chopped fine
½ small onion, minced very fine
5 tablespoons butter
Salt and pepper to taste
2 tablespoons fine dry bread crumbs
All-purpose flour for dusting
½ cup chicken broth or bouillon (or more)
¼ cup dry sherry or white wine
Few drops of beef extract

Have the veal cut as thin as possible; then pound well to make it thinner still, taking care not to tear it. Cut into pieces about 3 inches square.

Simmer the mushrooms and onion in 2 tablespoons of the butter until mushrooms change color and onion is transparent, about 5 minutes. Season to taste, add bread crumbs, and mix. Add more bread crumbs if the stuffing is too skimpy. Spread each piece of meat with a little of the mixture, roll, and secure with toothpicks or tie with white cotton thread. Dust rolls lightly with flour. Brown quickly in a skillet in remaining very hot butter. Transfer to a heavy kettle, being careful to arrange rolls tightly. Add a little of the broth and simmer, tightly covered, for about 45 minutes. Atfer the first 15 minutes, add the wine and beef extract. Continue adding more broth as sauce evaporates, rather than let the meat stew in all of the sauce at once. Be careful not to overcook. Serve with dilled new potatoes or pearl barley. Makes 4 servings.

Note: Veal slices may be stuffed with liver pâté (one 3-ounce can) instead of mushroom-onion-crumb mixture if desired.

PROSIĘ PIECZONE NADZIEWANE
(Roast Stuffed Suckling Pig)

1 whole suckling pig (10 to 12 pounds)
Salt
Stuffing
2 to 3 ounces salt pork for larding

½ cup butter, margarine, or other
fat for roasting
½ cup beer (optional) or cold water

Have the butcher dress the suckling pig, removing hoofs and reserving the liver, heart, and lungs; if possible, ask him to save the blood. Scald, scrub, rinse, and refrigerate for 2 days. About 1 hour before roasting, salt the meat inside and out. Stuff, truss, and lard with salt pork. Place in shallow roasting pan, preferably on rack, and smear with the butter. Start the roast in preheated hot oven (425° F.), basting frequently with pan fat, alternating with beer or cold water, until the skin is brown. Reduce the heat to moderate (350°F.) and continue cooking, basting occasionally, for 2½ to 3 hours. To test for doneness, pierce with a fork where meat is thickest; if the juice comes out watery, continue roasting a little longer; if fat flows, the meat is done. Makes 10 to 12 servings.

Note: Suckling pig is also delicious when roasted on a spit and is therefore ideal for a barbecue.

Stuffings

Groat Stuffing

2 cups buckwheat groats (kasha)
1 egg, lightly beaten
4 cups water
2 medium onions, diced and browned
in butter or fat
Podróbki (liver, heart, lungs, and any
available coagulated blood from
slaughter), chopped fine
Salt and pepper to taste
1 teaspoon crumbled dried marjoram

Prepare groats with egg, according to recipe for *Czarna Kasza* (page 1428), with the addition of onions to cooking water. When done, dry out in oven. Combine with *podróbki,* mix well, season to taste.

Note: Groat Stuffing may also be used for roast goose.

Bread-Crumb Stuffing

3 tablespoons butter
3 eggs, separated
2 medium onions, minced and braised
in a little butter or fat
Podróbki (liver, heart, lungs, and
coagulated blood from slaughter),
chopped fine
Salt, pepper, and dried marjoram
to taste

Cream butter and combine with egg yolks. Mix thoroughly and combine with onion and chopped *podróbki.* Season to taste with salt, pepper, and about 1 teaspoon marjoram. Beat egg whites until stiff and fold into the mixture.

POLĘDWICA WIEPRZOWA DUSZONA NA WINIE
(Pork Pot Roast in Wine)

1½ pounds pork tenderloin
Salt
2 tablespoons butter or margarine
1 small onion, sliced and cooked

only until limp
1 to 1½ cups diced vegetables
including any combination of
the following:
carrot
celery root
parsley root
celery stalk
Few parsley sprigs
Pepper to taste
Herbs and spices to taste: a few
peppercorns, allspice berries, caraway
seeds, whole or crushed, dried
marjoram and a dash of ground
ginger
½ cup dry red wine
1 ripe fresh tomato or 1 tablespoon
tomato paste
¼ teaspoon beef extract
1 teaspoon all-purpose flour
¼ cup beef bouillon

Rub meat with salt 1 hour before cooking time and allow to stand at room temperature. Sear on all sides in the butter and transfer to casserole. Add the onion, diced vegetables, parsley, and salt, pepper, herbs and spices to taste. Cover tightly and simmer without adding any liquid until the meat and vegetables begin to brown. Add the wine and tomato and continue simmering until tender, about 1 hour. Add the beef extract and dust with a little flour, taking care not to make sauce too thick. If necessary, add the bouillon. When the liquid bubbles up, cover, and simmer for another 10 minutes. Excellent served with red cabbage. Makes about 4 servings.

■ **Variation**—This dish may also be prepared from marinated fresh pork. In that case proceed as follows: Make a marinade by combining 1 part wine vinegar and 2 parts water (enough liquid to half cover the meat), 1 onion, sliced; 1 carrot, sliced; 1 bay leaf, 12 peppercorns, and 3 allspice berries. Boil until vegetables are limp.

Pour the boiling liquid over the meat and let stand in refrigerator for 24 hours, turning occasionally. Wipe meat dry and reserve marinade for basting. Omit the wine, using a little more bouillon if sauce is too scant. Otherwise prepare like Pork Pot Roast in Wine.

NÓŻKI WIEPRZOWE Z GROCHEM
(Pickled or Fresh Pigs' Knuckles with Split Peas)

6 pigs' knuckles, fresh or pickled,
cracked
½ pound diced mixed vegetables
(carrot, parsley root, parsnip, celery
rot, leaf celery)
1 medium onion, minced
1 bay leaf
Pinch each of ground coriander
and allspice
Salt and pepper to taste

If using pickled knuckles, scrape and rinse to remove saltpeter. Soak in water if very salty. Fresh knuckles need no preparation. Cover with boiling water and simmer, skimming, for 15 to 20 min-

utes. Add the diced vegetables, onion, bay leaf, and spices. Adjust seasoning, and continue to simmer until meat is very tender. Drain and serve very hot with split-pea purée and horseradish. Makes 6 servings.

BIGOS MYŚLIWSKI
(Hunters' Stew)

This dish, which got its name because traditionally it used to be served after the hunt, is an ideal one for a large dinner party since it requires a minimum of last-minute effort. It must, in fact, be prepared in advance, then reheated. The morning of the party will do, but it will taste better if cooked a day or two ahead of time. Also, the hostess will have time to recover and look fresh and relaxed!

Because it requires so many ingredients, it is seldom planned for less than a dozen people. The leftovers, if any, can be refrigerated; or it may be cooked in large quantities and frozen for use later on, for the more bigos is reheated, the better it tastes. Old-time cooks also used to advise that it be planned as a late-holiday-season menu or after a long weekend of entertaining "when there are many kinds of meats and poultry left over in the larder." No two cooks' recipes for it are alike, but if you know the principle, you can proceed safely with whatever meats are at hand, remembering only that the greater the variety, the better.

6 to 8 pounds sauerkraut
¼ pound bacon or salt pork, diced
3 ounces dried mushrooms
2 large onions, minced
2 tablespoons all-purpose flour
1 bay leaf
3 to 4 pounds roast or braised meats,
from any or all of these:
roast pork
roast or braised beef
roast or braised veal
½ pound Polish sausage
venison or hare
chicken
goose
duck
Salt, pepper, and sugar to taste
1 cup Madeira, sherry, or dry red wine

Rinse the sauerkraut in cold water, squeeze out juice, and reserve it. Put sauerkraut in a large kettle over low heat. While the sauerkraut heats, render the bacon or salt pork. At the same time cook the mushrooms in enough water to cover until they are tender; then cut them into thin strips. Crumble the bacon and add to the sauerkraut. Add the mushrooms, together with the liquid in which they cooked. Brown the onions in the bacon fat until limp and transparent. Add the flour and continue cooking until that browns. Add the mixture with the bay leaf to the sauerkraut. Simmer for 30 minutes.

Dice the meat, poultry, game, and

sausage and add to the pot. Add any meat sauce that is available. Mix thoroughly and season to taste with salt, pepper, and a dash of sugar, adding a little of the reserved sauerkraut juice for tartness. Simmer for another 30 minutes. Add the wine and let mixture bubble up. Cover and let stand until ready to use. Serve with potatoes. Makes 12 generous servings.

Note: If the meats for the *bigos* are prepared afresh—that is, if you start the dish from scratch—they must all be cooked separately. In that case they should be braised or baked covered, since roasting such small amounts would dry them out. Vegetables used in braising should *not* be added to the *bigos;* all meat juices, however, should be used.

BIGOS POLSKI
(Polish Bigos)

A simpler variation of the same dish, this bigos is to be found often in the average Polish home. It makes a satisfying cold-weather meal.

    1 pound sauerkraut
    1 pound fresh cabbage
    2 or 3 dried mushrooms,
       broken into bits
    ½ pound boneless fresh pork
       Fat for frying
    ¼ pound bacon
    2 ounces salt pork, diced
    1 medium-small onion, minced
    2 to 3 tablespoons all-purpose flour
    6 ounces sausage
    3 to 4 tablespoons tomato paste
       Salt and pepper to taste
       Sugar to taste (optional)
    ⅓ cup red wine

Cut up the sauerkraut, add a small amount of boiling water, and simmer until tender. Shred the fresh cabbage and cook in the same way, with the mushrooms added. In a hot skillet brown the pork on all sides in a little fat. Add to the sauerkraut together with the bacon and simmer, covered, until meat is tender. Render the salt pork, add crisp pieces to the sauerkraut, and use the pork fat for cooking onion until lightly browned. Add the flour, stirring to prevent lumping, and cook until that browns. Remove the fresh pork and bacon and cut into small pieces. Peel and dice the sausage. Combine the sauerkraut and cabbage, add the browned onion, flour, and tomato paste, and stir thoroughly. Return the meat to the pot, season to taste with salt and pepper, add a dash of sugar, and bring to a boil. Add wine and simmer for another few minutes. Serve with potatoes, sprinkled with parsley. Makes 4 servings.

ZAJĄC PIECZONY
(Roast Hare)

Hare is a popular dish in Poland. Its equivalent in this country is Canadian

Wielkanocna Babka   Sztufada

hare, gamy and with dark meat. However, rabbit may be substituted in this recipe, although it is more bland in flavor. Four pounds hare or rabbit will make about 6 servings.

Marinate the loin and the hind legs of a hare, well larded with salt pork, in Vinegar Marinade (page 1422), and proceed as for Marinated Duck or Goose (below), omitting ginger and nutmeg. Baste with dry red wine instead of marinade. Use either dairy sour cream or ½ cup red wine for sauce. Serve with potatoes, beets, red cabbage, and horseradish with cranberries.

POULTRY

KURA LUB KURCZĘTA PO POLSKU
(Roast Chicken or Pullets à la Polonaise)

2 large broiling chickens (2 pounds each), or 1 young roasting chicken (4 pounds), or 5 six-week-old pullets (individual servings, about 1 pound each)
Salt
¼ cup butter

Stuffing:

1½ cups bread crumbs
½ cup butter
¼ cup fresh dill or dill and parsley combined, chopped fine
Dash of ground nutmeg
Salt and pepper to taste
Chicken livers, mashed (optional)

Rub chicken with salt inside and out about 30 minutes before stuffing. Combine all the stuffing ingredients and mix thoroughly. (If chicken livers are used, sauté until done and mash with the butter before adding bread crumbs and other ingredients.) Stuff the cavity lightly, to allow for puffing up during the cooking. Secure with skewers or sew up cavity with cotton thread. Truss the bird, rub with butter, and roast in preheated hot oven (425°F.), basting frequently with butter and pan juices.

The pullets should not take longer than 45 minutes, the broilers about 1 hour. For large roasting chicken, allow 1½ to 2 hours. Serve with Cucumber Salad with Sour Cream *(Mizerja II),* page 1430, a green salad, or apple or pear compote. Makes 5 servings.

Note: For the larger birds, the stuffing may be varied by substituting stale white bread moistened in milk for the bread crumbs. In that case, add 3 eggs, separated, creaming the egg yolks with the other ingredients, then beating the egg whites until stiff and folding in last. This stuffing is also used for turkey. For squab, follow the same recipe as for pullets.

KACZKA LUB GĘŚ MARYNOWANA
(Marinated Duck or Goose)

Vinegar Marinade (page 1422)
1 duck (about 5 pounds) or ½ goose (8- to 10-pound goose)
Salt
1 garlic clove (optional)
1 medium onion, sliced
Bay leaf (optional)
Ground allspice, ginger, and nutmeg to taste
1 cup dairy sour cream
2 tablespoons all-purpose flour

Bring marinade to a boil and pour while hot over duck. Let stand for 1 or 2 days in refrigerator. Drain, reserving some of the liquid. Rub duck with salt and garlic and let stand for 1 hour.

Put bird, breast side up, in rack on shallow pan. Roast in preheated slow oven (325°F.) for 2 hours, or until done. Baste frequently, alternating the pan fat with the reserved marinade. Halfway through the cooking time, add the onion and bay leaf to the pan, and sprinkle meat with the spices. Continue roasting until the duck is tender and the skin very crisp.

Remove the bird to a hot platter for carving. Keep hot. Add a very little water to pan, scraping sides, and let sauce bubble up. Strain, skimming as much of the fat as possible. Add the sour cream and flour, and stir over low heat until smooth. Season to taste with more ginger and nutmeg. The sauce should have a tart flavor. Serve with roast or baked potatoes and sweet-and-sour red cabbage. Makes about 4 servings.

GĘŚ PO POLSKU
(Goose à la Polonaise)

1 small lean young goose (about 5 pounds)
Salt
1 garlic clove (optional)
1 cup diced mixed vegetables
1 medium onion, chopped
3 tablespoons goose fat or butter
3 scant tablespoons all-purpose flour
Pepper
1 teaspoon each of ground marjoram and freshly grated nutmeg
2 egg yolks, lightly beaten

Soak goose for 2 to 3 hours in cold water; rub with salt and let stand for 1 hour. Cut into halves, arrange in a large pan, skin side up, and pour about 4 cups boiling water over the bird. Cover and simmer until half cooked, less than 1 hour. Add the garlic, diced vegetables, and chopped onion, and continue simmering until done. The liquid should be reduced to 2 or 3 cups. Skim off as much fat as possible. Prepare a brown *roux* with melted goose fat or butter and the flour, and dilute with stock from goose. Add salt, a very little pepper, the marjoram, and nutmeg and stir until smooth and the sauce has thickened.

Carve the goose into serving pieces and

keep hot. Gradually beat the sauce into the egg yolks, taking care not to let the mixture curdle. Heat for 1 or 2 minutes, then pour over goose. Serve with barley groats and red cabbage or beets. Makes 7 or 8 servings.

MEATLESS MAIN DISHES

SIADLE MLEKO
(Clabber)

Clabber and potatoes is the dish that for centuries has been the mainstay of the Polish countryside; it makes a fine summer meal. However, getting pasteurized milk to set is somewhat tricky. Since the whole secret of good clabber is to have it set fast—slow souring gives it a bitter, cheeselike taste—when pasteurized milk is used, it requires an assist in the form of 1 tablespoon dairy sour cream for each 1 cup sweet milk.

Dissolve the cream in the milk thoroughly and place in a bowl, covered with cheesecloth, in a fairly warm spot in the kitchen, letting it stand overnight, or for about 24 hours. As soon as the milk sets, chill in refrigerator. Serve with hot boiled parsley potatoes and black or rye bread.

CZARNA KASZA
(Buckwheat Groats)

This has long been a staple of Poland's largely peasant population, for it is nourishing and cheap, and sticks to the ribs. It is an excellent source of Vitamins A and B as well as calcium and, of course, carbohydrates. Served with a mushroom sauce, it makes a balanced meatless meal. It is also a delicious addition to beef or pork dishes, especially when the meat dish is one with much sauce, for kasza is too dry to eat by itself.

In this country, buckwheat groats may be purchased in many food stores, in delicatessens, and speciality stores, especially in those neighborhoods where there is a large East-European or Jewish population. Groats are sold by variety: whole, coarse-cut, medium, and fine. Which kind to use is determined by personal preference, depending on whether one likes one's cereal mushy or dry. We happen to like ours dry, so that the grains are separate as in oriental rice. My own rule, therefore, is the coarser the better, but finding whole groats sometimes takes a bit of shopping around.

For fluffy *kasza*, proceed as follows:

1 cup groats
1 tablespoon butter or bacon fat, or 1 raw egg or egg white
2 cups briskly boiling water (a little less for very dry groats)
Salt to taste (about 1 teaspoon)

Brown the groats in a heavy skillet in the

butter; if egg is used, coat the grains first, allow to dry, then brown lightly. For coating without egg, add butter to the water. Pour the boiling water over the groats and reduce the heat at once. Add salt, cover tightly, and simmer until done, about 25 minutes, stirring once or twice to prevent sticking. Fluff with a fork if necessary before it is quite done. The cooking can also be done in the oven in a tightly covered casserole, in which case you may want to take the cover off for the final few minutes, to let the steam escape. Makes 4 generous servings.

KOTLETY Z GRZYBÓW
(Mushroom Patties)
¾ pound fresh mushrooms or 3 ounces dried mushrooms
1 small or ½ large onion, minced
2 tablespoons butter
  Salt and pepper to taste
2 to 3 tablespoons water
1 large roll or 4 slices of bread, stale, moistened with milk
1 whole egg, lightly beaten
1 tablespoon chopped fresh dill and parsley
  Bread crumbs
  Butter, margarine, or other fat for frying

Wash and chop the fresh mushrooms. If dried mushrooms are used, simmer in 1 cup water until tender enough to cut easily. Drain, reserving liquid for use in sauces. Combine mushrooms with onion and butter, season, and simmer, covered, until mushrooms are tender and onion transparent and lightly browned. If too dry, add a little water. Squeeze most of the milk out of the bread. Put bread and mushroom mixture through a meat grinder, or use a blender. Combine with the egg and chopped herbs, season to taste, and shape into patties. If the mixture is too wet, add 2 to 3 tablespoons dry bread crumbs.

Sauté patties in hot butter over a high heat, until golden brown on both sides, taking care not to burn. Arrange on hot platter and serve at once with Horse-radish Sauce (page 1422), potatoes, cooked cabbage, or a salad. Makes 4 servings.

LENIWE PIEROGI
(Lazy Dumplings)
2½ cups dry cottage cheese or pot cheese
4 eggs, separated, plus 1 egg white
6 tablespoons butter
  Salt to taste
¼ cup sifted all-purpose flour
2 to 3 tablespoons bread crumbs

Put cheese through a sieve. Combine egg yolks and half of the butter and cream well. Add the cheese and salt to taste, and cream again. Beat the egg whites until stiff and fold into the mixture. Sprinkle

the flour into the mixture and blend well. If necessary to make dough easy to handle, dust with more flour and mix lightly.

Using a floured board or wax paper, roll into the shape and thickness of long French bread (about 2 inches), flatten slightly, and cut into diagonal strips about ½ inch wide. Drop the *pierogi* into boiling water and cook until done, 12 to 15 minutes. Drain. Serve hot with a garnish made by browning the remaining butter and the bread crumbs. Makes 4 to 6 servings.

PIEROGI Z KASZY ZE SEREM
(Buckwheat Dumplings with Cheese)
2 cups buckwheat flour
3 cups boiling water
3 cups all-purpose flour
  Salt to taste
  Piece of salt pork or bacon, diced, for topping (or butter)
1 cup dry cottage cheese or pot cheese

Combine buckwheat flour and boiling water, and mix thoroughly. Add all-purpose flour, season, and mix again. Shape dumplings according to recipe for Lazy Dumplings. Drop into salted boiling water and cook, covered, until done, about 20 minutes. In the meantime, render the salt pork. Put cheese through a sieve or simply work with a fork so it is fluffy. Drain the dumplings, turn out onto a hot platter, mix with rendered fat and pork, and sprinkle with the cheese. Heat over boiling water for a few minutes before serving. Makes about 8 servings.

NALEŚNIKI
(Rolled Pancakes)
These may be eaten as a main dish or as dessert, depending on the filling. The basic recipe is the same for all, and approximates the standard recipe for Crêpes Suzette. The secret of good naleśniki *is to do them quickly in a very hot skillet (or in several skillets at once) rubbed with fat or butter.*

Spoon a little of the batter into a 7- or 8-inch skillet, and tip the pan so that the whole surface is covered. As soon as batter adheres to the surface, pour off excess. When nearly done, turn and brown on the other side. Transfer to a hot platter and keep hot in the oven until all are done. Then roll each separately, and brown quickly on both sides in hot melted butter.

Basic Dough:
1 cup of half milk and half water
1 egg, beaten
1 cup sifted all-purpose flour
  Salt to taste

Combine liquid and egg, add flour and salt, and mix thoroughly before using. Makes 10 to 12 large pancakes.

Fillings:
Groats and Mushroom Filling
2 or 3 dried mushrooms, simmered in 1½ cups water until soft
¾ cup buckwheat groats (kasha)
  Butter or bacon fat
  Salt and pepper to taste

Use liquid in which mushrooms have cooked for cooking the groats (follow recipe for *Czarna Kasza,* page 1428), adding 1 tablespoon butter. Cut mushrooms into bits. Combine all the ingredients and season to taste. Fill the *naleśniki,* roll and brown in butter or bacon fat.

Mushroom Filling
1 pound fresh mushrooms, caps and stems both, chopped
1 medium onion, minced
2 tablespoons butter or other fat
½ cup dairy sour cream
1 tablespoon all-purpose flour
  Salt and pepper to taste

Simmer mushrooms and onions in the butter until mushrooms change color and the onion is a light golden brown. Combine sour cream and flour, and add to mixture. Season to taste and continue to simmer until the mixture bubbles up. The filling should be thick and not runny. If too thin, add a little flour. Fill the *naleśniki,* roll, and brown in butter or bacon fat.

Cheese Filling
1 pound dry cottage cheese or pot cheese
2 eggs, lightly beaten
2 tablespoons dairy sour cream
2 tablespoons all-purpose flour
  A little grated lemon or orange rind
  Salt to taste
  Raisins and/or slivered almonds (optional)
  Sugar to taste (optional)

Work the cheese with a fork until fluffy; combine with eggs, sour cream, flour, lemon rind, and salt to taste. If the *naleśniki* are to be eaten as a main dish, omit other ingredients. For a dessert dish, sweeten filling to taste and add raisins and/or almonds. Fill the pancakes, roll, and brown lightly in butter.

Note: Cheese *naleśniki* may be served with drawn butter, or topped with sour cream and a little ground cinnamon and sugar.

Garnish:
All these *naleśniki* may be simply browned in butter or fat, but if served as a main dish they will have an added fillip if browned as described below:

1 large or 2 small eggs, lightly beaten
5 tablespoons bread crumbs
3 to 4 tablespoons butter or bacon fat

Dip the rolled *naleśniki* into egg, then into bread crumbs, and fry in hot butter.

STUFFED CABBAGE, VEGETABLES, SALADS, AND SAUCES

GOLĄBKI Z KAPUSTY
(Cabbage Birds or Stuffed Cabbage I)

1 large or 2 medium heads of cabbage
2 slices of stale bread or bread crumbs
¾ pound chopped beef
1 small onion, minced and cooked golden brown in 2 tablespoons butter, margarine, or bacon fat
1 egg
1¼ teaspoons salt
½ teaspoon pepper
1 cup beef bouillon (about)

Sauce:

3 tablespoons all-purpose flour
3 tablespoons butter or bacon fat
3 tablespoons tomato paste
Salt, pepper, and paprika to taste
Pinch of sugar (optional)

Parboil cabbage long enough so that the leaves separate without tearing. Select 10 or 12 of the largest leaves; trim off the midribs so leaves become easy to roll. Reserve remaining cabbage for other use. Soak the bread in water and squeeze out; or moisten the bread crumbs. Combine with meat and mix thoroughly. Add the onion, egg, and seasoning and mix again. Divide into as many portions as there are cabbage leaves.

Spread mixture evenly on leaves. Roll firmly, tucking edges inside so that stuffing will not escape, and secure with cotton string. If there are not enough large leaves, use 2 small leaves, letting them overlap. Arrange cabbage birds tightly in a saucepan, add a small quantity of bouillon, and simmer over low heat until tender. Remove string.

For the sauce, make a *roux* with the flour and butter, add tomato paste and bouillon from the stuffed cabbage, and stir until smooth and bubbly. Season to taste and let the sauce simmer for a few more minutes. Arrange cabbage on a hot platter, pour sauce over it, and serve with potatoes. Makes 5 or 6 servings.

■ **Variation**—Instead of the tomato sauce used above, these Cabbage Birds, as well as the two which follow, may be served with Mushroom Sour-Cream Sauce (at right).

Cabbage Birds II

For the same amount of cabbage, use:

2 dried mushrooms, simmered in very little water until soft, then chopped
½ pound boneless pork, chopped
½ cup rice or pearl barley, cooked according to directions on box
1 medium onion, minced and sautéed until golden brown
Salt and pepper to taste
Water or bouillon

Reserve liquid from the mushrooms for use in cooking. Combine all the ingredients, mix thoroughly, and stuff cabbage leaves as in the basic recipe. Add a little water or bouillon to mushroom liquid

and use in simmering.

Make sauce, using the ingredients and following directions given for Cabbage Birds I.

Goląbki Postne
(Meatless Stuffed Cabbage)

Follow the recipe for Cabbage Birds II, but use 1 cup rice or pearl barley and omit the meat. Add more onion and dried mushrooms (as much as double the amount) for a more pronounced taste.

GARNISH FOR VEGETABLES À LA POLONAISE

A typical way to serve vegetables in season, asparagus, cauliflower, Brussels sprouts, Savoy cabbage in particular, is with drawn butter and bread-crumb topping, a method which by now has been adopted internationally. Chefs are forever trying to dress it up, but it is best not to gild the lily.

3 tablespoons butter
3 tablespoons bread crumbs

Melt the butter and let it brown lightly. Add bread crumbs and let these brown too, taking care not to burn. Pour over vegetables and serve at once. Makes enough for 4 to 6 servings.

SAŁATKA PO POLSKU
(Salad Greens à la Polonaise)

2 hard-cooked egg yolks
2 tablespoons olive oil
¼ cup fresh lemon juice
1 teaspoon sugar (less according to taste)
Salt to taste
2 quarts tender young salad greens, such as Boston, Bibb, or oakleaf lettuce, romaine, endive

Mash the egg yolks and combine with other dressing ingredients. Vary proportions of oil and lemon juice according to personal preference. Coat salad greens with the mixture and serve at once. Makes 4 to 6 servings.

MIZERJA I
(Cucumber Salad)

2 or 3 fresh young cucumbers, sliced very thin
Salt
1 tablespoon each of olive oil and vinegar
Pepper to taste
Pinch of sugar (optional)

In a bowl arrange the sliced cucumbers, salting them in layers. Cover with a saucer and weigh down with something heavy. Let stand for several hours, or until juices run out. Pour off the cucumber juice, which will take care of most of the salt. Combine all other ingredients and add to the cucumbers. Mix and chill. Makes 4 to 6 servings.

Mizerja II
(Cucumber Salad with Sour Cream)

2 or 3 fresh cucumbers
¼ to ½ cup dairy sour cream
1 tablespoon vinegar
Pepper to taste
1 to 2 tablespoons chopped dill

Proceed as for *Mizerja I*, but omit olive oil and sugar and substitute sour cream and dill. Makes 4 to 6 servings.

MUSHROOM SWEET-CREAM SAUCE

1½ cups mushrooms, caps and stems both, washed and sliced*
½ medium onion
Water
Salt and pepper to taste
3½ tablespoons butter
2 to 3 tablespoons all-purpose flour
1 cup chicken or beef bouillon
½ cup sweet cream
½ cup dry white wine
Lemon juice to taste
2 egg yolks, lightly beaten

Combine mushrooms, onion, a little water, and seasoning, and simmer in the butter until mushrooms are tender; then add the flour and fry until lightly brown. Slowly add bouillon, stirring to prevent lumps. Let the sauce boil up, slowly add the cream, wine, and lemon juice, stirring all the time, until thick and bubbly. Adjust seasoning. Add egg yolks immediately before serving, taking care not to let the mixture curdle. Makes about 3 cups.

*A gourmet variation is to use dried mushrooms, but they are expensive and not always available in the stores, except in predominantly East-European neighborhoods. Dried Italian mushrooms may be substituted; these are considerably cheaper but are also more bland. When using dried mushrooms, allow a 1½-ounce package for the sauce recipe with sour cream. Simmer them in 1 cup water until tender enough to cut into strips. Reduce liquid to half or less, and add to sauce. Dried mushrooms are not recommended for the sweet-cream sauce, as their taste is too strong.

Note: The proportions of mushrooms to liquid may be varied, depending on how thick one wants the sauce. And this sauce, plus the one which follows, especially the latter, may both be used as a side dish with meat; in that case add more mushrooms, ¾ pound or even 1 pound, for 4 servings.

MUSHROOM SOUR-CREAM SAUCE

1½ cups mushrooms
1 small or ½ large onion, minced
Water
Salt and pepper
3½ tablespoons butter
1 tablespoon all-purpose flour
½ cup dairy sour cream
1 egg yolk, beaten (optional)
1 tablespoon chopped fresh dill (optional)

Wash mushrooms, slice thin, using both stems and caps, and combine with onion and a very little water. Season with salt and pepper to taste, and simmer in the butter until mushrooms are tender. Add the flour, coating the mushrooms, and if necessary moisten with a little water or broth to keep flour from sticking. Keeping the pan over low heat, stir in the sour cream and allow sauce to bubble up. Add egg yolk last, taking care not to let sauce curdle. Adjust seasoning. Sprinkle with chopped dill. Makes about 2 cups.

 **DESSERTS**

WIELKANOCNA BABKA
(Easter Babka)
½ cup soft butter or margarine
½ cup sugar
5 egg yolks
1 package active dry yeast or 1 cake compressed yeast
   Water*
   Grated rind of 1 lemon
1 teaspoon salt
½ teaspoon ground cinnamon
1 cup milk, scalded and cooled to lukewarm
4 cups all-purpose flour (about)
1 cup golden raisins
¼ cup sliced blanched almonds

Cream butter and sugar in large bowl. Beat 4 egg yolks until thick and lemon-colored. Stir into creamed mixture. Soften yeast in ¼ cup water. *Use very warm water (115°F.) for dry yeast; use lukewarm (80°F. to 90°F.) for compressed. Add to mixture with the lemon rind. Beat in salt and cinnamon. Add milk and flour to make a soft dough. Stir in raisins. Knead in bowl until dough no longer sticks to the hands. Cover and let rise in a warm place until doubled in bulk (about 2 hours). Butter a 3-quart bundt pan and shape dough to fit it. Put dough in pan, cover and let rise again until doubled (about 1½ hours). Beat remaining egg yolk slightly with 2 tablespoons of water. Brush on raised dough and sprinkle with almonds. Bake in preheated moderate oven (350°F.) for about 30 minutes.

CHRUST CZYLI FAWORKI
(Crunch Cakes or Favors)
2 tablespoons butter
2 cups sifted all-purpose flour
5 egg yolks, lightly beaten
¼ cup milk
¼ teaspoon salt
1 tablespoon rum
   Flour for flouring board
   Oil or shortening for deep frying
   Vanilla Confectioners' Sugar

Cut butter into the flour; add egg yolks and milk mixed with salt and rum. The dough should not be so wet that it will stick to the floured board. If too wet, add a little more flour. Beat the dough against the board until bubbles appear, then set aside, covered, for 30 minutes. Working with small amount of dough at a time, roll out to a sheet ⅛ inch thick. Cut into long strips, about 1 inch wide by 4 inches long, cutting ends diagonally. Make a slit 2 inches long in center of each strip and pull one end through the slit.

Heat oil to 350°F. on a frying thermometer. Fry only a few cakes at a time in order not to crowd. If frying in skillet in a few inches of fat, brown first on one side, then on the other. When ready, drain on paper towels. When all are done, sprinkle with Vanilla Confectioners' Sugar. Makes about 48.

Vanilla Confectioners' Sugar
Let 1 vanilla bean stand in 2 cups confectioners' sugar for 2 to 3 days.

BABKI ŚMIETANKOWE
(Cream Tarts)
Dough:
1 cup sifted all-purpose flour
4½ tablespoons butter, melted or very soft
2 egg yolks
3 tablespoons confectioners' sugar
   Butter for lining tart molds

Sift flour, combine with butter, egg yolks, and sugar, and divide dough into 3 parts. Roll out 2 parts. Butter fluted tart molds and line with the rolled-out dough. Set aside in a cool place. Roll out the remaining dough into a thin sheet and reserve.

Rich Cream Filling:
3 egg yolks
1 tablespoon sugar
½ teaspoon vanilla extract
1 cup heavy cream

Cream egg yolks and sugar, then add vanilla. In top part of a double boiler, combine cream with the egg and sugar mixture and cook, stirring constantly, until mixture thickens. Do not let it boil. Allow custard to cool and use it to fill the pastry-lined tart pans. Cover filled tarts with remaining dough. Press down and trim the mold edges. Bake in preheated moderate oven (350°F.) for about 30 minutes. Makes about 6 medium tarts.

MAZUREK MIGDAŁOWY
(Almond Mazurka)
2½ cups sifted all-purpose flour
1½ cups butter
¼ cup confectioners' sugar
2¼ cups almonds, including 2 or 3 bitter almonds, blanched and ground
   Vanilla extract to taste (½ to 1 teaspoon)
6 egg whites, beaten stiff
   Apricot preserves or rose petal jam for filling
   Pink or white prepared frosting

Sift flour, cut in butter, and combine with sugar, almonds, and vanilla. Fold in egg whites last. Bake in a flat oblong pan (15 x 10 x 1 inch) in preheated moderate oven (350°F.) until light brown, about 40 minutes. Allow to cool in pan. Remove from pan. Cut into halves. Spread one half of cake with preserves, cover with second half, and frost.

KISIEL OWOCOWY
(Fruit Dessert)
This is one of the most popular everyday desserts, akin to our gelatin desserts but more runny. It is generally served with light cream or with a milk-and-egg-yolk mixture.

1½ cups berries (strawberries, wild or cultivated; blueberries, currants, or raspberries), or 1 cup pitted cherries
2½ cups hot water
¾ cup sugar
6 tablespoons potato starch or cornstarch dissolved in ½ cup cold water

Combine the fruit and water, and cook until soft and mushy. Press through a sieve. Add sugar and reheat; then remove from the stove. Slowly add the dissolved potato starch, return to heat, and again bring to a boil, stirring constantly. If necessary, add more sugar. Pour into sherbet glasses, and sprinkle lightly with water. Allow to set. Chill before serving. Makes 4 to 6 servings.

KRUPNIK
(Hot Grog with Honey)
This is a drink, served during holidays, which is said to go to the feet rather than the head. It is also said to fell the mighty and conquer the conquerors. Not recommended as a stirrup cup.

1 cup dark honey
1 cup water
8 cinnamon sticks (1 ounce)
1½-inch piece of vanilla bean, crushed
¼ whole nutmeg, freshly grated
6 cloves, crushed
10 peppercorns (optional), freshly ground
   Piece of lemon or orange rind
1 pint vodka

Combine honey and water, add all the ingredients except the vodka, and simmer for 5 to 10 minutes. Set aside and let stand in a warm place for 30 minutes. Strain through cheesecloth, and again bring to a boil. Pour at once into a well-heated covered pitcher, add the vodka, and stir. Serve very hot in liqueur glasses or in preheated demitasse cups. Makes about 1 quart.

POLLACK or POLLOCK—A salt-water fish which resembles the cod. Also known as the coalfish, it is found in the Atlantic from Norway to the Mediterranean. A closely related species, the Alaska pollack, is plentiful in the Bering Sea and north Pacific waters.

The flesh is white, firm, and lean, with a pleasant, delicate flavor.

Availability and Purchasing Guide—Pollacks weigh from three to fourteen pounds market weight and are sold drawn, dressed, in steaks or fillets, fresh, frozen, or smoked. They are available year round.

Storage—See Perch, page 1362.

Nutritive Food Values—A good source of protein.

☐ 3½ ounces, raw = 95 calories
☐ 3½ ounces, cooked and creamed = 128 calories

Basic Preparation—See Perch, page 1363.

Polynesian Cookery

by William Clifford

Polynesia stretches all the way from Hawaii to New Zealand, with Samoa and Tonga, the Cook Islands and Tahiti in between. This is a considerable part of the Pacific Ocean and, except for what lives under water, virtually all of it is empty. There are probably fewer than half a million Polynesians on all the islands combined. Papeete, the metropolis of Tahiti and capital of French Oceania, recently discovered it had problems of urbanization when the population rose to 24,000.

Besides its vast emptiness, other impressive features of the area are its natural beauty and the ease of living. Tahiti is as colorful as Gauguin's paintings, with raven-haired girls in bright-flowered sarongs strolling down the road, playing on the beach, or lolling by the brook where a violet-colored horse reaches down to drink. Every coral reef and blue lagoon is breathtakingly beautiful, especially as you catch sight of it after hours of flying over nothing but ocean. Fruit virtually falls into your hands from the trees; fish leap out of the sea. Flowers are everywhere, worn by men as well as women, expressing the joyful acceptance of beauty, woven into leis to say welcome or farewell.

Except for the Maoris of New Zealand, all Polynesians live in the tropics, where life inevitably moves at a leisurely pace. They have some trouble with disease, and there aren't enough doctors, but they have few problems of clothing and shelter, for their needs are minimal. They don't allow food to become overly troublesome or complicated, but their cooking is still distinctive and delicious. They eat fish every day, either broiled over an open fire, baked in leaves or other wrappings, simmered in chowder, or raw—marinated but uncooked. They enjoy all the familiar species of fish and shellfish (whatever happens to swim past the spear or into the net), plus dolphin. Octopus is a particular favorite.

Polynesians eat more fruit than vegetables—all the tropical varieties of bananas, papayas, pineapples, avocados,

Io Pua

tangerines, and grapefruit or pomelo. Coconut is much appreciated everywhere, for its water, milk, meat, oil, and husks which are made into cordage. When a coconut palm is felled, the heart of the tree provides a delicacy somewhat like white asparagus. Breadfruit, a nearly tasteless food, is steamed or baked and eaten as a bland accompaniment to seasoned dishes. In Pago Pago I found it slivered and fried crisp, like Hawaiian coconut chips.

The common meats of Polynesia are pork and chicken. Much cooking is done without fat, but lard and coconut oil are both available. Favorite vegetables are yams and taro leaves, resembling spinach. Poi, a pounded paste made from boiled taro roots, is the basic starch. In modern Honolulu you can buy it canned, bottled, or frozen. It's relatively flavorless in all forms.

Hawaii, our fiftieth state, was originally settled by Polynesians, and although it is today different from the rest of Polynesia in almost every way, Hawaii's luaus compare favorably with those I enjoyed in Samoa and Tahiti. The traditional luau is a feast built around a whole pig baked in a fire pit. To prepare it you must get up early, dig a hole in the ground, and line it with stones. Build a good fire in the hole, enough to make lots of long-lasting coals, and add some stones to get heated through. Dress a 100-pound pig for baking and rub it well with rock salt. Place hot stones in its cavity, wrap in leaves and burlap, and lower the bundle into the pit. Wrap yams, bananas, and breadfruit in leaves, and place them in the pit. Wrap anything else you want to cook, such as chickens. Cover the pit with leaves and earth, and go away for a swim in the lagoon. Come back later in the day with some fresh-caught fish, which you proceed to clean, cut into bites, and marinate in lime juice. After an hour change the marinade to coconut milk, and add garlic and ginger. Now dig everything out of the pit, open it all up, carve the pig, and serve.

If you think this sounds like too much work for easygoing people to do very often, you're right. Once you sail south of the Royal Hawaiian Hotel, life gets simpler. However, you can still enjoy a native cookout on the beach by just grilling a fish on an open fire. Never mind the pig and the pit. If you have the cash and if you think about it far enough in advance, there may be a bottle of beer cooling in the nearby stream. Or perhaps your neighbor has fermented some ti root, coconut, palm nuts or sugar cane.

After dinner somebody will bring out a kava bowl, and a couple of women will chew and scrub the fiber until the juice is ready to drink. It isn't alcoholic, but kava anesthetizes your mouth and tongue, and somehow it makes you want to dance. However, you'd better watch your step. In Samoa they may invite you to do the fire dance with real swords, and the Tahitian hula is about seven times as fast as the harmless one in Hawaii.

I'A OTA
(Marinated Fish)

This is a Tahitian version of raw fish marinated in lime and coconut milk, as prepared at the old bungalow hotel "Les Tropiques" just outside Papeete. Did migrants on giant rafts bring this dish from South America? It resembles the seviche of Peru, and supports the idea of Thor Heyerdahl's Kon-Tiki expedition. Incidentally, a strong acid like lime juice breaks down the large protein molecules of the fish exactly as heat would do it, so you may say the fish is cooked in lime if you like. Use any very fresh salt-water fish, filleted and trimmed of fat or tough fiber. Fresh tuna and striped bass are both good.

1 pound ocean fish, cut into bite-size chunks
1 small onion, sliced thin
1 garlic clove, mashed
½ cup fresh lime juice
½ cup coconut milk (page 1370)
  Salt and pepper
  Finely shredded carrot

Combine fish, onion, garlic, and lime juice, and marinate in refrigerator for 4 hours, stirring once or twice. Drain. Add coconut milk, and salt and pepper to taste; chill thoroughly. Serve garnished with carrot. Makes 4 servings.

OPIHI
(Hawaiian Marinated Scallops)

1 pound sea scallops, halved or quartered (small bites)
¾ cup fresh lemon juice
¼ teaspoon hot pepper sauce
½ teaspoon monosodium glutamate
¼ cup coconut milk (page 1370)
2 tablespoons dairy sour cream
½ cup minced green onion
  Salt and pepper to taste

Combine scallops, lemon juice, hot pepper sauce, and monosodium glutamate. Marinate in refrigerator for 4 hours, stirring once or twice. Drain, add remaining ingredients and chill well. Makes 4 servings.

Note: The same recipe can be used for shrimps, small ones split into halves, large ones cut into bites. Hawaiians often omit the coconut milk on their marinated fish, and more and more of them are eating it without any marinating, as the Japanese do. Raw octopus, called *he'e*, seasoned with hot pepper and onion, makes a good hors-d'oeuvre, too.

OPAKAPAKA KOALA
(Grilled Red Snapper)

1 red snapper (2 to 3 pounds)
¼ cup cooking oil
½ teaspoon ground ginger
  Salt

Smaller or larger snapper are just as good, and many other fish may be grilled in the same way. Have the fish cleaned but head left on. Rub all over with oil, coconut oil if available, but any cooking oil will do. Rub inside cavity with ginger. Place fish on oiled grill over charcoal and cook just until flesh tests done. Turn carefully and grill other side. Or broil for 15 minutes on each side. Season with salt to taste. Makes 4 servings.

PAPAI
(Kona Crab)

Mantis shrimps, Samoan and Kona crabs, spiny lobsters—these are some of the tropical Pacific's many shellfish. They are never better than when steamed or boiled as simply as this: Heat a large pot of sea water if available, or fresh water with salt and a little vinegar. Drop in as many Kona crabs as you want for the people you have to feed. Substitute Dungeness crabs on the West Coast, blue or rock crabs in the East. Cook for 10 minutes after water returns to boil. Cool under running water, remove claws and legs, and crack each one. Lift and tear off tail, lift off top shell, and remove spongy fingers and stomach. Break body into two pieces, sprinkle with fresh lime juice, and pick out meat.

IO PUA
(Roast Pork)

Assuming you don't want to cope with a 100-pound pig, this recipe will give you an acceptable substitute that can be done on a rotisserie over charcoal, or in the oven of your kitchen range.

½ cup soy sauce
4 garlic cloves, mashed
1 teaspoon ground ginger
½ cup firmly packed brown sugar
1 suckling pig (about 10 pounds) or 6-pound pork loin roast
  Salt

Combine soy sauce, garlic, ginger, and sugar. Rub over suckling pig inside and out. Place pig on spit and broil slowly for 3 hours, or until meat thermometer registers 185°F. Or roast in preheated slow oven (325°F.) until same temperature is reached. Season with salt to taste. Makes 8 or more servings.

UHA PUA
(Smoked Pork Chops)

6 smoked loin pork chops, cut thick
1 small fresh pineapple, cut into slices
  Salt and pepper

Place chops on rack or ribbed aluminum-foil tray. Cover each chop with a slice of pineapple. Roast in preheated slow oven

(300°F.) for 1 hour. Season with salt and pepper to taste. Makes 6 servings.

LAULAU PUA
(Pork and Salmon Packages)

Ti leaves or aluminum foil
1½ pounds taro leaves or spinach
1½ pounds boneless pork, cut into small cubes
½ pound smoked salmon or salted salmon, soaked
Salt and pepper

The taro plant, whose root gets pounded into poi, has tasty green leaves that resemble spinach. The leaves of the ti palm, whose root becomes an alcoholic drink (*okolehao*), are not edible, but they make excellent wrappers, as well as table decorations. *Laulaus* are wrapped in them the way tamales are wrapped in corn husks, but aluminum foil will serve the purpose. Take a 6- to 8-inch square of foil and place on it several whole taro leaves. Place 3 or 4 small cubes of pork and a bit of salmon in the center and sprinkle lightly with salt and pepper. Fold in the leaves and fold the foil, crimping or twisting the edges tight. Portion out ingredients to make 12 of these small packages. Place in steamer for 4 hours. For the final hour add whole yams (*uhi*) and bananas (*maia*) in their skins, to serve with *Laulau*. Makes 6 servings.

LAULAU I'A
(Fish Packages)

Laulaus can be made of many different ingredients, seasoned in many ways, and cooked by steaming, boiling, or baking.

2 pounds fish fillets
Aluminum foil
1 pound spinach
1 cup coconut milk (page 1370)
Salt and pepper

Divide the fish into 6 portions and cut squares of aluminum foil large enough to hold each one comfortably. Line foil with spinach leaves, top with piece of fish, and add the coconut milk, 2½ tablespoons per package, and salt and pepper to taste. Fold up tightly and bake in preheated moderate oven (375°F.) for 30 to 40 minutes. Makes 6 servings.

MOA NIU
(Coconut Chicken)

If you want something like a laulau *without the package, try this.*

¼ cup lard or butter
6 small chicken breasts, boned and cubed
1 package (10 ounces) frozen spinach
½ cup coconut milk
1 garlic clove, minced
Salt and pepper
½ cup macadamia nuts, chopped

Heat lard and stir-fry chicken until white. Cook spinach with coconut milk and garlic. Add to chicken. Season with salt and pepper to taste and garnish with macadamia nuts. Makes 6 servings.

LIMU NIU
(Coconut Spinach)

Similar to the preceding dish, this omits the meat and is garnished differently.

2 packages (10 ounces each) frozen spinach
½ cup coconut milk (page 1370)
2 tablespoons coconut oil or any cooking oil
Salt and pepper
1 small onion, minced
½ cup Hawaiian coconut chips, crushed

Cook spinach with coconut milk. Add oil and salt and pepper to taste. Garnish with raw onion and coconut chips. Makes 6 servings.

KUMU NIU PU'UWAI
(Hearts of Palm)

When they started clearing land to build more bungalows at the hotel where I lived in Tahiti, fresh hearts of palm appeared on the dinner menu. Fortunately coconut palms or cabbage palms (palmettos) are always being cut down somewhere, and this delicacy comes to us in cans. It should be treated like canned asparagus. Serve it cold as a salad: drain palm hearts, chill, cut into convenient-size pieces, and cover with your favorite oil and vinegar dressing. Or heat palm hearts in liquid from can, drain, and serve with hollandaise sauce. Hearts of palm may also be chopped and combined with chicken or sweetbreads to fill a patty shell. One can (14 ounces) makes 4 or more servings.

MAIA KALUA
(Baked Banana)

Fresh fruit is the favorite Polynesian dessert. Ices and ice cream are also popular. Here is something a bit fancier.

6 large bananas
¼ cup firmly packed brown sugar
½ to ¾ cup rum
1 cup coconut, toasted

Bake bananas in their skins in luau pit or in preheated hot oven (400°F.) for about 15 minutes. Remove bananas from skins and place on individual serving plates. Cover evenly with brown sugar, spoon on rum, and set aflame. When flame dies, sprinkle with coconut. Makes 6 servings.

POMANDER—An old-fashioned way of sweetening the air. A pomander ball is an orange, lemon, or lime studded with cloves and made fragrant with cinnamon and orrisroot. Its origins go back to the Middle Ages, when primitive sanitary conditions made the sweetening of the air imperative. But even in our super hygienic age pomander balls add great fragrance to closets, garment bags, and bureau drawers. They are extremely easy to make. The orrisroot required is available at drugstores.

HOW TO MAKE POMANDER BALLS

Oranges, lemons, or limes
Whole cloves
Ground cinnamon
Orrisroot

Wash oranges and wipe dry. Insert whole cloves in skins so that the whole surface of the fruit is covered, using a skewer or bobby pin to start holes if you find skins are difficult to pierce. If cloves are inserted in a straight line the skins are apt to crack. Mix equal parts of ground cinnamon and orrisroot and put a heaping teaspoon in a small bag along with 1 clove-stuck fruit. Shake bag to coat well with the mixture. Wrap loosely or place in a foil-covered tray or basket. Store in a dry place until fruit shrinks and hardens, usually 3 to 4 weeks. Wrap pomander ball in a cradle of net and tie with a colored ribbon.

OLD ENGLISH APPLE POMANDERS

Select small apples. Press whole cloves into apples, row after row, covering entire fruit. Dust with cinnamon. Let stand for a week; tie with narrow ribbon.

POMEGRANATE—The fruit of a bush or small tree with bright green leaves and orange-red flowers. Pomegranates are one of nature's most startling fruits, about the size of a large orange, with a vaguely six-sided shape, and a hard, leathery skin which can range in color from light yellow to deep purplish-red, but is most often a pinkish- or brownish-yellow. The flesh is a brilliant red, enveloping a large quantity of little seeds. In fact, pomegranates, to the eye and taste, appear to have more seeds than flesh. But what flesh there is has a delicious sweet, pleasantly acid taste. Pomegranate is eaten as a fruit, in salads, and sprinkled over desserts. Grenadine, a syrup especially popular in France, is made from pomegranates. The roots of the tree and the rinds and seeds of the fruit are used in medicine.

The tree is thought to be indigenous to Persia, but has been cultivated in the Mediterranean littoral and throughout southern Asia as far east as India for thousands of years. Its botanical name, *Punica granatum,* comes partly from its early Roman designation *malum punicum* or "apple of Carthage" and partly from *malum granatum* or "apple of many seeds."

The seeds of the pomegranate have long symbolized fertility in the mythology of many countries. Famous kings and heroes cultivated pomegranates. King Solomon had an orchard of the fruit and they are said to have grown in the fabulous Hanging Gardens of Babylon. The Greeks believed that the fruit was from the blood of Dionysius, a figure of life force and energy.

The Greeks also blamed the fact that winter must replace summer on the deliciousness of the pomegranate. Persephone, daughter of Demeter, the Greek goddess of agriculture, was captured by Pluto and taken off to the underworld. She was instructed to eat nothing during her stay. Unfortunately she succumbed and ate a few pomegranate seeds. For every seed that she had eaten she had to remain one month each year in the underworld, and during her annual stay, mourned by her mother, winter reigns on earth.

Pomegranates have been grown in this country since the middle of the 18th century. Although the tree will flourish in a variety of climates, it produces the best fruit in areas where the ripening period takes place in high temperatures and a dry atmosphere, and is most successfully grown in California and some of the Gulf states.

Availability and Purchasing Guide—In season from late September to November.

Select pomegranates that are heavy for their size with thin skin of bright color and fresh appearance.

Storage—Store in a cool dry place, or refrigerate for 2 to 3 days.

Caloric Value
☐ 3½ ounces, raw pulp = 63 calories
Basic Preparation—Cut into halves. With the fingers pull apart membranes. Carefully remove outer rind and inner membranes which have a bitter flavor. Collect the pulp capsules, eating the flesh. The seeds may be used as a colorful garnish.
☐ **To Make Juice**—Cut pomegranates into halves and press out juice on a reamer as you would the juice of an orange.

POMEGRANATE NECTAR
8 large pomegranates

Juice of 1 lemon
⅔ cup sugar, or to taste

Cut pomegranates into halves. Squeeze out juice on orange or lemon juicer, the way you would that of an orange or lemon. Strain juice. Add lemon juice and sugar. Chill. Serve diluted with water or soda, or over crushed ice. Makes 4 servings.

Pomegranate Ice
Make Pomegranate Nectar as above. Freeze in refrigerator trays until mushy. Beat to break up ice crystals. Refreeze.

ORANGE AND POMEGRANATE COMPOTE
4 navel oranges
2 pomegranates
1 tablespoon fresh lemon juice
1 tablespoon rosewater
  Sugar

With a sharp knife pare yellow rind and white skin off oranges. Cut into thin slices on plate to catch juice. Remove seeds. Place orange slices in glass serving dish. Cut pomegranates into quarters. Remove seeds. Remove white membranes between seeds. Sprinkle seeds over orange slices. Sprinkle with lemon juice, rosewater, and sugar to taste. Chill until ready to serve. Makes 4 servings.
Note: Rosewater can be bought in specialty stores and in some drugstores.

POMELO—Another name for grapefruit. The word would seem to be an early misspelling of "pummelo," a citrus fruit which is native to the East Indies and which the grapefruit greatly resembles.

POMPANO—An important salt-water food fish which ranges Atlantic waters from Cape Cod to Brazil, but is found in quantity only in the warm waters of Florida and the Gulf of Mexico. The pompano, related to the mackerel, reaches a length of about eighteen inches and has a silvery blue skin that is highly polished with gold reflections, and touches of orange on the fins. Its tail is deeply forked. Its rich yet delicate flavor makes it beloved by gourmets. New Orleans is famous for its pompano, served *en papillote,* in a paper bag.

Availability and Purchasing Guide—Sold fresh, whole or filleted. The market weight

is about one and a half pounds; the quantity is limited. The season is from January to April.

Select fish with firm flesh, clear full eyes, red gills and a shiny skin.
Storage—Wrap in moisture-proof paper or place in tightly covered container in coldest part of refrigerator.
☐ Refrigerator shelf, raw: 1 to 2 days
☐ Refrigerator shelf, cooked: 3 to 4 days
☐ Refrigerator frozen-food compartment, prepared for freezing: 2 to 3 weeks
☐ Freezer, prepared for freezing: 6 months
Nutritive Food Values—A good source of protein and fat.
☐ 3½ ounces, raw = 166 calories
Basic Preparation—See Perch, page 1363.
☐ **To Freeze**—Eviscerate and remove head and tail. Wash thoroughly and drain. Fillet fish if desired. Dip fish into a solution of 2 teaspoons ascorbic acid in 4 cups cold water for 20 seconds. Drain and wrap fish in moisture-vapor-proof wrapping, excluding as much air as possible. Seal.

SIMPLE POMPANO EN PAPILLOTE
4 squares of parchment paper
8 pompano fillets
1½ teaspoons butter
1½ teaspoons all-purpose flour
½ cup chicken bouillon
  Salt and pepper
8 large shrimps, cooked and chopped
½ cup chopped cooked crabmeat

Cut parchment paper large enough to enclose 2 fillets of pompano for each serving. Put 2 fillets on each piece of parchment. Melt butter and stir in flour. Gradually stir in bouillon and cook over low heat, stirring constantly, until smooth and thickened. Season to taste with salt and pepper. Spoon sauce over fish fillets. Top with chopped shrimps and crabmeat. Fold parchment over fish fillets and bake in preheated very hot oven (450°F.) for about 15 minutes, or until paper is puffed and brown. Serve immediately. Makes 6 servings.

POPCORN—A variety of edible corn, *Zea everta,* with small ears about six inches long. The kernels are very hard, small, pointed or round, depending on type, with a proportionately large amount of endosperm. Dry heat causes the moisture and air inside the kernel to explode into a starchy wrong-side-out white popped corn many times larger than its unpopped size. Popping quality depends on correct variety and proper uniform drying process. Popcorn, either whole or ground, is also consumed as a breakfast food.
Availability and Purchasing Guide—Available popped, plain or sweetened and in

specialty combinations. It is also available dry unpopped, in vacuum cans or packaged in a popping utensil.

□ 1 cup unpopped = 5 cups popped

Storage—Opened containers of uncooked popcorn, as well as unopened packages, must be kept dry.

□ Kitchen shelf, dry kernel, unopened: 1 year

□ Kitchen shelf, popped, in plastic bags: 2 weeks

□ Kitchen shelf, popped, opened: 2 days

Caloric Values

□ Plain, 3½ ounces, popped = 386 calories

Basic Preparation—Use metal popper or wire mesh basket, skillet, electric popper, or package where packed as a popper container. For electric and package-popper, follow manufacturer's directions. For metal poppers, baskets, and skillets, use only a small amount of dry popcorn to permit space for the corn as it pops. An exploded kernel may be 20 times its original size. Shake over hot heat until popping ceases. Add butter or margarine and salt, mixing well.

For skillet popping, butter is melted in heated pan *before adding* popcorn; about ½ cup is added. Sprinkle with salt. Follow directions given above for metal poppers.

CARAMEL POPCORN

1 cup sugar
½ cup light corn syrup
2 tablespoons dark molasses
½ cup water
2 tablespoons margarine
1 teaspoon vinegar
2 quarts popped corn

Combine all ingredients except corn. Cook syrup mixture until brittle when a little is tried in cold water (270°F. on a candy thermometer). Pour gradually over popped corn in large bowl. Mix and pour on buttered platter. Makes 2½ quarts.

CURRIED POPCORN

1 quart popped corn
¼ cup margarine
¼ teaspoon curry powder

Keep popped corn hot in the oven. Melt margarine, add curry powder, and pour over popped corn, mixing thoroughly. Makes 1 quart.

SUGARED POPCORN BALLS

2 cups sugar
⅔ cup light corn syrup
⅔ cup water
½ cup margarine
2 teaspoons salt
1½ teaspoons vanilla extract
6 quarts popped corn

Mix sugar, corn syrup, water, margarine, and salt in saucepan; cook until mixture becomes brittle when tried in cold water (270°F. on a candy thermometer). Add vanilla and stir; pour slowly over popped corn; mix. Grease fingers with extra mar-

garine and form into popcorn balls. Makes 24 medium balls.

MOLASSES POPCORN WITH PEANUTS

½ cup sugar
⅔ cup dark molasses
⅓ cup water
1 tablespoon vinegar
¼ teaspoon salt
1 tablespoon margarine
⅛ teaspoon baking soda
5 cups popped corn
1½ cups shelled peanuts

Mix sugar, molasses, water, vinegar, and salt; cook until syrup becomes brittle when a little is tried in cold water (270° F. on a candy thermometer). Add margarine and baking soda. Stir well and pour gradually over popped corn and peanuts, tossing until cool. Makes about 2 quarts.

POPOVER—A quick bread made from an egg-rich batter. A well-made popover is large, light, puffed up on top, with firm crisp brown walls. The center cavity is moist and yellow. Since popovers are steam-leavened, the thin batter must be baked in a hot oven in order to form steam rapidly. The egg protein allows the batter to expand and hold the steam and then coagulates to form the crusty walls. The walls should be firm before popovers are removed otherwise they will collapse. Popovers should be served while hot.

Caloric Value

□ 3½ ounces, baked = 224 calories

POPOVERS

2 eggs
1 cup milk
1 cup sifted all-purpose flour
¼ teaspoon salt

Beat eggs slightly; add milk. Then add flour and salt. Beat vigorously for 2 minutes. Pour batter into very hot greased custard cups or iron popover pans, filling two thirds full. Bake in preheated hot oven (425°F.) for about 40 minutes. Serve at once. Makes 6 large popovers.

Cheese Popovers

Use recipe for Popovers. Sprinkle filled pans with ¼ cup grated sharp Cheddar cheese before baking.

Almond Popovers

Use recipe for Popovers. Add ⅓ cup ground blanched almonds to sifted flour and salt. Mix and bake.

Whole-Wheat Popovers

Use recipe for Popovers. Add 2 teaspoons melted butter to eggs and milk. Substitute ½ cup whole-wheat flour for half of the white flour. Mix and bake.

POPPY SEED—The minute seeds of an annual species (*Papaver somniferum*) of the large Poppy family. The seeds make an excellent food flavoring and are used extensively in Austrian, Czechoslovakian, and Hungarian cooking and baking.

The little bluish-gray seeds look round to the eye, but they are actually kidney-shape. They scarcely ever grow more than 3/64 inch in length. Although small, they have a delicious crunchy texture and nutty flavor. They are especially popular sprinkled on rolls, bread, cake, cookies, and pastries. Sometimes they are crushed and sweetened and used as a filling for cakes, coffeecakes, and pastries. Added to cooked noodles and various kinds of salads they contribute both taste and texture.

Poppy seed can be bought whole in small containers in food stores, or in bulk, both whole and ground, in food stores specializing in Hungarian or Czechoslovakian products.

POPPY-SEED TORTE

8 eggs, separated
1½ cups sugar
½ cup raisins, plumped (in rum or brandy preferably) and dried
1 tablespoon grated lemon rind
1 teaspoon ground cinnamon
½ teaspoon ground cloves
½ pound ground poppy seed*
Sweetened whipped cream flavored to taste

Beat egg yolks until thick and lemon colored. Beat in sugar gradually. Add raisins, lemon rind, cinnamon, cloves, and poppy seed, beating well after each addition. Beat egg whites until stiff. Fold into mixture with hands. Grease two 9-inch pans and line with wax paper. Bake in preheated moderate oven (350°F.) for 30 to 35 minutes. Remove from pans and cool on rack. Put layers together with sweetened whipped cream. Makes 6 to 8 servings.

* Poppy seeds cannot be ground in a nut grinder or even in an electric blender, but ground poppy seeds can be bought in Hungarian and Czechoslovakian food stores. Do not try to substitute whole for ground ones, since their volume is very different.

HUNGARIAN POPPY-SEED KRINGLE

¼ cup milk, scalded
3 tablespoons sugar
¼ teaspoon salt
2¼ cups sifted all-purpose flour
⅓ cup shortening
1 package active dry yeast or 1 cake compressed yeast
¼ cup warm water*
1 egg, beaten
Poppy-Seed Filling
Confectioners'-Sugar Glaze
Candied fruits for decoration
Poppy seeds for decoration

Cool milk to lukewarm. Mix together next 3 ingredients. Cut in shortening with 2 knives or pastry blender until mixture resembles coarse meal. *Use very warm water (105°F. to 115°F.) for dry yeast; use lukewarm water (80°F. to 90°F.) for compressed. In large mixing bowl sprinkle yeast over warm water and stir until dissolved. Stir in milk. Add egg; gradually stir in flour mixture. Blend well for about 2 minutes. Place in greased bowl, turning dough over to grease top. Cover with foil or clean cloth and let rise in warm place until almost doubled in bulk, about 2 hours. Punch down and roll out on lightly floured board to a rectangle 8 x 16 inches. Spread with Poppy-Seed Filling. Starting at long end, roll up as for jelly roll. Place on a lightly greased cookie sheet. Turn ends in to form horseshoe or circle. Let rise until almost doubled in bulk, about 30 minutes. Bake in preheated moderate oven (350°F.) for 25 minutes. Cool on wire rack. Frost with Confectioners'-Sugar Glaze and decorate with candied fruits and poppy seeds. Makes 8 to 10 slices.

Poppy-Seed Filling

½ cup sugar
½ cup water
1 cup poppy seeds
¼ teaspoon ground cinnamon
½ cup seedless raisins
2 tablespoons honey
Grated rind of 1 lemon

Cook sugar and water together over medium heat, stirring until all sugar is dissolved. Boil for 5 minutes. Add remaining ingredients. Bring to boil and boil for 3 minutes longer, stirring constantly. Cool before using.

Confectioners'-Sugar Glaze

Mix ½ cup sifted confectioners' sugar with 2 teaspoons water and ⅛ teaspoon vanilla extract. Spread thinly over top of kringle.

POPPY-SEED COCONUT BARS

2 cups sifted cake flour
¼ teaspoon each of salt and baking soda
1¼ cups sugar
½ cup butter or margarine, melted
⅓ cup honey
1½ teaspoons vanilla extract
½ teaspoon almond extract
4 egg whites
2 tablespoons milk
1 cup flaked coconut
⅓ cup poppy seed

Sift the first 4 ingredients into a mixing bowl. Add the next 6 ingredients and mix well. Stir in coconut and poppy seed. Pour into 2 well-greased, wax-paper lined baking pans (9 x 9 x 2 inches). Bake in preheated moderate oven (350°F.) for 30 minutes, or until top is firm when pressed lightly with finger. Turn out on racks and peel off paper. Cool and cut each cake into 16 bars. Store airtight. Makes 32.

PORGY—The name applied to various marine food and game fish of the sea bream family. One genus, *Pagrus,* found in the Atlantic and the Mediterranean, is crimson with blue spots, and is called the red porgy. The variety familiar in Atlantic coastal waters from Cape Cod to South Carolina belongs to the *Stentotomus* genus and in New England is more commonly known as the scup. Its back is brown, tinged with pink, its underside is silvery. It grows up to eighteen inches long, with an average length of about twelve inches. The weight averages between one and two pounds. Smaller and lighter (half-pound) fish are also caught. Rarely filleted, usually served whole, the fish is tender, flaky, and of good flavor.
Availability—Sold fresh, whole. Season January to November.
Purchasing Guide—See Perch, page 1362.
Storage—See Perch, page 1362.
Nutritive Food Values—Good source of protein.
☐ 3½ ounces, raw = 112 calories
Basic Preparation—See Perch, page 1363. Porgies are particularly suitable for broiling, baking, and panfrying.

SAUTÉED PORGIES

Dip cleaned porgies in milk and roll in all-purpose flour. Sauté fish in hot butter in skillet until well browned on one side. Turn and brown the other side. Remove to a hot platter, season to taste and sprinkle with chopped parsley. Add a little more butter to skillet, melt and pour over fish.

PORGIES BAKED WITH TOMATOES

4 porgies, dressed, about 1 pound each
Salt
1 small onion, chopped
3 tablespoons olive oil
½ teaspoon basil
1 bay leaf
¼ teaspoon pepper
4 large tomatoes
½ cup water
½ cup buttered cracker crumbs
Parsley

Wipe fish with damp cloth and sprinkle lightly inside and out with salt. Sauté onion in the oil for 3 minutes. Add basil, bay leaf, pepper, and ¼ teaspoon salt. Simmer for 2 minutes. Arrange fish in shallow baking dish and pour hot onion

mixture over top. Arrange tomatoes around fish. Add the water. Bake in preheated moderate oven (350°F.) for about 30 minutes. About 10 minutes before fish are done, sprinkle tomatoes with the cracker crumbs. When done, garnish with parsley. Makes 4 servings.

PORK—The flesh of domestic swine is called pork, and it has been a vital element in the diets of many of the peoples of the world since the wild swine was first domesticated, reputedly by the Chinese, around 2900 B.C.

"The Gentleman That Pays the Rent" is what Irish farmers called the pig, which gave them both food and cash to pay the land rent. For the pig, as the saying goes, is man's best friend: every part of him can be used but the squeal. Here are the makings of noble hams, toothsome bacon, great pork roasts, juicy pork chops, spicy sausages, and lard for the tenderest of pies. In addition there are skins for bags and gloves, and bristles for brushes.

Although all flesh of domestic swine may properly be called pork, once pigs, or hogs as older swine are called, are butchered, the word "ham" is used to describe the rear-leg cuts, particularly when they are cured and/or smoked; and the word "bacon" is used to describe the side meat, with spareribs removed, when it is cured and smoked.

FRESH PORK

Availability—All year round. Most plentiful from October through January. For information on the cuts of pork available see listing under Retail Cuts of Pork, page 1439.

The pork variety meats available are liver, kidneys, hearts, and tongues.

Canned barbecued spareribs are available. Among the many canned pork products are pork and gravy, pork chop suey, pork and beans, pork liver pâté, pickled pork hocks, pickled pigs' feet, and pork sausage.

Frozen sweet and sour pork is available, as is a freeze-dried pork chop dinner and freeze-dried boneless pork chops.
Purchasing Guide—In high-quality pork the layer of external fat is firm and

white; the color of the lean is grayish-pink in young pork and turns a delicate rose color in older animals; the lean is firm, fine-grained, and well-marbled with fat; the bones are porous and pinkish in color.

The following rule of thumb is suggested for the amount of pork to buy:

- ¼ to ⅓ pound per serving for boneless cuts
- ⅓ to ½ pound per serving for cuts with some bone
- ¾ to 1 pound per serving for bony cuts

Storage—Remove from market paper or loosen wrapper; store unwrapped or loosely wrapped in coldest part of refrigerator. If pork cannot be used within time suggested, wrap closely and seal tightly in moisture- vapor-proof material and freeze quickly.

- Fresh variety meats, refrigerator shelf: 1 to 2 days
- Fresh chops and spareribs, refrigerator shelf, raw: 3 days
- Fresh roasts, refrigerator shelf, raw: 5 to 6 days
- Fresh, refrigerator frozen-food compartment, raw or cooked, prepared for freezing: 2 to 3 weeks
- Fresh ground pork, freezer, prepared for freezing: 1 to 3 months
- Fresh cuts or pieces, freezer, prepared for freezing, raw: 3 to 4 months
- Fresh, freezer, prepared for freezing, cooked: 2 to 3 months

- Canned, kitchen shelf: 1 year
- Canned, refrigerator shelf, opened: 2 to 3 days

Do not refreeze pork once it is thawed.

Nutritive Food Values—A very good to excellent source of high-quality protein, fair to good in iron, fair to good in niacin, fair in riboflavin, and very good to excellent in thiamine.

All the caloric values below are given for a 3½-ounce edible portion of cooked pork.

- Boston butt = 389 calories
- Picnic shoulder = 420 calories
- Loin roast = 387 calories
- Spareribs = 467 calories

Basic Preparation—Pork should be thoroughly cooked to bring out its full flavor, as well as to kill any trichinae organisms present. This does not mean overcooking, which reduces juiciness, flavor, tenderness, and food value (vitamins). Low cooking temperatures are recommended.

Remember that when meat is cooked in liquid, vitamins are lost to the liquid. Use this liquid in gravies, sauces, soups.

- **To Roast**—If desired, sprinkle meat with salt and pepper. Put, fat side up, on rack in open roasting pan. Insert meat thermometer in center of thickest part of meat so that it doesn't touch a bone. Do not add water, do not cover, and do not baste. Roast in preheated slow oven (300°F. to 325°F.) until meat thermometer registers 185°F., or well done. See

Timetable for Roasting Fresh Pork, below, for approximate cooking times.

- **To Broil**—Broiling in a range is not recommended for pork since the high temperature toughens and dries out the meat. However, chops can be broiled or grilled over charcoal if a moderate temperature is used.
- **To Panbroil**—Put meat in heavy skillet. Do not add fat or water and do not cover. Cook slowly, turning occasionally. Pour off fat from skillet as it accumulates. Brown meat on both sides. When well done, season with salt and pepper.
- **To Panfry**—Brown meat on both sides in small amount of fat. Season with salt and pepper, if desired. Do not cover. Cook over moderate heat until done, turning occasionally.
- **To Braise**—Brown meat on all sides in small amount of fat in heavy skillet, kettle or Dutch oven. Season with salt and pepper, if desired. Add small amount of liquid if necessary. Cover tightly. Cook over low heat until tender. See Timetable for Braising Fresh Pork, below, for approximate cooking times.
- **To Cook in Liquid**—Brown meat on all sides without added fat. Or use a small amount of lard if necessary. Season with salt and pepper, if desired. Cover with water or other liquid, put lid on kettle, and simmer until tender. If desired, add vegetables just long enough before serving for them to cook.
- **To Freeze**—Wrap fresh pork in mois-

RETAIL CUTS OF PORK WHERE THEY COME FROM

TENDER

1. **Jowl Section**
   Jowl bacon
2. **Shoulder Section**
   Boston butt
   Rolled Boston butt
   Blade steak
   Smoked shoulder butt
   Arm roast
   Fresh picnic
   Smoked picnic
   Cushion picnic
   Rolled fresh picnic
   Arm steak
   Porklet
   Sausage
   Clear plate (for lard)
3. **Loin Section**
   Blade loin roast
   Center loin roast
   Crown roast
   Sirloin roast
   Blade chops
   Rib chops
   Loin chops
   Sirloin chops
   Country-style backbone
   Butterfly chops
   Top loin chops
   Smoked loin chops
   Back ribs
   Rolled loin roast

   Tenderloin
   Canadian-style bacon
   Fat back
4. **Belly Section**
   Spareribs
   Slab bacon
   Sliced bacon
   Salt pork
5. **Leg Section**
   Cured ham, shank portion
   Cured ham, butt portion
   Cured ham, center slice
   Fresh ham roast
   Rolled fresh ham
   Cured ham, boneless roll

LESS TENDER
   Shanks
   Hocks
   Knuckles
   Feet
   Tails

VARIETY MEATS
   Liver
   Kidneys
   Hearts
   Tongues

GROUND PORK
   Ground pork
   Meatloaf mixture
   (with beef and veal)

TIMETABLE FOR ROASTING FRESH PORK

CUT	APPROX. WEIGHT (POUNDS)	APPROX. COOKING TIME (MINUTES PER POUND)
Loin		
Center	3 to 5	35 to 40
Half	5 to 7	40 to 45
Blade Loin or Sirloin	3 to 4	45 to 50
Picnic Shoulder	5 to 8	30 to 35
Rolled	3 to 5	40 to 45
Cushion	3 to 5	35 to 40
Boston Butt	4 to 6	35 to 50
Leg (fresh ham)		
Whole (bone in)	10 to 14	25 to 30
Whole (boneless)	7 to 10	35 to 40
Half (bone in)	5 to 7	40 to 45

TIMETABLE FOR BRAISING FRESH PORK

CUT	AVERAGE WEIGHT OR THICKNESS	APPROXIMATE TOTAL COOKING TIME
Rib and loin chops	¾ to 1½ inches	45 to 60 minutes
Spareribs	2 to 3 pounds	1½ hours
Tenderloin		
Whole	¾ to 1 pound	45 to 60 minutes
Fillets	½ inch	30 minutes
Shoulder steaks	¾ inch	45 to 60 minutes

ture- vapor-proof wrapping, excluding as much air as possible. Seal and freeze.

Do not add salt before freezing as this develops rancidity.

CURED PORK
(preserved by salting)

Availability and Purchasing Guide—The pork cuts available cured and uncooked are smoked shoulder butt, picnic, loin, loin chops, and salt pork. Cooked smoked picnics, bone in, are also available. (Bacon, Canadian bacon, and cured ham are, of course, also cured pork, but they are thought of under those names, and are so treated in this Encyclopedia.)

Canned picnics and loins are available.

Storage—Refrigerate in original wrapper. Do not freeze. Canned cured pork should generally be refrigerated. Be sure to check label for special instructions.

☐ Cured pork, refrigerator shelf: 1 week
☐ Salt pork: 2 to 3 weeks
☐ Canned cured pork, refrigerator shelf, unopened: 1 year, unless label directs otherwise

Nutritive Food Values—Cured pork has approximately the same food value as fresh pork. All the caloric values below are given for a 3½-ounce edible portion of cured pork.

☐ Butt, roasted = 330 calories
☐ Picnic, roasted = 323 calories
☐ Loin, roasted = 300 calories
☐ Salt pork, raw = 783 calories

Basic Preparation

☐ **To Heat Ready-to-Eat Picnic Shoulder**—Put meat on rack in shallow roasting pan. Add no water and do not baste. Bake in preheated slow oven (325°F.) for 20 minutes to the pound, or until roast meat thermometer registers 130°F.

☐ **To Bake**—Put uncooked picnic shoulder or loin on rack in shallow roasting pan. Add no water and do not baste. Bake in preheated slow oven (325°F.) for 25 to 30 minutes to the pound, or until meat thermometer registers 170°F.

☐ **To Cook in Liquid**—Put uncooked picnic shoulder or butt in kettle and cover with water. Bring to boil, cover, and simmer for 45 to 50 minutes to the pound, or until tender.

☐ **To Pan-Broil Chops**—Put chops in cold skillet over medium heat and cook for about 5 minutes on each side, or until browned and done.

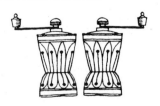

PORK COOK BOOK

FRESH PORK

SHOULDER

BRAISED PORK BUTT WITH CRANBERRIES

5- pound Boston butt
¾ cup water
½ teaspoon salt
½ teaspoon pepper
1½ cups whole cranberry sauce

Put meat in kettle just large enough to hold it. Add water and cook slowly until water has evaporated. Brown meat with fat left in pan. Pour off fat and add salt and pepper. Add cranberry sauce. Cover and simmer for 3 to 3½ hours, or until meat is tender. Check occasionally for dryness; add a little hot water if necessary, ¼ cup at a time. Makes 6 servings.

PORK BUTT WITH CARAWAY SAUERKRAUT

2 pounds lean Boston butt
¼ teaspoon peppercorns
2 pounds sauerkraut
2 tablespoons caraway seeds
½ cup firmly packed brown sugar
2 cups diced unpeeled green apples

Put pork in kettle containing 2 inches of boiling water and peppercorns. Simmer, covered, for 1½ to 2 hours, or until tender. Rinse sauerkraut under running cold water and drain thoroughly. Add sauerkraut, caraway seeds, sugar, and apples to pork. Cook for 20 minutes longer. Makes 4 to 6 servings.

Roast Pork with Oranges

PICNIC SHOULDER STUFFED WITH SAUERKRAUT

Buy a boned fresh picnic shoulder, allowing ½ pound for each serving. Sprinkle the inside with salt and pepper, and fill the pocket with sauerkraut. Sew or skewer the opening. Sprinkle with salt, pepper, and crumbled dried rosemary; dredge with all-purpose flour. Roast in preheated slow oven (325°F.) until meat thermometer registers 185°F. A 4-pound roast will take about 4 hours.

PORK STEAKS, BOUILLON

Dredge 4 pork-shoulder steaks with all-purpose flour and brown on both sides in 2 tablespoons hot shortening. Season with salt and pepper, and sprinkle with 1 chopped onion. Add 1 cup bouillon and ¼ teaspoon ground thyme. Cover and simmer for 35 to 40 minutes, turning several times. Makes 4 servings.

Tomato Pork Steaks

In Pork Steaks, Bouillon recipe, use tomato juice and marjoram for liquid and herb.

LOIN

CROWN ROAST OF PORK WITH SPROUTS AND CRANBERRIES

1 crown roast of pork (6 to 7 pounds)
  Salt and pepper
2 packages (10 ounces each) frozen Brussels sprouts, thawed
2 cups cooked rice (brown or wild)
1 cup fresh cranberries, rinsed and drained
¼ cup chutney, chopped
¼ cup sugar
½ teaspoon ground ginger

Sprinkle meat with salt and pepper. Chop 1 package of sprouts and mix with remaining ingredients. Put crown roast on a piece of foil in a shallow baking pan. Fill roast with stuffing. Bake in preheated slow oven (325°F.) for 3½ to 3¾ hours, depending on weight. During the last 30 minutes of cooking arrange remaining box of sprouts on bone ends. Brush occasionally with drippings. Makes 6 to 8 servings.

APPLE-STUFFED CROWN ROAST OF PORK

1 onion, chopped
¼ cup diced celery
2 cups diced tart apples
2 tablespoons butter or margarine
¼ cup molasses
¼ cup hot water
1 teaspoon grated lemon rind
  Juice of ½ lemon
1 teaspoon salt
½ teaspoon ground sage
4 cups bread cubes, toasted
1 crown roast of pork (7 pounds)

Cook onion, celery, and apples in butter for 5 minutes. Remove from heat and add remaining ingredients except pork.

Fill roast lightly with stuffing, heaping it up in the center. Roast, uncovered, in preheated slow oven (325°F.) for about 4 hours. Fasten paper frills to rib tips. Makes 8 servings.

ROAST PORK WITH SAGE ONIONS

3 pounds pork loin roast
  Salt
8 medium onions
½ to 1 teaspoon ground sage
3 tablespoons drippings from roast
  Pepper

Put pork on rack in shallow baking pan. Rub with salt. Roast in preheated slow oven (325°F.) for 2 hours, or until meat thermometer registers 185°F. Peel onions and cut into sixths. Sprinkle onions with sage and fry in drippings in skillet until golden-brown and tender. Season with salt and pepper to taste. Carve pork. Serve with onions. Makes 4 servings.

BARBECUED PORK, FOIL-BAKED POTATOES

5 pounds pork loin roast
¼ cup sugar
2 teaspoons each of paprika and salt
½ teaspoon each of pepper and garlic salt
1 teaspoon onion salt
1 tablespoon Worcestershire
½ teaspoon hot pepper sauce
½ cup fresh lemon juice
1 cup each of vinegar and water
6 large baking potatoes
⅓ cup melted butter or margarine

Put pork in open roasting pan. Mix remaining ingredients except last 2 in saucepan. Heat to boiling. Spoon some over meat. Roast in preheated slow oven (325°F.) for 3½ hours, or until a meat thermometer registers 185°F., brushing occasionally with sauce. About 1¾ hours before meat should be done, peel potatoes and cut into ¼-inch slices, putting each potato on square of foil. Brush generously with melted butter. Wrap tightly. Put in oven and bake for 1½ hours, or until done. Makes 6 servings.

PORK LOIN WITH SAUERKRAUT AND APPLES

5 pounds pork loin roast
  Salt and pepper
3½ cups (one 1-pound, 13-ounce can) sauerkraut, rinsed and drained
1 can (8 ounces) tomato sauce
¾ cup molasses
⅓ cup vinegar
3 medium apples, cored and sliced
⅓ cup melted butter or margarine
2 tablespoons fresh lemon juice
½ teaspoon ground cinnamon

Put pork on rack in shallow baking pan. Sprinkle with salt and pepper. Bake in preheated slow oven (325°F.) for 2½ hours. Combine sauerkraut, tomato sauce, ½ cup of the molasses, and the vinegar. Pour off excess fat from pan in which pork is roasting. Spread sauerkraut mixture over pork. Bake for 45 minutes longer, or until meat thermometer reg-

isters 185°F. Combine remaining molasses with apples, butter, lemon juice, and cinnamon. Cook, covered, over low heat for 20 minutes. Serve with pork and sauerkraut. Makes 6 to 8 servings.

FLORENTINE PORK COOKED IN MILK

4 pounds pork loin roast, boned
  Salt and pepper to taste
1 tablespoon crumbled dried rosemary
2 tablespoons butter or margarine
4 cups milk
1 can (4 ounces) mushrooms, drained, or ¼ pound mushrooms, sliced and sautéed in a little butter

Trim excess fat from meat. Rub with salt, pepper, and rosemary. Brown on all sides in butter. Add milk. Cover tightly and simmer over low heat for 2 to 2½ hours. Gravy will be thick and creamy and golden-brown. At serving time, place pork on hot serving platter and slice. Strain liquid if desired; add mushrooms. Thicken with flour-and-water paste if desired. Pour gravy over sliced pork. Makes 6 to 8 servings.

ROAST PORK AU VIN BLANC

Rub 5-pound piece of pork loin roast with ½ lemon, 1 cut garlic clove, and crumbled dried marjoram, salt, and pepper to taste. Roast in preheated moderate oven (375°F.) for 2½ to 3 hours, or until a meat thermometer registers 185°F. Remove meat and keep warm. Heat ⅓ cup dry white wine in pan. Stir in ¾ cup dairy sour cream and season to taste with salt and pepper. Serve with the pork. Makes 6 to 8 servings.

ROAST PORK WITH BROWNED VEGETABLES

Put a 5-pound piece of pork loin roast, fat side up, in open roasting pan. Rub with cut garlic clove. Roast in preheated slow oven (325°F.) for about 4¼ hours. About 1¼ hours before meat is done, put 12 peeled small potatoes, 12 carrots, and 12 white onions around the roast. Season with salt and pepper to taste. Turn vegetables occasionally. Makes 6 servings, with some meat left over.

CHINESE BROILED PORK

Split 3 pounds boned pork loin roast into halves lengthwise through thickest part and put in a shallow pan. Mix 1 cup soy sauce, ½ cup sherry, 2 crushed garlic cloves, and 1 teaspoon ground ginger. Pour over pork and let stand for 2 hours, turning meat occasionally. Broil slowly about 8 inches from hot coals, turning occasionally, for about 1 hour. When done, slice thin and serve with hot mustard. Makes 6 servings.

CARIBBEAN LOIN OF PORK IN BLACK SAUCE

4 to 5 pounds pork loin roast, with or without bones

2 teaspoons salt
1 teaspoon pepper
¼ cup lard
2 large onions, thickly sliced
¼ cup vinegar
12 ripe olives, pitted and chopped
1 tablespoon capers
⅓ cup seeded raisins, chopped
1 tablespoon brown sugar or molasses
4 cups water, about
2 large or 4 small onions, chopped
1½ pounds potatoes, pared and quartered (4 to 6 medium)

Sprinkle meat with salt and pepper. Brown on all sides in hot lard with sliced onions. The meat must be thoroughly browned. Discard onions. Pour off excess fat. Sprinkle meat with vinegar. Add olives, capers, raisins, sugar, and water. Bring to boil; lower heat. Simmer, covered, for 1½ to 2 hours. Turn meat occasionally. Add chopped onions and simmer for 30 minutes longer. Add potatoes and cook for 30 minutes longer, or until potatoes are done and sauce thickens. This dish must be cooked over very low heat. Makes 6 to 8 servings.

ROAST PORK WITH YAMS AND WHITE ONIONS

4 to 5 pounds pork loin roast
2 teaspoons salt
½ teaspoon pepper
6 medium yams, cooked and peeled
2 pounds small white onions, peeled and cooked
¾ cup apple juice or cider

Trim excess fat from meat. Rub with salt and pepper. Put on rack in shallow baking pan. Roast in preheated slow oven (325°F.) for 35 to 40 minutes to the pound, or until meat thermometer registers 185°F. Arrange yams and onions on rack beside pork. Bake for 15 minutes longer, basting frequently with apple juice. Garnish serving platter with spiced pears if desired. Makes 6 servings.

ROAST PORK WITH ORANGES

4 pounds pork loin
1 teaspoon powdered sage
Salt and pepper
1 cup water
1 tablespoon red currant jelly
Grated rind and juice of 1 orange
½ cup sherry
3 to 6 oranges, peeled and sectioned slightly on top*
Watercress

Rub pork with sage, salt, and pepper. Put on rack in shallow roasting pan and add the water. Roast, uncovered, in preheated slow oven (325°F.) for 2 hours, or until meat thermometer registers 170°F. About 45 minutes before meat is done, remove from oven and pour off fat, leaving pan juices. Spread jelly over meat and sprinkle with orange rind. Pour orange juice and sherry over meat. Finish roasting. Five minutes before meat is done, add oranges to heat slightly. Put meat on platter and surround with

oranges. Garnish oranges with sprigs of watercress. If desired, make gravy with the pan juices. Makes 6 servings.

*Allow ½ to 1 whole orange per serving.
Note: This is good with parsley potatoes and steamed cabbage wedges sprinkled with chopped pimiento.

CHOPS

BREADED PORK CHOPS, APPLE RINGS

8 thin center-cut loin pork chops (about 2 pounds)
Seasoned all-purpose flour
1 egg
2 tablespoons water
Fine dry bread crumbs
Fat for deep frying
2 large unpeeled red apples
2 tablespoons butter or margarine

Dredge pork chops with flour. Dip into egg beaten with water. Roll in bread crumbs. Fry in deep hot fat (375°F. on a frying thermometer) until golden-brown and done. Meanwhile, core unpeeled apples. Cut into ½-inch slices. Cook in butter in skillet until lightly browned and tender. Arrange chops and apple rings on hot platter. If gravy is desired, use a can of mushroom or celery soup thinned with a little milk and served piping hot. Makes 4 servings.

BARBECUED PORK CHOPS

¾ cup each of vinegar and ketchup
1½ cups water
1 medium onion, chopped
1 garlic clove, minced
2 teaspoons salt
½ teaspoon pepper
1 tablespoon Worcestershire
¼ teaspoon hot pepper sauce
3 tablespoons brown sugar
8 thick center-cut loin pork chops (about 3 pounds)

In saucepan mix vinegar and ketchup, water, onion, garlic, salt, pepper, Worcestershire, hot pepper sauce, and brown sugar. Simmer, uncovered, for 20 minutes, stirring occasionally. Pour over pork chops in a deep bowl; cool. Let stand in refrigerator for several hours or overnight. When ready to cook, arrange chops in shallow baking dish or roasting pan. Add the sauce. Bake, uncovered, in preheated moderate oven (350°F.) for

1½ hours, or until chops are tender, basting occasionally with the sauce. Makes 4 generous servings.

SMOTHERED PORK CHOPS

6 end loin pork chops (about 2¼ pounds)
Seasoned all-purpose flour
Shortening
½ cup water

Dredge pork chops with flour. Brown on both sides in small amount of shortening in skillet. Pour off shortening. Add water. Bring to boil; cover, lower heat, and simmer for 1 hour, or until chops are tender. Arrange chops on hot platter. If necessary, thicken drippings in skillet with a little flour blended with cold water. Season to taste and pour over chops. Serve with buttered yellow turnips if desired. Makes 6 servings.

PORK CHOPS, SWEET POTATOES, AND APPLES

About 3½ cups (one 1-pound, 13-ounce can) dry-pack sweet potatoes
2½ cups (one 1-pound, 4-ounce can) sliced apples
Salt and pepper to taste
4 end loin pork chops (about 1½ pounds)
½ cup water

Slice sweet potatoes and arrange with sliced apples in 1½-quart casserole. Sprinkle lightly with salt and pepper. Brown pork chops on both sides in skillet. Sprinkle with salt and pepper. Arrange on top of mixture in casserole. Add water. Bake, uncovered, in preheated moderate oven (350°F.) for 1¼ hours, or until chops are tender. Makes 4 servings.

ITALIAN PORK CHOPS WITH HERBS

1 to 2 teaspoons crushed dried rosemary
1 to 2 teaspoons ground sage
½ teaspoon garlic salt
⅛ teaspoon salt
¼ teaspoon pepper
4 large pork chops
Water
½ cup dry white wine

Combine herbs and seasonings. Rub mixture on both sides of chops and put chops in skillet. Pour water over chops to cover. Cook, covered, over low heat for about 1 hour. When the water has evap-

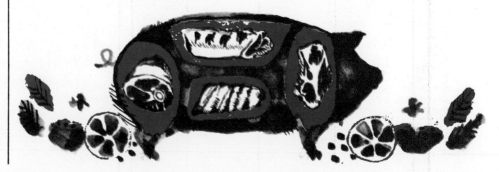

orated, the chops will begin to brown. Turn several times until browned on both sides. When chops are browned, add wine. Bring to boil and remove from heat. Put chops in heated serving dish and pour sauce over top. Makes 4 servings.

BAKED BONELESS PORK CHOPS

½ cup all-purpose flour
2 teaspoons paprika
1½ teaspoons salt
¼ teaspoon pepper
2 pounds boneless pork chops
½ cup butter or margarine
1 medium onion, minced
½ cup minced green pepper
1 can (4 ounces) sliced mushrooms, drained
2 cups milk
Juice of 1 lemon

Mix ¼ cup of the flour, the paprika, salt, and pepper. Dredge chops lightly with mixture. Heat butter in heavy skillet. Brown chops on both sides in it. Transfer to shallow baking dish. Add onion, green pepper, and mushrooms to skillet. Cook until onion is soft and golden. Stir in remaining flour. Blend in milk, stirring constantly, and cook until sauce is smooth and thickened. Season. Remove from heat; stir in lemon juice. Pour sauce over chops. Bake, covered, in preheated moderate oven (350°F.) for 1 hour. Makes 4 to 6 servings.

ORANGE PORK-CHOP SKILLET

6 pork chops, ½ inch thick
2 tablespoons butter or margarine
1 acorn squash
1 can (6 ounces) frozen orange juice, undiluted and thawed
2 tablespoons brown sugar
1½ teaspoons ground ginger
½ teaspoon ground allspice
¼ teaspoon hot pepper sauce
2 oranges

Trim pork chops of excess fat. Brown on both sides in butter; pour off all fat. Cut squash into ¾-inch-thick rings. Remove seeds and cut rings into halves. Arrange chops and squash in skillet. Combine orange juice, brown sugar, ginger, allspice, and hot pepper sauce. Pour over pork chops. Simmer, covered, for 45 minutes, or until chops are tender. Baste occasionally during cooking time. Cut oranges into ¼-inch slices; remove seeds. Cut slices into halves. Put orange slices on pork chops during the last 5 minutes of cooking time. Makes 6 servings.

HERB-STUFFED PORK BIRDS

8 very thin end loin pork chops
1 onion, chopped
2 tablespoons chopped parsley
2 tablespoons chopped celery and leaves
2 tablespoons butter or margarine
Salt
Dash of pepper
½ teaspoon poultry seasoning
2 cups soft bread crumbs
2 tablespoons all-purpose flour

2 tablespoons shortening
⅓ cup bouillon or water

Cut bones out of chops. Pound meat slightly. Make stuffing: Cook onion, parsley, and celery in butter; add ½ teaspoon salt, the pepper, and poultry seasoning; mix with bread crumbs; add a little water to moisten. Put some stuffing on each chop. Roll, and tie with string. Roll in flour; brown in shortening in heavy skillet. Add bouillon; cover; simmer for 1¼ hours. Makes 4 servings.

SIMPLE CHOUCROUTE GARNIE

6 thick slices of bacon
1 quart sauerkraut, rinsed and drained
6 pork chops, about ¾ inch thick
1 medium onion, sliced
12 peppercorns
6 juniper berries
2 cups chicken bouillon and 1 cup dry white wine or 3 cups chicken bouillon

Arrange bacon in bottom of large saucepan or deep skillet. Top with sauerkraut and pork chops. Combine remaining ingredients and pour over chops. Cover and simmer for about 1 hour. Makes 6 servings.

PORK TAMALE PIE

4 end loin pork chops
¾ cup yellow cornmeal
1½ teaspoons salt
1 small onion, chopped
½ cup diced celery
1½ cups (one 12-ounce can) tomatoes
½ cup canned whole-kernel corn
1 teaspoon chili powder
1 egg, beaten
¼ cup sliced stuffed olives

Trim any excess fat from chops and reserve. Cover chops with boiling water; bring to boil and simmer, covered, for 1 hour, or until meat is tender. Strain, reserving broth. Cool chops. Add enough water to broth to make 4 cups. Put in saucepan and bring to boil. Gradually add cornmeal and cook for 15 minutes, stirring frequently. Add salt. Fry 2 tablespoons chopped pork fat in skillet until crisp and browned. Add onion and celery and cook for a few minutes longer. Add to cornmeal mixture. Remove meat from bones and cut into small pieces. Add with next 4 ingredients to cornmeal mixture. Add olives. Put in shallow baking dish and bake in preheated moderate oven (350°F.) for about 1 hour. Makes 4 servings.

PORK CHOPS WITH PRUNES

6 center-cut pork chops, cut 1 inch thick
1 teaspoon salt
Dash of pepper
1 cup cooked chopped prunes
½ cup each of minced celery and finely chopped nuts
¼ teaspoon salt
1 thick slice of bread, cubed
Dairy sour cream (optional)

Sprinkle chops on both sides with salt and pepper. With a sharp knife cut a pocket into side of each chop. Mix remaining ingredients except cream and stuff mixture into chops. Place chops in a skillet and brown on both sides. Place chops in a well-greased casserole. Cover and bake in preheated moderate oven (350°F.) for 45 minutes, or until chops are tender. Chops may be spread with sour cream just before serving. Makes 6 servings.

ORANGE-BAKED PORK CHOPS

2 pounds thick lean pork chops
Salt and pepper
2 tablespoons all-purpose flour
1 to 2 oranges, sliced thin
½ cup fresh orange juice

Arrange meat in casserole. Sprinkle with salt, pepper, and flour, and top with orange slices. Pour orange juice over meat and oranges. Cover. Bake in preheated moderate oven (350°F.) for 1½ hours, or until tender. Makes 4 to 6 servings.

FRENCH COUNTRY-STYLE PORK CHOPS

4 medium carrots
2 small white turnips
2 celery stalks
4 leeks, white part only, or 8 green onions, white part only
4 small white onions, chopped
3½ cups (one 1-pound, 13-ounce can) tomatoes
⅛ teaspoon ground marjoram
1 bay leaf
¼ cup chopped parsley
¾ teaspoon salt
½ teaspoon pepper
⅓ cup consommé
1½ to 2 pounds blade pork chops, trimmed of excess fat

Cut carrots, turnips, celery, and leeks into 1½-inch-long julienne strips. Combine with next 7 ingredients in large heavy kettle. Add consommé; bring to a boil. Simmer, covered, for 5 minutes. Put pork chops on top of vegetables. Cover and simmer for about 1 hour, or until

thoroughly done. At serving time, place vegetables in center of serving dish and surround with pork chops. Makes 4 servings.

HUNGARIAN PORK CHOPS

6 pork chops, about ½ inch thick
Salt and pepper
1 medium onion, chopped
1 garlic clove, minced
3 tablespoons butter or margarine
1 bay leaf
¾ cup chicken bouillon
1 cup dairy sour cream
2 teaspoons paprika

Trim excess fat from pork chops and sprinkle chops with salt and pepper. Sauté onion and garlic in hot butter until soft and golden. Push aside or remove from skillet. Add pork chops and brown on both sides. Pour off fat. Lower heat and add bay leaf and bouillon. Cook, covered, over low heat for about 1 hour. Transfer chops to hot serving plate and keep hot. Reduce pan juices to half by cooking over high heat. Add sour cream and paprika and blend thoroughly with pan juices. Heat through, but do not boil. Pour sauce over chops. Makes 4 to 6 servings.

GEORGIA PORK CHOPS

4 large lean pork chops
Shortening
4 thick onion slices
¼ cup peanut butter
½ can (10½-ounce size) condensed mushroom soup
¼ cup milk
1 teaspoon each of Worcestershire and salt
⅛ teaspoon pepper

Brown pork chops on both sides in small amount of shortening. Pour off shortening. Top each chop with a slice of onion. Mix peanut butter, mushroom soup, milk, Worcestershire, salt, and pepper. Pour over chops. Cover and cook slowly for 45 minutes. Makes 4 servings.

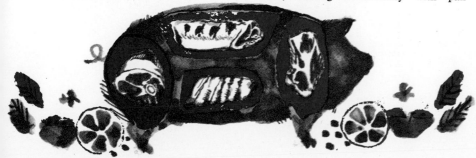

TENDERLOIN

BAKED PORK TENDERLOIN

2 small pork tenderloins
Salt and pepper
All-purpose flour
2 tablespoons cooking oil
1 celery stalk, sliced
1 small onion, chopped
1 envelope mushroom-soup mix

1½ cups water

Season small pork tenderloins with salt and pepper and roll in flour. Brown on all sides in hot oil. Remove to shallow baking dish. Lightly brown celery and onion in drippings. Put with meat. Mix mushroom-soup mix and water. Pour over meat. Cover; bake in moderate oven (350°F.) 2 hours. Makes 6 to 8 servings.

TOMATO PORK TENDERLOIN

1 large pork tenderloin
Salt and pepper
2 tablespoons all-purpose flour
3 tablespoons shortening
1 small onion, chopped
1 garlic clove, minced
1 beef or chicken bouillon cube
1 cup water
½ cup tomato juice

Slice tenderloin into 2-inch pieces and flatten slightly. Season with salt and pepper and roll in flour. Brown on both sides in shortening. Remove meat and lightly brown onion and garlic in drippings in skillet. Add remaining ingredients and bring to boil, stirring constantly. Return pork to skillet, cover; simmer 30 minutes. Makes 4 servings.

SAVORY PORK TENDERLOIN

Roll 8 thin slices of pork tenderloin in all-purpose flour. Brown on both sides in a little shortening. Drain off shortening and sprinkle meat with salt and pepper. Add 1 chopped medium onion, 1 teaspoon each of Worcestershire and sugar, ½ teaspoon chili powder, and 1 cup canned tomatoes. Cover; simmer for 1 hour, turning meat occasionally. Makes 4 servings.

STUFFED PORK TENDERLOIN

1 large pork tenderloin, split lengthwise
Salt and pepper
1 cup chopped cooked Brussels sprouts
½ cup chopped peeled cooked Italian chestnuts
3 tablespoons melted butter or margarine

Lay tenderloin out flat and sprinkle both sides with salt and pepper. Mix remaining ingredients and spread on meat. Roll up crosswise and tie. Put on rack in baking pan and bake in preheated very hot oven (450°F.) for 15 minutes. Reduce heat to slow (325°F.) and bake for 1 hour, basting occasionally with pan

liquid. Untie and slice. Makes 4 servings.

SPARERIBS

SPARERIBS SOYA

5 pounds spareribs
¼ cup all-purpose flour
1 tablespoon shortening
1 tablespoon ground ginger
½ cup soy sauce
Juice of 1 lemon
2 garlic cloves, crushed

Cut spareribs into 2-rib portions. Roll in flour. Melt shortening in Dutch oven and brown spareribs, a few pieces at a time. When all are browned, pour off shortening. Mix ginger, soy sauce, lemon juice, and garlic. Pour over ribs. Cover; bake in preheated slow oven (325°F.) for 2½ hours, basting with the sauce several times. Makes 6 servings.

PORK SPARERIBS, CHINESE STYLE

Spareribs cooked over charcoal are delectable. The spit method of cooking spareribs requires practically no attention, but they have to be watched and turned constantly when they are broiled. In either case, leave them in one piece and marinate for 4 to 5 hours in this: Combine ½ cup water or chicken broth, ¼ cup soy sauce, ¼ cup each of orange marmalade or honey and tomato ketchup, and 2 crushed garlic cloves. Drain; weave on the spit or broil over a slow fire for 1 to 1½ hours, basting with the marinade occasionally. The fat should be crisp, the meat tender and beautifully glazed. Cut ribs apart to serve.

Note: Pork tenderloins, soaked in this same marinade, are also delicious broiled, sliced very thin, and served with Chinese mustard as an appetizer.

FRESH HAM

ROAST FRESH HAM

1 fresh ham
1 garlic clove, cut
Salt and pepper
1 tablespoon caraway seeds
4 onions, sliced
2 carrots, sliced
2 medium celery stalks, sliced
1 bay leaf
3 whole cloves
1 cup water
1 cup dry white wine

Score skin of ham in two directions, making a diamond pattern. Rub meat on all sides with garlic, salt, pepper, and caraway seeds. Put onions, carrots, celery, bay leaf, and cloves on bottom of large baking pan. Add water. Put ham, skin side down, on vegetables. Roast, uncovered, in preheated slow oven (325°F.) for 1 hour. Baste frequently with pan

Caribbean Loin of Pork in Black Sauce

French Country-Style Pork Chops

juices and wine. Turn meat skin side up and roast until done. Roasting time is 25 minutes per pound, from the time meat is put in the oven. Or roast to 185°F. on a meat thermometer. Baste often with pan juices and wine. Serve with gravy or with raisin sauce, made with pan juices. Allow ½ pound uncooked meat for each serving.

BAKED FRESH HAM, SOUTHERN STYLE

- 6 pounds fresh ham
- 2 bay leaves
- 1 hot dried red pepper
- 1 cinnamon stick
- 2 tablespoons salt
- 1 tablespoon powdered mustard
- 1 tablespoon horseradish
- 1 garlic clove
  Whole cloves
- ½ cup firmly packed brown sugar

Put meat in kettle and cover with boiling water. Add next 4 ingredients. Bring to boil, cover, and simmer for 2 hours. Cool in the broth and refrigerate overnight. Remove rind from ham. Mix mustard and horseradish, and rub on fat. Insert garlic in the fat. Put on rack and bake in preheated slow oven (300°F.) for 2 hours. Score fat with a knife, stud with cloves, and sprinkle with the sugar. Bake for 1 hour longer, basting occasionally with drippings in the pan. Makes 8 to 10 servings.

ROAST FRESH HAM WITH SAVORY STUFFING

- 1 fresh ham, about 8 pounds
- 3 tablespoons butter or margarine
- ½ cup each of chopped onion and celery
  Ground sage
  Salt
  Seasoned pepper
- ¼ teaspoon paprika
- ⅛ teaspoon garlic salt
- ½ cup water
- 2 cups soft stale-bread crumbs
- ½ cup chopped parsley

Have the butcher remove the aitchbone and leg bone from the ham, leaving the shank bone in. Melt butter; add onion and celery, and cook slowly for about 10 minutes, stirring occasionally. Add 1½ teaspoons sage, ½ teaspoon salt, ¼ teaspoon pepper, the paprika, and garlic salt. Add the water and bring to boil. Stir in crumbs and parsley. Fill pocket in ham left by removing the leg bone. It is possible to remove the bone without cutting the meat, but if the meat is cut, tie together securely with cord. Score fat, leaving skin on shank. (When ready to serve, cut off skin and break up to serve.) Put meat, fat side up, on rack in shallow roasting pan. Sprinkle with salt, pepper, and a little sage. Do not cover, do not add water, and do not baste. Insert the point of a meat thermometer into center of thickest part of meat, not touching bone, fat, or stuffing. Roast in preheated

slow oven (325°F.) for about 4½ hours, or until meat thermometer registers 185° F. Makes 12 to 16 servings.

BARBECUED ROAST FRESH HAM

- 1 boned and rolled fresh ham, about 7 pounds
- 1 garlic clove, cut
- ¼ cup each of ketchup and vinegar
- ½ cup water
- 2 teaspoons salt
- ½ teaspoon pepper
- 1 teaspoon powdered mustard
- 1 teaspoon Worcestershire
  Dash of hot pepper sauce

Put meat on rack in shallow roasting pan. Rub with garlic. Mix remaining ingredients and brush meat with some of the mixture. Insert the point of a meat thermometer into thickest part of the meat. Cover and roast in preheated moderate oven (350°F.) for 2 hours, basting twice with the sauce. Uncover, reduce heat to slow (325°F.), and roast for 2½ hours longer, or until meat thermometer registers 185°F., basting several times with the sauce. Makes 10 servings.

VARIETY MEATS, PIGS' FEET, KNUCKLES, AND CRACKLINGS

BRAWN

Boil a pig's head, tongue, and heart until tender. They must be kept covered, simmering gently in just enough water to keep them stewing. When tender, remove the meat and cut into small dice. Boil down the liquid until about 3 cups remain. Strain and add salt and pepper to taste, 1 teaspoon grated lemon rind, a little ground cloves or mace, and ⅔ cup each of dry white wine and vinegar. Stir the meat into the sauce and simmer together for 10 minutes. Pour into a loaf pan (9 x 5 x 3 inches) and chill until set. Makes 6 to 8 servings.

Note: 4 to 5 pounds pigs' knuckles can be used in place of pig's head.

OLD-FASHIONED PORK-LIVER PUDDING

- 1 large veal shank
- 2 quarts water
- 1 bay leaf
- 2 parsley sprigs
- ½ teaspoon powdered thyme

- 1 celery stalk, diced
- 1 large onion, chopped
- 1 carrot, chopped
  Salt and pepper
- 2 pounds pork liver
- 1 pound boned fresh picnic shoulder
- 1 onion

Put veal shank, water, bay leaf, parsley, ¼ teaspoon thyme, celery, chopped onion, carrot, and salt and pepper to taste in kettle. Bring to boil and boil until liquid is reduced to 3 cups. Reserve liquid. Force liver, shoulder, and onion through food chopper, using medium blade. Add remaining thyme and salt and pepper; mix well. Put mixture in 3-quart casserole and strain a little of the hot reserved broth over it. Bake, covered, in preheated moderate oven (350°F.) for 1½ hours, basting every 15 minutes with remaining broth. Remove cover and bake for 1 hour longer. Cool; then chill. Let stand overnight in refrigerator before slicing. Serve as cold meat or for sandwiches. Makes 12 servings.

PIGS' FEET AND SAUERKRAUT

- 4 pigs' feet
  Water
- 1 large onion, quartered
- 2 teaspoons salt
- 1 quart fresh sauerkraut
- 1 tablespoon brown sugar
- 2 tablespoons ketchup
- ½ teaspoon caraway seed
- 1 teaspoon fresh lemon juice
- ¼ teaspoon pepper

Buy pigs' feet already cleaned. Put in large kettle with water to cover. Bring to boil, drain, and cover again with water. Repeat. Cover with 2 quarts water. Add the onion and salt. Bring to boil, cover, and simmer for 2 to 2½ hours, or until meat begins to fall from bones. Add more water if necessary during cooking. Transfer to a 3-quart casserole. Rinse sauerkraut and mix with meat and remaining ingredients. Bake in preheated moderate oven (375°F.) for 20 minutes, or until heated through. Good with boiled potatoes and applesauce. Makes 4 servings.

SPICY PICKLED PIGS' FEET

- 4 pigs' feet
- 3 cups cold water
- 3 cups cider vinegar
- 1 onion
- 12 peppercorns

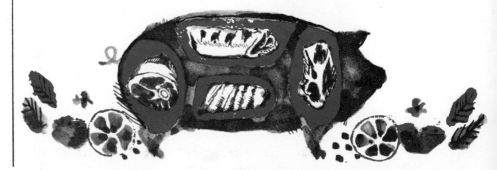

6 whole cloves
1 bay leaf
1 tablespoon salt

Have butcher split pigs' feet. Wash thoroughly and put in kettle. Add cold water and vinegar; bring to boil and skim. Add remaining ingredients and cover. Simmer gently for 2½ to 3 hours, or until meat is tender. Cool in liquid. Drain and chill. Makes 4 servings.

PORK HOCKS WITH VEGETABLES

4 pork hocks
  Water
1 bay leaf
1 garlic clove
2 teaspoons salt
¼ teaspoon pepper
4 sweet potatoes, peeled
4 large white turnips, peeled

Put hocks in kettle and cover with water. Add seasonings, cover, and simmer for 2 hours. Add potatoes and turnips cut into quarters. Cook for 30 minutes. Skin hocks and arrange on hot platter with vegetables. Makes 4 servings.

BREADED PIGS' KNUCKLES

6 pigs' knuckles
  Boiling water
1 medium onion, stuck with 3 cloves
2 teaspoons salt
1 egg, beaten
  Fine dry bread crumbs
½ cup shortening

Put pigs' knuckles in kettle with boiling water to cover. Cook for 15 minutes. Remove from boiling water with slotted spoon; reserve liquid. Plunge knuckles into cold water. Pull off skins. Return knuckles to liquid. Add onion and salt. Cook, covered, until meat falls off bones, about 2 hours. Drain. Pick meat off bones and cut into bite-size pieces. Dip first into egg, then into crumbs. Sauté on all sides in hot shortening until brown. Makes 4 servings.

PIGS' KNUCKLES, SAUERKRAUT, AND BISCUIT DUMPLINGS

3 pounds pigs' knuckles
2 pounds sauerkraut
6 cups water
2 tablespoons caraway seeds
  Salt
2 cups sifted all-purpose flour
2 teaspoons baking powder
1 tablespoon shortening
¾ cup milk

Put pigs' knuckles, sauerkraut, and water in kettle; cover and simmer for 3½ hours, or until meat is tender. Add caraway seeds and salt to taste. To prepare dumplings: Sift flour, baking powder, and ½ teaspoon salt. Cut in shortening. Stir in milk. Drop dumpling batter by tablespoonfuls into kettle. Cover and steam for 12 to 15 minutes without removing cover. Makes 4 servings.

PORK-TAIL STEW

2 pounds pork tails
2 tablespoons lard or other fat
2 small onions, sliced
1 large carrot, cut into thick slices
¼ cup diced celery
6 tablespoons all-purpose flour
2 cups hot water
1 cup canned tomatoes
3 whole cloves
3 bay leaves
  Salt and pepper

Have butcher cut tails into 2- or 3-inch pieces. Wash thoroughly twice in boiling water. Rinse in cold water and dry on absorbent paper. Brown lightly in the lard in kettle or Dutch oven. Add onion, carrot, and celery, and cook for 8 to 10 minutes. Brown flour in skillet and sprinkle over meat and vegetables. Add remaining ingredients. Bring to boil, cover, and simmer until meat begins to fall from bones, about 2 hours. Add more salt and pepper if necessary. Good with parsley potatoes, green beans, and red cabbage. Makes 4 servings.

CRACKLINGS AND LARD

Cut pork fat into small pieces. Put in skillet and fry until bits of fat are crisp and browned. Remove and drain on absorbent paper. These cracklings are delicious sprinkled with salt and served as a snack or added to corn-bread batter. Strain the remaining fat and keep in a cool place to use for making piecrust, biscuits, etc.

GROUND

DANISH PORK BALLS

2 pounds lean pork, ground
½ cup all-purpose flour
1 egg
1 tablespoon grated onion
1 teaspoon grated lemon rind

2 teaspoons salt
½ teaspoon pepper
½ cup carbonated or cold water
3 tablespoons butter or margarine
½ to ¾ cup light cream

Combine pork, flour, egg, onion, lemon rind, and salt and pepper. Blend thoroughly with a fork. Stir in water. Shape into meatballs, using hands. Heat butter in skillet. Brown pork balls on all sides. Lower heat and cook for 20 minutes, or until done. Transfer pork balls to heated serving dish and keep hot. Add cream to pan juices. Bring to a boil, stirring constantly. Pour over pork balls. Good with hash-browned potatoes. Makes 4 to 6 servings.

BOILED BEEF AND PORK LOAF WITH VEGETABLES

1 pound fresh pork
1 pound ground beef
1 medium onion, chopped
1 tablespoon salt
½ teaspoon pepper
1 teaspoon poultry seasoning
1 egg
¾ cup milk
⅓ cup fine dry bread crumbs
1 medium yellow turnip, peeled and cut into strips
2 packages (10 ounces each) frozen Lima beans
  Dairy sour cream

Have butcher grind pork; or force through food chopper twice, using medium blade. Combine with remaining ingredients except vegetables and sour cream and mix well. Shape into rounded loaf about 8 inches long. Put loaf on a square of cheesecloth. Roll up, and tie ends with cord. Put on trivet in large kettle; add 2 quarts lightly salted water. Cover, bring to boil, and simmer for 1¾ hours. Add turnip strips to meat during last 25 minutes of cooking. Add some of liquid to Lima beans and cook for 15 to 20 minutes. Slice meat and put on platter. Surround with vegetables. Spoon sour cream over meat. Makes 4 to 6 servings.

CHILI PORK BALLS IN TOMATO SAUCE

1 pound lean pork, ground
½ pound ground beef
1 tablespoon instant minced onion
¼ teaspoon each of pepper and garlic salt
2 tablespoons chili seasoning
1 tablespoon dried parsley
1 teaspoon salt
½ teaspoon crumbled dried oregano
1½ cups fine dry bread crumbs
¾ cup grated sharp Cheddar cheese
2 eggs, well beaten
  Tomato Sauce

Mix all ingredients except Tomato Sauce until well blended. Shape into 1½-inch balls. Brown in shortening. Drop meatballs into simmering Tomato Sauce and simmer, covered, for 45 minutes. Serve on rice. Makes 6 to 8 servings.

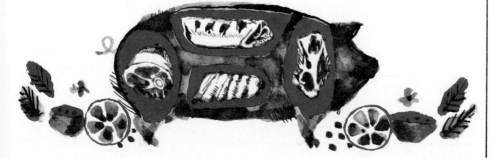

Tomato Sauce

3½ cups (one 1-pound, 13-ounce can) tomatoes
¼ cup instant minced onion
2 teaspoons salt
1 teaspoon sugar
¼ teaspoon each of garlic salt, pepper, and red hot sauce
1 teaspoon each of chili seasoning and crumbled dried oregano

Mix all ingredients together. Bring to boil, cover, and simmer for 30 minutes.

PORK BALLS WITH NOODLES

3 slices of white bread
⅓ cup milk
1 pound ground pork
1 small onion, chopped
1 teaspoon salt
¼ teaspoon pepper
Dash of ground nutmeg
1 egg
Cornstarch
2 tablespoons margarine
2 chicken bouillon cubes
1½ cups water
1 garlic clove, minced
6 ounces medium noodles
Chopped parsley

Soak bread in milk; crumble. Mix well with pork, onion, salt, pepper, nutmeg, and egg. Shape into 12 balls, roll in cornstarch, and brown in margarine. Add bouillon cubes, water, and garlic. Cover and simmer for 30 minutes. Add noodles and cook for 20 minutes longer, adding more water if necessary. Sprinkle with parsley. Makes 4 servings.

SMALL BONELESS CHUNKS OF PORK

MEXICAN PORK AND HOMINY

2 medium onions, chopped
2 tablespoons bacon fat or lard
2 tablespoons chili powder, or more if desired
2 pounds lean pork, cubed
1 bay leaf
1 teaspoon salt
½ teaspoon crumbled dried oregano
4 cups hot water
2 cups cooked hominy

Cook onions in hot bacon fat until soft and golden. Remove. Stir chili powder into fat. Add pork and brown on all sides. Add onions and all other ingre-

dients except hominy. Simmer, covered, for 2½ hours, or until meat is tender. Add hominy and heat. Makes 4 to 6 servings.

SWEET AND PUNGENT PORK

1½ pounds lean pork, cut into ½-inch cubes
¼ cup cooking oil
2 green peppers, cut into eighths and seeded
2½ cups (one 1-pound, 4-ounce can) sliced apples
1 cup chicken bouillon
3 tablespoons cornstarch
2 to 3 tablespoons soy sauce
½ cup vinegar
½ cup sugar
½ teaspoon salt
¼ teaspoon pepper
Hot rice

Brown pork on all sides in hot oil. Add green peppers, apples, and ⅓ cup bouillon. Simmer, covered, for 20 minutes, stirring frequently. Blend together until smooth remaining bouillon, the cornstarch, soy sauce, vinegar, sugar, and salt and pepper. Add slowly to pork mixture. Cook until sauce thickens, stirring. Serve over rice. Makes 4 to 6 servings.

CURRIED PORK

½ cup all-purpose flour
Salt and pepper
½ teaspoon ground ginger
2 pounds lean pork, cut into 1-inch cubes
¼ cup butter or margarine
1 tablespoon curry powder
⅛ teaspoon chili powder
1 cup chopped onions
¾ cup chopped green peppers
2 cups hot bouillon or water

Combine flour, 1 teaspoon salt, ¼ teaspoon pepper, and the ginger. Coat pork with this mixture. Brown on all sides in hot butter, stirring occasionally. Stir in curry and chili powder. Add onions, green peppers, and bouillon. Simmer, covered, for 1¼ to 1½ hours, or until pork is tender, stirring occasionally. Makes 6 servings.

CHINESE-PORK-FRIED RICE

1 pound pork
1 garlic clove, minced
1 onion, chopped
1 cup uncooked rice
Salt and pepper

1 can (3 ounces) sliced mushrooms, undrained
1¾ cups water
1 egg
Soy sauce

Cut pork into thin strips. Brown in skillet with garlic and onion. Add rice and cook until lightly browned, stirring frequently. Add 1 teaspoon salt, ¼ teaspoon pepper, the mushrooms, and the water. Bring to boil; cover and simmer for 25 minutes, or until rice is tender. Beat egg with salt and pepper to taste. Put in hot greased 8-inch skillet. Fry until firm, turning once; cut into strips. Put rice mixture in serving bowl; arrange egg strips on top. Serve at once with soy sauce. Makes 4 servings.

BAKED PORK AND NOODLES

3½ pounds pork
1 onion, chopped
1 cup sliced celery
1 teaspoon salt
½ teaspoon crumbled dried thyme
¼ teaspoon pepper
1 can (10½ ounces) condensed mushroom soup
1 cup water
3 cups uncooked wide noodles
1 cup (one 8½-ounce can) peas, undrained
1 can (3 ounces) chopped mushrooms
2 pimientos, diced
½ cup grated Cheddar cheese
Buttered bread crumbs

Remove excess fat from pork. Render some of the fat in skillet. Cut meat into small cubes; brown in the fat. Add onion, celery, salt, thyme, pepper, mushroom soup, and water. Cover; simmer for 1 hour. Cook and drain noodles. Add with peas, mushrooms, pimientos, and cheese to first mixture. Pour into large shallow baking dish. Top with buttered bread crumbs; bake in preheated moderate oven (375°F.) for 30 minutes. Makes 6 to 8 servings.

PORK HAWAIIAN

1½ pounds pork
1 egg, well beaten
1 tablespoon milk
3 tablespoons all-purpose flour
½ teaspoon salt
¼ cup margarine
1 garlic clove, minced
1 beef bouillon cube
1 cup hot water
1 cup pineapple tidbits, drained
½ cup pineapple juice
1 carrot, sliced
2 tablespoons each of vinegar and soy sauce
1 tablespoon sugar
1 green pepper, seeded and cut into eighths
2 tablespoons cornstarch

Cut pork into ½-inch strips. Mix until smooth egg, milk, flour, and salt. Dip pork strips into mixture; fry in 3 tablespoons of the margarine until browned and done. Sauté garlic in remaining margarine for 1 minute. Add bouillon cube,

hot water, pineapple tidbits and juice, carrot, vinegar and soy sauce, sugar, and green pepper. Simmer for 5 minutes. Add meat; thicken with cornstarch mixed with cold water. Serve on rice. Makes 4 servings.

PORK, STROGANOFF STYLE

1 pound lean pork
¼ cup seasoned all-purpose flour
2 tablespoons hot shortening
1 cup water
1 beef bouillon cube
3 tablespoons ketchup or tomato purée
1 teaspoon Worcestershire
1 can (3 ounces) sliced mushrooms with liquid
1 cup dairy sour cream

Cut pork into thin strips and dredge with seasoned flour. Brown in hot shortening. Add water, bouillon cube, ketchup, Worcestershire, and mushrooms with the liquid. Cover and simmer for about 30 minutes. Just before serving, stir in sour cream. Serve with hot rice. Makes 4 servings.

AUSTRIAN PIQUANT PORK WITH HORSERADISH

2 pounds lean pork, cut into 1½-inch cubes
2 tablespoons butter or margarine
2 cups water
1 cup vinegar
1 medium onion, stuck with 3 cloves
1 medium carrot
1 small celery root (celeriac), peeled, or 1 celery stalk
1 tablespoon salt
1 teaspoon caraway seeds
½ teaspoon pepper
¼ cup prepared horseradish
Boiled potatoes

Brown pork in hot butter on all sides in deep kettle. Add water and all other ingredients except last 2. Simmer, covered, for 1½ hours, or until tender. Transfer meat to hot platter; keep hot. Force liquid and vegetables through sieve, or purée in electric blender. Pour sauce over meat. Sprinkle with horseradish. Serve with potatoes. Makes 4 to 6 servings.

PORK-VEGETABLE SKILLET

2 teaspoons sugar
1 pound boneless pork, diced
¼ cup all-purpose flour
2½ cups water
1 teaspoon salt
Dash of pepper
1 teaspoon Worcestershire
Dash of hot pepper sauce
1 onion, sliced
4 green peppers
3 carrots, sliced
Hot cooked rice

Melt sugar and cook in large skillet until dark brown. Add pork and cook until browned. Stir in flour and brown lightly. Add water and seasonings. Simmer, covered, for 30 minutes. Add onion; simmer for 30 minutes longer. Add peppers cut into eighths and the carrots. Simmer

again for 30 minutes. Serve on rice. Makes 4 servings.

ITALIAN STEWED PORK WITH CELERY

1 garlic clove
2 tablespoons olive or cooking oil
1 carrot, minced
2 pounds lean pork, cut into bite-size pieces
1 cup dry red or white wine
1½ teaspoons salt
½ teaspoon pepper
2½ cups sliced celery
Bouillon or water
1 cup chopped fresh or canned tomatoes

Brown garlic in oil and discard garlic. Add carrot, pork, wine, salt, and pepper. Cook, covered, over low heat for 1½ hours. Cook celery in bouillon until almost tender. Drain. Add cooked celery and tomatoes to pork mixture for the last 15 minutes of cooking time. Makes 4 to 6 servings.

PORK-VEGETABLE BAKE

1 pound pork
2 onions, sliced
1 green pepper, seeded and cut into rings
1 potato, peeled and thinly sliced
1 cup raw rice
3⅔ cups (one 1-pound, 13-ounce can) tomatoes
1 small eggplant, peeled and diced
1 cup drained canned okra
Salt and pepper

Cube pork and brown in hot greased skillet. Add onions and green pepper; sauté for 5 minutes. Season. Grease a 3-quart casserole and line with potato. Sprinkle with ½ cup of the rice and half of the tomatoes. Season. Add eggplant and pork mixture. Sprinkle with remaining rice and the okra. Add rest of tomatoes; season with salt and pepper. Cover; bake in preheated moderate oven (375° F.) for 1 hour. Uncover; bake for 15 minutes longer. Makes 6 servings.

LEFTOVER COOKED PORK

PORK CHOW MEIN

2 onions, sliced
2 cups sliced celery
1 tablespoon cooking oil
2 cups diced cooked pork
2 cups water
3 tablespoons soy sauce
1 tablespoon molasses
1 can (19 ounces) bean sprouts, drained
3 tablespoons cornstarch

Sauté onions and celery in oil for 5 minutes. Add pork, water, soy sauce, and molasses. Simmer for 15 minutes. Add bean sprouts; heat. Stir in cornstarch blended with a little cold water. Cook until thickened. Serve on chow-mein noodles. Makes 4 servings.

CREAMY PORK HASH

1 medium onion, sliced
3 tablespoons butter or margarine
1 can (10½ ounces) condensed cream-of-mushroom soup
½ cup milk
1 teaspoon Worcestershire
½ teaspoon hot pepper sauce
1 cup diced cooked pork
1 cup diced cooked potatoes
½ cup cooked peas
1 teaspoon paprika

Sauté onion in hot butter until soft and golden. Blend in soup, milk, Worcestershire, and hot pepper sauce. Add remaining ingredients. Cook over low heat for 10 minutes, or until heated through, stirring often. Makes 4 servings.

BROWN PORK HASH

2 cups chopped cold roast pork
2 cups chopped cold boiled potatoes
¼ cup butter or margarine
1 large onion, sliced
1½ teaspoons salt
½ teaspoon pepper
Boiling water or bouillon
2 tablespoons sherry (optional)

Brown meat and potatoes in hot butter. Add onion, salt, pepper, and enough boiling hot water or bouillon to cover. Bring to boil; reduce heat. Cover and simmer for 45 minutes. The water must be absorbed. Stir in sherry. Makes 4 to 6 servings.

LEFTOVER PORK IN OLIVE SAUCE

2 tablespoons all-purpose flour
2 tablespoons shortening
½ teaspoon salt
½ teaspoon paprika
2 tablespoons brown sugar
1 tablespoon fresh lemon juice
1 tablespoon chopped onion
1 cup water
2½ to 3 cups cold cooked pork, cut into strips
½ cup chopped pimiento-stuffed olives

Stir flour into hot shortening and cook until light brown. Add all except last 2 ingredients. Blend thoroughly. Cook over low heat for 5 minutes, stirring constantly. Put meat in sauce. Cook, covered, over low heat until meat is heated through, about 10 minutes. Stir occasionally. Add olives and cook for 5 minutes longer, or until heated. Makes 4 servings.

LEFTOVER-PORK CASSEROLE

2 slices of bacon
1 large onion, chopped
1 can (10½ ounces) condensed tomato soup
4 cups cooked dried Lima beans
2 cups diced cooked pork
½ cup water
Salt and pepper to taste
½ cup buttered soft bread crumbs

Cook bacon until crisp; drain and crumble. Brown onion in fat. Add remaining ingredients except bread crumbs and mix thoroughly. Transfer to 2-quart casserole. Sprinkle with bread crumbs. Bake in preheated hot oven (425°F.) for 15 minutes, or until crumbs are browned. Makes 4 to 6 servings.

CURED PORK

SIMMERED SMOKED PICNIC SHOULDER WITH CURRANT-MUSTARD SAUCE

1 uncooked smoked picnic shoulder, about 6 pounds
1 cup red currant jelly
1 teaspoon powdered mustard
2 teaspoons white vinegar
2 tablespoons dark corn syrup

Put pork in kettle and cover with water; bring to boil and simmer, covered, for about 3½ hours. Mix remaining ingredients in small saucepan and bring to boil, stirring until jelly is melted and ingredients are blended. Serve with the pork. Makes 8 servings.

SMOKED BUTT BOILED DINNER

1 smoked boneless shoulder butt (about 3 pounds)
4 peppercorns
1 onion
4 medium sweet potatoes, peeled
1 pound green beans
4 to 6 ears of corn, husked

Cover smoked butt with water. Add peppercorns and onion; simmer for 2 hours, or until tender. Add sweet potatoes during last 35 minutes of cooking. Add small amount of liquid to beans and cook for 15 minutes, or until tender. Remove meat and potatoes from liquid and keep hot. Add corn and boil for 5 minutes. Makes 4 servings, with meat left over.

Note: Dilute liquid with water to use in making bean or pea soup. Leftover meat can be served cold or sliced thin, browned lightly, and served with eggs.

BROWN GLAZED PORK BUTT

1 smoked shoulder butt (about 2½ pounds)
Water
4 orange slices
4 pineapple slices
4 sweet potatoes, cooked
Corn syrup
Brown sugar

Cover butt with water. Simmer until tender, allowing about 50 minutes per pound. Remove to baking dish; slice. Arrange orange and pineapple slices and potatoes around meat. Pour a little corn syrup over meat and sweet potatoes. Sprinkle all with brown sugar. Bake in preheated hot oven (400°F.) for about 25 minutes, until browned and glazed. Makes 4 servings.

SMOKED LOIN OF PORK WITH BURGUNDY-CHERRY SAUCE

7 pounds smoked pork loin
2 cups (one 1-pound can) black cherries in syrup
2 tablespoons cornstarch
¾ cup Burgundy wine
2 tablespoons wine vinegar
¼ cup light corn syrup
2 teaspoons fresh lemon juice

Put pork loin on rack and bake in preheated slow oven (325°F.) for about 3½ hours. Drain cherries, reserving ¾ cup of the syrup. Blend the reserved syrup with cornstarch. Add Burgundy, vinegar, and corn syrup. Bring to boil, stirring constantly. Add lemon juice. Serve hot with the pork. Makes 10 servings.

PORK AND POTATO SCALLOP

4 cups sliced peeled raw potatoes
1 small onion, sliced
2 tablespoons all-purpose flour
Salt and pepper
1½ cups hot milk
4 smoked pork loin chops (about 1½ pounds)

Put a layer of potatoes and onion in 2-quart casserole. Sprinkle with some of the flour, salt, and pepper. Repeat, ending with layer of potatoes. Add milk, or enough almost to cover potatoes. Brown pork chops on both sides in hot skillet. Arrange chops on top of potatoes. Bake, covered, in preheated moderate oven (350°F.) for 45 minutes. Uncover and bake for 15 minutes longer, or until potatoes are tender. Makes 4 servings.

BAKED SALT PORK AND POTATOES

½ pound salt pork, diced
6 medium potatoes, peeled
Salt and pepper

Brown salt pork lightly and drain off fat. Cut potatoes into ½-inch slices. Wash and dry on absorbent paper. In 2½-quart casserole, put a layer of pork; add a layer of potato slices and continue alternating layers until all ingredients are used, sprinkling the potato layers lightly with salt and pepper. Cover, and bake in preheated moderate oven (350°F.) for 1½ hours, or until potatoes are tender. Add a little water or consommé during baking if necessary to keep mixture from becoming dry. Makes 4 to 6 servings.

PORRIDGE—A dish made by boiling a grain or vegetable in water or milk to make a thickened soup to be eaten with a spoon. Originally the dish was made of meat and vegetables, and often thickened with barley or another cereal. It was for centuries the subsistence of millions of people throughout the whole of Europe. Later, the word came to be used chiefly in connection with boiled grains, and although a porridge can be made from any grain, the word is now associated mostly with oatmeal.

Porridge, which Robert Burns called "chief o' Scotia's food" is the national breakfast dish there. The Scottish speak of it in the plural and some of their customs of eating it are interesting. For one, it used to be eaten standing up, on the principle that "a staunin' sack fills the fu'est." In cooking it, when it was stirred with a stick called a spurtle or a theevil, people were guided by an old Scotch saying "when the porridge begin to say 'Gargunnock' or 'Perth,' it's time they were dished." The proper way to dish the porridge was to ladle it into wooden porringers, and to serve it with individual bowls of cream, milk, or buttermilk. One took a spoonful of porridge, dipped in into the bowl of one's choice, and ate it.

OLD-FASHIONED OATMEAL PORRIDGE

2½ cups water
½ teaspoon salt
½ cup Scotch or Scotch-style rolled oats

Bring water and salt to a boil. Sprinkle in the oats, stirring constantly to prevent lumping. Reduce heat, cover, and simmer for about 25 minutes, stirring occasionally. Serve hot with milk or cream, and with honey, maple syrup, or fruits, if desired. Makes 6 servings.

PORT—The vineyards of the Oporto district of Portugal produce a sweet wine that, when fortified, is known as port. It is the best known of all after-dinner wines.

Port, like sherry, is a fortified wine. That is to say, brandy is added to the wine at various stages of the fermentation. Port has an average of seventeen to twenty-five per cent alcohol.

There are four main varieties of port: vintage port, crusted port, ruby port, and tawny port. The vintage port, deep red in color, is a blend of great wines of an outstanding year, and is aged in the bottle for twenty years or more. Crusted port is a little less fine than the vintage port, and is aged in the bottle for about ten years. Both these ports must be decanted because they form a crusty sediment in the bottle. Ruby port is a young wine matured in the cask. It is light, with an agreeable, fruity flavor. Usually a mixture of various vintages, it is, as its name implies, a deep ruby-red in color. Tawny port is an older ruby port that has faded to a tawny color and become mellower. It is aged for a long time, usually about twenty years, in the cask, and the wood gives it its characteristic flavor. There is some white port made from white grapes.

PORTUGUESE COOKERY
by Lea Maidman

Portuguese food offers three delightful surprises to the newcomer: its remarkable affinity to the American palate; its unexpected individuality; an unusual delicacy certain to titillate the taste buds of the most sophisticated epicurean. It is easy to prepare, easy on the digestion, and easy on the eye, and the Portuguese have a happy simplicity in their culinary approach. They believe in getting the ultimate nutritional value and flavor out of their food and have the highest respect for quality. The result is an exquisitely refined cuisine, which is altogether different, on a low-cost budget.

As in most interesting situations, there are certain inconsistencies. For example, despite their profuse, constant use of olive oil, Portuguese food is neither rich, heavy, nor greasy. Discreet in their use of seasoning, no kitchen is considered functional without a fair supply of garlic. Yet it is seldom overused. Again, innumerable tasty sauces are put together with a minimum of effort, but the Portuguese custom of reshaping the common potato into small barrel forms is so prevalent, one might think potatoes grow that way in Portugal.

Faithful to the blessings of their fertile lands and spawning seas, their fish, fruits, and vegetables are used with delightful originality and good cooking sense. Everything seems to grow to extra perfection in this magnificent country, flowers blooming everywhere with such beauty as to effect masterpieces of artificial artistry.

Soup and fish are Portugal's most popular eating. And while most of their recipes are classics sentimentally handed down from generation to generation, every locale has its own variation. Salt cod, which Escoffier once said put the world in Portugal's debt for having discovered this dry fish (long before refrigeration), is still the national favorite.

Fish common to the Portuguese table may sound like denizens of an aquarium to us, but they are daily fare in the markets: moray, conger, sea bream, frogfish, turbot, plaice, octopus,

and barnacles, to name a few. All of these and many, many others have a happy get-together in that most delectable of fish stews—*Caldeirada*. Said to have inspired the French and Spanish bouillabaisse, when the Portuguese get going on this one the password is "The more variety, the merrier!"

In *Caldeirada* and many other Portuguese specialties, coriander is the favorite seasoning. As common in the markets as parsley, this herb, used fresh, has an originality and delicate pungency well worth home cultivation. Meanwhile, the dry herb can provide the flavor if not the full fragrance. Another interesting substitute is improvised by mashing tender fresh mint leaves with garlic and salt. If and when fresh mint is not available, parsley makes a good substitute for the substitute.

Another Portuguese fetish is olive oil. It's as common to see a ten-gallon oil dispenser in a Portuguese kitchen as a ten-gallon hat on a Texan. Also, a jar of used oil, re-used and re-used (especially for deep-frying fish or for a fish-oil flavor), is a common sight around the stove.

Like the Japanese, the Portuguese save every smidgen of fish broth for their soup and rice dishes. The recipe may call for water, but they really mean fish broth, if possible. Since cod is always on the menu and boiled fish (served with melted butter or a thin béchamel sauce) is a two to one favorite, the Portuguese always have a supply of fish broth on hand. This base is practically the only soup stock used. And a lovely, piquant flavor it has indeed! If it is born out of a fatty fish, they abstain from adding the butter or oil which otherwise provides the body.

Most Portuguese soups are made of vegetables puréed in their own liquid. Extremely easy to make on short order, they can be aesthetically thin or very fortifying, depending upon appetite, imagination, and leftovers. For seasoning soups, coriander is, again, the heavy favorite.

As may well be expected, the Portuguese are quite iconoclastic about their world-famous sardines. But consistent with their good taste in not spoiling a good thing, the fresh sardine is revered and relished in one classic form: broiled over a charcoal brazier in the open. Typical of the character of these charming, honest people, the Portuguese are the first to caution you that any variation on the theme is a poor substitute for the real thing. To appreciate fully the flavor of a fresh sardine, one must really go to Portugal.

All things considered, Portuguese food like Portugal itself is very worthwhile.

SOUPS & STEWS

SOPA DE AMEIJOAS
(Clam Soup)

4 to 5 pounds small clams
  Salt
2 ounces fat bacon
1 large onion
¼ cup olive oil
1 tablespoon butter
  Parsley
2½ quarts water
1½ cups uncooked rice
1 package (10 ounces) frozen peas

Leave clams overnight in salted water and then wash thoroughly in several waters to be sure they are completely free of sand and grit. Dice bacon and onion and sauté with oil and butter in a deep pot or Dutch oven. Add clams and a parsley sprig. Cover and allow to simmer slowly for about 20 minutes, stirring from time to time so onions do not burn. Add water. When this comes to a boil, add rice. Add frozen peas to the soup when rice is soft. Allow to come to a boil again and then turn heat down, allowing soup to simmer slowly until rice has softened almost to a paste. Remove all empty shells which have loosened from the clams. Makes 8 servings.

SOPA DE CAMARÕES
(Shrimp Bisque)

1 large onion
1 garlic clove (optional)
1 carrot
2 tomatoes
2 tablespoons olive oil or butter
4 tablespoons white wine
1 tablespoon brandy or port
1 quart water or fish stock
1 pound shrimps
¼ cup uncooked rice
  Salt and pepper

Slice onion, garlic, carrot, and tomatoes, and sauté them in 1 tablespoon of hot olive oil. Add white wine, brandy, and water. Poach raw shrimps, which have been thoroughly washed, in this base. When shrimps are cooked, remove them from pot and add rice along with a little salt and pepper. Shell shrimps and after

Sardinhas de Caldeirada

grinding three quarters of them, return to soup. For extra flavor, pound shrimp shells, blend with a little boiling water and strain back into soup. Continue to boil, covered, and when rice is soft, purée the soup through a sieve. Before serving, blend in the remaining olive oil and add remaining shrimps. Makes 4 servings.

Note: Flour may be used instead of rice, the quantity depending upon the thickness desired. For a smooth bisque, whirl a few minutes in an electric blender.

SARDINHAS DE CALDEIRADA
(Boatman's Stew)

¾ teaspoon salt
2 pounds fish*
2 large onions, sliced
½ cup olive oil
2⅓ cups (one 1-pound, 3-ounce can) tomatoes
1 can (8 ounces) tomato sauce
1 teaspoon crushed sweet red pepper
  Salt and pepper to taste
½ bunch of parsley
½ cup white wine
1½ cups water

Salt fish for a few hours. Make a sauce by browning the onions in olive oil. Add tomatoes, tomato sauce, crushed sweet red pepper, salt, pepper, parsley, wine, and water. Allow to simmer for 30 minutes. Add fish. Continue to simmer until fish is cooked. Serve in deep plates over French or Italian bread. Makes 4 servings.

*Whole small fish of any type can be used, or frozen fish, such as cod or haddock.

CALDEIRADA DE PEIXE
(Potato Fish Stew)

¾ cup olive oil
6 large onions, sliced
6 large peeled tomatoes or canned equivalent
1 bunch parsley, chopped
  Salt and pepper
3 pounds of different small fish and shellfish (such as flounders, bass, perch, whiting, shrimps, clams, etc.)
6 medium potatoes, sliced
  Toast

Pour oil into a casserole or Dutch oven over low heat. When hot, add onions. When these are soft, add tomatoes, parsley, and salt and pepper. Let simmer for about 15 minutes. Put in a layer of sliced fish, boned and skinned if preferred, then potatoes and remaining fish. When fish and potatoes are cooked through, serve at once from the same casserole over slices of toasted bread. Makes 6 to 8 servings.

FISH AND SHELLFISH

PEIXE A ALENTEJANA
(Fish Alentejo Style)

½ cup olive oil
4 medium onions, sliced
2 garlic cloves, minced

2 tablespoons chopped parsley
  Pepper to taste
2 or 3 fresh coriander sprigs or 3 or 4 coriander seeds, crushed
1½ pounds fish fillets
1½ pounds potatoes, sliced
1¼ cups (one 10-ounce can) tomatoes or 1 can (8 ounces) tomato sauce
1 bay leaf

Heat half of the oil in heavy skillet. When hot, add onions, garlic, parsley, pepper, and coriander. Place a layer of the fish over the onions and then a layer of the potatoes. Add tomatoes, bay leaf, and the rest of the olive oil. Cover tightly and allow to simmer over low heat until potatoes are done. Makes 6 servings.

FILÉS DE PEIXE RECHEADOS
(Stuffed Fillets of Fish)

2 pounds fish fillets
2 tablespoons fresh lemon juice
¼ cup olive oil
½ cup white wine
  Salt and pepper
  White sauce
1 cup cooked shrimps, cut into small pieces
  Fine dry bread crumbs
1 egg, beaten
  Fat for deep frying
  Grated Parmesan cheese

Cut fillets into servings and marinate for 1 hour in a mixture of lemon juice, oil, wine, and salt and pepper. Meanwhile, make ½ cup thick white sauce (see any standard cookbook) to which shrimps are added. After allowing this to chill, use it to stuff the fillets. Roll fish and secure with toothpicks. Now roll fish in bread crumbs, then in beaten egg, and again in bread crumbs. Deep fry in hot fat until brown. Remove toothpicks. Place in casserole, sprinkle top with cheese, and put into preheated hot oven (400°F.) for 8 to 10 minutes. Serve with creamed shrimps or tomato sauce. Makes 4 to 6 servings.

MEXILHÕES DE AVEIRO
(Aveiro Mussels)

2 pounds small mussels or clams
1 onion
¼ cup olive oil
3 garlic cloves, halved
¼ cup white wine
  Pepper to taste
⅛ teaspoon ground saffron
1 cup uncooked rice
2 cups hot fish broth or boiling water

Wash and scrub mussels thoroughly and then rinse in several waters to make sure they are free of all sand and particles. Chop onion and brown lightly in hot olive oil in a heavy skillet. Add mussels and cover tightly to allow them to steam, shaking pan from time to time. When shells open, take mussels out of pan and remove empty shells, being careful to retain all the juice which is returned to pan with the shelled mussels. Now, add garlic cloves, wine, pepper, saffron, and then rice, letting it brown slightly before

gradually adding fish broth. Cook over low heat until rice is thoroughly cooked. Stir occasionally so that rice does not stick to the pan. Makes 4 to 6 servings.

LINGUADO RECHEADO
(Ana of Povoa's Stuffed Sole)

1 large sole
½ cup chopped cooked bacon or ham
1 onion, diced
1 tablespoon olive oil
1 tablespoon melted butter
  Salt and pepper
2 egg yolks, beaten
  Bread crumbs
2 tablespoons port
1 tablespoon fresh lemon juice
  Mashed potatoes
  Parsley

Skin sole and remove backbone. Fill space with bacon. Put diced onion and fish in a flat casserole which has been spread with olive oil. Pour melted butter over fish. Season with salt and pepper. Cover fish with beaten egg yolks, then sprinkle with bread crumbs. Add wine and lemon juice. Bake in preheated moderate oven (375°F.) for about 30 minutes. Border with mashed potatoes or potato chips. Bake for about 5 minutes longer. Garnish with parsley. Makes 3 or 4 servings.

Note: As a variation, chopped shrimps, clams, or scallops can be used for the filling.

FILÉS COM MÔLHO DE LARANJA
(Fish Fillets with Orange Sauce)

1½ pounds fish fillets
2 tablespoons fresh orange juice
2 tablespoons melted butter or margarine
  Salt and pepper
½ teaspoon grated orange rind
  Buttered walnut halves

Place fish in broiler pan. Blend orange juice with melted butter and pour half over the fish. Sprinkle with salt, pepper, and orange rind. Broil for 2 minutes, then pour remaining sauce over top and broil until fish is done. If fish seems dry, add a little dry white wine. If desired, season and butter tomato halves and broil for 4 minutes along with the fish. A minute before removing from oven, scatter some buttered walnut halves over fish. Makes 4 servings.

AMEIJOAS PORTUGUESAS
(Portuguese Clams)

3 garlic cloves
¼ cup olive oil
2 pounds small clams or mussels
  Salt and pepper
  Juice of ½ lemon
1 bunch of parsley, chopped
  Lemon wedges
  French bread, toasted

Halve garlic and sauté it lightly in oil. When hot, add clams which have been thoroughly rinsed in several waters. Season with salt and pepper. Cover with tight lid and steam until clams open. Add lemon juice and parsley. Then shake pan to distribute and leave over heat for a few minutes longer. Serve piping hot with lemon wedges and slices of bread. Makes 4 servings.

AMEIJOAS A BULHÃO PATO
(Clams à la Bulhao Pato)

- 4 dozen soft-shell clams
- 2 garlic cloves, well mashed
- ½ teaspoon salt
- ½ cup olive oil
- 2 tablespoons water
- 1 bunch of parsley, chopped
- 1 bunch of coriander or a few coriander seeds, crushed

Scrub clams thoroughly and rinse in cold running water until all sand is removed. Mash garlic with salt and fry in oil. Add clams, water, parsley, and coriander. Cook slowly, covered, for 20 minutes, or until shells open. Serve at once. Makes 4 servings.

OSTRAS LUSITANAS
(Lusitanian Oysters)

- 2 dozen oysters
- 1 garlic clove
- 3 tablespoons olive oil
- 2 tablespoons chopped parsley
  White wine
  All-purpose flour
- 2 egg yolks, beaten
  Fresh lemon juice
  Grated Parmesan cheese
  Bread crumbs
  Lemon wedges

Scrub oysters thoroughly. Open, and then cook for a few minutes in a little water. Remove from shells. Sauté garlic in oil in a skillet and then add parsley, some of the oyster liquid, and a little white wine. Boil for a few moments, then thicken sauce with a little flour. Cool; stir in well-beaten egg yolks and a few drops of lemon juice. Place oysters in a casserole and then pour all the sauce over them. Sprinkle with cheese and bread crumbs. Put into preheated hot oven (400°F.) for a few minutes. Then place under low heat to brown. Serve piping hot with lemon wedges. Makes 4 servings.

MEAT

BIFES COM AZEDAS
(Sorrel and Spinach Steaks)

- 2 pounds spinach
  Salt and pepper
  Butter
- 2 tablespoons chopped sorrel
- 1½ pounds round steak, ground
  Lard or butter for frying
- 8 egg yolks, poached

Wash spinach thoroughly; or if packaged, rinse with water. Put in saucepan without water. Sprinkle with salt and cook gently, uncovered, until greens are thoroughly wilted and tender. Drain well and force through a food mill or fine sieve. Reheat and season with salt, pepper, and butter

to taste. Add sorrel. Season steak with salt and pepper and divide into 8 portions. Shape into 8 patties with a depression in the center of each. Panfry in hot lard. Reheat spinach and arrange patties on top. Put a poached egg yolk in the center of each patty. Serve with the pan juices. Makes 4 servings.

ALMÔNDEGAS
(Meatballs)

- 1 pound ground beef
- 1 teaspoon salt
- ¼ teaspoon pepper
- 2 eggs, beaten
- ¼ pound bacon, diced
- ¼ cup chopped parsley
- 1 garlic clove, minced (optional)
  All-purpose flour
- 1 onion, chopped
  Shortening for frying
- 4 tomatoes, peeled and chopped
- 2 tablespoons beef bouillon or water

Season meat with salt and pepper. Add the eggs. Cook bacon until browned, drain, and add to meat with half the parsley and the garlic, if used. Shape into walnut-size balls and roll in flour. Next cook the onion in hot shortening until golden, add tomatoes, remaining parsley, and the bouillon. Add meatballs and simmer, uncovered, for about 30 minutes. Makes 4 to 6 servings.

CARNEIRO TRANSMONTANO
(Lamb from over the Hills)

- 1 leg of lamb (6 pounds)
- 1 tablespoon salt
  Lard
- ½ cup white wine
- ½ cup bouillon or water
- 1 small onion, sliced
- 2 eggs, beaten
  Fine, dry bread crumbs (about 6 tablespoons)

Rub the lamb all over with salt and then with lard. Put on a rack in shallow roasting pan and add the white wine, bouillon, and the onion. Bake in preheated slow oven (325°F.) for about 2½ hours, basting frequently with the drippings in the pan and adding more lard if necessary. When the meat is tender, remove from oven and brush with the eggs. Sprinkle with bread crumbs. Return to the oven to brown lightly. Makes 8 to 10 servings.
Note: The Portuguese prefer this dish cold, but it may also be served hot.

CARNE DE PORCO A ALENTEJANA
(Pork with Mussels)

- 1 pound mussels, in shells
- 1 cup water
- 1 pound lean boneless pork
- 1 tablespoon lard
- 2 tablespoons olive oil
- 2 large onions, sliced
- 2 large tomatoes, peeled and chopped
- 1 bay leaf
- 1 teaspoon salt
- ½ teaspoon paprika

Scrub mussels, discarding any open ones, or any with cracked or broken shells. Steam mussels in the water for about 5

minutes. Discard any shells that have not opened, and reserve remainder in their shells. Cut pork into small pieces and cook in hot lard until nearly done. In the meantime, heat olive oil in a Dutch oven. Add onions, tomatoes, and bay leaf. Sauté until onion is tender. Add the salt, paprika, pork, and the reserved mussels in their shells. Cook all together for a few minutes. Remove the bay leaf before serving. Makes 4 servings.

COUVE-LOMBARDA RECHEADA
(Stuffed Cabbage)

- ½ pound bacon, finely diced
- 1 pound round steak, ground
- 1 onion, chopped
- ½ cup chopped parsley
  Salt and pepper
- 1 large white cabbage
- 1 tablespoon each of olive oil and lard
- 2 onions, sliced
- 2 carrots, sliced
- 2 tomatoes, peeled and cut into chunks
  Water

Partially cook bacon in skillet. Add beef and the chopped onion and cook for 5 minutes. Drain off fat. Mix parsley with the meat mixture and season with salt and pepper. Wash the cabbage well. Remove the outer leaves. Then cut a large round piece out of the top. Scoop out the inside. Fill with the meat mixture. Then close with the piece of cabbage cut from the top. Put the olive oil and lard in a large kettle. Heat. When hot, put the cabbage upright in the kettle. Arrange sliced onions, carrots, and tomatoes around cabbage. Add salt and pepper to taste and a little water. Cover tightly and cook gently for 45 minutes, or until the cabbage is tender. Serve with the cooked vegetables. Makes 6 servings.
Note: Large onions, eggplants, cucumbers, zucchini, and tomatoes are also delicious when stuffed and cooked in this way.

ISCAS
(Sliced Liver with Spleen Sauce)

- 2 pounds beef or calf's liver, sliced
- 1½ cups white wine
- 3 garlic cloves, sliced
- 2 bay leaves
- 6 tablespoons vinegar
- 2 teaspoons salt
- ½ pound spleen
- ¼ cup butter or margarine
  Boiled potatoes

Marinate the liver in the wine for 2 hours, together with garlic, bay leaves, vinegar, and salt. Remove the skin from the spleen and with a fork scrape spleen free of tissue and tendons. Remove the liver slices from the marinade and drain them. Strain the marinade and reserve. Add the spleen to the marinade, mix well, and simmer until spleen turns color and is cooked. Heat the butter in a skillet and quickly sauté the liver slices. Arrange liver in a deep serving dish, cover with the spleen sauce, and serve with boiled potatoes. Makes 8 servings.

RECHEIO A MODA DE LISBOA PARA PERU
(Lisbon Turkey Stuffing)

½ pound bacon
Uncooked giblets from 1 turkey, chopped
1 large onion, chopped
½ pound pork, ground
½ pound veal, ground
Salt and pepper to taste
Poultry seasoning
4 egg yolks
3 cups soft stale-bread crumbs
8 black olives, pitted and chopped

Mince bacon and sauté lightly in large skillet. Add giblets, onion, and ground meats. Sauté all together gently, adding more salt and pepper and a little poultry seasoning. When browned and cooked, stir in egg yolks, crumbs and olives. Makes enough stuffing for a 6- to 8-pound turkey.

Note: Although this stuffing is generally used for roast turkeys in Portugal, it may also be used for any other farmyard bird. When stuffed, the turkey should be roasted gently with plenty of fat until tender.

DESSERTS

PUDIM DE OVOS A MODA DE COIMBRA
(Coimbra Egg Pudding)

1 cup sugar
⅓ cup water
8 egg yolks
1 tablespoon butter, softened or
½ cup port

Put sugar in a pan with the water and bring to a boil. Simmer until the mixture sticks to a spoon. In the meantime, blend the egg yolks with the butter and when the sugar mixture has cooled, add the egg-yolk mixture slowly, beating all the time. Pour into buttered 9-inch pan and bake in preheated slow oven (325°F.) for 35 minutes, or until set. For added zest, the egg yolks can be beaten with ½ cup port instead of the butter before adding to the syrup. Makes 6 servings.

TOUCINHO-DO-CÉU
(Bacon from Heaven)

3⅓ cups sugar
1 cup water
1 pound shelled almonds, blanched and finely ground, or 1 can (1 pound) almond purée
6 egg yolks, beaten

Put the sugar and water in a saucepan and boil until the syrup sticks to a spoon. Remove from heat and cool slightly. Add the almonds and the egg yolks. Stir over low heat until slightly thickened. Put in a buttered 9-inch pie pan and bake in preheated slow oven (325°F.) for 45 minutes, or until firm. Makes 6 to 8 servings.

QUEIJADINHAS DE AMÊNDOAS
(Almond Cheesecakes)

2¼ cups sugar
⅔ cup water
4 ounces shelled almonds, blanched and finely ground, or canned almond purée
3 whole eggs
9 egg yolks
Grated rind of 1 lemon

Put the sugar and water in a saucepan and boil until the syrup sticks to a spoon. Then add the almonds. When the mixture has come to a boil again, remove from heat and let it cool. In the meantime, beat whole eggs and egg yolks. Add the lemon rind and stir all into the sugar and almond mixture. Return the saucepan to a low heat and stir constantly until the mixture sticks to the spoon. Remove from heat and allow to cool. Butter 2½-inch tart pans and half-fill with the mixture. Bake in preheated slow oven (300°F.) for 35 minutes, or until firm. Makes 8 servings.

PUDIM DE BANANAS
(Banana Pudding)

12 bananas
Water
½ cup white port
3 tablespoons butter
1 cup sugar
6 eggs, beaten

Cook bananas in a little water. When soft, drain and force through a sieve or food mill into a bowl. Add the wine and butter, and beat well together; then add sugar and beaten eggs. When the mixture is quite smooth, pour into a buttered 2-quart soufflé dish and bake in preheated slow oven (325°F.) for 45 minutes to 1 hour. Makes 8 servings.

DOCE DE CASTANHAS
(Chestnut Sweet)

2¼ cups sugar
1 cup water
1 can (1 pound) chestnut purée
6 to 8 blanched almonds, finely ground
Cream

Put the sugar in a saucepan with the water and boil. When it sticks to the spoon, add it to the chestnut purée with the almonds. Return it to the heat, stirring all the time with a spoon. When the mixture thickens, it is ready. Serve cold with cream. Makes 6 servings.

SONHOS
(Dreams)

¼ cup water
Dash of salt
¼ cup butter
½ cup all-purpose flour
4 eggs
Cooking oil or fat for frying
Sugar
Cinnamon

Heat the water with the salt and butter. When boiling, blend in the flour quickly and smoothly. Remove from heat and beat the mixture with a whisk until it is

cold. Then add the eggs, one at a time, continually beating. The mixture should be well whipped and then left to rest for 15 minutes. Heat oil in deep fryer. When the oil is boiling, drop in 3 or 4 teaspoonfuls of the mixture. Stir the oil all the time with a fork or wooden spoon to make the *sonhos* rise well. They should fry slowly to rise well. When pale brown, remove, drain, and keep them in a warm oven while cooking the others. Sprinkle with sugar and a little cinnamon. Makes about 18.

Note: This is a favorite provincial sweet which should be served piping hot.

POSSET—A beverage made from hot milk curdled with wine or lemon juice. It is sweetened with sugar or molasses and sometimes thickened with flour or bread. It is a time-honored drink for invalids.

BRANDY OR SHERRY POSSET

Bring 2 cups milk to boil. Cut crusts from 2 thin slices of stale bread and dice bread. Put bread in soup bowl and sprinkle with a pinch of salt, a little grated nutmeg, and 1 tablespoon sugar. Pour milk over bread, cover and let stand for 10 minutes. Then stir in 1 tablespoon brandy or sherry. Serve at once. Makes 1 serving.

MOLASSES POSSET

Bring 1 cup milk to boil. Add 2 tablespoons molasses and juice of ½ lemon. When curdled, strain through muslin or cheesecloth. Makes 1 serving.

POTATO by *James A. Beard*—The white potato (botanical name, *Solanum tuberosum*) is a starchy tuber of the nightshade family and was one of the New World's greatest emissaries to the Old. Oddly enough, in the beginning it was considered food suitable only for chickens and pigs. The white potato (sweet potatoes and yams belong to two completely different plant families) was originally cultivated in Peru and probably Ecuador, where the varied soils produce variations in the potato as well. It is an astonishing experience to visit the marketplace in Lima and see there potatoes in all shapes, sizes, and colors, many kinds completely unknown in the rest of the world.

It is said that the potato had to cross the Atlantic seven times to become popular in the American Colonies, long after it had been accepted in England, Ireland, and to some degree on the Continent, during the 16th century. Although the potato was introduced in France as an ornamental plant in the same century, it remained highly suspect for eating until the great agriculturist and botanist Antoine-Auguste Parmentier (1737-1817) proved its beneficial qualities in 1771.

While some very sophisticated recipes were to develop around the potato, in Ireland it was loved for itself alone. Eliza Acton, in her magnificent book of *Modern Cookery,* published in London in 1848, quotes the following "genuine Irish receipt" for boiling potatoes:

Potatoes, to boil well together should be all of the same sort and as nearly equal in size as may be. Wash off the mould, and scrub them very hard with a hard brush, but neither scoop nor apply a knife to them in any way, even to clear the eyes.* Rinse them well, and arrange them compactly in a saucepan, so that they may not lie loose in the water, and that a small quantity may suffice to cover them. Pour this in cold, and when it boils, throw in about a teaspoonful of salt to the quart, and simmer the potatoes until they are nearly done, but for the last few minutes let them boil rapidly. When they are tender quite through, which may be known by probing them with a fork, pour all the water from them immediately, lift the lid of the saucepan to allow the steam to escape, and place them on a trivet, high over the fire or by the side of it, until the moisture has entirely evaporated; peel them and send them to the table as quickly as possible either in a hot napkin, or in a hot dish, of which the cover is so placed that the steam can pass off. There should be no delay for serving them after they are once taken from the fire. Irish families usually prefer them served in their skins. Some kinds will be done in twenty minutes, others in less than three quarters of an hour. We are informed "that the best potatoes average five to six to a pound, with few eyes, but those pretty deep and distributed well over the surface." We cannot ourselves vouch for the correctness of this assertion, but we think it may be relied upon.

*Because, in the words of our Irish correspondent, "the water through these parts is then admitted to the very heart of the vegetable; and the latent heat, after cooking, is not sufficient to throw it off; this renders the potatoes very unwholesome."

Simply cooked potatoes, such as this Irish version, used to be the mainstay of many diets, sometimes with the addition of milk, butter, or cheese. In England the use of the potato was extended to dishes that included meat or fish. And in France, after Parmentier, some of the most imaginative of all potato dishes were created—among them, Potatoes Anna (layers of thin slices, cooked in butter in a hot oven till crisp and brown) and Soufflé Potatoes (crisp, puffy and airy), created by mistake when, as one story has it, a chef refried potatoes for a royal feast. He could not have known what trouble he was to cause cooks for generations after.

Each of the potato-consuming countries of the world has added its own distinctive recipes. The Teutonic countries created a potato salad, tossed with oil, vinegar, and seasonings that has become standard; the Swiss produced *roesti;* and the Italians developed those ambrosial little dumplings called *gnocchi.*

In the United States we discovered the potato chip, again by mistake, when a chef in Saratoga cut his potatoes too thin for ordinary frying and so hit upon a way to his and other people's fortunes. Another of our specialties is the baked potato, which came about because of the variety of potato grown in certain volcanic soil found in Idaho, similar to some of the fine potato soil in Peru. The sudden vogue for the baked potato was dramatized earlier in this century when competitive railroads, the Northern Pacific and the Great Northern, vied with each other for the claim of serving the biggest baked potatoes in their dining cars. Now the baked potato is an institution, and, so prized has it become, the raw product is frequently sold individually wrapped in foil. Some people love to lather their baked Idaho with butter, others with cream, and still others (I among them) prefer it merely with coarse salt and freshly ground black pepper. Those who first ventured to eat the skin found another delight, and at least one fashionable hostess has offered the skins buttered and grilled as an elegant hors-d'oeuvre.

Perhaps the most elevated use of the potato is in the potato cake, which used to be a feature at basket socials and church fairs. Rich with chocolate, this specialty attracted those with a fondness for layer cakes with fluffy icing. There are still few light cakes its equal.

To my mind, one of the most satisfying forms of potato I have experienced in this country or in Europe, as anyone who has lived near the soil will understand, are tiny marble-size new potatoes. When freshly dug, quickly boiled, and buttered copiously there is nothing in the potato repertory to match them. They may be scraped, left in their skins, or partially peeled, with a band cut around their circumference.

Nowadays, of course, the reigning potato dish is "French" fries, cooked, usually, as no Frenchman ever thought of doing. They are consumed daily by the countless tons and are almost as popular in Europe as they are in the United States. The French serve them crisp and brown with salt and pepper; the Dutch offer them in small cornucopias with a dollop of mustard mayonnaise, as do the Belgians; the English prefer them with a sprinkling of vinegar; the Spanish and Portuguese are content with pepper; and we in America douse them with ketchup. The quality can be as varied as the condiments, anywhere from excellent to indigestible.

In recent years frozen foods have given us prepared potatoes with very little work left to do in the kitchen except heating, in most cases. Wondrous packages yield everything from ready-mashed to scalloped potatoes.

In summary let us list a few of the great potato dishes of the world: a plain boiled potato, served fresh and hot; a good baked potato; Potatoes Anna; *roesti;* tiny new potatoes, as served in France or England; the yellow potatoes one gets in France, Belgium, and Holland; a perfect potato salad; and well-prepared puréed (or mashed, as they are often called) potatoes. It is interesting to note that M. Dumaine, the great French chef of this century, stated that potatoes should never be whipped but mashed with a down motion only, lest they become stringy and tough. The number of potato dishes seems infinite. Without doubt, in the realm of gastronomy the potato is one of nature's greatest triumphs.

Availability—Year round, with new potatoes in food stores in the spring and summer.

Canned potatoes are available whole, julienne, and in sticks; and as an ingredient in stews, etc. Packaged chips and fried shoestring potatoes are available.

Frozen potatoes available include: whole potatoes in moisture-proof bags; French-fried, puffs, whipped, au gratin, hashed brown, patties, tiny potato bites. Cream of potato soup is available, and potatoes are an ingredient in frozen dinners and main-dish pies.

Mashed-potato flakes and granules, scalloped and au gratin potatoes are available dried, and potatoes are an ingredient in freeze-dried dinners.

Purchasing Guide—New potatoes should have a thin feathery skin of red or white that breaks easily. They are particularly good for boiling and for salads.

Mature potatoes, which include mealy and waxy types, should be clean, firm, free from cuts, growth, cracks or surface defects. They should be well-shaped, have shallow eyes, and be of medium size. Avoid dirty, withered, leathery, discolored, sprouting or green-colored (sunburned) potatoes.

The mealy potatoes, also known as all-purpose potatoes are good for baking and mashing and include such varieties as Idaho, Maine, and Long Island potatoes. Waxy potatoes, which hold their shape well, are good for creaming, scalloping, frying, and use in salads. They include such varieties as Early Rose, Green Mountain, and Cobblers.

Storage—Keep potatoes in a cool dark well-ventilated place. Refrigerate new potatoes. Do not freeze uncooked potatoes.

☐ Refrigerator shelf, cooked: 4 to 5 days

☐ Frozen products; or cooked, refrigerator frozen-food compartment: 2 to 3 months

☐ Frozen products; or cooked, freezer: 1 year

☐ Canned, kitchen shelf: 1 year

Nutritive Food Values—One medium-size potato is a fair source of vitamin C. This can be significant when eaten in quantity. Potatoes are a fair source of thiamine and niacin. The caloric values given below are for 3½ ounces, edible portion.

☐ Baked in skin = 93 calories

☐ Boiled in skin = 76 calories

☐ Boiled, pared before cooking = 65 calories

☐ French-fried = 274 calories

☐ Fried = 268 calories

☐ Mashed, milk and table fat added = 94 calories

☐ Canned, solids and liquid = 44 calories

☐ Frozen, hash-browned = 224 calories

☐ Frozen French-fried, heated = 220 calories

☐ Frozen mashed, heated = 93 calories

☐ Potato chips = 568 calories

Basic Preparation—Scrub potatoes. To get the most food value leave the skins on whenever possible. If potatoes are peeled, keep the parings thin. There is less loss of nutrients in cooking if the potatoes are left whole; however, the cooking time is shortened if cut into pieces. Pared potatoes usually retain their whiteness better during cooking than those cooked in their "jackets." If potatoes are not cooked immediately after paring, cover with cold water to prevent darkening.

☐ **To Boil**—Cook, covered, in 1 inch of boiling salted water until tender, whole for 30 to 40 minutes, very small or sliced for 20 to 25 minutes. To speed cooking cut potatoes into pieces and cook in as little water as possible in a tightly covered pan.

☐ **To Boil New Potatoes in Jackets**—Scrub potatoes thoroughly. Cut off a strip of peel around center of each potato. Put in saucepan and add boiling water almost to cover. Add a pinch of salt. Bring to boil, cover, and cook until tender. Drain and put into serving dish. Add melted butter or margarine.

☐ **To Make Mashed Potatoes**—Peel washed potatoes of even size. If necessary, cut larger potatoes into halves or quarters. Put in saucepan, and add boiling water almost to cover. Add a pinch of salt. Bring to boil, cover, and cook until tender. Drain and put over low heat to dry out, shaking pan gently. Mash with potato masher or in electric mixer, or force potatoes through ricer. Add small amount of combined hot milk and butter or margarine. Beat until fluffy; season with salt and pepper to taste.

☐ **To Rice**—Peel washed potatoes of even size. If necessary, cut larger potatoes into halves or quarters. Put in saucepan and add boiling water almost to cover. Add a pinch of salt. Bring to boil, cover, and cook until tender. Drain and put over low heat to dry out, shaking pan gently. Add melted butter or margarine and turn with fork until potatoes are well coated. Force through potato ricer.

Note: Melted butter or margarine can be poured over potatoes after ricing if preferred.

☐ **To Bake**—Scrub medium or large potatoes, and dry. To keep skins soft, rub with a little shortening. Arrange on small cookie sheet, pie pan, or rack in oven. Bake in preheated very hot oven (450° F.) for 45 to 50 minutes, or until done. (They are usually done if they feel soft when pressed.) Cut a 1½-inch cross in center top of each potato. Hold with clean towel and press at bottom until potato bursts through top. Fluff up potato with fork, and add a square of butter, if desired.

☐ **To Pan Roast**—Peel medium potatoes and cook for 10 minutes in boiling salted water. Drain. Arrange in roasting pan or shallow baking dish. Brush with fat or drippings. Bake in preheated hot oven (400°F.) for about 45 minutes, turning occasionally and brushing with fat.

☐ **To French Fry**—*Single-Frying Method (for small amount):* Peel potatoes. Heat ¾ inch of shortening in large skillet to 285°F. on a frying thermometer. Cut potatoes into ½-inch slices, then into ½-inch strips. Rinse in cold water and dry. Put potatoes in hot fat; fry for 20 to 30 minutes, or until tender and brown. Drain on absorbent paper. Sprinkle lightly with salt.

Double-Frying Method (for large amount): Peel potatoes. Heat shortening in skillet or fryer to 370°F. on a frying

thermometer. Cut potatoes and put, a few at a time, into shortening; fry for about 8 minutes, or until tender, but not brown. Drain on absorbent paper. Continue until all potatoes are cooked. Shortly before serving, heat shortening to 390° F. Put potatoes in shortening and fry until brown. Drain on absorbent paper and sprinkle with salt. Keep hot in oven until all are fried.

French-Fried Potato Twists: Peel potatoes. With knife or vegetable peeler, cut round and round, making long, thin curls. Fry, using single-frying method.

Lattice-Fried Potatoes: Cut peeled potatoes with lattice cutter. Use single-frying method and fry for a few minutes in shortening heated to 385°F. on a frying thermometer.

Oven French-Fries: Cut potatoes and rinse in cold water, drain, and dry on absorbent paper. Arrange on shallow baking pan. Brush generously with melted butter or margarine. Bake in preheated very hot oven (450°F.) for 35 to 40 minutes, or until golden-brown and tender; turn occasionally. Sprinkle with salt.

☐ **To Hash-Brown Potatoes**—For 4 servings mix 3 cups chopped cold boiled or baked potatoes, 3 tablespoons all-purpose flour, and ¼ cup milk. Season to taste with salt and pepper. Add instant minced onion or chopped parsley if desired. Heat 2 tablespoons fat in heavy 9-inch skillet. Add potato mixture and pack with spatula in a large cake. Cook over medium heat until brown and crusty, shaking the pan to keep potato from sticking. Turn out on flat plate. Wipe pan free of crumbs and add 1 tablespoon fat. Slide potato back into hot pan, brown side up. Cook until bottom is brown, packing edges with spatula and shaking pan.

☐ **To Freeze**—*French-fried potatoes:* Fry as usual and drain on absorbent paper. Cool to room temperature and pack into containers leaving ½-inch headspace. Potato chips can also be frozen in this way. Both should be reheated or crisped again in fat before serving.

Baked Stuffed Potatoes: Bake and stuff potatoes as usual; cool to room temperature, and wrap separately, excluding as much air as possible.

Mashed Potatoes: Prepare as usual, cool to room temperature, and pack into containers, leaving ½-inch headspace. Can also be packed in patties as you would hamburgers with 2 thicknesses of freezer paper between each 2 patties.

POTATO COOK BOOK

A collection of delicious recipes for potatoes:
baked, scalloped, creamed, or crisply fried; as an accompaniment
for entrées and in soups, salads, and pies, plus the
greatest potato dish of them all, fluffy chocolate cake.

SOUPS

CURRIED POTATO SOUP

3 cups diced raw potatoes
2½ cups boiling water
3 chicken or beef bouillon cubes
¾ teaspoon salt
1 garlic clove, minced
1¾ teaspoons curry powder
1 small onion, chopped
2 cups milk
2 tablespoons butter or margarine
¼ teaspoon pepper

Combine potatoes, water, bouillon cubes, salt, garlic, curry powder, and onion. Cover and cook until potatoes fall apart, 40 to 50 minutes. Remove from heat and mash potatoes in the liquid. If necessary put mixture through a sieve or whirl in blender. Add milk, butter, and pepper. Heat only until hot. Makes 6 servings.

POTATO AND CARROT SOUP

2 slices of bacon, diced
1 onion, minced
3 cups diced potatoes
3 cups water
1 cup grated raw carrot
2 teaspoons salt
¼ teaspoon pepper
2 tablespoons all-purpose flour
3 cups milk

Cook bacon in kettle until golden-brown. Remove bacon. Add onion to fat remaining in kettle and cook until golden. Add potatoes and water, cover and simmer for 15 minutes, or until tender. Add carrot and seasonings. Blend flour with a little of the milk. Stir into hot mixture and cook, stirring, until slightly thickened. Add remaining milk and heat. Sprinkle with bacon. Makes 4 servings.

SALT-PORK AND POTATO CHOWDER

¼ pound salt pork, minced
1 large onion, chopped
½ cup finely diced celery and leaves
3 cups diced potatoes
3 cups water
3 cups milk
Salt and pepper
8 saltine crackers

Fry salt pork in kettle until golden-brown. Remove pork. Add onion, celery, and potatoes to fat remaining in kettle. Cover and cook for 10 minutes, stirring several times. Add the water, cover, and simmer for 15 minutes, or until potatoes are tender. Add milk and heat. Season with salt and pepper to taste. Just before serving add pork and crumbled crackers. Makes 4 servings.

 ## SALADS AND MAIN DISHES

GERMAN POTATO SALAD

Peel, cook, and drain 6 medium potatoes.

Cut into very thin slices. Put in shallow baking dish and season with salt and pepper. Dice 4 slices of bacon and cook with 1 sliced onion. Add 2 tablespoons vinegar and heat to boiling. Pour over potatoes. Cover and let stand in preheated slow oven (300°F.) until warm. Toss lightly. Makes 6 servings.

POTATO SALAD WITH EGGS

4 cups hot diced potatoes
⅓ cup French dressing
Salt, pepper, and cayenne
1 cup sliced celery
½ cup chopped sweet pickle
½ cup mayonnaise
2 hard-cooked eggs
Parsley

Mix potatoes lightly with French dressing; season with salt, pepper, and cayenne to taste. Add celery, pickle, mayonnaise, and chopped egg whites. Add more seasoning if necessary. Just before serving, garnish with parsley and hard-cooked egg yolks forced through ricer or sieve. Makes 4 servings.

HOT CREAMY POTATO-EGG SALAD

2 tablespoons butter or margarine
2 tablespoons all-purpose flour
1½ teaspoons salt
Pepper to taste
1 cup milk
4 cups diced cooked potatoes
1 onion, minced
1 pimiento, diced
1 cup diced celery
⅓ cup minced ripe olives
6 hard-cooked eggs, chopped
⅔ cup salad dressing or mayonnaise

Melt butter and blend in flour and seasonings. Gradually stir in milk and cook, stirring, until thickened. Add potatoes and heat gently. Just before serving, add remaining ingredients, reserving some of the chopped egg to garnish top. Mix lightly. Add more seasoning if necessary. Makes 4 servings.

POTATO SALAD WITH SOUR CREAM

5 cups sliced cooked potatoes
½ cup minced celery
4 green onions, sliced
¼ cup French dressing
1 cup dairy sour cream
Salt, pepper, and cayenne
Finely sliced green-onion tops
Paprika

Combine potatoes, celery, and onions. Pour French dressing over mixture and let stand in refrigerator for several hours. Just before serving, fold in sour cream. Season with salt, pepper, cayenne to taste. Sprinkle with onion tops and paprika. Makes 4 servings.

HOT POTATO SALAD

2 slices of bacon
1 onion, chopped
1 tablespoon all-purpose flour
¼ cup vinegar
½ cup water
½ teaspoon salt

1 teaspoon sugar
⅛ teaspoon pepper
3 tablespoons prepared mustard
5 cups sliced cooked potatoes
Chopped parsley

Cook bacon until crisp; crumble; remove. Cook onion in bacon fat until lightly browned. Blend in flour; add bacon, vinegar, water, and seasonings; bring to boil. Add potatoes, mixing lightly; heat. Sprinkle with parsley and serve. Or let cool, store in refrigerator, and reheat before serving. Makes 4 servings.

HOT MASHED-POTATO SALAD

To 6 cups hot mashed potatoes add ½ cup diced celery, ¾ cup salad dressing, 1 minced onion, ¼ cup each of milk and vinegar, and 1 tablespoon powdered mustard; season with salt and pepper to taste. Mix well and garnish with paprika and green-pepper rings. Makes 6 servings.

TEXAS POTATO SALAD

4 medium potatoes
1 can (10½ ounces) condensed consommé
1 garlic clove
3 tablespoons tarragon vinegar
2 tablespoons olive or cooking oil
1 teaspoon salt
¼ teaspoon pepper
Few parsley sprigs, chopped
1 small onion, chopped
¼ cup grated Parmesan cheese
Salad greens

Cook peeled potatoes in consommé with the garlic until potatoes are tender. Drain and discard garlic. (Liquid can be used later in soups or gravies.) Dice potatoes while still warm. Mix remaining ingredients except greens to make dressing. Alternate potatoes and dressing in bowl. Cool, then cover and chill for several hours or overnight. Serve with the salad greens. Makes 4 servings.

POTATO WAFFLES

3 eggs
1 cup sifted all-purpose flour
2 teaspoons baking powder
½ teaspoon salt
1 cup milk
1 tablespoon melted shortening
2 cups cold riced cooked potatoes
Butter
Maple syrup

Beat eggs until light. Add sifted dry ingredients, milk, and shortening; mix until smooth. Add potatoes and mix well. Bake in hot waffle iron. Serve hot with butter and syrup. Makes 4 servings.

POTATO-TUNA CASSEROLE

2 cups mashed potatoes
1 can (7 ounces) tuna fish
1 tablespoon minced onion
½ teaspoon curry powder
¼ cup crushed potato chips

Mix all ingredients except potato chips, and put in shallow baking dish. Sprinkle with potato chips. Bake in preheated

moderate oven (350°F.) for about 30 minutes. Makes 4 servings.

HAMBURGER POTATO-CHEESE PIE

1 pound ground beef
1 teaspoon salt
¼ teaspoon pepper
1 teaspoon instant minced onion
¼ cup fine dry bread crumbs
½ cup milk
1 egg
1 envelope instant mashed potatoes
¾ cup shredded sharp Cheddar cheese
Paprika

Mix meat, salt, pepper, onion, bread crumbs soaked in milk, and egg. Spread in 9-inch pie pan. Bake in preheated moderate oven (350°F.) for 35 minutes. Top with potatoes made according to package directions. Sprinkle with cheese. Bake for 10 minutes longer, or until cheese is melted and potatoes are hot. Sprinkle with paprika. Makes 4 servings.

POTATO-TOPPED LUNCHEON MEAT

1 can luncheon meat, sliced
3 cups mashed potatoes
2 tablespoons minced green onion
¼ cup chopped stuffed olives
1 tablespoon chopped parsley
    Dash of pepper
    Paprika

Place meat in shallow casserole. Combine potatoes with remaining ingredients except paprika; moisten with a little milk if necessary. Mix well. Spread on meat. Sprinkle with paprika. Bake in preheated moderate oven (350°F.) for 35 minutes. Makes 4 servings.

POTATO, CHEESE, AND ONION PIE

3 cups sliced onions
2 tablespoons butter or margarine
1 can (10½ ounces) cream-of-mushroom soup
½ cup water
    Salt and pepper to taste
    Pinch of ground sage
6 medium potatoes, cooked and sliced
¼ pound Cheddar cheese, sliced
    Pastry (recipe using 2 cups flour), unbaked

Brown onions lightly in butter; cover and cook slowly until tender. Add soup and water; season with salt, pepper, and sage. Arrange potatoes and half of cheese in 2-quart casserole. Pour onion mixture over ingredients in casserole and top with remaining cheese. Bake in preheated hot oven (400°F.) for 15 minutes, or until mixture is heated and cheese is lightly browned. Top with baked pastry wedges. Makes 4 servings. To make pastry wedges:

Roll pastry ½ inch thick to form a round that fits top of casserole. Cut into 4 wedges, and brush with beaten egg yolk or cream. Bake on cookie sheet in oven with potatoes for 15 minutes.

POTATOES HUNGARIAN

6 medium potatoes
4 hard-cooked eggs
½ cup butter or margarine
2 cups dairy sour cream
1½ teaspoons salt
¼ teaspoon pepper
6 slices of toast, crushed fine, or 1 cup fine dry bread crumbs
    Paprika

Peel, cook, and slice potatoes. Slice eggs. Melt butter, add cream and seasoning, and mix well. Put potatoes, eggs, cream mixture, and crumbs in layers in shallow baking dish. Repeat, ending with crumbs. Sprinkle with paprika. Bake in preheated moderate oven (350°F.) for about 30 minutes. Makes 6 servings.

SCALLOPED POTATOES WITH PORK CHOPS

Follow recipe for Scalloped Potatoes (page 1467), omitting butter. Brown 4 large pork chops (about 1½ pounds) on both sides. Arrange chops on potato. Bake as directed for Scalloped Potatoes. Makes 4 servings.

SCALLOPED POTATOES WITH HAM

Follow recipe for Scalloped Potatoes (page 1467); put four ½-inch thick serving pieces of ready-to-eat ham in casserole before adding top layer of potato. Proceed as directed. Or use 1½ cups diced cooked ham and put some on each potato layer. Makes 4 servings.

HOPPEL POPPEL

½ cup butter or margarine
1 large onion, sliced
8 medium potatoes, cooked, peeled, and sliced
1 teaspoon paprika
2 tablespoons chopped parsley
8 eggs
½ cup light cream
1 teaspoon salt
½ teaspoon pepper

Heat butter and sauté onion in it until golden brown. Add potatoes, paprika, and parsley. Sauté until potatoes are golden. Beat eggs with cream, salt, and pepper. Pour eggs over potatoes. Cook, stirring, until eggs are set. Makes 6 to 8 servings.

 ## SIDE DISHES: BOILED

POTATO GNOCCHI

7 medium potatoes, peeled
1 cup all-purpose flour (about)
    Boiling salted water
2 cups homemade or canned tomato sauce, heated
2 tablespoons grated Parmesan cheese

Cook and drain potatoes. Mash until smooth. Put on a floured board and mix with the flour. (Use enough flour to make a dough that can be kneaded. Amounts will depend on the moisture in the potatoes.) Knead dough well. Roll into finger-thin roll and cut into 2-inch pieces. Press each piece lightly with fork. Drop, about 20 at a time, into boiling salted water. When they come to the surface, remove from water with skimmer and put in serving dish. Keep water boiling briskly and repeat until all are cooked. Mix with the hot sauce and sprinkle with cheese. Makes 4 to 6 servings.

PARSLEYED POTATO BALLS

4 large potatoes
    Salt
¼ cup melted butter or margarine
2 parsley sprigs, chopped

Peel potatoes and put in cold water. With melon-ball cutter, cut potatoes into balls. Cook in boiling salted water until just tender. Drain and shake over low heat to dry out slightly. Add butter and parsley. Makes 4 servings.

POMMES FONDANTE

Prepare mashed potatoes. (See page 1460.) Put into a casserole, having them

O'Brien Potatoes **Stuffed Baked Potatoes** **Pommes Anna** **Potato Pancakes**

about 2 inches thick. Float ¼-inch layer of heavy cream over the top, completely covering potatoes, then sprinkle with coarse dry bread crumbs, not too thickly. Put in preheated hot oven (400°F.) until brown on top; serve at once.

CHANTILLY POTATOES

Make these like *Pommes Fondante,* page 1463, but whip the cream before spreading on top. Use ½ cup before whipping, for each 3 cups of mashed potatoes. Pile potatoes in baking dish, cover with whipped cream, and sprinkle top with ¼ cup grated Parmesan cheese; finish as for *Pommes Fondante.*

MASHED POTATOES WITH SAGE ONIONS

6 medium potatoes
  Salt
½ cup hot milk
½ cup butter or margarine
  Pepper
4 medium onions, sliced thin
½ teaspoon ground sage

Cook peeled potatoes in boiling salted water until tender; drain. Mash well with hot milk and ¼ cup butter; season with salt and pepper to taste. Keep warm. Cook onions in ¼ cup butter until golden brown and tender. Sprinkle with sage, salt, and pepper. Serve on potatoes. Makes 4 servings.

CURRIED POTATOES

Cook 1 minced small onion in ¼ cup butter or margarine for 5 minutes. Add 3 cups diced cold cooked potatoes and cook until butter is absorbed. Add 1½ teaspoons each of curry powder and fresh lemon juice and ½ cup chicken bouillon; season. Cook for a few minutes longer. Makes 4 servings.

SOUR-CREAM POTATOES

4 medium potatoes
1 small onion, minced
1 teaspoon salt
  Dash of pepper
½ cup boiling water
¼ cup dairy sour cream

Chantilly Potatoes

Paprika and chopped parsley

Peel potatoes and cut into ¾-inch cubes. Put in skillet with onion, salt, pepper, and boiling water. Bring to boil, cover, and simmer for 15 minutes, or until tender. Do not drain. Add sour cream and toss lightly with fork. Put in hot serving dish and sprinkle with paprika and parsley. Makes 4 servings.

MEXICAN PANNED POTATOES

1 onion, minced
1 small garlic clove, minced
2 tablespoons bacon fat
1 teaspoon chili powder
¼ teaspoon crumbled dried oregano
1 teaspoon salt

1 cup water
4 medium potatoes, peeled
  and quartered

Brown onion and garlic lightly in fat. Add seasonings and water; bring to boil. Add potatoes and simmer, stirring occasionally, for 30 minutes, or until potatoes are tender. Makes 4 servings.

DOUBLE-BOILER CREAMED POTATOES

½ cup dry skim milk
3 tablespoons all-purpose flour
1 teaspoon salt
¼ teaspoon pepper
  Little grated onion
3 cups finely diced
  raw potatoes

1 tablespoon butter
  or margarine
  Water

In top part of double boiler mix dry skim milk, flour, and seasonings. Add onion and potatoes; stir until coated. Add butter and 1¼ cups water. Cook over boiling water for about 1 hour, or until potatoes are tender, stirring occasionally. Makes 4 servings.

GOLDEN POTATOES

6 potatoes, boiled
1 medium onion, grated
½ teaspoon salt
¼ teaspoon pepper
¼ cup yellow cornmeal
2 tablespoons shortening

Dice potatoes into bowl containing onion, seasonings, and cornmeal; mix well. Heat shortening in skillet. Add potatoes, and cook until brown and crusty, stirring frequently. Makes 4 servings.

POTATOES IN MUSTARD SAUCE

8 to 12 small new potatoes
    Salt
1½ tablespoons butter
    or margarine
1½ tablespoons all-purpose flour
½ cup water
¾ cup undiluted
    evaporated milk
1 tablespoon prepared mustard
½ cup chopped watercress

Cook potatoes in jackets in boiling salted water until tender. Meanwhile, make sauce. Melt butter in saucepan. Add flour, stir in water, and bring to boil, stirring constantly. Add evaporated milk, mustard, and 1 teaspoon salt; bring again to boil. Add hot peeled potatoes; heat thoroughly. Add watercress just before serving. Makes 4 servings.

NEW POTATOES AND PEAS IN CREAM

1 pound small new potatoes
1 teaspoon salt
2 cups boiling water
1 package (10 ounces)
    frozen peas
⅔ cup heavy cream
⅛ teaspoon pepper

Peel potatoes and cook with salt in boiling water until almost tender. Add peas; continue cooking until vegetables are tender. Drain; add cream and pepper; heat well. Makes 4 servings.

CARAWAY POTATOES

Scrub 8 small new potatoes and cook in boiling salted water until tender. Drain and peel. Melt 2 tablespoons butter or margarine; add 1 tablespoon caraway seeds and the potatoes and toss until well coated with butter and seeds. Put into serving dish; sprinkle with paprika and chopped parsley. Makes 4 servings.

SIDE DISHES: BAKED

POMMES ANNA

2 pounds potatoes, peeled
    Butter or margarine
    Salt and pepper

Slice potatoes 1/6 inch thick; rinse and dry. Cut a circle of brown paper to fit the bottom of a round shallow baking dish with a cover or a 10-inch pie pan. Butter pan generously, put paper in the bottom and butter paper. Arrange a layer of overlapping slices of potato in the pan, starting in the middle and making concentric circles to the edge. Pour over the layer about 1 tablespoon melted butter. Sprinkle with salt and pepper and continue adding more layers of potatoes, buttering and seasoning each layer. There will be 3 or 4 layers. Pour another tablespoon of butter on top, cover, and bake on the bottom shelf of preheated hot oven (425°F.) for 50 minutes, or until fork-tender. Drain off butter and reserve for later uses. Then carefully turn potatoes upside down on a round plate and peel off paper. The potatoes should be well browned on the bottom. If not, put under broiler for a minute or two. Makes 6 servings.

POTATO MOUNDS, AMANDINE

1½ pounds potatoes
    Salt
¼ cup butter
    or margarine
¼ cup hot milk
1 egg
    Pepper
¼ cup slivered
    blanched almonds

Peel potatoes, cut into pieces, and cook in boiling salted water until tender. Drain and force through ricer. Add 2 tablespoons butter, the milk, and egg; beat until light and fluffy. Season with salt and pepper to taste. Drop from spoon in 12 mounds on greased cookie sheet. Mix remaining butter and almonds; sprinkle on mounds. Bake in preheated hot oven (400°F.) for 15 minutes, or until lightly browned. Makes 4 servings.

BAKED HERBED POTATOES

8 cups diced potatoes
1 onion, minced
1 cup minced celery
    and leaves
⅓ cup melted butter
    or margarine
¼ cup minced parsley
2 teaspoons salt
¼ teaspoon pepper
1 teaspoon poultry seasoning

Cook potatoes in small amount of boiling water for 5 minutes; drain. Add remaining ingredients and mix well. Put in shallow baking dish and bake in preheated moderate oven (375°F.) for about 30 minutes. Makes 6 servings.

POTATO PUFF

Force enough cold boiled potatoes through ricer to make 2 cups. Add 2 tablespoons melted butter or margarine, ⅓ cup hot milk, ½ cup grated Cheddar cheese, ½ teaspoon salt, ¼ teaspoon pepper, and 2 slightly beaten eggs. Pour into greased 1-quart casserole. Bake in preheated moderate oven (350°F.) for 30 minutes, or until set. Makes 4 servings.

STUFFED BAKED POTATOES

Bake large potatoes. (See page 1460.) When they are done, cut them into halves lengthwise and quickly scoop out the insides. Mash potatoes well and for each one add 1 tablespoon of butter and also 1 tablespoon of cream. Season to taste with salt and pepper and return to the shells. Brush tops with melted butter, then sprinkle with grated cheese and brown in preheated hot oven (425°F.).

BAKED POTATOES RECTOR

Bake large potatoes. (See page 1460). Cut a large oval piece of skin from the top of each potato, and scrape all the potato from the shell into a warm bowl. Season potato with salt, pepper, and paprika. Mash well and beat in a little heavy cream. Add some chopped green onions and fill potato shells lightly with the mixture. Put in hot oven until lightly browned.

SAVORY STUFFED POTATOES

4 large baking potatoes
¼ cup hot milk
    Salt and pepper
1 can (3 ounces) chopped
    mushrooms, drained
    Melted butter
    Chopped chives

Bake potatoes as directed on page 1460. Cut a slice from top of each; scoop out potato into a bowl. Add milk and beat until fluffy. Season with salt and pepper. Add mushrooms and 2 tablespoons melted butter. Pile lightly in potato shells. Brush with butter and top with chives. Brown lightly in preheated very hot oven (450°F.). Makes 4 servings.

POTATOES BAKED IN SPAGHETTI SAUCE

8 medium potatoes
½ teaspoon salt
2 tablespoons olive oil
1 can (10½ ounces)
    meatless spaghetti sauce
1 garlic clove, minced
1 small onion, minced
1 tablespoon chopped parsley

Peel potatoes and cook in boiling salted water until partially tender. Drain and coat with oil. Put in shallow baking dish. Pour spaghetti sauce over potatoes and sprinkle with remaining ingredients. Bake in preheated moderate oven (350°F.) for 1 hour, or until potatoes are tender. Makes 4 servings.

POTATO SOUFFLÉ

3 tablespoons butter
   or margarine
3 tablespoons all-purpose flour
1 cup light cream
1 teaspoon instant minced onion
1 cup mashed potatoes
3 eggs, separated
   Salt and pepper

Melt butter and blend in flour. Add cream and cook, stirring, until thickened. Add onion and potatoes; heat, stirring. Quickly stir in beaten egg yolks. Season, and fold in stiffly beaten egg whites. Pour into 1½-quart soufflé dish or casserole, and bake in preheated moderate oven (350°F.) for 30 minutes, or until puffed and firm. Makes 4 servings.

CRISP NEW POTATOES

12 small new potatoes
2 tablespoons melted
   shortening
2 tablespoons all-purpose flour
1 teaspoon salt
   Dash of pepper
½ teaspoon paprika
¼ cup chopped stuffed olives

Boil potatoes and peel; roll in shortening, then in mixed flour and seasonings. Put in shallow baking dish, sprinkle with olives, and bake in preheated hot oven (425°F.) for about 20 minutes. Makes 4 servings.

POTATOES AU GRATIN

3 cups diced cold
   cooked potatoes
6 tablespoons butter
   or margarine
3 tablespoons all-purpose flour
1½ cups milk
¼ pound sharp Cheddar
   cheese, grated
   Salt and pepper
¾ cup soft bread crumbs

Put potatoes in shallow broilerproof baking dish. Melt 3 tablespoons butter; blend in flour. Add milk gradually and cook, stirring, until smooth and thickened. Add cheese and stir until melted. Season to taste with salt and pepper. Pour over potatoes and mix lightly with fork. Melt remaining butter and mix with crumbs. Sprinkle over contents of baking dish. Put in broiler under medium heat and broil until golden brown. Makes 4 servings.

SCALLOPED POTATOES

4 cups very thinly sliced potatoes
1 onion, thinly sliced
2 tablespoons all-purpose flour
   Salt and pepper
2 tablespoons butter or margarine
   Hot milk (about 1½ cups)

Put a layer of potato and onion in 1½-quart casserole. Sprinkle with some of the flour, salt, and pepper. Dot with butter. Repeat; top with a layer of potato. Dot with butter. Add enough hot milk almost to cover potato. Bake, covered, in preheated moderate oven (375°F.) for 45 minutes. Uncover and bake for 15 minutes longer. Makes 4 servings.

CHIVE POTATOES

4 cups quartered potatoes
   Butter (about ⅓ cup)
   Salt and pepper to taste
   About 1 cup hot rich milk
   Minced chives (about ⅓ cup)
   Paprika

Boil potatoes in salted water until done. Drain. Mash with ¼ cup butter, seasonings, and milk. Whip until like slightly wet mashed potatoes. Stir in ¼ cup chives gently and place in greased shallow baking dish. Bake in preheated hot oven (425°F.) for 20 minutes. Dot with butter and place under broiler until brown. Sprinkle with more chives and a little paprika. Makes 4 servings.

POTATO-SPINACH CASSEROLE

1 pound (2 large) potatoes
   Salt
1 package (10 ounces) frozen chopped
   spinach
2 tablespoons light cream
2 tablespoons butter or margarine
1 egg
   Pepper and ground nutmeg

Peel potatoes, cut into quarters, and cook in boiling salted water until tender. Drain and force through ricer. Meanwhile, cook spinach as directed on package. Drain; add to potatoes. Add cream, butter, and egg; beat until light and fluffy. Season to taste with salt, pepper, and nutmeg. Pile in 1-quart casserole and bake in preheated hot oven (400°F.) for 15 minutes. Makes 4 servings.

SIDE DISHES: FRIED

O'BRIEN POTATOES

Peel and dice small 1 pound (4 medium) potatoes and sauté in ¼ cup shortening in a heavy skillet, turning more or less constantly, until brown and tender. If desired, 1 finely chopped onion may be added as the potatoes begin to brown. Chop 4 canned pimientos and add, mixing gently. When hot, turn out on a

serving dish and sprinkle with minced parsley. Makes 4 servings.

LYONNAISE POTATOES

Boil 1 pound (about 4 medium) potatoes; cool, peel, and dice. Cook ½ cup chopped onion in ¼ cup butter until lightly colored. Add the potato cubes, sprinkle with salt and pepper, and mix well, then add 3 tablespoons consommé or light cream. Cover and cook over low heat until brown on the bottom. Fold like an omelet, slide onto a heated dish, sprinkle with minced parsley or paprika, and serve. Makes 4 servings.

SWISS RÖSTI POTATOES

New, very waxy potatoes should be boiled in their jackets or baked, although the former is desirable. (Baked ones will require much more butter.) Cool the cooked potatoes, peel and grate them coarsely. Melt a little lard or vegetable fat in a pan. A rounded-edged 8-inch skillet is the preferred one. The smallish black iron pans are excellent. Add 1½ to 2 cups of the grated potatoes and cook over brisk heat, shaking the pan from time to time. Add bits of butter, in all about 1 tablespoon, to the potatoes and push the potatoes over the butter with a spatula, lifting the edge of the potatoes to see if they are becoming too brown on the bottom. Continue shaking the pan. When they are nicely browned on the bottom, turn the potatoes with a heavy spatula and continue in the same manner on the other side. Each cake will serve 2 or 3.

Note: Sometimes a little grated onion is added to the *Rösti*. At other times, grated Gruyère or Sapsago cheese.

SOUR-CREAM POTATO PATTIES

2 cups grated cooked potatoes
½ teaspoon salt
1 cup sifted all-purpose flour
   About 1 cup dairy sour cream
   Fat for frying

Mix first 3 ingredients. Add enough sour cream to make a soft dough, as for biscuits. Roll to ⅛-inch thickness on floured board. Cut with floured 2-inch cutter. Fry in small amount of hot fat in skillet until golden brown on both sides and done. Makes 6 servings.

RISSOLÉ POTATOES

3 cups cubes of cold cooked potatoes
   Fat for deep frying
½ medium green pepper, chopped
2 pimientos, chopped

2 tablespoons butter
or margarine

Fry potatoes in deep hot fat (375°F. on a frying thermometer) until crisp and golden brown. Drain on absorbent paper and put in hot serving dish. Cook pepper and pimientos in butter for 2 or 3 minutes. Sprinkle on potatoes and serve at once. Makes 4 servings.

COUNTRY-FRIED POTATOES
6 cold cooked medium potatoes
3 tablespoons shortening
Salt and pepper

Slice potatoes. Heat shortening in skillet, add potatoes, and cook until potatoes are golden brown on one side. Turn, and brown on the other side. Sprinkle with salt and pepper. Makes 4 servings.

SKILLET POTATOES, ONIONS, AND BEANS
6 medium potatoes
3 tablespoons shortening
2 large onions, sliced
1½ cups cooked
green beans
½ cup vegetable
cooking water
Salt and pepper

Scrub unpeeled potatoes well, but do not peel. Cut into thin slices. Heat shortening in large skillet. Add potatoes and onions. Cook slowly, turning carefully as vegetables brown lightly. When cooked, add beans and water. Season with salt and pepper to taste. Simmer for 5 minutes, stirring gently to prevent sticking. Makes 4 servings.

SOUFFLÉED POTATOES
Peel oval baking potatoes and cut them into uniform ovals about ⅛ inch thick. Wash the potatoes to remove any extra starch and dry them thoroughly on paper towels.

Have ready 2 kettles of frying fat. Heat one kettle to 350°F. and the other to 400°F. on a frying thermometer. Put a single layer of potatoes (do not put any more) into frying basket. Lower basket into 350°F. fat. Without raising the temperature, cook the potatoes until they begin to brown and puff slightly. Remove the basket from the kettle and plunge it at once into the kettle of 400°F. fat. The potatoes will puff at once. Continue to cook them in this fat until they are richly browned. Drain them on absorbent paper toweling. Sprinkle with salt and serve at once. The potatoes will deflate if allowed to stand, but they may be puffed again in hot fat.

POTATO PANCAKES
4 large potatoes
1 small onion
½ cup milk
1 teaspoon salt
1 egg, beaten
2 tablespoons all-purpose flour
Shortening for frying

Peel potatoes; grate potatoes and onion into milk. Mix with remaining ingredients except shortening. Drop by tablespoonfuls into hot shortening in skillet. Brown on both sides, and serve at once. Makes 6 servings.

POTATO CAKES ALLA CALABRESE
1 cup mashed potatoes
1 cup all-purpose flour
3 teaspoons baking powder
Few parsley sprigs,
finely chopped
½ cup grated
Parmesan cheese
2 eggs, slightly beaten
Salt and pepper to taste
Cooking oil

Mix all ingredients except oil. Shape into rolls about 3 inches long and 1 inch in diameter. Fry in 1 inch of hot oil in skillet until golden-brown and done. Serve hot as a vegetable or as a bread. Makes 4 to 6 servings.

POTATO-AND-ONION CAKE
4 medium potatoes
Butter or margarine
3 onions, chopped
Salt and pepper to taste
Fine dry bread crumbs

Peel potatoes and slice very thin. Melt butter in heavy skillet. When hot, add alternate layers of potatoes, onions, and seasonings. Sprinkle top layer with crumbs. Cook slowly until well browned on bottom and nearly done. Turn out on flat plate. Add more butter to skillet and slide potatoes back into pan, brown side up. Cook until browned. Turn out to serve. Makes 4 servings.

PRINCESS POTATOES
3 cups large cubes of cold cooked
potatoes
Fat for deep frying
2 tablespoons butter or margarine
2 tablespoons all-purpose flour
¼ teaspoon salt
⅛ teaspoon pepper
1 cup milk
1 bouillon cube
2 parsley sprigs, chopped

Fry potatoes in deep hot fat (375°F. on a frying thermometer) until golden brown. Melt butter in saucepan. Blend in flour and seasonings. Gradually add milk and cook, stirring, until smooth and thickened. Add bouillon cube and stir until dissolved. Put potatoes in serving dish; top with sauce and sprinkle with parsley. Makes 4 servings.

POTATO DISHES WITH FROZEN FRENCH FRIES
Each of the following recipes uses unthawed frozen French-fried potatoes (two 9-ounce packages) and makes 4 generous servings.

EASY O'BRIEN: Sprinkle 2 boxes French fries with salt, and heat in oven as directed on the label. Chop ½ medium green pepper and 1 small onion. Cook for 5 minutes in ¼ cup margarine. Add 1 canned pimiento, snipped into pieces with scissors. Pour over potatoes.

DEVILED: Mix ½ teaspoon each of chili powder, garlic salt, and powdered mustard. Sprinkle mixture on 2 packages French fries. Heat in oven as directed on the label.

ONION: Heat 1 can (10½ ounces) undiluted onion soup in large skillet. Add 2 packages French fries. Cover and heat slowly, separating potatoes with fork.

VERMONT: Heat 1 can (10¾ ounces) beef gravy and ½ teaspoon each of onion salt and seasoned salt in large skillet. Add 2 packages French fries. Cover and heat slowly, separating potatoes with fork.

SAVORY: Sprinkle 2 packages French fries with 2 teaspoons dry garlic-flavored French-dressing mix. Heat in oven as directed on the label. Just before serving, stir in ¼ cup grated Parmesan cheese.

SOUTHERN: Sprinkle 2 packages French fries lightly with salt and ½ teaspoon poultry seasoning. Heat in oven as directed on the label. Dice fine ¼ pound salt pork and cook until browned and crisp. Drain; sprinkle on potatoes.

SUNDAY: Heat 1 can (10 ounces) frozen potato soup, 1 cup milk, and 1 cup (one 8-ounce can) onions, drained. Pour over 2 packages French fries in shallow 1½-quart baking dish. Sprinkle with paprika and chopped parsley. Bake in preheated hot oven (400°F.) for about 25 minutes.

ZIPPY: Put 2 packages French fries in shallow baking pan and sprinkle with celery salt. Heat in oven as directed on the label. Remove from oven; onto potatoes drop in dabs ½ cup process American cheese spread. Put under broiler for a few minutes until browned.

 DESSERTS

CHOCOLATE POTATO CAKE
¾ cup butter or
margarine, softened
1½ cups sugar
4 eggs, separated
1 cup hot riced potato
1½ cups sifted all-purpose flour
2 teaspoons baking powder
½ teaspoon salt
½ cup cocoa
1 teaspoon ground cinnamon
½ teaspoon ground nutmeg
¼ teaspoon ground cloves
1 cup milk
1 teaspoon vanilla extract
1 cup chopped nuts
Fluffy White Frosting

Cream butter and 1 cup sugar until light.

Add egg yolks and beat well. Add potato and mix thoroughly. Add sifted dry ingredients alternately with milk, beating until smooth. Add vanilla and nuts. Beat egg whites until stiff but not dry. Gradually add remaining sugar, beating until very stiff. Fold into first mixture. Pour into pan (13 x 9 x 2 inches), lined on the bottom with wax paper. Bake in preheated moderate oven (350°F.) for about 45 minutes. Cool and frost with Fluffy White Frosting.

Fluffy White Frosting

In top part of small double boiler, combine 2 egg whites, 1½ cups sugar, ⅛ teaspoon salt, ⅓ cup water, and 2 teaspoons light corn syrup. Put over boiling water and beat well with rotary beater or electric mixer for 7 minutes, or until mixture will stand in stiff peaks. Fold in 1 teaspoon vanilla extract.

POTATO DOUGHNUTS

2 eggs
1 cup sugar
2 tablespoons melted butter
1 cup mashed potatoes
  (may be leftovers)
1 cup buttermilk
4½ cups sifted all-purpose flour
4 teaspoons baking powder
1 teaspoon each of baking
  soda and salt
½ teaspoon each of ground
  cinnamon and nutmeg
Fat for deep frying

Beat eggs with sugar. Stir in butter, mashed potatoes, and buttermilk. Sift flour with baking powder, baking soda, salt, cinnamon, and nutmeg. Add to egg mixture and blend. Chill dough for 1 to 2 hours. Roll out to ½-inch thickness. Cut into rounds with doughnut cutter or glass. Fry in deep hot fat (365°F. on a frying thermometer) for a few minutes on each side, or until light brown. Drain on paper towels. Dust with sugar if desired. Makes about 4 dozen.

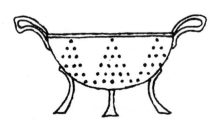

Potato Dishes from France

by Olga Kevorkoff

 SOUPS

POTATO SOUP PARMENTIER

4 medium potatoes
3 or 4 leeks without their greens
Sweet butter
Salt to taste
1 cup milk brought to a boil
1 egg yolk or 1 whole egg
White bread, cut into squares and
  browned in butter

Peel and dice potatoes. Chop leeks fine, browning them very lightly in a little butter. Put both in a covered pot; add water to cover, and salt. Cover pot; let cook on medium to slow heat until both vegetables are done. Pass entire mixture through food mill; add the milk. Add enough water to make soup of the right consistency. Bring to boil. Remove from heat. Beat egg yolk or egg. Add a small amount of soup to egg, stirring constantly. Return mixture to soup in pot. Mix well. Pour into serving bowl; add 1 tablespoon sweet butter and the bread squares. Serve. Makes 6 to 8 servings.

POTATO SOUP AMPHITRYON

To 1 quart Potato Soup Parmentier add 2 or 3 tomatoes, previously cooked (steamed) or canned. Add ½ cup cooked rice. Serve with a sprinkling of parsley.

 ## SALADS AND MAIN DISHES

SALAD LORRAINE

4 to 6 medium potatoes
2 cups light cream
1 teaspoon wine vinegar
3 or 4 small sour gherkins and/or 1
  tablespoon capers, chopped
  Dash of English mustard
  Salt and pepper to taste

Cut boiled potatoes into ¼-inch slices. When cool (do not ice), mix with the cream, to which the other ingredients

have been added. Makes 4 servings.

SALAD ALSACE

4 to 6 potatoes
2 cups dry white wine
1 small onion, chopped
  Salt to taste
1 tablespoon white-wine vinegar
  Pepper to taste
2 to 3 tablespoons salad oil
  Chopped fresh parsley and dill

Boil potatoes and cut into ¼- to ½-inch slices. While still warm, put into bowl and pour on the wine, letting it penetrate before proceeding. Drain off excess wine. Mix onion with potatoes. Dissolve good pinch of salt in the vinegar and dress the potato-onion mixture; add pepper and oil. Sprinkle on and mix into the salad a liberal amount of chopped parsley and fresh dill. Serve preferably lukewarm, or cold, but never iced. Makes 4 servings.

BIARRITZ

4 medium potatoes
½ pound salt pork, diced
1 bunch of parsley, chopped
1 garlic clove, minced
  Salt and pepper (preferably paprika)
2 pounds codfish or similar fish
2 tablespoons olive oil
  All-purpose flour

Peel raw potatoes and cut into rounds. Put in a covered pan a layer of half of the salt pork, some of the parsley, and some of the garlic; cover with a layer of potatoes, salt, and pepper, then fish broken up into large flakes, salt, and pepper. Cover with remaining salt pork, parsley, and garlic, and finally with remaining potatoes, salt, and pepper. Add water just to cover the last layer and add the oil. Let boil, covered, over medium heat until potatoes are done. Thicken with a little flour if desired. Serve very hot. Makes 4 to 6 servings.

CHEESE POTATOES

½ recipe Duchesse Potatoes (page 1470)
¼ to ½ pound cheese (Pont l'Evêque,
  Bel Paese, Muenster, or equivalent
  soft cheese, cut into large cubes)
1 egg, beaten
½ cup soft bread crumbs

Grease with butter about a dozen 6-ounce custard cups. Fill with Duchesse Potatoes, up to 1 inch from top. Put 1 cube of cheese in center of each, pressing down halfway. Brush with egg, and sprinkle with bread crumbs. Bake in preheated hot oven (425°F.) for about 6 minutes; serve while hot. Makes 6 servings.

CUILETS

1 recipe Duchesse Potatoes (below)
½ cup butter
8 to 10 chicken livers, chopped into very small pieces
¼ cup sherry
½ cup mushrooms, sliced
¼ cup minced boiled ham
¼ teaspoon each of salt and pepper
1 egg, beaten
1 cup dry bread crumbs

Prepare potatoes. Melt butter in pan and half cook chicken livers carefully over low heat; add sherry, mushrooms, ham, and salt and pepper; cook gently until liquid is almost absorbed. Form the potatoes into patties, enclosing 1 heaping tablespoon of the liver mixture inside each patty. Dip into egg, then into bread crumbs; place in buttered baking dish. Bake in preheated moderate oven (350° F.) for about 15 minutes, or until golden brown. Serve immediately. Makes 4 to 6 servings.

SIDE DISHES: BOILED

DUCHESSE

2 pounds potatoes
½ cup sweet butter
½ teaspoon salt
¼ teaspoon pepper
1 egg yolk

Peel potatoes, cut into quarters, and cook until done. Drain off water, and let dry, if possible in preheated hot oven (400° F.), for 10 minutes. Mash well, add butter, salt, and pepper, and mix well over low heat, stirring until smooth. A double boiler is recommended. Remove from heat, add egg yolk, and mix well, for about 5 minutes, if possible in top part of double boiler to retain heat. Serve hot. Makes 4 to 6 servings.

À LA PARISIENNE

With a melon-ball cutter cut potatoes into very small balls, *noisettes,* about 1 inch in diameter. Boil gently; when done, immerse in sauce of meat roast which accompanies the meal, or which has been put aside for this purpose, and let simmer on side of heat, without boiling. Strain off surplus sauce, sprinkle with parsley, and serve with any meat.

À LA CRÈME

2 pounds potatoes
½ teaspoon salt
¼ teaspoon pepper
⅛ teaspoon ground nutmeg
¼ cup butter or margarine
½ cup milk
¾ to 1 cup heavy cream

Peel potatoes, cut into quarters, and boil until done. Drain well; over low heat, preferably in top part of a double boiler, mash. Add salt, pepper, nutmeg, and butter; mix well. Add milk, stirring con-

stantly for 5 minutes longer. Put mixture into covered serving dish, cover it with preheated (but not boiled) cream, and let stand, covered, for about 5 minutes before serving. Place serving dish in hot water to keep warm. Makes 6 to 8 servings.

BOULES

6 medium potatoes
2 cups potato flour
2 eggs
Salt to taste
White bread, cut into cubes and sautéed in butter (croutons)

Peel potatoes, boil and let cool. Add potato flour; mash and mix well. Add the eggs, one by one, and season with salt. This should give a doughlike mass. Form orange-size balls, incorporating in the center of each 4 or 5 croutons. Boil in large pot of strongly boiling salted water. The *boules* will rise when ready. Drain. Serve with pot roast or any goulash. Makes 4 to 6 servings.
Note: Leftover *boules* are excellent if sliced into ½-inch disks and fried in a little butter.

BORDEAUX

4 medium potatoes
1 garlic clove
1 tablespoon cooking oil
2 tomatoes, diced
¼ teaspoon each of salt, pepper, and ground thyme

Peel potatoes and boil until done. Cut into thin slices. Brown garlic lightly in oil; remove garlic; add tomatoes, salt, pepper, and thyme. Cook gently for 5 minutes. Add potatoes and cook for 5 to 10 minutes longer. Serve immediately. Makes 4 servings.

SIDE DISHES: BAKED

SAVARIN

Peel raw potatoes and cut into thin matchlike sticks. Wash and dry well on paper towels. Put into a 6-cup ring mold. Press down, and add a liberal amount of butter. Bake in preheated very hot oven (500°F.) for at least 20 minutes, or until potatoes are done, the butter is absorbed, and the potatoes browned and crusted. Turn over onto a hot serving dish. Serve with the following sauce: In 2 tablespoons butter, over low heat, lightly brown 2 tablespoons all-purpose flour; when pasty, slowly stir in 1 cup milk and 1 cup heavy cream. Add salt, pepper, ground nutmeg, ¼ cup port, 1 tablespoon grated cheese (Parmesan is especially good in this), and 2 teaspoons paprika. Cook over low heat until smooth and thickened.

JEANETTE

4 medium potatoes
¼ cup melted butter
½ cup consommé
½ teaspoon each of salt and pepper
½ cup grated Swiss-type cheese
¼ cup sweet butter

Peel potatoes and slice into ½-inch rounds. Cook over low heat in the melted butter until they begin to be tender, adding some of the consommé as may become necessary. Put potatoes and remaining consommé in buttered 1-quart baking dish; sprinkle with salt and pepper. Cover with grated cheese and dot with butter. Bake in preheated hot oven (400°F.) for 10 minutes. Makes 3 or 4 servings.

GRATIN AUX CHAMPIGNONS

4 or 5 medium potatoes
¼ teaspoon each of salt and pepper
1½ pounds mushrooms
1 garlic clove
1 cup Swiss-type cheese, grated
Small bunch of parsley, chopped
1 small onion, minced
2 cups heavy cream
½ cup butter or margarine

Peel raw potatoes and slice into thin rounds; wash, dry, and sprinkle with salt and pepper. Wash, dry, and slice mushrooms. Rub a 2-quart baking dish with garlic and butter it well. Put in successively 1 layer of potatoes and 1 layer of mushrooms. Sprinkle over the layer some of the cheese, parsley, and onion. Repeat until supply is used, finishing with a layer of potatoes. Cover the last potato layer with cream. Sprinkle on another layer of cheese and dot top with butter. Bake in preheated moderate oven (375° F.) until potatoes are easily pierced. Serve very hot. Makes 6 to 8 servings.

GALETTE

4 or 5 medium potatoes
½ cup butter or margarine
1 cup consommé, warmed
Salt and pepper to taste
2 medium onions, chopped
Ground nutmeg (optional)

Peel potatoes, dice, and boil in lightly salted water until done. Pour off water and mash potatoes while still warm. In pot, preferably top part of a double boiler, mix into this mash ¼ cup of the butter and the consommé, and season with salt and pepper, stirring all the time. In 2 tablespoons butter lightly brown onions. Add the potato mash and mix well; add nutmeg, if desired, after mixture is removed from heat. Put into a 1-quart baking dish; dot top with remaining butter. Bake in preheated hot oven (400°F.) to form a brown crust. Serve hot. Makes 4 servings.

MONT D'OR

Prepare Duchesse Potatoes (at left) Mix with grated Swiss-type cheese in the proportion of about 1 part cheese to 6

parts potatoes. Place the mixture in a baking dish, forming a pointed peak, like a mountain, in the center. Sprinkle liberally with grated cheese, and place in preheated extremely hot oven (500°F.) for 5 or 6 minutes, or until deep golden-brown. Makes 4 to 6 servings.

 ### SIDE DISHES: FRIED

BRETONNE

4 or 5 medium potatoes
1 medium onion, chopped
1 tablespoon butter
2 ounces salt pork, diced
  Salt and pepper to taste

Peel potatoes and boil until almost tender. Slice potatoes into ¼-inch rounds. Sauté onion in butter; add potatoes and salt pork, and let brown without burning, turning from time to time. Season with salt and pepper. Serve immediately. Makes 4 servings.

CHASSEUR

Prepare potatoes as for Bretonne; in addition to salt pork, add 2 beaten eggs when potatoes are almost done; mix in. Mixture is cooked until eggs are set. Also, a liberal sprinkling of chopped parsley before serving is recommended. Makes 4 servings.

VICHY

½ recipe Duchesse Potatoes (page 1470)
½ cup all-purpose flour
1 egg, beaten
1 cup fine dry bread crumbs
2 cups cooking oil

Form the Duchesse mixture into croquettes, either balls or finger-shape, about 1½ inches thick. Roll in flour, then in egg, then in bread crumbs. Fry in deep hot oil (375°F. on a frying thermometer) until very brown. Let drain on absorbent paper, and serve. Makes about 6 servings.

SAUCISSES

3 medium potatoes
½ cup sweet butter
  Salt
  Ground nutmeg, if desired
  All-purpose flour in same quantity as the potatoes after being mashed (about 3 cups)
3 or 4 eggs

Prepare separately:

1. Bake potatoes in preheated moderate oven (350°F.) for 1 hour, or until tender. Take out pulp, mash, adding half of butter, a little salt, and pinch of nutmeg. 2. Boil 2 cups salted water with ¼ cup butter. When boiling point is reached, stir in flour, stirring constantly. Resume cooking over low heat and stir until thick and creamy. Remove from heat; add the eggs, one by one, mixing well.

In about equal parts, mix the potatoes (1) and the flour mixture (2). Season with salt, if necessary.

This mash, which should be fairly thick, can then be formed into sausage-like shapes and either fried in deep hot cooking oil (375°F.) on a frying thermometer), or dropped into gently boiling water, in which case they should be served with a sauce according to taste. Makes 4 to 6 servings.

FRITES PROVENÇALES

6 to 8 medium potatoes
  Salt
  Cooking oil sufficient for potatoes to float
1 garlic clove

Peel raw potatoes and slice into sticks ½ inch thick. Sprinkle liberally with salt; tilt so that liquid will drain off, and let stand in this position for 1 hour. Dry in towel; put into heated oil (375°F. on a frying thermometer), into which a cut garlic clove has been dropped. Fry until golden brown. Drain on absorbent paper. Sprinkle with salt, and serve. Makes 3 or 4 servings.

POTATO FLOUR or STARCH—A very fine flour made from potatoes ground to a pulp and freed from their fibers. The residue is flour.

Potato flour is an old product, but corn flour or cornstarch has taken its place in most American households. In Europe, however, potato flour is still widely used, both for cooking, as in gravies, sauces, and stewed fruits thickened with potato flour to make a pudding, and for baking, where it gives a dry texture to cakes.

For delicate gravies and sauces, potato flour is preferable to cornstarch as a thickener since it does not carry a raw flavor even when cooked for only a short time. It also gives the sauce a little transparency. In fruit puddings, it gives the dish an attractive, clear appearance. However, when potato flour is boiled it will thin out. Serve sauce at once as sauces thickened with potato flour have little holding power.

In using potato flour, one tablespoon will thicken one cup of liquid to a medium consistency. If substituting potato flour for other thickeners, one and a half teaspoons potato flour equals one tablespoon all-purpose flour; generally speaking, potato flour can be substituted measure for measure for cornstarch, but to be on the safe side, the recipe should be tested with each.

Availability—Potato flour is found in health-food stores and in some general food stores, especially those catering to people of German and Scandinavian descent. It can be found in Jewish markets during Passover when it is used instead of flour.

Storage—Potato flour is apt to deteriorate far more quickly than cornstarch and it should not be stored longer than a month or two.

Nutritive Food Value—Contains some protein, calcium, phosphorus, riboflavin, thiamine, niacin, and vitamin C.
☐ 3½ ounces = 351 calories

NORWEGIAN DALESMAN CAKES

1 cup butter or margarine
1 cup sugar
1 cup heavy cream, whipped
1 cup potato flour
2 cups sifted all-purpose flour
1½ cups minced blanched almonds
1 teaspoon vanilla extract

Cream butter until light and fluffy. Beat in sugar until mixture whitens. Beat in whipped cream. Stir in potato flour, all-purpose flour, almonds, and vanilla. Drop by teaspoonfuls onto lightly greased cookie sheets. Bake in preheated moderate oven (350°F.) for 10 to 12 minutes, or until golden brown. Makes 50 to 60 cookies.

POT-AU-FEU—Literally translated the phrase means "pot of fire" and it is the French version of a boiled dinner. Generally it consists of one or more meats, or chicken and meat, and a variety of vegetables cooked in liquid which is then served as a gravy with the meat and vegetables.

POT HERB—Any herb whose leaves, stems, or blossoms are cooked like a vegetable. Some of the commonest ones are: borage, chervil, chicory, lovage, sorrel, sweet cicely, and rampion. When cooking pot herbs, boil leaves as you would spinach, roots as you would turnips.

POT LIQUOR or LIKKER—The liquid left in the pot after cooking vegetables. In the Southeastern states, vegetables are often cooked for a long time in large amounts of water and with such meat as pigs' tails or salt pork. Several vegetables, potatoes, greens, and turnips, for example, may be cooked together. When the vegetables are done, they are removed with the meat to a serving dish. The fat is then skimmed from the liquid, and spooned over the vegetables. Any remaining liquid is poured into cups and served to the children.

POT PIE—A meat or poultry pie, usually made with vegetables and potatoes, and baked in an uncovered casserole with a single or double crust of pastry or biscuit dough.

VEAL-AND-HAM POTPIE

  1 pound boneless veal shoulder, cut into ½-inch cubes
  ½ pound smoked ham, cut into ½-inch cubes
  ¼ cup all-purpose flour
  3 tablespoons fat
  1 can beef gravy
  1 teaspoon Worcestershire
  ¼ pound mushrooms, sliced
  1 large potato, peeled and diced
  2 celery stalks, diced
  8 small white onions, peeled
1½ cups biscuit mix
  ½ cup milk

Dredge meats with flour and brown on all sides in the fat in a Dutch oven or large skillet. Pour off fat. Add remaining ingredients except biscuit mix and milk; pour into 2-quart casserole. Cover and bake in preheated slow oven (325°F.) for 1½ hours, or until meat is tender. Remove casserole from oven and increase oven heat to very hot (450°F.). Prepare biscuit mix with the milk and roll out on lightly floured board. Cut into rounds and put on mixture in casserole. Bake for 15 minutes. Makes 4 servings.

POTPOURRI—A mixture of flower petals and spices which can easily be made at home. It was particularly popular in Victorian and Edwardian times, when bowls of potpourri (silver ones, preferably) stood in all the best drawing rooms, giving the air a lovely, haunting fragrance.

HOW TO MAKE A ROSE POTPOURRI

  6 cups dried rose petals
  ½ teaspoon each of ground cloves, cinnamon, allspice
  ½ teaspoon mint flakes
1½ tablespoons orrisroot*

Pick the freshest blossoms of several varieties of fragrant roses. Separate the petals and spread them in single layers on a dry cloth or in bottom of a large shallow cardboard box. Place in a dry shady spot for 3 to 4 days, or until they are thoroughly dry. Add spices and orrisroot. Mix well. Pack into a large jar. Cover tightly and let stand for 4 to 5 weeks, stirring every 2 or 3 days. Tie in sachet bags with colorful ribbon.
*Orrisroot is available at drugstores.

POT ROAST—A term applied to larger cuts of meat which are cooked by braising, that is cooked slowly in a small amount of liquid or in steam. The meat may or may not be browned in a little fat before it is braised.

Lean or less tender cuts of meat, those which would be too dry or too tough if roasted, are generally used for pot roasts, although any meat or poultry, including tender cuts, can be used. When there is no qualifying adjective used to describe it, a pot roast is assumed to be made of beef.

The beef cuts most suitable for pot roast are: blade, arm, boneless shoulder (or chuck), Boston (or English) cut, rolled boned rump, eye of the round, heel of the round, boned and rolled sirloin tip, brisket, and flank.

Lamb is such a tender meat that all its cuts may be roasted. However, for pot-roasting these cuts can be used: square-cut shoulder, rolled shoulder, cushion shoulder, breast, and rolled breast.

Like lamb, pork cuts are so tender that they are usually roasted. However, any of these cuts can be pot-roasted: Boston butt, rolled Boston butt, arm roast, fresh picnic, rolled fresh picnic, loin, and leg (fresh ham).

The veal cuts best for pot roast are: blade, arm, breast, rolled shoulder, and boned and rolled rump.

Among the variety meats whole livers, kidneys, and hearts can be pot-roasted.

Whole chickens, ducklings, and small turkeys can be pot-roasted.

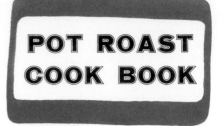

COMPANY YANKEE POT ROAST

  4 pounds beef for pot roast
    Salt
  ¼ cup water
  1 medium onion, sliced
  ½ cup diced turnip
  ½ cup diced carrot
  ¼ cup sliced celery, with leaves
  2 tablespoons chopped parsley
  ½ cup cooked peas
  1 can (3 ounces) sliced mushrooms, drained

Brown meat on all sides in heavy kettle, adding 1 tablespoon shortening if necessary. Sprinkle with salt. Put a rack in kettle under meat; add water and onion. Simmer, covered, for 3½ to 4 hours. Add remaining ingredients except peas and mushrooms. Simmer for 30 minutes, or until vegetables are done. Then remove meat and thicken liquid with a flour-and-water paste if desired. Add peas and mushrooms and heat. Season to taste. Makes 6 servings.

SPICED BEEF POT ROAST

  5 pounds of beef for pot roast
  2 tablespoons shortening
  2 cups water
  2 tablespoons mixed pickling spice
  2 teaspoons salt
  1 pound mixed dried fruits
    Buttered cooked noodles

Brown meat on all sides in hot shortening in large heavy kettle. Remove meat and pour off fat. Add water and bring to boil. Put meat on rack in kettle; add pickling spice. Simmer, covered, for 2½ hours. Add salt and fruits; simmer for 1 hour longer, or until meat is tender. Slice meat and serve with the liquid poured over top. Garnish with dried fruits. Serve with noodles. Makes 6 servings, with meat left over.

WEST INDIAN POT ROAST

  1 can flaked coconut
1¼ cups boiling water
  3 pounds beef for pot roast
    All-purpose flour
  2 tablespoons shortening
    Salt and pepper
  1 onion, sliced
  1 garlic clove, minced

Put coconut in bowl and cover with boiling water; let stand until cold. Strain, reserving liquid. Dredge meat with flour and brown on all sides in shortening in heavy kettle. Season with salt and pepper to taste; add coconut liquid, onion, and garlic. Simmer, covered, for 3 to 3½ hours, or until tender, adding water if necessary. Remove meat and thicken liquid if desired. Makes 4 servings.

CHILI-SAUCE-BEEF POT ROAST

3 pounds beef for pot roast
1 tablespoon shortening
  Salt and pepper
¼ cup water
3 onions, sliced
1 bottle (12 ounces) chili sauce
2 dill pickles, chopped

Brown meat in shortening in kettle. Add salt and pepper. Put a rack in kettle under meat; add water and onions. Simmer, covered, for 2 to 2½ hours. Add chili sauce and pickles and simmer for 1 hour longer, or until meat is tender. Makes 4 servings.

GINGER BEEF POT ROAST

4 pounds beef for pot roast
1 teaspoon ground turmeric
2 teaspoons ground ginger
2 teaspoons salt
2 tablespoons shortening
2 onions, chopped
2 garlic cloves, minced
1 cup canned tomatoes
1 cup beef bouillon
2 dried red peppers, crushed

Rub meat with turmeric, ginger, and salt. Brown on all sides in shortening in heavy kettle. Put meat on rack in kettle. Add remaining ingredients. Simmer, covered, for 3½ hours. If desired, thicken liquid with a flour-and-water paste. Makes 6 servings.

POT-ROASTED FLANK STEAK WITH VEGETABLES

1 flank steak (about 2 pounds)
½ cup chopped celery tops
1 onion, chopped
  Few parsley sprigs, chopped
½ teaspoon crumbled dried thyme
2 teaspoons salt
½ teaspoon pepper
1 tablespoon shortening
1 cup water
8 small whole carrots
8 small potatoes

Put steak on board and pound with rolling pin or mallet until both sides are slightly flattened. Sprinkle with celery tops, onion, parsley, thyme, half of salt, and the pepper. Roll up jelly-roll fashion, beginning at the pointed end. Tie with string. Brown on all sides in hot shortening in heavy kettle. Add water. Simmer, covered, for 1½ hours, turning meat occasionally, and adding more water if necessary. Add vegetables and remaining salt and pepper. Simmer for 30 minutes longer. To serve, slice meat diagonally. Makes 4 servings.

PEPPERY BEEF POT ROAST

4 pounds boneless beef brisket
1 tablespoon peppercorns

1½ teaspoons salt
¼ teaspoon ground allspice
2 tablespoons fine dry bread crumbs
1 teaspoon garlic salt
1 cup hot water
1 onion, sliced

Have butcher pound brisket flat. Put on board; with a heavy knife score the meat lengthwise and crosswise on both sides. Put peppercorns in a small cloth bag and crush with hammer or mallet. Sprinkle meat with crushed peppercorns, salt, allspice, bread crumbs, and garlic salt. Roll very tightly lengthwise. Cut into two crosswise pieces. Tie firmly with string. Put on a rack in heavy kettle. Add hot water and onion. Simmer, covered, for 4 hours, or until tender, adding more water if necessary. Serve hot; or cool in the broth, then chill. Makes 8 servings.

BEEF BRISKET WITH MUSHROOM GRAVY

4-pound piece of boneless fresh beef brisket
1 onion, sliced
  Salt and pepper
  All-purpose flour
½ pound fresh mushrooms, sliced
2 tablespoons butter or margarine

In large heavy kettle brown beef in its own fat. Pour off fat. Add onion. Cook, covered, over low heat for 1 hour. Put meat in shallow pan to cool. Cut into attractive serving slices. Return to kettle and sprinkle with salt and pepper. Cover and simmer for 2 hours, or until tender. Turn slices once. Remove meat to hot platter. To make gravy: skim off fat, add a little flour and water paste, and cook until slightly thickened. Brown mushrooms lightly in the butter; add to gravy. Makes 6 servings.

COFFEE POT ROAST WITH VEGETABLES

2 pounds beef for pot roast
1 cup each of tomatoes, water, and black coffee
  Salt and pepper
1 onion, chopped
6 carrots, peeled and diced
2 cups diced potatoes
1 package (10 ounces) frozen peas

Brown meat on all sides in heavy kettle, adding a small amount of fat if necessary. Add tomatoes, liquids, salt, and pepper. Bring to boil, cover, and simmer for 1 hour. Add onion and carrot; simmer for 15 minutes. Add potatoes and cook until vegetables are tender; then add peas and cook for a few minutes. If desired, thicken gravy with flour blended with a little cold water. Makes 6 servings.

POT ROAST FONTAINE

5 pounds beef for pot roast
2 garlic cloves, split
  Salt and pepper
  All-purpose flour
2 tablespoons olive oil
¼ cup brandy
1 bay leaf

  Pinch each of crumbled dried thyme and marjoram
2 onions, sliced
½ cup chopped celery
4 carrots, split
2 tomatoes, cut up
1 cup dry red wine
½ cup water
½ cup cooked or canned sliced drained mushrooms
1 tablespoon cornstarch

Make small cuts in meat and stuff with slivers of garlic. Sprinkle with salt and pepper and rub with flour. Brown on all sides in oil. Slip rack under the meat. Turn off heat, add brandy (be sure the kettle is away from everything as flame will come up over meat), and ignite. Let the brandy blaze until the flame dies down. Then cover to put out flame. Add bay leaf, thyme, marjoram, onions, celery, carrots, tomatoes, wine, and water. Cover and simmer for 3½ hours, or until meat is tender. Remove meat and carrots, strain liquid for gravy, and add a little water, if necessary. Add mushrooms. Mix cornstarch with a little cold water. Add to gravy and cook until thickened. Season to taste with salt and pepper. Slice meat and serve with gravy and mashed potatoes, or rice, if desired. Makes 6 servings, with meat left over for the next day.

POT ROAST À LA ESZTERHAZY

3 pounds beef round for pot roast
8 slices of bacon, cut into ¼-inch strips
  Salt
2 tablespoons lard
2 medium onions, chopped
2 medium carrots, chopped
2 parsnips, diced
2 celery stalks, diced
1 bay leaf
10 peppercorns
½ teaspoon crumbled dried thyme
¼ teaspoon each of ground allspice and nutmeg
2 cups beef bouillon
2 tablespoons all-purpose flour
½ cup dairy sour cream
  Grated rind of 1 lemon
1 teaspoon chopped capers

Lard beef with fat parts of bacon. (Use a larding needle or push bacon into meat with knitting needle.) Salt meat. In a Dutch oven brown beef in hot lard. Remove. Sauté vegetables in same fat until lightly browned. Add herbs and spices and half the bouillon. Return beef to Dutch oven. Cook, covered, in preheated moderate oven (350°F.) for 3 hours, or until meat is tender. Add remaining bouillon as needed during cooking. Remove beef to warm platter. Skim fat from gravy. Beat flour into sour cream. Gradually add to gravy while stirring and simmer, stirring constantly, over low heat until sauce is well blended. Stir in lemon rind and capers. Add salt to taste. Slice beef and pour sauce over meat. Makes 6 servings.

Spiced Beef Pot Roast

Note: For authenticity the gravy must not be strained.

POT-ROASTED BREAST OF LAMB WITH DILL SAUCE

3 pounds breast of lamb
1 cup water
1 teaspoon dillseed
1 teaspoon salt
4 peppercorns
 Dill Sauce

Put lamb in kettle and add water and seasonings. Simmer, covered, for 1½ hours, or until meat is tender, adding more water if necessary. Remove meat and strain liquid. Prepare Dill Sauce, using liquid, and pour over meat. Makes 4 to 6 servings.

Dill Sauce

Melt 2 tablespoons butter or margarine and blend in 2 tablespoons flour. Add 1¼ cups strained liquid, 1 teaspoon sugar, and 1 teaspoon vinegar. Cook until thickened. Beat 1 egg yolk; stir in small amount of sauce; add to remainder of sauce and mix well. Season to taste.

POT-ROASTED BREAST OF LAMB, ROSÉ

3 pounds breast of lamb
 Salt and pepper to taste
1 cup chicken broth
¼ cup currant jelly
¼ cup boiling water
½ cup rosé wine
 Few parsley sprigs, chopped

Brown meat on all sides in heavy kettle. Pour off fat and sprinkle meat with salt and pepper. Add broth, cover, and simmer for 2 hours, or until meat is tender. Dissolve jelly in the boiling water. Add wine and parsley; pour over meat. Simmer for about 15 minutes longer, basting several times with the liquid in kettle. Serve meat with the liquid; thicken, if desired, with a small amount of flour-and-water paste. Makes 4 servings.

MEXICAN PORK POT ROAST

5 tablespoons olive oil
3 garlic cloves, minced
¼ pound hot Spanish or Italian sausage
4 pounds pork loin
3 onions, chopped
2 tomatoes, peeled and chopped
1 cup chicken bouillon
6 green peppers, sliced thin
 Salt and pepper
 All-purpose flour

Heat 3 tablespoons of the oil in heavy kettle. Add garlic and sausage cut into small pieces. Cook until well browned: remove sausage. Brown pork loin on all sides. Remove pork and pour off fat. Return pork to kettle with half of onions, the tomatoes, bouillon, and sausage. Simmer, covered, for about 2½ hours. In skillet heat remaining oil. Add remaining onions and the peppers. Cook, stirring occasionally, until tender; season. Remove pork and slice. Arrange on hot platter; thicken the liquid in kettle with a flour and water paste; add salt and pepper and pour some of the gravy over pork. Top with peppers and onions. Serve remaining gravy in bowl. Makes 6 servings.

SPICED PORK POT ROAST
1 fresh ham (about 5 pounds)
1½ cups water
1 teaspoon each of salt, crumbled dried thyme, ground sage, and whole cloves
1½ teaspoons whole allspice
1 bay leaf, crumbled
1 tablespoon slivered lemon rind
2 tablespoons fresh lemon juice
1 medium onion, chopped
1 large carrot, diced

Brown meat on all sides in heavy kettle. Pour off fat. Place meat on rack and put in kettle. Add remaining ingredients. Simmer, covered, for 4 hours, or until meat is tender, basting occasionally with liquid in kettle. Add more water if necessary. Thicken liquid if desired. Makes 8 servings.

FRESH PORK PICNIC POT ROAST WITH VEGETABLES
3 pounds rolled fresh picnic
All-purpose flour
Salt, pepper, and paprika
2 tablespoons fat
2 cups water
1 bay leaf
1 garlic clove
4 sweet potatoes
4 large white turnips
½ medium head cabbage

Rub meat with flour, salt, pepper, and paprika. Brown on all sides in hot fat in Dutch oven or heavy kettle. Add water, bay leaf, and garlic. Bring to boil, cover, and simmer for 1½ hours. Add potatoes, and turnips cut into quarters. Cook for 15 minutes. Add cabbage, cut into 4 wedges. Cook for 20 minutes. Arrange meat and vegetables on hot platter. Makes 4 servings.

POT-ROASTED FRESH BOSTON BUTT WITH VEGETABLES
1 fresh rolled Boston butt (about 2 pounds)
Salt and pepper
2 tablespoons fat
2 cups water
1 onion, sliced
8 small carrots
2½ cups potato balls or cubes
2 cups fresh or frozen Lima beans
4 ears corn

Rub meat with salt and pepper, and brown on all sides in hot fat in Dutch oven or heavy kettle. Add water and onion, bring to boil and simmer, covered, for 2 hours, or until meat is almost

tender. Add carrots, potatoes, and Lima beans. Cover, and simmer for 20 minutes. Put corn on top, cover, and cook for 10 minutes, or until tender. Serve meat surrounded with vegetables. Makes 4 servings.

VEAL

VEAL POT ROAST WITH RAISIN SAUCE
3 pounds veal breast
2 tablespoons all-purpose flour
¼ cup butter or margarine
1 can (13¾ ounces) condensed chicken broth
2 tablespoons sherry
1 bay leaf
¾ cup raisins
1 can (4 ounces) sliced mushrooms, drained
1 tablespoon currant jelly
1 cup dairy sour cream
Salt and pepper

Rub veal on both sides with the flour. Brown in 2 tablespoons hot butter in heavy kettle. Add broth, sherry, and bay leaf. Simmer, covered, for 2 hours, or until meat is tender. Cook raisins and mushrooms lightly in remaining butter; stir in jelly. Remove meat and slice. Add raisin mixture and sour cream to liquid in kettle. Heat gently and season with salt and pepper. Serve with the veal. Makes 6 servings.

Lamb with Raisin Sauce
Use recipe above; substitute lamb for veal.

SPICY VEAL POT ROAST
5 pounds rump of veal
1 tablespoon each of brown sugar, powdered mustard, and salt
½ teaspoon pepper
2 tablespoons cooking oil
2 tablespoons vinegar
1 teaspoon crumbled dried basil
1 garlic clove, minced
½ cup water

Rub veal with mixture of sugar, mustard, salt, and pepper. Brown on all sides in oil in heavy kettle. Put meat on rack. Add remaining ingredients. Simmer, covered, for 2½ hours, or until meat is tender, basting occasionally with liquid in kettle. Add more water if necessary. Makes 8 servings.

VEAL POT ROAST, FILIPINO
2 pounds veal breast
¼ cup soy sauce
1 tablespoon vinegar
½ teaspoon each of salt and pepper
1 teaspoon ground ginger
¼ cup all-purpose flour
3 tablespoons shortening
¾ cup boiling water
About 1 cup (one 8-ounce can) white onions, drained

Put veal in deep bowl. Mix soy sauce, vinegar, and seasonings. Pour over veal and let stand for at least 30 minutes,

turning meat several times. Lift meat from marinade; roll in flour and brown in hot shortening. Put a small rack under meat in kettle. Add marinade and boiling water. Simmer, covered, for 2 hours, or until veal is tender. Add onions and heat. Makes 4 servings.

VARIETY MEATS

DANISH POT-ROASTED CALF HEARTS
2 calf hearts (about 1½ pounds)
6 parsley sprigs, chopped
2 onions, thinly sliced
1 tablespoon fat
½ bay leaf
1 teaspoon salt
4 peppercorns
Dash of pepper
2 small carrots, diced
1 celery stalk, diced
1 cup water
¼ cup heavy cream

Wash hearts and remove large tubes. Stuff hearts with parsley and half the onion. Close openings with skewers or sew with string. Brown on all sides in fat in Dutch oven or heavy kettle. Add remaining onion, seasonings, carrot, celery, and water. Cover, and simmer for 2 hours, or until hearts are very tender. Strain broth, add cream, and pour over hearts. Makes 4 servings.

POT-ROASTED VEAL KIDNEYS AU CITRON
4 veal kidneys with the fat
¼ cup water
Salt and pepper
Lemon wedges

Put kidneys in large heavy kettle. Add water, cover, and cook over very low heat for 3 hours, or until no blood comes out when kidneys are pierced with a fork. Remove fat and slice kidneys. Season to taste with salt and pepper, and serve with lemon wedges. Makes 4 servings.

POT-ROASTED PORK LIVER WITH BARBECUE SAUCE
Water
1 pork liver (about 2 pounds)
2 tablespoons all-purpose flour
6 tablespoons bacon fat or margarine
1¼ teaspoons salt
2 medium onions, chopped
¼ cup vinegar
½ cup ketchup
2 tablespoons Worcestershire
¼ teaspoon cayenne
½ teaspoon chili powder

Pour 1½ cups boiling water over liver. Drain, reserving water. Remove tough outer membrane from liver. Dry meat and dredge with the flour. Brown on all sides in 4 tablespoons of the fat. Add reserved water and ¼ teaspoon salt. Cover and simmer for 1½ hours, or until tender. Cook onions in remaining fat for 2 or 3 minutes. Add remaining salt, 1 cup water, and remaining ingredients.

Bring to boil, cover, and simmer for 45 minutes. Slice liver and serve with the sauce. Makes 6 servings.

POULTRY

POT-ROASTED STUFFED CHICKEN WITH POTATOES

1 roasting chicken, about 4 pounds
  Bread stuffing
  Vegetable oil
  Salt and pepper
¾ cup water
4 medium potatoes, peeled

Fill chicken with Bread Stuffing and sew up openings. Tie legs together. Brown on all sides in small amount of oil in heavy kettle. Pour off fat and put chicken on rack in kettle. Season to taste with salt and pepper. Add water, cover, and simmer for 1 hour. Add potatoes and season. Simmer, covered, for 45 minutes longer, or until chicken and potatoes are tender. Makes 4 servings.

Note: A 4- to 6-pound turkey may be pot-roasted in the same way.

Bread Stuffing

1 cup chopped celery and leaves
1 cup chopped onion
½ teaspoon each of thyme and sage
¼ teaspoon celery salt
¼ cup butter or margarine
½ cup chicken broth or water
3 cups soft stale-bread cubes
  Salt and pepper

Cook celery, onion, thyme, sage, and celery salt in the butter for 5 minutes. Add broth, crumbs, and salt and pepper to taste. Makes about 4 cups.

POT-ROASTED CHICKEN, JAMAICA STLYE

1 roasting chicken (about 4 pounds)
2 tablespoons butter or margarine
1½ cups chicken broth
¾ cup sliced celery
1 medium onion, chopped
½ teaspoon garlic salt
2 dried red peppers, crushed
1 tablespoon vinegar
¼ teaspoon ground allspice
½ cup sliced green olives
1 medium green pepper, sliced
2 tablespoons cornstarch
  Salt and pepper

Brown chicken on all sides in the butter in heavy kettle. Put chicken on rack in kettle. Add next 7 ingredients, cover, and simmer for 1½ hours, or until chicken is tender. Add olives and green pepper; cook for 10 minutes longer. Remove chicken to a hot platter and thicken liquid in kettle with cornstarch blended with a little cold water. Season to taste with salt and pepper; pour over chicken. Makes 4 servings.

POT-ROASTED DUCKLING, SPANISH STYLE

1 duckling (4 to 5 pounds)
1 onion, chopped
1 cup chicken broth

1 teaspoon salt
¼ teaspoon pepper
¼ teaspoon garlic salt
1 can (8 ounces) tomato sauce
1 tablespoon paprika
1 can (4 ounces) mushroom stems
  and pieces, drained
¼ cup dry sherry

Brown duckling slowly on all sides in heavy kettle; pour off fat. Put duckling on rack in kettle and add remaining ingredients except last 2. Simmer, covered, for 1½ hours, or until duckling is tender, basting frequently with the liquid in kettle. Remove duckling to a hot platter. Add mushrooms and sherry to liquid in kettle, heat, and pour over duckling. Makes 4 servings.

POTTED—The word is most often used to describe meat, poultry, or fish ground into a fine paste, lightly seasoned, and packed. Among the most popular potted meats are ham, chicken, and tongue. Fish available are shrimp, crab or salmon potted in butter, and sardines potted in tomato. Many types of cheese are potted, often with wines or brandy. Formerly many foods were potted at home, including baked beans which were mashed into a paste and stored to be used for sandwiches.

Potted also refers to food stewed in a deep pot, in which case the term is used interchangeably with "jugged," jugged hare and chicken, for example; and potted is sometimes used to describe products packaged or served in a small vessel or pot such as a custard cup or an earthenware dish.

SAVORY POTTED SHRIMPS

1 pound shrimps, cooked,
  shelled, and cleaned
1 small onion
½ cup soft butter
  or margarine
  Worcestershire, celery salt,
  and cayenne

Force shrimp through food chopper, using fine blade. Peel onion and force through food chopper. Mix shrimp, onion, and butter, and season to taste with Worcestershire, celery salt, and cayenne. Chill until firm. Makes 8 to 10 servings.

POULTRY—A word describing all domesticated birds bred and raised for use as human food. The most common are chickens, Rock Cornish hens, ducks, turkeys, geese, guinea fowls, and pigeons, the last marketed as squabs (birds from three-and-a-half to four-and-a-half weeks old). Other birds occasionally domesticated for the same purpose are peafowl

(peacocks), quail, pheasants, and swans. Wild ducks and wild turkeys are considered game birds, not poultry.

Nutritive Food Values—Poultry ranks as high nutritionally as it does in popularity. Since poultry contains many essential nutrients, protein being chief among them, it is recognized as one of the important members of the meat group, one of the four food groups essential for a balanced diet. (The other three are the milk, bread-cereal, and vegetable-fruit groups.)

The dietary value of protein is determined by the kinds and amounts of amino acids it contains. At least eighteen different amino acids commonly occur in our food supply. Some are more important than others and many can be synthesized by the body from materials supplied by proteins and other food ingredients. Eight of these are recognized as essential and must come directly from our food supply since our bodies cannot synthesize them. When a food contains all of the essential amino acids in significant amounts and in proportions similar to those found in body proteins, it is classified as a complete protein. Poultry qualifies as one of these foods.

In addition to its excellent qualifications as a protein food, poultry is a good source of calcium, phosphorus, and iron, minerals essential to the maintenance of good health. Important vitamins present in poultry are riboflavin, thiamine, and niacin.

Small amounts of fat in meats makes them more palatable and satisfying. Fat improves the utilization of proteins and facilitates the utilization of fat-soluble vitamins. The favorable proportion of fats and proteins in poultry meat makes it both satisfying and nutritious.

Availability and Purchasing Guide—Good quality-controlled poultry, the result of years of research and work in the development of meatier, tenderer and more nutritious birds, is available year round throughout the country.

In general look for a bird that is wide-bodied, plump and round-breasted, with short legs. Look for streaks of fat down the back, sides, and thighs. The skin should be clean and soft without bruises. Larger birds have more meat in proportion to bone than smaller birds.

Fresh chickens, turkeys, ducklings, and geese are available live, dressed, or ready-to-cook. Fresh squab and guinea hens are available ready-to-cook.

☐ **Live**—Poultry selected alive by the customer from a live-poultry market or from a farmer. The dealer may or may not dress and draw birds after purchase.

☐ **Dressed**—Poultry has been bled and the feathers have been removed. Head and feet are still on and the viscera have not been drawn. The dealer will usually remove viscera after purchase.

☐ **Ready-to-Cook**—Poultry has been fully drawn, pinfeathered, and cleaned inside and out, ready for cooking. It can be bought whole with the giblets and neck, wrapped separately, in the body. Chickens are also available cut up, as broiler-fryers; chicken and turkey parts, such as thighs, breasts, drumsticks, wings and backs are available.

Available frozen are whole chickens, whole stuffed chickens and chicken parts; whole turkeys, whole stuffed turkeys, half turkeys, and turkey rolls; whole ducklings; whole geese; whole Rock Cornish hens and whole stuffed Rock Cornish hens; whole squab and guinea hens.

Canned poultry products include whole chickens, chicken pieces, a large variety of soups, stews, noodle combinations, à la kings, pâtés, and spreads.

Storage

Uncooked Poultry:

■ Unwrap poultry and remove market paper. Wash and pat dry before storing or just before cooking, if preferred.

■ Loosely wrap in wax paper or foil, leaving ends open. It may be kept one to two days.

■ Store in meat compartment or coldest part of food compartment of refrigerator.

■ Variety meats should be cooked within one to two days or wrapped for freezing and frozen.

Some chicken is freeze-dried and can be stored at room temperature. It is generally sealed in an airtight container made of foil, or in a can. It is a part of some of the mixes featuring chicken. Freeze-dried chicken products can be found in camping supply stores.

Uncooked Frozen Poultry:

■ Keep poultry frozen until ready to use, allowing sufficient time for thawing before cooking. Follow package directions for thawing.

Cooked Poultry:

■ Cooked poultry should be cooled quickly, uncovered, then covered or wrapped and stored promptly in the refrigerator. Do not allow poultry to stand at room temperature longer than two hours. Refrigerate meat and gravy in separate containers. Remove any stuffing from stuffed birds and refrigerate in a covered container. Poultry cooked in liquid may be cooled quickly in the liquid by putting the pan containing the poultry where there is a good circulation of cool air. Or it can be cooled by setting the pan in cold or running water.

Freezing Poultry

Uncooked Poultry—Poultry freezes satisfactorily if properly wrapped, frozen quickly, and kept at 0°F. or below. To insure good quality remember the following:

■ Freeze poultry while it is fresh and in top condition. It will not improve in the freezer.

■ Select proper wrapping materials. Choose a moisture- vapor-proof wrap so that air will be sealed out and moisture locked in. Pliable wraps such as freezer foil, transparent moisture- vapor-proof wraps, and certain types of plastic bags are good for wrapping whole birds, since these wraps can be molded to the shape of the bird.

Freezer papers and cartons coated with cellophane, polyethylene, or wax; laminated freezer paper; plastic bags and certain types of waxed cartons are suitable for some poultry. Casserole dishes containing poultry sometimes are frozen in the dish in which they will be reheated or baked.

■ Allow space for air between packages during initial freezing time. Try to avoid freezing such a large quantity of poultry at one time that the freezer is overloaded and the temperature therefore raised undesirably.

■ Maintain freezer temperature at 0°F. or lower during freezer storage. Higher temperatures and fluctuations above that temperature impair quality.

■ Refreezing of defrosted poultry is not recommended except in emergencies. There is some loss of juices during defrosting and the possibility of deterioration of poultry between the time of defrosting and refreezing.

■ Prepare poultry for freezing before wrapping:

Whole Birds—Be sure that birds are well cleaned. Remove any bits of lung, etc.

Do not stuff birds. (Bacteria may develop during the time it takes to heat stuffing. This does not apply to commercially stuffed birds which are handled differently.)

Wrap giblets and livers separately. Giblets may be placed inside the body cavity and wrapped with the bird.

Tuck legs under band of skin to hold them near the body. Fold the neck skin under body.

Put in a moisture- vapor-proof plastic bag, press out all the air, and fasten with a twist-seal. Or mold heavy-duty foil tightly around the bird to exclude the air.

Label, date, and freeze at once at 0°F. or below.

Cut-up Poultry—Wash pieces and dry on absorbent paper.

Sort meaty pieces such as legs, thighs, and breasts from the bony pieces such as neck, back, and wing tips.

Place meaty pieces close together in layers with 2 sheets of freezer paper between or lay each piece in a fold of freezer paper. Pack close together in moisture- vapor-proof bags or cartons. Seal, label, date, and freeze at once at 0°F. or below.

Put broiler halves together with 2 pieces of freezer paper between. Wrap with foil or put in moisture- vapor-proof plastic bags and press out as much air as possible before tying with a twist seal.

Package the bony pieces for making broth.

Label, date, and freeze.

RECOMMENDED STORAGE PERIODS FOR UNCOOKED POULTRY AT 0°F.

Kind of poultry	Months
Chickens	12
Ducks, geese, and turkeys	6
Giblets and livers	3

Cooked Poultry—Frozen cooked poultry will retain its good quality for up to 3 months.

■ Remove meat from bones. (If desired, use bones for making soup or stock or soup which can be frozen in freezer jars or containers. Leftover gravy can also be frozen in this way.)

■ Separate large slices from scraps.

■ Package types and amounts of meat for the particular recipes in which you plan to use it.

■ Tear off generous strips of heavy-duty foil, put meat in the center, and fold ends over tightly, making several double folds. Fold sides in the same way.

■ Secure with string or freezer tape.

■ Label the contents: white-meat slices for pie; chopped light and dark for salads; mixed light and dark strips for turkey stew, etc.

■ Date packages and freeze at once at 0°F. or lower.

Basic Preparation—It is generally best to use a low temperature for cooking poultry as this causes less shrinkage and results in juicier meat with more flavor and less drippings. Two methods are used in poultry cookery: Dry heat, which includes oven-roasting, broiling, sautéing, and panfrying; moist heat, which includes braising, pot-roasting, and cooking in liquid. (The latter is used for stewing chickens especially, which are less tender than other birds.)

☐ **To Oven-Roast**—If stuffing is used, stuff neck cavity lightly and pull neck skin to back over stuffing. Fold ends of skin under and secure with skewer to back of bird. With bird breast-side up, lift each wing up and out, forcing tip back until it rests flat against neck skin. Stuff body cavity loosely. With poultry pins, draw body opening together at regular intervals. Lace shut with twine and tie, leaving long ends. Cross ends on bird and wind around leg ends, draw close and tie around tail. (Truss even if roasting bird unstuffed.)

Put bird, breast-side up, on rack in shallow roasting pan. If roast-meat thermometer is available, insert it into inside thigh muscle adjoining body of bird. Roast in preheated slow oven (325°F.) until thermometer registers 190°F. (Dry birds such as guinea hens may have a few strips of salt pork put on breast before roasting.) Do not add water, baste, or turn. When done, drumstick should move up and down easily. Remove skewers and string before serving. **Note:** Roast stuffed whole squabs in extremely hot oven (500°F.) for 15 minutes; then at 400°F. for 30 minutes, basting every 10 minutes with drippings.

☐ **To Broil** (chicken, turkey, duckling, squab)—Preheat broiler. Line broiler pan with foil. Arrange halves, quarters, or pieces of poultry, skin-side down, in bottom of broiler pan without rack. Sprinkle with salt and pepper. Brush with melted butter or margarine, or vegetable oil. (Omit, if broiling duckling.) Broil slowly 7 to 9 inches from heat, turning every 15 minutes and brushing with melted butter. When done, skin should be brown and crisp and drumstick and wing joints should move easily.

☐ **To Sauté** (chicken, squab)—Dust cut-up chicken or split squab lightly with flour, if desired. Brown quickly on all sides in hot butter, margarine, or vegetable oil. Reduce heat, season as desired, cover, and cook slowly, turning occasionally, until fork-tender.

☐ **To Panfry** (chicken, turkey)—Have bird cut into serving-size pieces. Dredge with seasoned flour or dip into mixture of 1 egg and 2 teaspoons water before coating with the flour. Brown in ½ inch of hot cooking oil or shortening in chicken fryer or large skillet, cover and cook until tender.

☐ **To Braise** (chicken, duckling, turkey)—Have bird cut into serving-size pieces. Dredge with seasoned flour and brown in hot fat or shortening in a heavy kettle or Dutch oven. Add a small amount of liquid, cover tightly, and simmer until tender. Add more small amounts of liquid if necessary to prevent sticking. The cooking can also be completed in a preheated moderate oven (350°F.), covered, for the same length of time.

☐ **To Pot-Roast** (whole chicken, duckling, or small turkey)—Brown bird slowly on all sides, in small amount of fat in heavy kettle or Dutch oven. When browned, pour off fat. Add 1 to 2 cups liquid, cover tightly, and simmer until tender. Remove bird to a hot platter and

thicken liquid with a flour-and-water paste.

☐ **To Cook in Liquid** (stewing chicken)—Put chicken, whole or cut up, in a heavy kettle or Dutch oven. Add enough water or stock to cover and add seasonings such as 1 bay leaf, 1 onion, and a few celery leaves. Simmer (do not boil), covered, until tender.

☐ **To Cook Frozen Poultry**—Birds purchased already stuffed should not be thawed before cooking. Follow directions on package for cooking. It is possible to cook unstuffed poultry from the frozen state but thawing is preferred. Some thawing is always necessary to remove giblets from whole birds, and cut up poultry must be thawed to separate the pieces for browning. Thaw birds in the wrapper, preferably in the refrigerator since it is more uniform than thawing at room temperature. Large birds may be started thawing in the refrigerator and the final thawing completed in cold water. For this, it is best if the bird is in its watertight wrapper. Keep cold water running gently over bird or allow it to stand in cold water, changing the water frequently. Once birds are thawed, they should not be refrozen, but cooked promptly.

POULTRY SEASONING—A commercial blend of ground sage, thyme, marjoram, and savory, sometimes with rosemary added. Poultry seasoning is used with poultry, pork, veal, and fish, in croquettes and meat loaf, in stuffings and biscuits. It is only available ground.

POUNDCAKE—A compact, fine-grained, easily sliced cake which, as its name suggests, traditionally contained a pound of sugar (2¼ cups), a pound of butter (2 cups), a pound of eggs (2 cups, about 8 large eggs), a pound of all-purpose flour (4 cups), a flavoring such as vanilla and/or mace, and no chemical leavening agent. Through the years this has been modified by varying the amounts of the ingredients and even adding chemical leavening and some liquid.

The secret of making the cake is to beat the batter until it is silky and smooth. To make this easy to do, all ingredients should be warmed to room temperature. Vanilla, brandy, rosewater, and small amounts of spices can be added to enhance the flavor of the cake; mace and brandy are a particularly appealing combination. The best beating of the batter can only be achieved with an electric mixer. (Some old cookbooks casually stated "Beat for 1 hour.") When the

batter has been beaten, it is poured into paper-lined pans, usually loaf pans, and baked in a moderate oven (350°F.) for about 1 hour, depending on the size of the pan.

Poundcake keeps well and, when properly wrapped, freezes well. Its simple flavor and firm texture allow it to be sliced, toasted, cubed and covered with pudding, crumbled, cut into finger lengths, made into sandwiches, soaked in wine, and mixed with fruit and many other ingredients.

Commercially made poundcake is sold in food stores in loaves and slices, plain, with raisins, and marbled. It is also available frozen and comes in a mix for those who enjoy the odor of baking in the house. The mix can be blended with candied fruits, spices, nuts, raisins, coconut, etc.

POUNDCAKE

```
   2 cups butter
2¼ cups sugar
   8 eggs (2 cups)
   5 cups sifted cake flour
 ½ teaspoon salt
   1 teaspoon ground mace
```

Cream butter; add sugar gradually, beating until light and fluffy. Add eggs, one at a time, beating well after each. Sift together dry ingredients and add to creamed mixture, a few spoonfuls at a time. Mix just enough to blend in flour mixture after each addition. Pour into one greased and floured loaf pan (9 x 5 x 3 inches) and one 1½-quart tube mold; or pour into 2 loaf pans. Bake in preheated very slow oven (275°F.) for about 2½ hours. Cool for 5 minutes. Turn out on rack to complete cooling.

CHOCOLATE POUNDCAKE

```
   1 cup soft butter or margarine
1¼ cups sugar
   1 teaspoon vanilla extract
   5 eggs, separated
   2 ounces (2 squares) unsweetened
       chocolate, melted
   2 cups sifted all-purpose flour
 ½ teaspoon baking powder
 ½ teaspoon salt
```

Cream butter until light and fluffy. Add 1 cup sugar gradually, beating until light and fluffy. Add vanilla, then egg yolks, one at a time, beating well after each. Blend in cooled chocolate. Add sifted flour, baking powder, and salt; beat until smooth. Beat egg whites until stiff but not dry. Gradually beat in ¼ cup sugar. Fold into first mixture. Pour into loaf pan (9 x 5 x 3 inches) lined on bottom with greased wax paper. Bake in preheated slow oven (300°F.) for about 1¾ hours. Cool for 5 minutes. Turn out on rack and peel off paper. When cool, sift confectioners' sugar over top, if desired.

SOUR-CREAM POUNDCAKE

1 cup soft butter
2¾ cups sugar
6 eggs
3 cups sifted all-purpose flour
½ teaspoon salt
¼ teaspoon baking soda
1 cup dairy sour cream
1 teaspoon flavoring: vanilla, lemon,
   orange, or mixture
   Double recipe Confectioners'-Sugar
   Glaze (page 1438), flavored as desired
   Red candied cherries
   Angelica or green candied cherries

Cream butter and sugar until light. Add eggs, one at a time, beating thoroughly after each addition. Sift dry ingredients 3 times and add alternately with sour cream to first mixture, beating until smooth. Add flavoring. Pour into 9-inch tube pan lined on the bottom with wax paper. Bake in preheated moderate oven (350°F.) for 1⅓ hours, or until done. Let stand in pan on rack for about 5 minutes. Turn out and peel off paper. Cool; cover top with Confectioners'-Sugar Frosting, allowing it to run down sides. Decorate with whole red cherries and leaves of angelica. Store airtight.

PRALINE—Nowadays the word is used to describe any confection made of nut kernels and sugar, although a praline was originally an almond candy, and even more specifically one made with burnt almonds. In the South the word is used to describe sugared coconut or pecan meats, especially the latter, a candy which may be described as native to Louisiana. Coconut pralines are made with white sugar and may be either white or colored pink. Pecan pralines are brown from the brown sugar used.

The term "praline" is often used to describe other foods made with brown sugar and pecans, such as praline topping for cakes and praline confections. Candies made with maple syrup or sugar or with caramelized white sugar, having flavors which simulate brown sugar, can also be called pralines when made in patty shapes with pecans added.

As long as two centuries ago the praline was famous around New Orleans. In the *History of Louisiana* written by Le Page du Pratz, a French explorer, and published in 1758, the great value of the pecan to the French colonists is discussed and the praline (then made from wild pecan kernels) is most highly praised.

CARAMEL PRALINES

4 cups sugar
1 cup light cream or rich milk
1 teaspoon grated orange rind
1 teaspoon vanilla extract
2½ cups pecans
   Dash of salt

Boil 3 cups sugar with the cream and rind in a large saucepan until a small amount of mixture forms a soft ball when dropped into very cold water (236°F. on a candy thermometer). Meanwhile, melt remaining 1 cup sugar in heavy skillet, stirring until it reaches the brown caramel stage. When both mixtures are ready, carefully add the caramel to the first mixture, stirring with a long spoon. Test for soft ball and if done, remove and cool to lukewarm. If not done, cook to soft-ball stage. Add vanilla, nuts, and salt, and beat until stiff and creamy. Drop onto a buttered cookie sheet. Let cool before removing from sheet. Makes about twenty 3-inch pralines.

FRESH-COCONUT PRALINES

2 cups sugar
1 cup coconut milk and water
   (see page 1370)
½ teaspoon vanilla extract
   Red food coloring
1 cup grated fresh coconut
   Candied cherries, diced

Mix sugar and coconut milk and water in saucepan. Bring to boil and cook until a small amount of mixture forms a soft ball when dropped into very cold water (240°F. on a candy thermometer). Pour onto a wet platter and let stand until lukewarm. Add vanilla and beat until thick and creamy. Knead until smooth. Divide into halves and add a few drops of red coloring to one half. Leave remaining half white. Sprinkle coconut on a cookie sheet. Dry in preheated very slow oven (250°F.) for about 15 minutes. Work half of coconut into each mixture. Heat each mixture over boiling water until softened. Drop by teaspoonfuls onto wax paper and flatten slightly. Put a bit of cherry in the center of each. Let stand until firm. Makes about 20.

PRALINE CONFECTIONS

20 to 24 graham crackers
1 cup butter or margarine
1 cup firmly packed light
   brown sugar
1 cup chopped pecans

Line a jelly-roll pan (15 x 10 x 1 inches) with whole graham crackers. Bring the butter and sugar to a rolling boil and boil for 2 minutes. Remove from heat; when bubbling has stopped, add the nuts. Spoon over graham crackers. Bake in preheated moderate oven (350°F.) for 10 minutes. Cool slightly; cut into 1-inch squares. Makes about 10 dozen.

BROILED PRALINE TOPPING

¼ cup butter or margarine
¾ cup firmly packed
   brown sugar
1½ tablespoons milk
¾ cup chopped pecans

Cream butter and sugar. Add milk and beat until smooth. Fold in nuts. Spread on a hot baked plain or chocolate cake in pan (8 x 8 x 2 inches) and broil for 3 minutes, or until topping is bubbly. Makes about 1¼ cups topping.

ALMOND PRALINE

Toast ½ cup slivered almonds in preheated moderate oven (350°F.) for about 10 minutes. Put ½ cup sugar and 2 tablespoons water in heavy saucepan and boil until sugar caramelizes. Stir in almonds, bring just to a boil, and pour out onto a greased marble slab, enamel kitchen table, or platter. Cool, break into pieces and force through food chopper, using coarsest blade. Use as a topping for cakes or ice cream. Makes about 1 cup.

HOW TO MAKE SOUTHERN PRALINES

by Dorothy C. Bishop

Walking through the French quarter of New Orleans, the pungent fragrance of boiling brown sugar leads you to an old-fashioned kitchen where an iron caldron bubbles with a mouth-watering brew.

Here a Negro woman, with expert timing converts the sweet brown syrup into a thin, crisp, pecan-filled concoction called pralines.

New Orleans pralines are true to their dictionary description: "A confection of nut kernels . . . roasted in boiling sugar until brown and crisp."

Here are two recipes for a praline that is creamy instead of crunchy, soft instead of sugary. One is a handed-down recipe which my mother called Southern pralines to distinguish them from the French ones; the other is a streamlined, economy-minded adaptation.

The original recipe reads:

3 cups light brown sugar
   (tightly packed)
¼ cup butter
1 cup heavy sweet cream
   Pinch of cinnamon
1½ cups pecan meats

Mix sugar, butter, and cream in heavy pan or kettle. Cook until soft-ball stage (236°F. on a candy thermometer). Remove from heat. Add cinnamon. Beat until almost cold. Add nuts. Drop by spoonfuls onto marble slab or wax paper. Makes about eighteen 3-inch pralines.

The recipe warns against too much cinnamon.

The only tricky part in making pralines is knowing when to remove the syrup from the heat and when to stop beating and start "spooning." A candy thermometer eliminates the first problem; a tip on the second is to beat until mixture changes color and you can see the bottom of the pan. If the candy should harden before you finish dropping it by spoonfuls, add a little cream.

For the modified recipe, instead of three cups of "tightly packed" brown sugar, use contents of a one-pound package. Substitute one small can (6 ounces) of evaporated milk for the cream, and margarine for butter. Makes about fifteen 3-inch pralines.

If you want the pralines to look like the New Orleans ones, make them large and thin. Individually wrapped and tied with ribbon, they make unusual party favors. Smaller pralines, about two-bite size, are easier to handle and go further. The small ones will fit in well with other dainties for the tea table. Fill a gaily decorated tin box or a candy box wrapped in a dime-store bandana with the small pralines for a thoughtful gift.

This recipe is a large one but pralines will keep well in a tight container, provided you can find a safe hiding place. Mother never could.

PRAWN—A shrimplike crustacean of the genus *Peneus setiferus,* abundant in all tropical and temperate waters, both fresh and salt. Prawns range in length from one inch to six inches, and in the tropics may grow to a length of two feet.

Prawns are sold as shrimps, both fresh and quick-frozen, year round; the only distinction made between them is on the West Coast where prawns and large shrimps are called "prawns" and small shrimps are called "shrimps."

PREHEAT, TO—As the word is applied to cooking, preheating is the process of heating a utensil, for example a skillet or Dutch oven, an oven or broiler, or a cooking medium such as fat or water to a given temperature before putting the food into it to cook.

A utensil is preheated so that food can be browned or its cut edges seared to keep juices from escaping. An oven or fat is preheated to enable a food to start cooking as soon as it is put into it. This not only permits standardization of time and temperature in recipes, but also affects the texture, appearance, and the flavor of the cooked foods.

PRESERVE—Broadly speaking a preserve may be any fruit processed for future use by any method. Thus, fruit butters, conserves, jams, jellies, marmalades, and canned fruits are all preserves. In common American usage, however, the term *fruit butter* is used to describe a product that is thick, smooth, has the spreading consistency of butter, and a larger proportion of fruit to sugar than there is in jam. The word *jam* is applied to crushed fruits and sugar when they are boiled to a thick consistency, with the crushed particles remaining part of the product. *Jelly* describes a translucent quivery fruit juice-and-sugar mixture; and *marmalade* a soft jelly with pieces or slices of the fruit plus pieces of the rind suspended in it. *Conserve* is a word often used interchangeably with jam or preserve, but it, too, has come to have a more restricted meaning: as a preserve similar to jam in consistency, but generally made from a mixture of fruits rather than one, and sometimes with the addition of nutmeats or raisins. The general word, *preserve*, is reserved, then, for a fruit cooked whole or in large pieces with sugar so as to keep its shape.

Fruits suitable for preserves are cherries, peaches, pears, pineapples, quinces, raspberries, strawberries, and tomatoes. If spices are used, they should be tied in a cheesecloth bag so that the flavor is delicate and the color of the preserve is clear and bright. The fruit is cooked with sugar and a little water until tender. Then the fruit is allowed to stand in the hot syrup so that it will absorb some of the juice and plump up. The fruit should be packed into sterilized glasses and the syrup spooned into the jar to cover the fruit. Then it should be sealed and cooled.

All preserves prepared as above can be kept without spoiling at room temperature while sealed. Once a jar is opened, it should be refrigerated.

DRIED-APRICOT PRESERVES

1 box (11 ounces) dried apricots
Water
1 lemon
2 cups sugar
¼ cup honey

Soak apricots in 2 cups water for about 2 hours. Drain, reserving 1½ cups of the water. Cut yellow from lemon peel and cut into thin strips. Squeeze out juice from lemon. Cover yellow peel with water and simmer for 10 minutes, or until tender; drain. Mix 1½ cups water, lemon juice and peel, sugar, and honey in saucepan. Cook until mixture forms a thick syrup. Add apricots and simmer until transparent. Put in hot sterilized jars and seal. Makes about two ½-pint jars.

SWEET-CHERRY PRESERVES

2½ pounds fully ripe
   sweet cherries (about)
5 cups sugar
⅓ cup fresh lemon juice
½ bottle fruit pectin

Steam and pit cherries. Measure 5 cups (firmly packed without crushing) into a large saucepan. Add sugar. Let stand for 30 minutes, stirring occasionally. Then put over high heat and bring to a full rolling boil, stirring carefully. Remove from heat and let stand for 3 to 4 hours. Add lemon juice to fruit in saucepan. Put over high heat, bring to a *full rolling boil* and *boil hard for 2 minutes,* stirring carefully. Remove from heat and at once stir in pectin. Skim off foam with metal spoon. Then stir and skim for 8 to 10 minutes. Ladle into hot sterilized jars and seal. Makes about six ½-pint jars.

FIG PRESERVES

7 cups sugar
¼ cup fresh lemon juice
1½ quarts hot water
2 quarts peeled, firm-ripe
   figs (about 4½ pounds
   before preparing)
2 lemons, thinly sliced

Add sugar and lemon juice to hot water. Cook until sugar dissolves. Add figs and cook rapidly for 10 minutes. Stir occasionally to prevent sticking. Add sliced lemons and cook rapidly for 10 to 15 minutes, or until figs are clear. (If syrup becomes too thick before figs are clear, add boiling water, ¼ cup at a time.) Cover, and let stand for 12 to 24 hours in a cool place. Pack into hot sterilized jars, leaving ¼-inch headspace. Adjust caps. Process in hot-water bath at 180°F. to 185°F. for 30 minutes. Makes about ten ½-pint jars.

BRANDIED PEACH PRESERVE

3 cups sugar
2 cups water
5 pounds small peaches
   Salt, or ascorbic-acid tablets used
   according to package directions
   Brandy

Bring sugar and water to boil, stirring down crystals from sides of pan. Cover peaches with boiling water; let stand for 1 minute; cool quickly under running water. Peel and put in pan of cool water, with either slight amount of salt or ascorbic-acid tablets added to prevent browning. Do not let stand for more than 15 to 20 minutes. Add 8 to 10 peaches at a time to syrup; simmer for 10 minutes, or until tender. Lift out into hot sterilized jars, filling to ½ inch from top. Put lids on to keep peaches hot. Spoon 2 to 4 tablespoons brandy into each jar. Bring syrup to boil and fill jars clear to top; seal. Makes 4 to 6 pints.

PEAR PRESERVES

3 cups sugar
3 cups water
6 medium hard-ripe pears, cored,
   pared and cut into halves or quarters
   (about 2 pounds before preparing)
1 lemon, thinly sliced

Combine 1½ cups sugar and the water. Cook rapidly for 2 minutes. Add pears and boil gently for 15 minutes. Add remaining sugar and the lemon, stirring until sugar is dissolved. Cook rapidly for 25 minutes, or until fruit is clear. Cover and let stand for 12 to 24 hours in a cool place. Pack fruit into hot sterilized jars, leaving ¼-inch headspace. Cook syrup for 3 to 5 minutes, or longer if very thin. Pour, boiling hot, over fruit, leaving ¼-inch headspace. Adjust caps. Process in hot-water bath at 180°F. to 185°F. for 20 minutes. Makes about five ½-pint jars.

PLUM PRESERVES

5 cups pitted tart plums
   (about 2½ pounds)
4 cups sugar
1 cup water

Combine all ingredients in kettle. Bring slowly to a boil, stirring until sugar is dissolved. Cook rapidly until mixture almost sheets from spoon, about 15 minutes. Stir frequently to prevent sticking. Pour into hot sterilized glasses and seal. Makes about five ½-pint jars.

QUINCE PRESERVES

7 cups quartered, cored,
   pared quinces (about 3 pounds
   before preparing)
3 cups sugar
2 quarts water

When preparing quinces, discard all gritty parts. Mix sugar and water, and boil for 5 minutes. Add quinces and cook until fruit has a clear, red color and syrup almost sheets from a spoon, about 1 hour. As mixture thickens, stir frequently to prevent sticking. Pour into hot sterilized jars and seal. Makes about four ½-pint jars.

STRAWBERRY PRESERVES

4 cups hulled strawberries
3¾ cups sugar

Put half of berries and half of sugar in a large heavy saucepan. Bring very slowly to boiling point, stirring frequently. Boil for 10 minutes. Add remaining berries and sugar; reheat slowly, stirring occasionally to dissolve sugar. Bring to boiling point, and boil rapidly for 10 to 15 minutes, or until syrup sheets from spoon, stirring occasionally to prevent sticking. Skim, and pour into bowl; let stand overnight. Fill sterilized jars with cold preserves; seal. Makes about 3 pints.

Note: For perfect results, do not try to make these preserves with more than 4 cups strawberries in each batch.

RIPE WATERMELON PRESERVE

4 quarts diced red watermelon meat,
   seeded
5 cups sugar
¼ teaspoon salt
½ cup cider vinegar
2 lemon slices
1 tablespoon cracked whole cinnamon
1 teaspoon whole cloves

Put diced melon in colander and with the hands squeeze out as much juice as possible. Let drain for 1 hour. Put melon, sugar, salt, vinegar, and lemon in large heavy kettle. Add spices tied in cheese-cloth bag. Cook slowly for 50 to 60 minutes. Stir occasionally to prevent sticking. Pack at once in hot sterilized jars and seal. Makes about 2 pints.

PRESERVE, TO—To prepare perishable food so that it can be kept for long periods of time. Food can be preserved by refrigeration, canning, freezing, irradiation, freeze drying, dehydration, salting, brining, smoking, and by the addition of sugar and acids as in pickles and preserves.

PRESS—In culinary usage the word is used to describe an apparatus or instrument used 1) to *express* liquid, as in the extraction of juice from grapes in jelly-making; 2) to *compress* a food to make it denser or more compact, as in making pressed duck; and 3) to shape a food, as in making pressed cookies.

Many special presses are available: Among them garlic, wine, duck, cookie, pretzel, and spaetzle presses.

PRESSURE COOKER—A utensil, electric or non-electric, which can be either a saucepan or a canner. The distinction is chiefly one of size since both operate on the same principle and canning in small amounts can be done in the saucepan, while cooking in quantity can be done in the canner.

Both the saucepan and the canner consist of a pan, a sealing ring or gasket, a lid which fastens tightly to the pan, and an air vent or safety fuse with accompanying weight which prevents dangerous or excessive pressures from building up within the pan. Pressure cooking is a very quick method of cooking, dependent upon the fact that food, cooked with moisture under pressure, has a higher boiling point than food cooked at normal atmospheric pressures. At these higher temperatures (250°F. at fifteen pounds

pressure, 240°F. at ten pounds pressure and 228°F. at five pounds pressure—all at sea level; slightly lower at higher altitudes) the food cooks in a fraction of the time necessary to cook the same food on a range or in a conventional oven. Manufacturer's directions should be followed very carefully with special attention given to the instructions about the air vent or safety fuse.

PRETZEL—A long roll of dough traditionally twisted into the shape of a loose knot or the letter B. There are two kinds of pretzels, hard and soft, and either may be salted or unsalted. Hard salted pretzels are now also made in the form of sticks and bite-size balls. The soft pretzel is a round roll-like pastry in pretzel shape and has the longest history, dating back to the Middle Ages, while the hard pretzel is relatively new.

The name, which seems as strange as the shape, may come from the Middle Latin *bracciatello*, little arms. Tradition supports this interpretation by claiming that pretzels were first baked by an Italian monk as a reward for children learning their prayers. The other explanation of the word is that it comes from *pretiola* which means "small gift" in Middle Latin. Although etymologically this is not so likely, the monk legend tends to give credence to this theory as well.

Pretzels are popular in central Europe. The pretzel bakers of Vienna have a pretzel in their coat of arms; they were awarded this insignia after their heroic turning back of Turkish invaders in the siege of Vienna in 1510. In Switzerland and Germany a gilt pretzel hanging over a door identifies a baker's shop.

Pretzels came to America early in this country's history. There are court records of 1652 which show that pretzels were being sold to the Indians at that time. Pretzels were made at home and in small bakeries, especially in regions heavily populated by people of German origin. They were often served as snacks. A commentator writing in the *Atlantic Monthly* of May, 1867, mentions a German restaurant in New York which had "baskets full of those queer twisted briny cakes which go variously, I believe, by the names of *Pretzel* and *Wunder*."

The first commercial pretzel bakery was opened in 1861 in Lititz, Pennsylvania. Its owner, Julius Sturgis, had a recipe for hard pretzels, and the date is regarded as the start of a new era in pretzel making.

PRICKLY PEAR—A name given to a cactus, and its fruit, of the genus *Opuntia*. Native to the western hemisphere, the Spaniards found the Indians cultivating prickly pears at the time of the discovery of America. It was the Spaniards who then introduced it to the Mediterranean region, and various species of prickly pear now grow throughout the world.

Some species of prickly pear have edible fruit. Among them are *O. vulgaris*, or barberry fig, which grows in the eastern United States; *O. ficus-indica*, or Indian fig, and *O. tuna*, or tuna, common in the southwestern United States.

The tuna, the prickly pear most often found in markets, varies from pear-shape to round and is yellowish-rose in color when ripe. Sweet, flavorsome, and juicy, it may be peeled, sliced, chilled and served with lemon juice, or lemon juice and sugar; or with cream and sugar. Prickly pears can also be served whole. The ends are sliced off and an incision made the full length of the fruit. The skin is then laid back and the pulp eaten with a spoon. Prickly pears can be made into preserves and jelly. The Mexicans make a paste of the fruit similar to guava paste.

Availability and Purchasing Guide—In food stores during late September and early October only.

Select firm ripe fruit with a yellowish-rose color. Fruit should not be dry or shrunken in appearance.

Nutritive Food Value—Small amounts of potassium, calcium, and phosphorus, and vitamins A and C.

☐ 3½ ounces, raw = 42 calories

PRICKLY-PEAR JELLY

3 pounds prickly pears
6 cups water
¼ cup strained fresh lemon juice
7½ cups sugar
½ bottle fruit pectin

Wash pears and very carefully rub off the spines with a thick cloth. Cut pears into halves and put in kettle. Add water and cook until fruit is soft and almost pulpy. Put in jelly cloth or bag and squeeze out juice. Measure 4 cups into a very large saucepan. Stir in lemon juice and sugar. Put over high heat and bring to a boil, stirring constantly. At once stir in pectin. Then bring to a full rolling boil and boil hard for 1 minute, stirring constantly. Remove from heat, skim off foam with metal spoon, and pour quickly into hot sterilized jars; seal. Makes about eight ½-pint jars.

PROFITEROLE—A miniature cream-puff pastry made from puff or chou paste which can be filled with either meat, poultry, or cheese mixtures for appetizers or with sweet custard, flavored whipped cream, or jam for dessert.

PROSCIUTTO—The Italian word for ham. In the United States the word stands for ready-to-eat ham cured and smoked Italian style. The taste is slightly smoky and salty, a cross between Canadian bacon and American country-cured hams. It is served as an antipasto, on sandwiches, or with fresh melon as a first course, and it is used in cooking. To taste right, prosciutto must be sliced so thinly that the slices are almost transparent.

In Italy, a distinction is made between *prosciutto cotto*, cooked ham, and *prosciutto crudo*, which means literally "raw ham," but is in actuality anything but raw, being the ready-to-eat smoked ham we Americans know as prosciutto. The former is plain boiled ham, the ordinary sandwich ham. Good *prosciutto crudo* is highly prized, and it ranks among the great hams of the world. As with all hams, the taste depends on the pigs' food, the cure, and the smoking.

Prosciutto hams are now also made by American meat packers and both domestic and imported prosciutto is widely available.

PRUNE—A plum dried without fermentation. Prunes are made from several varieties of cultivated plums, most often blue-purple freestone prune-plums.

Drying plums is an important industry on the west coast of the United States. Europe also dries them in large amounts. Commercially prepared prunes are dried by dehydration rather than sun-dried, to control the amount of moisture left in the prunes so that they remain soft and require less cooking.

The preparation of prunes dates back to the days before modern food-preservation methods. The northern countries of Europe relied on prunes for winter fruit; and in Holland, Germany, and the Scandinavian and Slavic countries, prunes were used as a stuffing for meats and poultry as well as an accompaniment for main dishes or as a compote.

Availability and Purchasing Guide—Available all year round. Prunes vary in size and are small, medium, large, extra large, and jumbo. They are packed in plastic bags, wrapped cartons, or in plastic bags in a carton, or sold in bulk. They are also available in combination with other dried fruits.

Cooked and ready-to-serve prunes are available in cans and jars. Prune purée, chopped prunes, and prune butter are also sold. Prune juice is available canned and bottled.

Storage—Store in a cool dry place. In summer refrigerate.

☐ Kitchen shelf: 6 to 8 months
☐ Refrigerator shelf, cooked: 4 to 5 days

Nutritive Food Values—Good source of iron and a concentrated source of energy.

☐ 3½ ounces, uncooked = 255 calories
☐ 3½ ounces, cooked, fruit and liquid without added sugar = 119 calories
☐ Juice, 3½ ounces, canned or bottled = 77 calories

Basic Preparation—Rinse prunes.

☐ **To Plump**—Use one of the following methods:

Boiling-Water Method—Cover prunes with boiling water and let stand for 24 hours while stored in the refrigerator.

Steaming Method—Put prunes in a colander over boiling water and steam, covered, for 30 minutes.

Cold-Water Method—Cover prunes with water and let stand in the refrigerator until tender.

☐ **To Stew**—Cover prunes with water, bring to a boil, lower heat, and simmer for 10 to 20 minutes, or until prunes are tender. For a change of flavor, they may be cooked in tea or in wine, port being the best for the purpose.

SPICED HAMBURGER BALLS WITH PRUNES

1 cup prunes
1½ cups water
1 pound hamburger
1 onion, grated
¼ cup undiluted evaporated milk or 1 egg
1½ teaspoons salt
⅛ teaspoon each of pepper, ground ginger, and cloves
2 tablespoons all-purpose flour
2 tablespoons fat
2 tablespoons cider vinegar
2 cups (one 5-ounce package) noodles (about), cooked

Soak prunes in water for about 2 hours; remove pits. Mix hamburger, onion, milk, and seasonings. Lightly shape into 12 balls; roll in flour and brown on all sides in hot fat. Add vinegar and prunes with water in which they were soaked. Cover and simmer for about 1 hour, adding a little water if needed. Serve with hot noodles. Makes 4 servings.

FRUITED VEAL STEW

2 pounds boneless veal for stew, cut into 1½-inch cubes
5 tablespoons all-purpose flour
2 teaspoons salt
¼ teaspoon pepper
⅛ teaspoon ground ginger
¼ teaspoon ground cloves
3 tablespoons lard or other fat
1½ cups water
1 cup prunes
½ cup fresh orange juice

Prune-Pineapple Dessert   **California Prunes in Claret**   **Prune Whip**

Dredge veal with 3 tablespoons flour, salt, pepper, and spices mixed together. Brown meat on all sides in hot lard in kettle. Pour off drippings; add water and prunes. Bring to boil, cover and simmer for 1½ hours. Add orange juice. Blend remaining flour with a little cold water and use to thicken stew. Makes 6 servings.

Fruited Lamb Stew
Follow recipe above, substituting lamb for the veal.

PRUNE-NUT SANDWICHES
- 1 cup peanut butter
- 1 jar (5 ounces) junior prunes
- ½ cup chopped nuts
- ½ cup chopped shredded coconut
- 16 slices of bread
- 3 eggs, slightly beaten
- ¾ cup milk
- ⅛ teaspoon salt
  Butter or margarine

Mix peanut butter, prunes, nuts, and coconut. Spread on half of bread slices and top with remaining slices. Mix eggs, milk, and salt. Dip sandwiches into mixture and brown on both sides in hot butter in heavy skillet. Makes 8 sandwiches.

PEANUT-BUTTER AND PRUNE SANDWICHES
Mix equal amounts of peanut butter and chopped pitted soft prunes. Moisten with a little dairy sour cream or salad dressing. Spread between slices of buttered bread.

PRUNE-CHEESE SOUFFLÉ
- ½ cup butter or margarine
- ½ cup sugar
- 4 eggs, separated
- ¾ cup finely chopped uncooked prunes
- 1 cup cottage cheese, sieved
- 1 cup dairy sour cream
- 1 tablespoon fresh lemon juice
- ⅛ teaspoon salt
  Whipped cream

Cream butter and sugar until light. Beat in egg yolks. Add prunes, cheese, cream, and lemon juice; mix well. Beat egg whites with salt until stiff but not dry. Fold into first mixture. Pour into buttered 2-quart baking dish and bake in pan of hot water in preheated moderate oven (350°F.) for 1 hour, or until firm. Serve with whipped cream. Makes 6 servings.
Note: Unlike most soufflés this one is also good cold.

PRUNE BRAN BREAD
- 2 packages active dry yeast or 2 cakes compressed yeast
- ¼ cup water*
- 2¾ cups buttermilk
- ¼ cup firmly packed light brown sugar
- 1½ teaspoons salt
- 1 teaspoon baking soda
- 2 cups all-bran
- 2 eggs
- ¼ cup cooking oil
- 5¾ cups sifted all-purpose flour
- 2 cups chopped pitted prunes

Sprinkle dry yeast or crumble cake yeast into warm water. *Use very warm water (105°F. to 115°F.) for dry yeast; use

lukewarm water (80°F. to 90°F.) for compressed. Let stand for a few minutes, then stir until dissolved. Heat buttermilk to lukewarm. Stir in dissolved yeast, sugar, salt, baking soda, bran, eggs, and oil. Blend well. Beat in 2 cups of the flour. Add prunes and remaining flour. Blend well. Turn out dough on a lightly floured board and knead until smooth and elastic. Put dough in a greased bowl and let rise until doubled in bulk. Punch dough down and shape dough into 3 loaves. Put dough into 3 greased loaf pans (8½ x 4½ inches). Let rise until doubled in bulk. Bake in preheated moderate oven (350°F.) for 40 to 50 minutes. Turn out and cool on a rack.

PRUNES IN PORT
Cover prunes with equal parts of port and water. Simmer, covered, for 10 minutes. Cool and chill overnight. Serve prunes with some of the sauce.

CALIFORNIA PRUNES IN CLARET
Wash 1 pound prunes and put in deep bowl. Cover with 2 cups claret wine and ½ cup water. Cover and let stand overnight in refrigerator. Next day simmer in same liquid until tender. Add ⅓ cup sugar; simmer for a few minutes. Cool and refrigerate.
Note: Serve as dessert or relish.

PRUNE WHIP
- ¾ cup prune juice
- ½ cup sugar
- 1 envelope unflavored gelatin
- 1 cup prune pulp (made from stewed prunes or baby-food prunes)
- 2 to 3 tablespoons fresh lemon juice
- ¼ teaspoon salt
- 2 egg whites, stiffly beaten

Heat ½ cup prune juice combined with the sugar. Soften gelatin in ¼ cup cold prune juice. Let stand for 5 minutes. Add hot prune juice mixture and stir until gelatin is dissolved. Add prune pulp, lemon juice to taste, and salt. Let cool over ice water or in the refrigerator until slightly thickened while you beat egg whites to stiff peaks. Fold whites gently but thoroughly into cooled prune mixture and spoon into a fancy mold or individual sherbet glasses. Chill until firm, about 3 hours. Serve with whipped cream and a dusting of ground mace or nutmeg. Makes 4 servings.

FROZEN PRUNE WHIP
- 1 cup undiluted evaporated milk
- ⅓ cup sugar
  Dash of salt
- ½ cup fresh orange juice
- 1 tablespoon fresh lemon juice
- 1 cup chopped pitted cooked prunes

Chill evaporated milk in refrigerator tray until nearly frozen. Beat with rotary beater or electric mixer until stiff; add sugar and salt and continue beating until no grains of sugar remain. Fold in juices

and fruit. Freeze. Makes 4 servings.

PRUNE CRUMBLE PUDDING
- 1½ cups pitted cooked prunes
  Juice of 1 lemon
- ¼ cup liquid from prunes
- 6 tablespoons all-purpose flour
- ¼ cup firmly packed dark brown sugar
- 2 tablespoons shortening
- 1 teaspoon salt

Put prunes in greased 1-quart shallow baking dish. Add lemon juice and prune liquid. Work remaining ingredients together to consistency of fine crumbs; sprinkle over prunes. Bake in preheated moderate oven (375°F.) for about 20 minutes. Serve warm with milk. Makes 4 servings.

HONEY-PRUNE PUDDING
- 1 cup chopped pitted cooked prunes
- ½ cup honey
- ½ cup chopped nuts
  Grated rind of 1 lemon
- ½ cup milk
- 1 tablespoon melted butter
- ½ cup crumbled dry bread
- 1 teaspoon baking powder
  Light cream

Mix all ingredients except cream in order given. Pour into 1-quart baking dish. Set in shallow pan of hot water. Bake in preheated moderate oven (350°F.) for about 35 minutes. Serve warm, or cold, with cream. Makes 4 servings.

PRUNE-PINEAPPLE DESSERT
- 1 cup diced cooked prunes
- 1 can (9 ounces) crushed pineapple, well drained
- 12 large marshmallows, cut into quarters
- 1 tablespoon fresh lemon juice
- 1 cup heavy cream, whipped
- 2 tablespoons sugar

Mix prunes, pineapple, and marshmallows; sprinkle with lemon juice. Lightly fold in the whipped cream and sugar. Pile in sherbet glasses. Makes 6 servings.

PRUNE COTTAGE PUDDING WITH ORANGE SAUCE
- ¼ cup shortening
- ½ cup sugar
- 1 egg
  Grated rind of 1 orange
- 1 cup sifted cake flour
- ½ teaspoon each of baking soda and baking powder
- ¼ teaspoon salt
- ⅓ cup buttermilk
- 1 cup chopped pitted cooked prunes
  Orange Sauce

Cream shortening. Add sugar gradually, beating until light and fluffy. Add egg and orange rind and beat thoroughly. Add sifted dry ingredients alternately with buttermilk, beating until smooth. Fold in prunes. Pour batter into greased medium-size muffin tins. Bake in preheated moderate oven (350°F.) for about 40 minutes. Turn out on rack. Serve hot with Orange Sauce. Makes 9 servings.
Note: 1 cup chopped cooked dried apricots may be substituted for prunes.

Orange Sauce

- 2 egg yolks
- ¼ cup sugar
- 1 cup fresh orange juice
  Grated rind of 1 orange

Beat egg yolks until thick, then beat in sugar gradually. Add orange juice and rind and cook slowly until slightly thickened, stirring constantly. Serve hot.

CALIFORNIA PRUNE PUDDING

- 4 slices of bread
- 2 teaspoons butter
- 1 cup chopped pitted cooked prunes
- 2 tablespoons brown sugar
  Ground cinnamon or allspice

Spread bread lightly with half of butter. Cover with prunes; sprinkle with sugar and cinnamon. Dot with remaining butter. Bake for 20 minutes in preheated moderate oven (350°F.). Makes 4 servings.

PRUNE CHOCOLATE CAKE

- ½ cup shortening
- 1 cup sugar
- 2 eggs, separated
- 1 jar (5 ounces) strained prunes
- 2 ounces (2 squares) unsweetened chocolate, melted and cooled
- 1 teaspoon vanilla extract
- 1¾ cups sifted all-purpose flour
- 1 teaspoon each of baking powder and baking soda
- ½ teaspoon salt
- 1 cup warm water
  Prune Frosting
- ½ cup chopped nuts

Cream shortening and sugar; add egg yolks; beat. Add prunes, cooled chocolate, and vanilla; beat for 1 minute. Add sifted dry ingredients alternately with water. Beat until smooth. Fold in stiffly beaten egg whites. Pour into pan (13 x 9 x 2 inches) lined on bottom with greased wax paper. Bake in preheated moderate oven (350°F.) for about 30 minutes. Cool and spread Prune Frosting. Sprinkle with nuts.

Prune Frosting

In saucepan mix 1 cup sugar, ¼ cup strained prunes, 2 ounces (2 squares) unsweetened chocolate, 2 tablespoons butter or margarine, ⅓ cup milk, and ⅛ teaspoon salt. Bring to boil and cook until a small amount of mixture forms a soft ball when dropped into a little cold water (234°F. on a candy thermometer). Remove from heat; add ½ teaspoon vanilla extract; beat.

PRUNE UPSIDE-DOWN CAKE

- 1½ cups pitted cooked prunes
- ½ cup dark corn syrup
  Few walnuts, if desired
  Corn Syrup Spongecake Batter

Put prunes in bottom of well-greased 8-inch square pan; add corn syrup. Place walnuts among prunes if desired. Pour Corn-Syrup Spongecake Batter over prunes and bake in preheated moderate oven (350°F.) for about 30 minutes. Cool slightly before turning upside down. Makes 6 servings.

Corn-Syrup Spongecake Batter

- 2 eggs, separated
- ¼ teaspoon salt
- 6 tablespoons light corn syrup
  Pinch of grated lemon rind
- ½ cup sifted cake flour
- ¼ teaspoon baking powder

Beat egg whites with salt until stiff but not dry. Heat corn syrup to boiling in small saucepan; pour slowly over beaten whites, beating constantly with rotary beater. Add lemon rind to yolks and beat well; fold into whites. Fold in sifted flour and baking powder.

DUTCH PRUNE CAKE

- 2 cups prepared biscuit mix
  Ground cinnamon
- ⅔ cup liquid from cooked prunes
- 1 egg
- 1 cup pitted cooked prunes
- 2 tablespoons sugar

Mix biscuit mix with ½ teaspoon cinnamon; add liquid and beaten egg to make a soft dough. Spread dough in greased 1½-quart round baking pan; arrange prunes over top and sprinkle with sugar and a little cinnamon. Bake in preheated hot oven (400°F.) for about 30 minutes. Makes 6 servings.

PRUNE-WHIP PIE

- 1 pound prunes, cooked, pitted, and cut up
- ½ cup sugar
- ¾ cup chopped nuts
- ⅛ teaspoon salt
- 1 teaspoon grated lemon rind
- 1 tablespoon fresh lemon juice
- 2 egg whites
  Standard Pastry for 1-crust 9-inch pie shell, baked (page 1399)
- ½ cup heavy cream
  Few drops of almond or rum extract

Mix first 6 ingredients. Fold in stiffly beaten egg whites. Pour into pie shell and bake in preheated slow oven (325°F.) for 20 minutes, or until set. Cool. Whip cream and add flavoring. Spread on pie. Makes 6 servings.

PUCHERO—Also called *Olla Podrida,* this is a rich stewlike dish of Spanish origin, which has spread throughout the Latin American countries. It usually contains chick-peas, sausage, cabbage, and several meats. *Puchero* is in some respects a Spanish version of a boiled dinner.

PUCHERO

- 1 cup dried chick-peas
- 6 cups water
- 2 pounds beef short ribs
- 1 pound lean fresh pork, diced
- 1 frying chicken, about 3 pounds, cut up
- ½ pound chorizos or hot Italian sausage
- 8 small white onions
- 8 small carrots
- 2 garlic cloves, minced
- 2 teaspoons salt
- ¼ teaspoon pepper
- 1 pound yellow squash, peeled and sliced
- 4 tomatoes, quartered
- 1 small head cabbage, cut into eighths
- 1 large green pepper, chopped
- 4 potatoes, peeled and quartered
- 6 leeks, cut into halves lengthwise
  Few sprigs of parsley, minced

Cover chick-peas with the water, bring to boil, and boil for 2 minutes. Cover, and let stand for 1 hour. Bring again to boil, and add the beef and pork. Cover, and simmer for 1 hour. Add the chicken, sausages, onions, carrots, and garlic. Cover, and simmer for 45 minutes. Add remaining ingredients except parsley. Cook for 45 minutes. Add parsley. Arrange meat and vegetables on a platter. Serve remaining broth in soup bowls. Makes 8 to 10 servings.

PUDDING—The word is used to describe a wide variety of baked, boiled, or steamed soft foods, either savory or sweet, served hot or cold, as main dishes, side dishes, or desserts. Pudding is also another name for blood sausage.

The chief types of puddings are: unsweetened boiled or baked dishes, usually with a cereal base and a texture resembling custard, such as corn pudding; sweetened boiled or baked dishes of a soft, spongy or thick creamy consistency, such as chocolate pudding; and suet-based or suet-custard dishes, such as plum pudding, which were originally boiled in a bag, but are now often baked or steamed.

There seems to be no end to the variety of puddings, both savory and sweet. Puddings have had a long culinary history and there has been time for cooks to develop all sorts of recipes. The name itself may be related to older Germanic words meaning "sausage" or "swollen." Certainly blood puddings, such as Haggis, that Scottish conglomeration Robert Burns called the "great chieftain o' the pudding race," are swollen. Also swollen and encased like a sausage are the early English "puddynges" of the 14th century. These were often suet crusted, such as the now popular steak and kidney pudding, or suet based, such as plum pudding. Steamed within a bag or cloth in a huge kettle along with the rest of the dinner, they became swollen. The bag or cloth took the place of the sausage casing.

Sweet dessert puddings are relatively modern. It was only when sugar became widely available in the late 18th and early 19th centuries that sweet puddings came into their own. The sweet puddings were of such great variety that Englishmen now often use the word to mean dessert.

Americans inherit the English enjoyment of puddings. The early settlers of New England ate their puddings as a first course. It may have well been an Indian pudding, made with the cornmeal the Indians had introduced to the colonists. For the early Americans used native ingredients to build upon the foundations of English pudding cookery. Hasty pudding, for instance, was quickly made in England with wheat flour. Here, where wheat flour was not available, the colonists used cornmeal or a mixture known as rye 'n Injun. Sweetened with maple sugar, the New England hasty pudding was and is a delight.

Today, in addition to the almost endless number of puddings to be made from scratch at home, there is available a wide variety of canned puddings and packaged pudding mixes.

PUDDING COOK BOOK

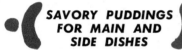

SAVORY PUDDINGS FOR MAIN AND SIDE DISHES

BREAD AND CHEESE PUDDING

    6 slices of dry bread
    ½ pound Cheddar cheese, sliced
    1¾ cups milk
    1 onion, grated
    2 eggs, beaten
    1 teaspoon salt
      Dash each of cayenne and paprika
    ½ teaspoon steak sauce

Arrange alternate layers of bread and cheese in shallow 1½-quart baking pan, ending with a layer of cheese. Heat milk with the onion. Pour slowly over eggs combined with the seasonings, stirring constantly. Pour milk mixture over bread and cheese. Let stand for 5 minutes or longer. Bake in preheated moderate oven (375°F.) for 20 minutes, or until pudding is set and bread and cheese are puffy. Makes 4 servings.

CHICKEN AND CORN PUDDING

    1 cup diced cooked chicken
    2 cups cooked whole-kernel corn
    1 cup milk
    2 eggs, beaten
    ½ green pepper, minced
    1 teaspoon instant minced onion
    ¾ teaspoon seasoned salt
    ¼ teaspoon pepper
      Dash of ground nutmeg
    ½ cup grated Cheddar cheese

Mix all ingredients and put in shallow 1½-quart baking dish. Bake in preheated slow oven (325°F.) for 1 hour, or until firm. Makes 4 servings.

GREEN-PEA PUDDING

    2 tablespoons butter or margarine
    ½ teaspoon garlic salt
    1 teaspoon paprika
    ½ teaspoon salt
    ½ teaspoon pepper
    2 medium onions, coarsely chopped
    4 eggs, beaten
    2 tablespoons heavy cream or undiluted
      evaporated milk
    2 cups cooked peas

Heat butter in heavy skillet. Stir in garlic salt, paprika, salt, and pepper. Cook for 1 minute. Add onions and cook until soft and golden. Remove from heat. Beat eggs and cream together. Add to onion mixture. Add peas. Pour into greased 1½-quart casserole. Set dish in a pan of hot water. Bake in preheated moderate oven (350°F.) for 40 to 45 minutes, or until knife inserted in middle comes out clean. Makes 4 to 6 servings.

FRESH-CORN PUDDING

    3 cups fresh corn pulp or cream-style
      corn
    1 egg, separated
    2 teaspoons sugar
    1 teaspoon salt
      Butter or margarine (about ¼ cup)

Combine corn pulp, egg yolk, sugar, salt, and 2 tablespoons melted butter. Fold in stiffly beaten egg white. Pour into buttered shallow 1-quart baking dish and dot with butter. Bake in preheated moderate oven (350° F.) for 45 minutes, or until golden brown. Makes 6 servings.

FISH PUDDING

    1 pound haddock or cod fillets
    1½ teaspoons salt
    ¼ teaspoon each of white pepper and
      ground nutmeg
      Dash each of ground allspice and
      cloves
    1 tablespoon all-purpose flour
      Melted butter or margarine
    1¾ cups milk
      Fine dry bread crumbs

Wipe fish with damp cloth, cut into small pieces and force through food chopper twice, using finest blade. Add seasonings and flour, and force through food chopper 4 or 5 more times. Beat in 3 tablespoons butter and the milk, adding a little at a time. Butter a 1-quart casserole or mold and dust with crumbs. Pour in fish mixture, set in pan of hot water and bake in preheated moderate oven (350° F.) for 45 minutes, or until firm. Unmold, if desired, and serve with melted butter. Makes 6 servings.

NOODLE COTTAGE-CHEESE PUDDING

    8 ounces wide noodles
    1 pound dry cottage cheese or pot
      cheese
    2 eggs, beaten
    1 tablespoon sugar (optional)

    ¼ cup butter or margarine, melted
    ½ cup dairy sour cream
    1 teaspoon salt
    ⅛ teaspoon white pepper

Cook and drain noodles. Mix with remaining ingredients. Pour into greased 1½-quart casserole and bake in preheated moderate oven (375°F.) for about 45 minutes. Makes 6 servings.

BAKED ONION PUDDING

    3 cups coarsely chopped onions
    ½ teaspoon poultry seasoning
    1½ tablespoons butter or margarine
    1½ tablespoons flour
    1½ cups milk
    ¾ cup fine dry bread crumbs
    2 eggs, separated
      Salt and pepper
      Chopped parsley

Cook onions with poultry seasoning in small amount of boiling salted water until tender. Drain. Melt butter, stir in flour, and add milk. Cool until thickened, stirring constantly. Add drained onions, ½ cup bread crumbs, and slightly beaten egg yolks. Season with salt and pepper to taste. Fold in stiffly beaten egg whites. Turn into buttered 1½-quart casserole. Sprinkle with remaining bread crumbs. Bake in preheated moderate oven (350° F.) for 40 minutes, or until set. Sprinkle with chopped parsley. Makes 4 to 6 servings.

YORKSHIRE PUDDING

    1 cup sifted all-purpose flour
    ½ teaspoon salt
    2 eggs
    1 cup milk
    ¼ cup hot beef fat and drippings

Set 4 custard cups in moderate oven (350°F.) to heat. Combine all ingredients except fat in large mixing bowl. Beat vigorously with rotary beater for 2 minutes. Put 1 tablespoon fat and drippings from roast meat into each heated custard cup. Pour batter into hot fat in custard cups. Return cups to oven and bake for 30 minutes. Roast and pudding can be baked at the same time. Serve at once. Makes 4 servings.

SWEET DESSERT PUDDINGS

Top-Stove Puddings

BUTTERSCOTCH-PEANUT TAPIOCA PUDDING

    1 tablespoon butter
    ¾ cup firmly packed light brown sugar
    3 tablespoons quick-cooking tapioca
    ¼ teaspoon salt
    2 eggs, separated
    2 cups milk, scalded
    ½ cup chopped peanuts
    1 teaspoon vanilla extract

In top part of a double boiler heat butter and sugar, stirring, until a golden

Jellied Fruit-Cream Pudding

Steamed Carrot-Suet Pudding

Lemon Cream Rice Pudding

syrup forms. Add tapioca, salt, beaten egg yolks, and milk. Cook over simmering water for 10 minutes, or until tapioca is translucent, stirring frequently. Stir into stiffly beaten egg whites and fold in peanuts and vanilla. Cool, stirring once or twice. Chill. Makes 6 servings.

Butterscotch-Date Tapioca Pudding
Follow recipe above; substitute 1 cup diced dates for peanuts.

ENGLISH TRIFLE
    1 cup soft custard*
    6 ladyfingers
      Strawberry or raspberry jam
   12 almond macaroons
   18 almonds, blanched and slivered
      Grated rind of ½ lemon
      Sherry (about ⅓ cup)
    1 cup heavy cream, whipped
      Candied cherries, angelica,
      pistachio nuts

*In top part of a double boiler make a soft custard using 2 egg yolks, 2 tablespoons sugar, 1 cup scalded milk. Cool slightly.

Split ladyfingers and spread with jam. Arrange in a serving dish. Cover with whole macaroons; sprinkle with almonds and grated lemon rind. Pour sherry over to soak cookies. Spoon custard over all; top with whipped cream. Garnish with candied cherries, strips of angelica, and chopped pistachio nuts. Refrigerate for several hours before serving. Makes 8 servings.

JELLIED FRUIT-CREAM PUDDING
    2 envelopes unflavored gelatin
    ¾ cup sugar
    ¼ teaspoon salt
   1½ cups milk
    4 eggs, separated
    1 teaspoon vanilla extract
    ¼ cup light rum
    ¼ cup chopped almonds
    ¼ cup each of raisins and chopped
      pitted dates
    ½ cup chopped candied cherries
    ⅓ cup heavy cream, whipped
      Whipped topping
      Whole candied cherry, strip of
      angelica

In top part of a small double boiler mix gelatin, ¼ cup sugar, and the salt. Add milk and beat in egg yolks. Put over simmering water and cook, stirring constantly, until mixture coats a metal spoon. Remove from heat and add vanilla, rum, nuts, and fruits. Chill until almost firm. Beat egg whites until frothy; gradually add ½ cup sugar and beat until stiff. Fold into first mixture with whipped cream. Pour into 1½-quart mold and chill until firm. Unmold and decorate with whipped topping, whole cherry, and angelica strips. Makes 8 to 10 servings.

SABAYON
    5 egg yolks
    1 tablespoon cold water
    ¾ cup sugar
    ⅛ teaspoon salt

½ cup marsala, port, or sherry

In top part of a double boiler beat egg yolks with water until they are foamy and light. Whisk in sugar, salt, and wine. Beat over hot, not boiling water, until thickened and fluffy. This will take only a few minutes. Pile into sherbet glasses; serve hot. Makes 6 servings.

Sabayon with Fresh Strawberries or Peaches
Follow recipe for Sabayon. Cool; fold in 5 stiffly beaten egg whites. Pile in a pretty serving bowl and garnish with fruit.

Chocolate Sabayon
Follow recipe for Sabayon; stir 2 ounces grated sweet chocolate into the dessert when it is taken from the heat.

Frozen Sabayon
Follow recipe for Sabayon. Cool; add 2 cups heavy cream, whipped, ¼ cup diced candied cherries, ½ cup diced candied pineapple, and ½ cup chopped pecans. Freeze in parfait glasses; garnish with candied cherries and bits of angelica. Or pour into ice-cube trays and freeze in refrigerator, or in mold in freezer. Makes 10 to 12 servings.

VANILLA CORNSTARCH PUDDING
    3 cups milk
    ¼ cup cornstarch
    ½ cup sugar
    ¼ teaspoon salt
   1½ teaspoons vanilla extract

Scald 2⅔ cups of the milk. Mix cornstarch, sugar, and salt. Then stir in remaining milk until smooth. Add to scalded milk and cook over low heat, or in top part of double boiler over boiling water, stirring constantly, until thickened. Continue cooking for about 5 minutes, or until cornstarch is completely cooked. Cool slightly, add vanilla, and pour into serving dish or dishes. Makes 6 servings.

Chocolate Cornstarch Pudding
Follow recipe above, adding 3 squares (3 ounces) unsweetened chocolate to milk to be scalded. When chocolate is melted and milk scalded, proceed as above.

Baked Puddings

BLUEBERRY BREAD PUDDING
    4 cups bread cubes
    ¼ cup butter or margarine, cut into
      pieces
    ½ to ¾ cup sugar
    ¼ teaspoon salt
    1 pint fresh blueberries, washed and
      drained
    ¼ cup water
    2 tablespoons fresh lemon juice
      Cream or Hard Sauce (page 1493)

Combine all ingredients except cream and pack into a well-greased 1½-quart baking dish. Bake in preheated moderate oven (350°F.) for 40 minutes. Serve hot or cold with cream. Makes 6 servings.

ORANGE-DATE BREAD PUDDING

- 4 cups milk
- 3 cups soft bread cubes
- 2 tablespoons butter or margarine
- 1 cup sugar
- ¼ teaspoon salt
- 1 cup chopped pitted dates
  Grated rind and juice of 1 orange and 1 lemon
- 2 whole eggs
- 4 eggs, separated
  Orange marmalade

Scald milk and pour over bread cubes. Add butter, ¾ cup sugar, the salt, dates, grated rinds and juices, beaten whole eggs and egg yolks. Mix well and pour into 1½-quart casserole. Set in pan of hot water and bake in preheated moderate oven (350°F.) for 1¼ hours, or until set. Spread top with thin layer of marmalade. Beat egg whites until foamy; gradually add ¼ cup sugar and beat until stiff. Pile lightly on pudding. With pudding still in pan of hot water, bake in preheated hot oven (400°F.) for 5 minutes. Makes 6 servings.

PINEAPPLE BREAD PUDDING

- 1 cup (one 9-ounce can) crushed pineapple
- 2 cups soft bread crumbs
- 2 cups milk, scalded
- ½ teaspoon salt
- 2 eggs, beaten
- ⅓ cup honey
- 1 tablespoon fresh lemon juice
  Lemon Hard Sauce (page 1493)

Drain pineapple and add enough water or other fruit juice to syrup to make ¼ cup. Add with pineapple to remaining ingredients except sauce and mix well. Pour into 1½-quart baking dish. Bake in preheated slow oven (325°F.) for about 45 minutes. Serve with Lemon Hard Sauce. Makes 4 servings.

COCONUT APPLE BETTY

- 4 large tart apples, peeled and thinly sliced
- 1 cup soft bread crumbs
- 1 cup flaked coconut
- ½ cup firmly packed brown sugar
  Dash of salt
- ½ teaspoon ground cinnamon
- ¼ cup butter or margarine
- 12 salted almonds

Arrange layer of apple slices in shallow baking dish. Cover with some of bread crumbs and coconut. Sprinkle with some of sugar, salt, and cinnamon; dot with butter. Repeat until all ingredients are used. Arrange nuts around edge of mixture. Cover; bake in preheated moderate oven (350°F.) for 35 minutes. Uncover; bake for about 10 minutes longer. Makes 6 servings.

LEMON CAKE PUDDING

- 1 cup sugar
- 3 tablespoons soft butter
- 3 tablespoons all-purpose flour
- 2 eggs, separated
  Juice and grated rind of 1 lemon
- 1 cup milk

Cream sugar and butter. Add flour, beaten egg yolks, rind, juice, and milk. Mix well and fold in stiffly beaten egg whites. Pour into 1-quart casserole. Set in pan of hot water and bake in a preheated slow oven (325°F.) for about 1 hour. Makes 4 servings.

MERINGUE CAKE PUDDING

- 3 cups ½-inch day-old cake cubes
- ½ cup sugar
- ¼ teaspoon salt
- 2 eggs, separated
- 2 whole eggs
- 3 cups milk, scalded
- 1 teaspoon vanilla or rum extract
- ½ cup semisweet chocolate pieces

Put cake cubes in 1½-quart casserole. Add ¼ cup sugar and the salt to egg yolks and whole eggs and beat slightly. Add milk and flavoring; mix well and pour over cake. Set in pan of hot water and bake in preheated moderate oven (350°F.) for 50 minutes, or until firm. Sprinkle with chocolate. Beat 2 egg whites until foamy; gradually add ¼ cup sugar and beat until stiff. Spread lightly on pudding, covering top completely. With casserole still in hot water, bake in hot oven (400°F.) for 5 minutes, or until golden. Serve warm. Makes 6 servings.

COFFEE CUSTARD PUDDING WITH CARAMEL GLAZE

Caramel Glaze:

Caramelize ¾ cup sugar in heavy saucepan and pour into 1½-quart casserole, turning to glaze completely.

Coffee Custard:

- 6 eggs
- 5 tablespoons sugar
- ¼ teaspoon salt
- 1 cup strong coffee
- 1 cup light cream
- 3 tablespoons sherry

Beat eggs slightly; add remaining ingredients and mix well. Pour into caramel-glazed casserole. Set casserole in pan of hot water. Bake in preheated moderate oven (350°F.) for 40 to 45 minutes, or until a silver knife inserted in the custard comes out clean. Cool completely. Makes 6 servings.

COTTAGE PUDDING

- ½ cup soft butter or margarine
- ½ cup sugar
- 1 egg
- 1⅔ cups sifted all-purpose flour
- 2 teaspoons baking powder
- ½ teaspoon salt
- ½ cup milk

Cream butter and sugar until light. Beat

in egg. Add sifted dry ingredients alternately with milk, beating until smooth. Pour into greased pan (8 x 8 x 2 inches) and bake in preheated hot oven (400°F.) for 20 to 25 minutes. Serve warm with any dessert sauce. Makes 9 servings.

SOUR-CREAM INDIAN PUDDING

- 4 cups milk
- ¾ cup yellow cornmeal
- ¼ cup molasses
- 1 teaspoon each of ground ginger and cinnamon
- ½ teaspoon ground nutmeg
- 1 cup firmly packed brown sugar
- ½ teaspoon salt
- ½ cup soft butter or margarine
- 4 eggs, beaten
- 1 cup dairy sour cream
  Ice cream, whipped cream or Hard Sauce (page 1493)

Heat 3 cups of the milk in top part of double boiler over boiling water. Mix remaining 1 cup milk and the cornmeal. Stir into hot milk and cook, stirring, until slightly thickened. Remove from heat. Mix molasses and spices and stir into first mixture. Beat in remaining ingredients except ice cream. Pour into buttered 2-quart casserole and bake in preheated very slow oven (275°F.) for about 2 hours. Serve warm or cool with ice cream. Makes 8 servings.

BAKED MOLASSES PUDDING

- ½ cup soft shortening
- 1 cup sugar (granulated or firmly packed brown)
- ⅔ cup molasses
- 1½ cups sifted cake flour
- ¼ teaspoon salt
- ¾ teaspoon baking soda
- 1 teaspoon ground ginger
- 1½ cups soft bread crumbs
- 1 cup buttermilk
- 1 egg, beaten
  Lemon Sauce (page 1493)

Cream shortening and sugar until light; beat in molasses. Sift dry ingredients and add to first mixture with crumbs and buttermilk. Beat for 1 minute; add egg. Pour into greased pan (8 x 8 x 2 inches) and let stand for 30 minutes. Bake in preheated moderate oven (350°F.) for about 45 minutes. Serve warm with Lemon Sauce, or serve cold. Makes 8 servings.

NOODLE-APPLE PUDDING

- 1 package (8 ounces) wide noodles
- 4 medium apples, peeled, cored, and grated
- ½ cup chopped almonds
- ½ cup firmly packed brown sugar
- ½ teaspoon vanilla extract
- 1 teaspoon fresh lemon juice
- ½ teaspoon ground cinnamon
- 2 tablespoons fine dry bread crumbs
- 2 tablespoons butter or margarine

Cook noodles as directed on package; drain. Combine remaining ingredients except crumbs and butter. In buttered 1½-quart casserole, arrange alternate layers of noodles and apple mixture, beginning and ending with noodles. Sprinkle with the crumbs and dot with the butter. Bake in preheated moderate oven (375°F.) for about 45 minutes. Serve warm. Makes 6 servings.

ORANGE CREAM PUDDING

3 large oranges
1 cup sugar
⅓ cup all-purpose flour
¼ teaspoon salt
2 cups milk
1 whole egg
2 eggs, separated
1 tablespoon butter
1 teaspoon grated lemon rind

Peel and section oranges. Drain off excess juice and put oranges in 1½-quart casserole. In top part of a small double boiler mix well ¾ cup sugar, the flour, and salt. Add milk and stir until smooth. Put over boiling water and cook, stirring, until thickened. Cover and cook for 10 minutes, stirring occasionally. Stir small amount of mixture into whole egg and egg yolks, beaten together. Put back in double boiler and cook, stirring constantly, for 2 minutes longer. Add butter and lemon rind. Pour over oranges. Beat egg whites until foamy; gradually add ¼ cup sugar and beat until stiff. Pile lightly on pudding. Bake in preheated hot oven (400°F.) for 5 minutes. Cool. Makes 4 to 6 servings.

GINGER PEAR CRUMBLE

1½ cups gingersnap crumbs (thirty 2-inch cookies)
¼ cup butter, melted
3¾ cups (one 1-pound, 14-ounce can) pear halves
1 tablespoon fresh lemon juice
½ cup firmly packed brown sugar
¼ teaspoon salt
½ teaspoon ground cinnamon
¼ teaspoon ground nutmeg
Cream or vanilla ice cream

Mix crumbs and melted butter; put half in 1½-quart baking dish. Drain pears, reserving ¼ cup syrup. Put pears on crumbs and sprinkle with mixture of lemon juice and pear syrup. Mix sugar, salt, and spices; sprinkle on pears. Top with remaining crumbs. Bake in preheated moderate oven (350°F.) for about 25 minutes. Serve warm with cream. Makes 6 servings.

PUMPKIN CUSTARD PUDDING WITH SHERRY GINGER CREAM

2 cups canned pumpkin
1 cup firmly packed light brown sugar
1 tablespoon all-purpose flour
¼ teaspoon salt
1 teaspoon each of ground cinnamon, ginger, and nutmeg
2 tablespoons butter or margarine
1½ cups milk
4 eggs, slightly beaten
Sherry Ginger Cream (page 1493)

In saucepan mix pumpkin, sugar, flour, salt, spices, butter, and milk. Cook, stirring constantly, for 5 minutes. Cool slightly; pour over slightly beaten eggs. Pour into well-buttered 1½-quart casserole. Set in pan of hot water. Bake in preheated moderate oven (350°F.) for 1 hour, or until set. Serve with Sherry Ginger Cream. Makes 6 servings.

Note: To use fresh pumpkin, halve 3-pound pumpkin; remove seeds and stringy part. Pare, and cut into pieces. Cook, drain, and mash. Drain again.

EVERY-DAY RICE PUDDING

4 cups milk
3 tablespoons uncooked rice
½ teaspoon salt
⅔ cup sugar
1 teaspoon vanilla extract

Combine all ingredients. Pour into buttered 1½-quart casserole and bake in preheated slow oven (325°F.) for about 3 hours, stirring occasionally during the first hour. Makes 4 to 6 servings.

LEMON CREAM RICE PUDDING

3 cups milk
½ cup uncooked rice
1 cup sugar
Grated rind of ½ lemon
1½ tablespoons fresh lemon juice
¾ teaspoon salt
4 eggs, separated
Bright red jelly

Heat milk in top part of a double boiler. Stir in rice, cover, and cook over simmering water for 30 minutes, or until rice is tender. Beat ½ cup sugar, the grated rind, juice, salt, and egg yolks together. Stir in small amount of hot mixture. Put back in double boiler and cook, stirring constantly, for 2 or 3 minutes, or until mixture coats a metal spoon. Pour into shallow 1½-quart baking dish. Beat egg whites until foamy; gradually add ½ cup sugar and beat until stiff. Pile lightly on pudding. Bake in preheated hot oven (400°F.) for about 5 minutes. Top with jelly. Serve warm or cold. Makes 6 servings.

SPICY SWEET-POTATO PUDDING

¼ cup butter or margarine
½ cup firmly packed brown sugar
2 eggs, separated
¼ cup milk
½ teaspoon salt
¼ teaspoon ground nutmeg
⅛ teaspoon each of ground cinnamon, and ginger
1 cup mashed cooked sweet potatoes
Cream or Hard Sauce (page 1493)

Cream butter and sugar together. Add well-beaten egg yolks, milk, seasonings, and sweet potatoes. Beat egg whites until stiff and fold into mixture. Turn into 1½-quart casserole. Bake in preheated moderate oven (350°F.) for 40 minutes. Serve warm with cream. Makes 4 servings.

UPSIDE-DOWN PUDDING

¼ cup firmly packed brown sugar
¼ teaspoon ground cinnamon
¼ cup chopped almonds

About 3½ cups (one 1-pound 13-ounce can) sliced peaches
1½ cups sifted all-purpose flour
2 teaspoons baking powder
¾ teaspoon salt
¼ cup shortening
½ cup sugar
1 egg
½ cup milk
½ teaspoon vanilla extract
½ cup heavy cream, whipped

Grease bottom of 6- or 8-inch square glass baking pan and sprinkle with sugar, cinnamon, and chopped nuts. Place drained peaches in pan. Sift together flour, baking powder, and salt. Cream shortening; add sugar and cream until fluffy. Add egg, then dry ingredients alternately with milk mixed with vanilla. Spoon batter over fruit. Bake in preheated moderate oven, (350°F.) for about 45 minutes. Serve with whipped cream. Makes 9 servings.

Steamed Puddings

STEAMED CARROT-SUET PUDDING

½ cup each of grated peeled raw carrot and raw potato
½ cup brown sugar, firmly packed
½ cup chopped suet
1 cup seeded raisins, cut into pieces
½ cup dried currants
1 cup all-purpose flour
½ teaspoon baking soda
1 teaspoon baking powder
¼ teaspoon salt
1 teaspoon ground cinnamon
½ teaspoon each of ground cloves and nutmeg
Hard Sauce (page 1493) or Foamy Sauce (page 1492)

Mix carrot, potato, sugar, and suet. Add remaining ingredients except sauce and mix well. Pack into greased 1-quart pudding mold. Cover and steam for 2 hours, or until done. Serve warm, topped with Hard Sauce, garnished with a few strips of candied orange peel, if desired. Makes 6 servings.

STEAMED CRANBERRY PUDDING

1⅓ cups sifted all-purpose flour
1 teaspoon baking soda
½ teaspoon salt
½ cup molasses
⅓ cup boiling water
2 cups whole raw cranberries
Butter Sauce (page 1492)

Sift dry ingredients. Add molasses and hot water; stir in cranberries. Pour into a buttered 1½-quart mold; cover tightly with a lid or double thickness of wax paper or aluminum foil; secure with string. Place on rack in large kettle and add boiling water to half cover mold; cover. Steam for 2 hours. Unmold and serve hot with Butter Sauce. If desired, sprinkle with grated orange rind and chopped pistachio nuts. Makes 6 servings.

INDIVIDUAL STEAMED FIG PUDDINGS

1 cup finely chopped dried figs
1 cup raisins
½ cup chopped nuts
¼ cup diced citron
½ cup firmly packed finely chopped
suet
1½ cups sifted all-purpose flour
½ teaspoon each of baking soda
and baking powder
¼ teaspoon salt
1 teaspoon ground cinnamon
¼ teaspoon ground cloves
⅛ teaspoon ground nutmeg
½ cup molasses
½ cup undiluted evaporated milk
Hard Sauce (page 1493) or
Foamy Sauce (page 1492)

Put first 5 ingredients in large bowl. Sift in dry ingredients and mix well. Combine molasses and evaporated milk; add to fruit mixture and stir until well blended. Press into 8 buttered custard cups. Cover with transparent plastic wrap twisted to hold tightly or with squares of wax paper secured with string. Set on rack in large kettle with tight-fitting cover. Add boiling water to depth of about 1 inch. Bring to boil, reduce heat, and steam for about 40 minutes. Serve warm with Hard Sauce. Makes 8 servings.

MARMALADE PUDDING

½ cup shortening
¼ cup sugar
2 eggs
1 cup sifted all-purpose flour
1 teaspoon baking powder
½ teaspoon salt
¼ cup orange marmalade
Hard Sauce (page 1493)

Cream shortening and sugar together. Add eggs and beat until fluffy. Add sifted dry ingredients and marmalade. Fill 6 greased custard cups ⅔ full of batter, or put in 1-quart ring mold and cover center with small saucer. Cover and steam for 1¼ hours. Serve with Hard Sauce. Other preserves may be used instead of marmalade. Makes 6 servings.

BRANDY PLUM PUDDING

½ cup sugar
3 cups sifted all-purpose flour
1 teaspoon baking powder
1½ teaspoons salt
½ teaspoon each of ground ginger,
cloves, and nutmeg
1 teaspoon ground cinnamon
½ cup each of dry currants and raisins,
soaked overnight in ⅓ cup brandy
½ cup chopped nuts
¼ cup each of chopped citron and
candied orange peel
1 apple, grated
1 cup suet, chopped fine
1½ cups milk
½ cup molasses
½ cup brandy
Brandy Hard Sauce (page 1493)

Sift together dry ingredients; add currants, raisins, nuts, citron, orange peel, and grated apple. Stir in suet, milk, and molasses. Pour into two buttered 1½-quart molds. Cover tightly with a lid or

double thickness of wax paper or aluminum foil; secure with string. Place on rack in bottom of large kettle and add boiling water to half cover mold. Cover and steam for 3 hours. Unmold on large serving platter. Decorate top with sprig of holly; pour ½ cup heated and flaming brandy over pudding. Serve with Brandy Hard Sauce. Makes 8 servings.

STEAMED STRAWBERRY PUDDING

6 tablespoons shortening
¼ cup strawberry-flavored beverage mix
¾ cup sugar
½ teaspoon almond extract
½ teaspoon salt
1½ cups sifted cake flour
1½ teaspoons baking powder
½ cup milk
3 egg whites
2 packages (10 ounces each)
frozen sliced strawberries

Cream shortening, beverage mix, and ½ cup sugar until light. Add flavoring. Add sifted dry ingredients alternately with milk, beating until smooth. Beat egg whites until foamy; gradually add remaining sugar, continuing to beat until stiff. Fold into first mixture. Fill 7 or 8 greased 6-ounce custard cups or other individual molds two-thirds full of batter. Cover top of each loosely with wax paper; tie on firmly with cord. Put on rack in large kettle or skillet containing 1 inch of boiling water. Cover and steam for 30 minutes. Turn out and serve warm with berries. Makes 7 or 8 servings.

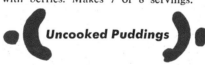

Uncooked Puddings

BRIDE'S PUDDING

2 envelopes unflavored gelatin
½ cup cold water
⅓ cup boiling water
6 egg whites
¼ teaspoon salt
¾ cup sugar
2 cups heavy cream, whipped
1 teaspoon vanilla extract
1 can (3½ ounces) flaked coconut

Soften gelatin in cold water; pour boiling water over gelatin and stir until dissolved. Cool. Beat egg whites with salt until frothy; gradually beat in sugar. Continue beating until mixture holds a peak. Slowly beat in gelatin. Fold in whipped cream and vanilla. Butter well a 9-inch springform pan; sprinkle thickly with coconut. Carefully pour pudding mixture into springform. Chill for at least 4 hours. Cut into wedges, and serve with fresh or frozen raspberries. Makes 10 to 12 servings.

GREEN GABLES ICEBOX PUDDING

1 pound marshmallows, quartered
9 candied cherries, minced
1 package (1 pound) dates, cut
½ cup walnuts
1 pound graham crackers, rolled
into crumbs

Mix all ingredients, saving about ½ cup of the crumbs. Shape into a roll and roll in reserved crumbs. Chill. When wrapped in foil, will keep "forever." Slice to serve. Makes 8 to 10 servings.

SHERRY ALMOND SNOW PUDDING

1 envelope unflavored gelatin
¼ cup cold water
⅓ cup boiling water
3 egg whites
⅛ teaspoon salt
½ cup sugar
¼ teaspoon almond extract
3 tablespoons sherry
⅓ cup toasted almond slivers
Sherry Custard Sauce (page 1493)

Soften gelatin in cold water; dissolve in boiling water. Refrigerate until it just begins to congeal. Beat until frothy. Beat egg whites with salt until stiff; gradually beat in sugar; add almond extract, sherry, and frothy gelatin. Pour into 1½-quart mold, alternating layers of gelatin mixture and almonds. Chill for at least 4 hours. Unmold and serve with Sherry Custard Sauce. Makes 6 servings.

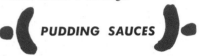

PUDDING SAUCES

BRANDY SAUCE

4 egg yolks
⅓ cup confectioners' sugar
¼ cup fresh orange juice
2 tablespoons brandy
¾ cup heavy cream, whipped

Beat egg yolks and sugar until thick and lemon colored. Fold in orange juice, brandy, and cream. Makes about 2 cups.

BUTTER SAUCE

Mix together ½ cup butter, 1 cup sugar, and ½ cup light cream. Cook until sugar is dissolved, stirring constantly.

CHOCOLATE SAUCE

In saucepan over low heat melt 2 ounces (2 squares) unsweetened chocolate in ¾ cup milk, stirring constantly. Beat until smooth. Add ¼ teaspoon salt, 1½ cups sugar, and 3 tablespoons light corn syrup. Cook, stirring occasionally, for 2 or 3 minutes. Add 2 tablespoons butter and 1 teaspoon vanilla extract. Makes 2 cups.

CUSTARD SAUCE

Scald 1½ cups milk in top part of a double boiler over simmering water. Mix ⅛ teaspoon salt, 3 egg yolks and 3 tablespoons sugar. Stir in small amount of hot milk; put back in double boiler and cook, stirring constantly, until thickened. Cool. Flavor sauce with vanilla or almond extract. Makes 1½ cups.

FOAMY SAUCE

In top part of a double boiler cream 1 cup confectioners' sugar and ½ cup soft butter or margarine. Add 2 egg yolks, beaten. Cook over simmering water, stirring constantly, until thickened. Fold in 2 stiffly beaten egg whites and 1 tablespoon brandy or rum. Serve warm. Makes 4 to 6 servings.

HARD SAUCE

Cream ½ cup soft butter with 1½ cups sifted confectioners' sugar until light and fluffy. Add 1 teaspoon vanilla extract or 2 tablespoons rum or brandy. Chill. Makes 8 to 10 servings.

BRANDY HARD SAUCE

Cream 1 cup sweet butter and 2 cups sifted confectioners' sugar; beat in 1 teaspoon vanilla extract and ¼ cup brandy. Makes 2 cups.

Lighted Hard-Sauce Stars—Spread hard sauce in shallow pan. Chill. Cut with 2-inch star cutter. Place small birthday candle in center of star. Place stars around pudding; light when served.

LEMON HARD SAUCE

Cream ⅓ cup soft butter or margarine and 1 cup sifted confectioners' sugar until light. Add 1 teaspoon grated lemon rind.

LEMON SAUCE

In saucepan mix ½ cup sugar, ⅛ teaspoon salt, and 2 tablespoons cornstarch. Gradually stir in 1 cup boiling water. Cook, stirring constantly, until thickened. Remove from heat; stir in 2 tablespoons butter, juice of 1 lemon, and 1 teaspoon grated lemon rind. Serve warm. Makes 1¾ cups.

SHERRY CUSTARD SAUCE

3 egg yolks, slightly beaten
2 tablespoons sugar
½ cup milk
Dash of salt
¼ teaspoon vanilla extract
½ cup heavy cream, whipped
1½ tablespoons sherry

In top part of double boiler over simmering water cook, stirring constantly, egg yolks, sugar, milk, and salt until mixture coats a spoon. Cool. Fold in vanilla, whipped cream, and sherry.

SHERRY GINGER CREAM

Mix 1 cup heavy cream, whipped, ¼ cup confectioners' sugar, 1 tablespoon sherry, and ¼ cup chopped preserved gingerroot.

VANILLA SAUCE

In small saucepan mix ½ cup sugar and 1 tablespoon cornstarch. Stir in 1 cup boiling water. Simmer for 5 minutes. Stir in 2 tablespoons butter and 1 teaspoon vanilla extract. Add dash of salt. Serve warm. Makes 1¼ cups.

PUERTO RICAN COOKERY
by Carmen Aboy Valldejuli

One of the most attractive spots in the Caribbean is the sunny island of Puerto Rico. It is frequently referred to as "the Crossroad of the Americas" because of its strategic position. Discovered by Christopher Columbus on his second voyage in 1493, it was settled by the Spaniards and remained a Spanish possession until ceded to the United States in 1898. Today, the island enjoys the status of a free commonwealth government under the American flag.

Because of its historical background, Puerto Rico is a land of contrasts, with two outstanding cultures, the Spanish and American. The charm of Old San Juan, with the magnificent walls of El Morro Castle, built four centuries ago; San Cristóbal, the historical fortress that withstood the attacks of the pirates who roamed those waters; and the legendary San José church, one of the oldest in the New World, keep alive the memories of the Spanish settlers. Even though it is only a few hours away from the mainland by air, Puerto Rico has maintained much of this Spanish culture.

The *cocina criolla* in Puerto Rico was started by its earliest inhabitants, the docile Arawak Indians and the ferocious Caribs. Through the centuries, the simple dishes prepared by the Indians have been enriched by the culinary skills of the descendants of the original settlers and by the African slaves brought over to toil in the green sugar fields. Today the tasty ingredients and flavorings added have resulted in a really distinctive cuisine.

One of the cooking secrets is *sofrito,* a combination of green peppers, sweet chili peppers, onions, garlic, tomatoes, oregano, and *cilantro* (fresh coriander), cooked together in lard or vegetable oil and used as a seasoning.

The Spaniards use saffron to color their delicious *paella,* but in Puerto Rico *achiote* (annatto seeds) is used to give coloring to this and many other native dishes. *Achiote* is tasteless; the coloring is obtained by slowly heating the seeds in lard or vegetable oil. The colored shortening is strained and used by spoonfuls in many recipes.

Rum manufacturing, a by-product of the sugar industry, is one of the most important sources of income of the island. Delicious rum drinks are a Puerto Rican specialty. One of the favorites is a pineapple-rum punch, which is prepared and set in the freezer. The remarkable thing is that it does not congeal; it keeps to the consistency of a frozen daiquiri. It is scooped from the freezer right into the cocktail glasses to the guests' amazement and delight!

Puerto Rico is blessed with a tropical climate all year round, beautiful mountain ranges, fishing villages, balmy beaches on a blue-green ocean, and delicious cookery based on the abundant fresh seafood, vegetables, and tropical fruits.

SOUP

SOPÓN DE GARBANZOS CON PATAS DE CERDO
(Chick-Pea Soup with Pigs' Feet)

½ pound dried chick-peas
2 pounds pigs' feet
Water
½ green pepper, seeded and chopped
1 garlic clove, peeled and chopped
1 onion, peeled and chopped
2 ounces cured ham, chopped
1 ounce salt pork, chopped
4 leaves cilantro (fresh coriander) chopped or 1½ teaspoons ground coriander
1 tablespoon achiote lard or vegetable oil
⅓ cup tomato sauce
½ pound pumpkin, pared and chopped
1 pound potatoes, pared and chopped
1 tomato, peeled and chopped
½ pound cabbage, chopped

Wash and soak chick-peas overnight. Rinse and drain. If the pigs' feet are salted, soak overnight. If unsalted pigs' feet are used, season to taste. Place in water and heat to boiling. Drain. Remove and discard any small loose bones.

Heat 4½ quarts water in a large pot. Add the pigs' feet, cover, and boil for 1½ hours. Add the drained chick-peas and the next 6 ingredients. Cover and cook for 1 hour. Add remaining ingredients, cover, and cook for 1¼ hours. If necessary, uncover to thicken sauce. Remove bones before serving. Makes 8 servings.

 **FISH**

MOJO ISLEÑO
(Fried Fish with Puerto Rican Sauce)

- 2½ pounds onions, peeled and sliced
- 1½ cups water
- 24 black olives
- 2 tablespoons capers
- ½ cup (one 4-ounce can) pimientos, cut into tiny slices, in their juice
- 2 cups (two 8-ounce cans) tomato sauce
- 2 tablespoons vinegar
- 2 bay leaves
- 3 tablespoons salt
- 1½ cups olive oil
- 4 pounds fish, cut into 1-inch slices
- 1 large garlic clove, peeled

Combine first 8 ingredients, 1 tablespoon of the salt, and ½ cup of the olive oil, and cook over moderate heat for about 1 hour. When sauce is nearly done, season fish with remaining salt. Put remaining oil and the garlic in a frying pan. Brown garlic over moderate heat. Remove garlic and place in the pan as many slices of fish as will fit. Fry each side over moderate heat for 7 minutes, or until done. Fry remaining slices in same way. Cover with the sauce and serve. Makes 12 servings.

PESCADO EN ESCABECHE
(Pickled Fish)

- 1 cup vinegar
- 12 peppercorns
- 2 bay leaves
- 1½ pounds onions, peeled and sliced
  Salt
- 3 cups olive oil
- 3 pounds firm-fleshed fish, cut into 1-inch slices
  Juice of 1 large lime
- ¼ cup all-purpose flour
- 2 large garlic cloves, peeled and crushed

Mix first 4 ingredients with ½ teaspoon salt and 2 cups of the olive oil in a large kettle; and cook slowly for 1 hour. Cool sauce. Rinse fish in running water and dry. Sprinkle lime juice over the fish slices and season with 1½ tablespoons salt. Sprinkle both sides of the slices lightly with flour when ready to fry. In a frying pan heat remaining olive oil with crushed garlic cloves. Remove garlic as soon as it is brown. Add as many fish slices as will fit in the pan and brown on both sides over moderate heat. Reduce heat and cook the slices for 15 minutes. Fry remaining slices in same way.

Remove fish and arrange in a deep glass dish as follows: Pour a little cool sauce over a few fish slices in bottom of dish. Fill dish with alternate layers of fish slices and sauce. Cover and put in refrigerator for at least 24 hours before serving. Serve cold. Makes 8 servings.

COCA DE SARDINAS
(Sardine Pie)

Pastry:

- 1½ cups all-purpose flour
- ¼ teaspoon salt
- 1 tablespoon baking powder
- 3 tablespoons cold butter
- 1 egg
- ⅓ cup cold milk (about)

Sift flour 3 times with salt and baking powder. Rapidly cut in butter, using 2 knives, until butter is cut into pieces the size of peas. Put egg in a measuring cup and stir with a fork just enough to mix yolk and white. Stir in milk until liquid measures ½ cup. Stir liquid into flour-butter mixture. Turn dough onto a floured board. Roll out a circle ¼ inch thick and large enough to cover a 9-inch pan. Prick dough in several places and press a fork moistened in milk around the edge. Bake in preheated moderate oven (350°F.) for 20 minutes.

Filling:

- 2 cups (one 1-pound can) sardines
- ¾ pound onions, peeled and sliced
- ⅓ cup olive oil
- 5 parsley sprigs, chopped
- ½ cup (one 4-ounce can) pimientos
- 6 tablespoons tomato sauce
- 1 teaspoon salt

Remove any bones from the sardines. Brown onions slowly in the olive oil for about 15 minutes, stirring occasionally. Add parsley. Chop the pimientos and add with their liquid. Add tomato sauce, salt, and sardines. Stir well and bring to a boil. Turn filling into baked pastry shell. Bake in preheated moderate oven (375° F.) for 10 minutes. Makes 6 servings.

 **MEAT AND POULTRY**

LECHÓN DE MECHAR
(Stuffed Eye Round)

  Beef eye round (4 to 4½ pounds)
  Stuffing
- ¼ cup lard
- 4 cups water
- 1 tablespoon salt
- 1 sweet chili pepper, seeded
- 3 leaves cilantro (fresh coriander) or ¼ teaspoon ground coriander
- 2 ounces cured ham
- ½ green pepper, seeded
- 1 medium onion, peeled
- 1½ pounds potatoes, pared and diced
- 2 tablespoons achiote lard or oil
- 1 tomato, chopped
- ½ cup tomato sauce

Wash and clean meat. With a sharp knife make a deep cut from both ends to the center. Stuff meat and skewer or sew opening closed. Melt lard in a large heavy kettle. When hot, add meat and brown on all sides over high heat for about 10 minutes. Add water and salt. Chop coarsely next 5 ingredients and add. Cover kettle and cook over moderate heat for 2½

Pollo en Vino Dulce

Sopón de Garbanzos con Patas de Cerdo

Sopa Borracha

Pineapple-Rum Punch

hours. Add remaining ingredients, and continue to cook, uncovered, for 45 minutes longer, or until sauce begins to thicken. Makes 6 servings.

Stuffing

2 ounces each of cured ham and salt pork
1 small onion, peeled
2 sweet chili peppers, seeded
½ green pepper, seeded
6 green olives, pitted
1 teaspoon capers
1 teaspoon crumbled dried oregano
1 tablespoon olive oil
1 teaspoon vinegar

Chop first 7 ingredients, and mix with oregano, olive oil, and vinegar.

PERNIL CON VINO AL CALDERO
(Pot of Fresh Ham with Wine)

7 pounds fresh ham
1 large garlic clove, peeled
6 peppercorns
2 teaspoons crumbled dried oregano
Salt
2 tablespoons olive oil
6 cups water
½ pound onions, peeled and sliced
2 bay leaves
2 cups muscatel
½ cup sugar (optional)
2 pounds potatoes, pared and halved

Remove skin and excess fat from meat. Make superficial crisscross gashes on top of meat. Crush next 3 ingredients with 2 tablespoons salt in a mortar and rub into meat. Place meat in a kettle with olive oil and brown well over high heat. Add water, onions, and bay leaves and bring to a boil. Cover and cook over moderate heat for 2½ hours. Turn meat occasionally. Add ½ teaspoon salt and remaining ingredients. When boiling, cover and cook for 45 minutes; if necessary, uncover and cook to thicken sauce. Serve meat in a platter with potatoes. Pour sauce into a glass container. Remove fat from top and serve sauce over meat. Makes 8 to 10 servings.

ARROZ CON POLLO
(Rice with Chicken)

1 frying chicken (2½ pounds), about 1½ pounds cleaned and dressed
1 teaspoon crumbled dried oregano
2 peppercorns
1 garlic clove, peeled
3¼ teaspoons salt
2 teaspoons olive oil
1 teaspoon vinegar
1 tablespoon lard or oil
2 ounces cured ham, chopped
1 ounce salt pork or 1 strip bacon, chopped
1 onion, peeled
1 green pepper, seeded
1 sweet chili pepper, seeded
2 leaves cilantro (fresh coriander)
6 green olives, pitted
1 teaspoon capers
1 tomato
2 tablespoons achiote lard or oil
¼ cup tomato sauce
2¼ cups uncooked rice, washed and drained
2 cups (one 1-pound, 1-ounce can) green peas

½ cup (one 4-ounce can) pimientos

Cut chicken into serving pieces. Mash in a mortar next 6 ingredients and rub mixture into chicken pieces. Place lard in a large deep kettle. Add cured ham and salt pork, and brown over high heat. Add chicken and brown lightly. Reduce heat to moderate. Chop next 7 ingredients and add; cook for 10 minutes. Add next 3 ingredients and cook for 5 minutes. Drain liquid from peas; measure and add enough water to make 3 cups. Reserve peas to be added later. Heat the 3 cups liquid to boiling and add to kettle. Mix well and cook rapidly, uncovered, until dry. With a large spoon turn rice from bottom to top. Cover and cook slowly for 20 minutes. Add peas, turn rice once more, cover, and cook for 10 minutes longer. Heat pimientos, drain, and garnish the rice. Serve at once. Makes 6 servings.

POLLO EN AGRIDULCE
(Sweet and Sour Chicken)

1 frying chicken (3½ pounds), cut up
2 cups water
Juice of 1 lime
1 garlic clove
1 teaspoon oregano
3 peppercorns
2¼ teaspoons salt
¼ cup butter or margarine
1 cup firmly packed brown sugar
¼ cup vinegar
2 chorizos (Spanish sausages), sliced

Wash chicken in mixture of the water and lime juice. Drain and dry on absorbent paper. Mash garlic with the seasonings. Rub well into both sides of chicken pieces. Melt butter in large skillet. Add chicken and brown quickly on both sides. Add remaining ingredients. As soon as sugar melts, turn heat to low, cover skillet, and cook for 30 minutes. Uncover, turn chicken pieces, and cook for 30 minutes longer, or until chicken is tender. Makes 6 servings.

POLLO EN VINO DULCE
(Chicken in Sweet Wine)

1 whole frying chicken (3½ pounds)
1 garlic clove
1 teaspoon oregano
3 peppercorns
2¼ teaspoons salt
¼ cup butter or margarine
1 cup water
3 medium onions, peeled and sliced
1 teaspoon capers
10 green olives, pitted
3 bay leaves
10 prunes, pitted
2 tablespoons seeded raisins
5 medium potatoes, peeled and cut into pieces
1½ cups muscatel
½ cup sugar

Wash and dry chicken. Mash next 4 ingredients together and rub chicken well inside and out with the mixture. Melt butter in a *caldero* (kettle). Add chicken and brown well on all sides. Add all remaining ingredients except wine and

sugar. Bring to boil, cover, and simmer for 15 minutes. Add wine and sugar, cover, and simmer for 15 minutes longer. Uncover and cook for 25 minutes longer, or until chicken is tender and sauce thickens slightly. Makes 6 servings.

VEGETABLES AND BREADS

REPOLLO EN SALSA DE QUESO
(Cabbage in Cheese Sauce)

2 pounds cabbage
2 quarts water
Salt
1 tablespoon sugar
2 cups milk
¼ cup cornstarch
¼ cup butter
¼ pound Swiss cheese, grated on half-moon side of a four-sided grater

Remove core from cabbage. Chop cabbage finely and combine with water, 1½ tablespoons salt, and the sugar. Heat to boiling, cover, reduce heat to moderate, and cook for 1 hour. Remove from heat and drain well. Combine next 3 ingredients and 1 teaspoon salt and stir over moderate heat until sauce boils; mix with drained cabbage. Set aside ¼ cup of the grated cheese. Add the rest of the cheese and mix well. Turn mixture into a 2-quart casserole. Sprinkle with reserved cheese and brown lightly under broiler heat. Makes 6 servings.

BERENJENA CON QUESO
(Eggplant with Cheese)

2 pounds eggplant
6 cups water
1½ tablespoons salt
¼ pound (1 cup) grated Parmesan cheese
1 egg
½ cup plus 2 tablespoons butter
3 tablespoons cracker crumbs

Wash eggplant and drop without peeling into the water with salt. Bring water to a boil, cover pot, and cook rapidly for 30 minutes. Remove eggplant from pot, peel, and mash with a fork. Add grated cheese, egg, and ½ cup butter. Mix well and put mixture into a greased glass baking dish (1 quart). Sprinkle with cracker crumbs and dot with remaining butter. Bake in preheated moderate oven (375° F.) for 30 minutes. Makes 4 servings.

TORTA DE MAÍZ TIERNO
(Fresh Corn Tart)

½ cup butter
1½ cups fresh corn grated from cobs
1 teaspoon salt
¾ cup sugar
3 eggs
1¼ cups milk
1 teaspoon vanilla extract

Melt butter and mix with corn, salt, and sugar. Break eggs with a fork, without beating; gradually add milk; then add vanilla. Mix and combine with corn mixture. Turn mixture into a greased 1½-quart baking dish. Bake in preheated moderate oven (375°F.) for 1 hour. Makes 6 servings.

PAPA EMPANADA AL HORNO
(Potato Soufflé)

6 medium potatoes
4 cups boiling water
Salt
¼ cup butter or margarine
2 tablespoons sugar
1½ cups hot milk
1 egg, well beaten
2 tablespoons fine cracker crumbs

Peel and halve potatoes. Cook in boiling water with 1 tablespoon salt for 25 minutes, or until tender. Drain and force through a ricer. Add butter, sugar, milk, and salt to taste; mix well. Fold egg into mixture. Grease a 1½-quart casserole and sprinkle with half the crumbs. Pour potato mixture into casserole and sprinkle with remaining crumbs. Bake in preheated hot oven (400°F.) for about 30 minutes. Makes 6 servings.

PASTELILLOS GALLEGOS
(Galician Turnovers)

2 cups all-purpose flour
1 cup water
2 tablespoons butter
1½ teaspoons salt
¼ pound cheese, preferably Cheddar, sliced
1 pound (2 cups) lard

Measure and sift flour. Heat to boiling the water, butter, and salt. Immediately add flour all at once. Cook for 1 minute, stirring to avoid lumps. Remove from heat and continue to stir until mixture is smooth. Turn mixture onto a lightly floured board while still hot. Knead rapidly for about 2 minutes. Shape dough into a ball. Place ball in a bowl and leave covered with a cloth for 1 hour.

Shape ball into a roll about 2 inches thick. Cut the roll into slices about ½ inch wide. Roll out slices thinly, one by one, with lightly floured rolling pin. Cut each slice into a circle the size of a doughnut. Two circles will make a *pastelillo*. Place one circle on top of the other with a slice of cheese between. Press the edges together first with the finger tips, then with a lightly floured fork. Lay the *pastelillos* on a lightly floured baking sheet, ready to be fried. Set in refrigerator until 30 minutes before frying. In the lard heated to 400° F. on a frying thermometer, fry 3 at a time until golden brown. Drain on absorbent paper. Makes about 30.

SURULLITOS DE MAÍZ
(Cornmeal Sticks)

2 cups water
1¼ teaspoons salt
1½ cups cornmeal
1 cup packed, grated Edam cheese

Combine water and salt in a saucepan; heat to boiling. Add cornmeal and mix

thoroughly. Cook over moderate heat for about 5 minutes, or until mixture separates from bottom and sides of pan. Remove from heat. Add grated cheese and mix well. Take mixture by teaspoonfuls and shape into balls. In the palms of the hands roll balls to ½-inch thickness, in the shape of small cigars. Fry in deep hot fat (370°F. on a frying thermometer) for 2 to 3 minutes, or until golden brown. Drain on absorbent paper. Makes 48.

DESSERTS AND BEVERAGES

HOJALDRE
(Sweet Cake)

1 cup butter
2 cups firmly packed brown sugar
6 eggs
3 cups unsifted all-purpose flour
2 teaspoons baking powder
2 teaspoons ground cinnamon
1 teaspoon ground cloves
2 teaspoons grated nutmeg
¼ teaspoon salt
1 cup milk
⅓ cup sweet wine
Confectioners' sugar

Cream butter and add sugar gradually. Add eggs, one at a time, beating well after each addition. Sift next 6 ingredients 3 times and add to egg mixture alternately with liquids. Butter tube pan (9 inches) and sprinkle lightly with flour. Pour mixture into pan and bake in preheated moderate oven (350°F.) for 1 hour. Cool, turn onto serving platter, and sprinkle with confectioners' sugar.

ARROZ CON LECHE
(Creamed Rice)

4 cups water
1 teaspoon salt
1 cup uncooked rice
1½ teaspoons lard
½ cup sugar
4 cups milk
Grated rind of 1 lime

In a deep kettle heat to boiling the water and salt. Wash rice in a colander under running water. Drain and add to the boiling water. Add lard and mix. Heat rapidly to boiling. Turn heat to low and cook for about 30 minutes, until liquid is absorbed. Do not stir during this cooking period. Combine sugar and milk and add. Add lime rind and mix all together. Heat rapidly to boiling. Turn heat to low and cook, uncovered, for about 30 minutes, turning rice over occasionally. Makes 6 servings.

BUÑUELOS DE VIENTO
(Wind Puffs)

Water
½ cup butter
½ teaspoon salt
1 cup sifted all-purpose flour
4 eggs
Cooking oil for frying
3 cups sugar
Peel of 1 lime

Place 1 cup water, the butter, and salt in a saucepan. Heat to boiling. Remove from heat and add flour all at once, stirring vigorously until well mixed. Add eggs, one at a time, mixing until well blended after each addition. In a deep kettle heat oil to 370°F. on a frying thermometer. Drop mixture into oil by tablespoonfuls, frying 5 at a time in the following way: Fry for 2 minutes uncovered, 2 minutes covered, 2 minutes uncovered. Drain on absorbent paper and place in dessert bowl. Mix remaining ingredients with 4 cups water and cook syrup until candy thermometer registers 222°F. Pour syrup over the fried *buñuelos* and serve warm. Makes 18.

ISLA FLOTANTE
(Floating Island)

Custard:

2 tablespoons cornstarch
6 cups milk
4 egg yolks
½ teaspoon salt
⅔ cup sugar
1 cinnamon stick or 1 teaspoon vanilla extract

Dissolve cornstarch in 2 cups of the milk. Mix with egg yolks. Combine rest of milk with remaining ingredients and heat to boiling without stirring. Gradually add egg-yolk mixture and cook, stirring rapidly with a wooden spoon, until custard boils. Immediately strain into individual custard cups.

Meringue:

4 egg whites
1 cup sugar
1 tablespoon fresh lime juice

Beat egg whites until stiff. Gradually beat in sugar and lime juice. Beat until fluffy. Garnish custard and set in refrigerator to serve cold. Makes 8 servings.

SOPA BORRACHA
(Tipsy Cake)

3 cups sugar
2 cups water
1½ cups muscatel
½ pound spongecake
2 egg whites
1 tablespoon tiny multicolored candies

Combine 2½ cups sugar and the water and boil until a heavy syrup is formed (240°F. on a candy thermometer). Remove from heat, add wine, and stir. Cut spongecake into 2-inch squares and place in individual custard cups. Pour the syrup over cake squares. Beat egg whites until stiff, add remaining sugar, and beat until fluffy. Top the cake with this meringue. Sprinkle with candies. Serve cold. Makes 8 servings.

CAZUELA
(Sweet-Potato and Pumpkin Dessert)

Water
Salt
2 pounds each of sweet potatoes and pumpkin, pared and chopped
1 cup coconut milk (page 1370)
¼ cup butter

3 eggs, beaten
2 cups sugar
¼ cup all-purpose flour
1 small piece of gingerroot, mashed
1 cinnamon stick
6 aniseeds
5 cloves
   Plantain leaves or parchment paper

Heat to boiling 2 quarts water and 1 tablespoon salt. Add sweet potatoes and pumpkin. Boil for 45 minutes and drain. Immediately mash vegetables and put through a ricer. Add next 5 ingredients with 1 teaspoon salt and mix thoroughly. Boil remaining ingredients except plantain leaves in ½ cup water for 5 minutes. Strain into the first mixture and mix well.

Butter generously a 3-quart casserole and cover bottom and sides with plantain leaves, washed and buttered, or with buttered parchment paper. Fill with the sweet-potato and pumpkin mixture. Bake in preheated hot oven (400°F.) for 1¾ hours. Cool completely before turning dessert onto platter. Makes 10 servings.

PINEAPPLE-RUM PUNCH

2 cups sugar
   About 6 cups (one 2-pound, 14-ounce can) pineapple juice
½ cup fresh lime juice
5 cups white Puerto Rican rum

Dissolve sugar in 2 cups of the pineapple juice over low heat. Remove from heat and mix with remaining pineapple juice. Add lime juice and rum. Mix well. Place in freezer. Scoop into daiquiri glasses at serving time. Makes about twenty 5½-ounce servings.

DAIQUIRI ON-THE-ROCKS

1 cup fresh lime juice
1 cup sugar
2 cups white Puerto Rican rum

Dissolve sugar in lime juice over low heat. Remove from heat and allow to cool. Add rum and chill in refrigerator for a few hours before serving. Mix well before serving over ice cubes in old-fashioned glass. Makes six 5½-ounce servings.

Note: For a stronger drink add an additional cup of rum.

PUFF—As applied to cooking, a puff is a light pastry frequently made hollow so that it can be filled, such as a cream puff. Sometimes the word is applied to other foods which become light and puffy while cooking, for example potato puffs.

PUFF PASTE—A very light flaky pastry which owes its tenderness and crisp quality to the large quantity of butter rolled into the basic flour-and-water dough. The paste expands a great deal in baking and is made up of many flaky layers. It is used in making Napoleons, cream horns, and many other sweet and nonsweet pastries.

PUMPKIN—The name of a gourd belonging to the *Cucurbitaceae* family which also includes melons, cucumbers, and squash. The pumpkin's flesh is orange-colored and has a distinctive sweet flavor. The word comes from the Old French *pompion,* in its turn derived from the Greek word *pepōn* meaning "cooked by the sun."

The pumpkin is probably native to Central America. It was being grown extensively by the Indians in North America when the first colonists landed in this country. The Indians boiled and baked pumpkin, made it into soup, dried and ground it into meal. The meal was used much as cornmeal was to make breads and puddings. The Indians cut pumpkins into rings and hung them to dry so as to have them throughout the winter.

A 17th-century writer reports on the New England method of cooking pumpkins: "The Housewive's manner is to slice them when ripe and then into Dice, and so fill a pot with them of two or three gallons and stew them upon a gentle fire the whole day. And as they sink they fill agin with fresh Pompions not putting any liquor to them and when it is stirred enough it will look like Baked Apples, this Dish putting Butter to it and a little Vinegar with some Spice as Ginger which makes it tart like an Apple, and so serve it up to be eaten with fish and flesh."

In the mountains of Virginia dried pumpkin was used as a substitute for molasses. Pumpkin pie was so associated with Thanksgiving that when a 17th-century Connecticut town could not get the molasses needed for the pie in time for Thanksgiving, the holiday was delayed. Americans have always loved pumpkin pie. The poet Whittier asked nostalgically: "What moistens the lip and what brightens the eye?/What calls back the past/, like the rich Pumpkin pie?"

The first New England pumpkin pie was made by cutting off a slice from the top of the pumpkin, taking out the seeds, and filling the cavity with milk and spices. Maple syrup or some natural sweetener was added and the whole was baked.

An old verse reports all the ways the early settlers used pumpkins:

> For pottage, and puddings, and custards, and pies,/Our pumpkins and parsnips are common supplies./We have pumpkins at morning and pumpkins at noon;/If it were not for pumpkins, we should be undoon.

Availability—Fresh pumpkin is available in the fall and winter months. Pumpkin is also sold canned and puréed. Some pumpkin pies are sold frozen.

Pumpkin seeds are dried and sold salted in the shell and salted shelled.

Purchasing Guide—Fresh pumpkins should have fairly firm rinds and be bright orange in color. They should be heavy for their size and free from blemishes. Small pumpkins have more tender flesh than large ones.

☐ 3 pounds fresh pumpkin = about 3 cups cooked and mashed

Storage

☐ Kitchen shelf, whole: about 1 month
☐ Refrigerator shelf, whole: 1 to 4 months
☐ Refrigerator frozen-food compartment, prepared for freezing: 2 to 3 months
☐ Freezer, prepared for freezing: 1 year
☐ Canned, kitchen shelf: 1 year
☐ Canned, opened; or fresh, cooked, refrigerator shelf: 4 to 5 days

Nutritive Food Values—Good source of vitamin A, fair source of iron.

☐ 3½ ounces, raw = 26 calories
☐ 3½ ounces, canned = 33 calories
☐ Pumpkin seeds, dry, 3½ ounces, shelled = 553 calories

Basic Preparation—If shell is desired whole for a jack-o-lantern, cut off top stem section. Remove seeds. Scrape out the meat with a spoon. Cook meat as directed below.

☐ **To Boil**—Halve pumpkin, and remove seeds and stringy portion. Cut pumpkin into small pieces, then peel. Cook in boiling salted water to cover for 25 to 30 minutes, or until tender. Drain and mash, or force through a food mill. Use in making pies or other desserts. Or reheat, season with butter, salt and pepper and serve as a vegetable.

☐ **To Bake**—Halve pumpkin, and remove seeds and stringy portion. Cut into 2-inch pieces and peel. Put in shallow baking dish and brush generously with melted butter or margarine. Sprinkle with salt and pepper. Bake, uncovered, in preheated moderate oven (350°F.) for 45 minutes, or until tender, brushing several times with melted butter. Serve as a vegetable.

□ **To Steam**—Halve pumpkin, and remove seeds and stringy portion. Cut into small pieces and peel. Put in a vegetable steamer, large strainer or colander. Put over boiling water, cover tightly and steam for about 50 minutes, or until tender. Mash or force through a food mill. Use in making pies or other desserts. Or reheat, season with butter, salt, and pepper and serve as a vegetable.

□ **To Freeze**—Boil or steam pumpkin as directed above. Mash. Cool. Spoon into freezer containers, leaving ½-inch headspace. Seal.

*Pumpkins
Have Many Faces*

by Doris E. Stebbins

The pumpkin is well known for its candle-lit jack-o'-lantern face that grins at you on Halloween, but it has many other faces as well. It looks up from a spicy chiffon pie gaily dotted with marshmallows, a cake trimmed with whipped cream flowers, cherries and candied ginger; it peeks out from a brown meringue crunchy with almonds, charms its way into ice cream and even pokes its nose into soufflés, preserves, bread, and soup, making all who look upon it grateful for the beholding.

This golden fruit of the vine supplies us generously with vitamin A in a multitude of delicious ways, and it's always available on the grocer's shelves. You don't have to wait for the holidays to enjoy it. Here, for your pleasure now and all year round, are a wide variety of delicious pumpkin recipes.

INDIAN PUMPKIN SOUP
About 2½ cups mashed cooked pumpkin
Approximately 3 cups water
1 tablespoon chopped onion, fried in shortening until transparent
1 cup milk or light cream
Salt
1 tablespoon curry powder (or more)
Dash of dried or fresh mint

Combine pumpkin and water; stir to form thin purée. Add onion. Boil for 3 minutes. Add milk or cream, salt to taste, and curry powder. Heat through, stirring constantly. Sprinkle mint over the top just before serving. Makes 6 to 8 servings.

PUMPKIN NUT WAFFLES
2½ cups sifted cake flour
4 teaspoons baking powder
1 teaspoon salt
¾ teaspoon ground cinnamon
¼ teaspoon ground nutmeg
3 eggs, separated
1¾ cups milk
½ cup melted shortening
½ cup canned pumpkin
¾ cup chopped pecans

Sift together dry ingredients. Beat egg yolks. Combine with milk, shortening, and pumpkin. Add to dry ingredients. Beat egg whites stiff. Fold into batter. Pour onto hot waffle iron. Sprinkle with a few chopped nuts and bake. Makes about 8 waffles.

RAISED PUMPKIN ROLLS
½ package active dry yeast or ½ cake compressed yeast
¼ cup water*
1 cup mashed cooked fresh pumpkin
1 egg, well beaten
½ cup sugar
¼ teaspoon salt
1 tablespoon butter or margarine
1 cup milk, scalded
4 cups unsifted all-purpose flour

Sprinkle or crumble yeast into water. *Use very warm water (105°F. to 115° F.) for dry yeast; use lukewarm (80°F. to 90°F.) for compressed. Let stand for a few minutes, then stir until dissolved. Combine pumpkin and egg, sugar, salt, butter, and milk. Cool to lukewarm. Add dissolved yeast and flour. Cover and let rise until doubled. Shape into rolls and let rise again until doubled, about 20 minutes. Bake in preheated moderate oven (350°F.) for 12 to 15 minutes. Makes about 1½ dozen rolls.

PUMPKIN BREAD
2 packages active dry yeast or 2 cakes compressed yeast
¼ cup water*
¼ cup sugar
1¾ cups milk, scalded
1 tablespoon salt
About 8 cups all-purpose flour
2 cups cooked pumpkin (canned or fresh)
¼ cup melted shortening or cooking oil

Sprinkle or crumble yeast into water. *Use very warm water (105°F. to 115° F.) for dry yeast; use lukewarm (80°F. to 90°F.) for compressed. Let stand for a few minutes, then stir until dissolved. Add 1 teaspoon sugar. Let stand for 10 minutes. Combine scalded milk, salt, and remaining sugar. Stir and cool until lukewarm. Combine yeast and cooled-milk mixtures and stir to blend. Add 2½ cups flour and beat until batter is very smooth. Add pumpkin and cooled shortening and mix well. Add enough of remaining flour to make a stiff dough. Turn dough out on lightly floured board. Cover with bowl, let rise for 10 minutes. Round up and place in a greased bowl; turn once to bring greased side up. Cover and let

stand in a warm place (86°F.); let rise until doubled in bulk, about 1 hour. Punch down dough, turn over in bowl, and let rise again until doubled in bulk, about 45 minutes. Turn out on board and divide into 3 equal portions. Quickly round up each portion, cover with bowls, and let rest for 10 minutes on board. Shape into loaves. Place in greased loaf pans. Cover and let rise in warm place until doubled in bulk. Bake in preheated hot oven (400°F.) for 15 minutes; reduce heat to moderate (375°F.) and continue baking for 20 to 30 minutes longer, or until well browned. Turn out on racks to cool, uncovered and away from drafts. Makes 3 loaves.

PUMPKIN SOUFFLÉ
1 cup canned or thick mashed cooked fresh pumpkin
½ teaspoon ground cinnamon
½ cup firmly packed brown sugar
3 egg whites
⅛ teaspoon salt

Combine pumpkin with cinnamon and sugar and mix well. Beat egg whites until stiff, add salt, and fold into pumpkin mixture. Fill greased 1-quart baking dish or individual molds about ⅔ full, and set in pan of hot water. Bake in preheated moderate oven (350°F.) for about 40 minutes for a large mold, 25 to 30 minutes for individual molds. Makes 4 to 6 servings.

PUMPKIN-ORANGE CUSTARDS
1 cup canned or mashed cooked fresh pumpkin
2 eggs, slightly beaten
½ cup firmly packed light brown sugar
½ teaspoon salt
Dash of ground ginger
½ teaspoon ground cinnamon
1 cup light cream or milk
⅛ teaspoon grated orange rind

Mix pumpkin with eggs, sugar, salt, and spices. Stir in cream and orange rind and pour mixture into custard cups. Set cups in a shallow pan of hot water high enough to come almost to the top of the cups. Bake in preheated slow oven (325° F.) for 40 to 50 minutes, or until custard is firm. Makes 4 servings.

TAWNY PUMPKIN PIE
1¼ cups pumpkin
¾ cup sugar
½ teaspoon salt
¼ teaspoon ground ginger
1 teaspoon ground cinnamon
1 teaspoon all-purpose flour
2 eggs, slightly beaten
1 cup undiluted evaporated milk
2 tablespoons water
½ teaspoon vanilla extract
Pastry for 1-crust 9-inch pie, unbaked

Combine pumpkin, sugar, salt, spices, and flour in mixing bowl. Add eggs; mix well. Add evaporated milk, water, and vanilla; mix. Pour into pastry-lined pie pan. Bake in preheated hot oven (425°F.) for 15 minutes; reduce heat to moderate (350° F.) and bake for 35 minutes longer, or until set. Makes 6 to 8 servings.

FROZEN GINGER-PUMPKIN PIE
1 pint vanilla ice cream
¼ cup chopped candied ginger
  Standard Pastry for 1-crust 9-inch pie, baked (page 1399)
1 cup canned pumpkin
1 cup sugar
½ teaspoon salt
1 teaspoon ground ginger
½ teaspoon ground nutmeg
1½ cups miniature marshmallows
1 cup heavy cream, whipped
  Chopped nuts
  Marzipan (optional)

Stir ice cream to soften. Quickly fold in chopped ginger and spread in pie shell. Freeze until firm. Mix pumpkin, sugar, salt, ginger, and nutmeg. Stir in marshmallows. Fold in cream. Pile on ice cream layer and sprinkle with nuts. Freeze until firm. To serve, remove from freezer and let stand in refrigerator for 5 to 10 minutes. Top with marzipan if desired. Makes 6 to 8 servings.

PUMPKIN-MINCE PIE
  Pastry (1 cup flour recipe)
1 package dry mincemeat
1 cup boiling water
1½ cups canned pumpkin
¾ to 1 cup firmly packed light brown sugar
½ teaspoon salt
1 teaspoon ground cinnamon
½ teaspoon ground ginger
1 tall can (14½ ounces) evaporated milk
2 tablespoons butter
2 eggs (1 white stiffly beaten)
  Few drops of lemon extract

Line a deep 10-inch pie pan with pastry. Chill. Break mincemeat into saucepan. Cook in boiling water for 3 minutes, stirring occasionally. Cool; then chill. Mix pumpkin, sugar, salt, and spices in another saucepan. Stir in milk; add butter; heat until butter is melted. Pour over slightly beaten eggs; add flavoring. Strain onto stiffly beaten egg white and mix. Cool. Spread mincemeat in bottom of pastry-lined pan; pour pumpkin mixture over top. Bake in preheated extremely hot oven (500°F.) for 5 minutes. Reduce heat to slow (325°F.) and continue baking for 25 to 35 minutes, or until set. Makes 8 servings.

PUMPKIN CHIFFON MERINGUE
1 envelope unflavored gelatin
½ cup firmly packed brown sugar
½ teaspoon salt
½ teaspoon each of ground cinnamon and nutmeg
¼ teaspoon ground ginger
2 eggs, separated
½ cup milk
1¼ cups canned pumpkin
¼ cup granulated sugar
½ cup heavy cream, whipped
½ cup chopped toasted almonds (optional)

9-inch meringue shell, baked

Combine gelatin, brown sugar, salt, and spices in top part of a double boiler. Stir in slightly beaten egg yolks, milk, and pumpkin. Cook over hot water for about 5 minutes, stirring constantly. Remove from heat; chill until slightly thickened. Beat egg whites until foamy; add granulated sugar, 1 tablespoon at a time, beating well after each addition; continue beating until stiff peaks form; fold into pumpkin mixture. Fold in whipped cream and almonds. Turn into cooled meringue shell; chill for 2 to 3 hours, or until firm. Garnish with whipped cream if desired.

Meringue Shell
Beat 3 egg whites until stiff but not dry. Beat in ¼ teaspoon cream of tartar. Gradually beat in ¾ cup sugar and continue beating until very stiff. Spread over bottom and up sides of greased 9-inch pie pan. Bake in preheated very slow oven (275°F.) for about 1¼ hours.

PUMPKIN CHIFFON CAKE
2 cups sifted cake flour
1½ cups sugar
3 teaspoons baking powder
1 teaspoon salt
1 teaspoon ground cinnamon
½ teaspoon each of ground cloves and nutmeg
½ cup cooking oil
8 egg yolks
½ cup water
¾ cup canned or thick mashed cooked fresh pumpkin
½ teaspoon cream of tartar
1 cup (8) egg whites

Sift first 7 ingredients into mixing bowl; make well in center. Add in order: cooking oil, egg yolks, water, pumpkin. Beat until satin smooth. Add cream of tartar to egg whites; beat to very stiff peaks. Pour egg-yolk batter in thin stream over entire surface of whites, gently folding to blend. Bake in ungreased 10-inch tube pan in preheated slow oven (325°F.) for 55 minutes; then increase heat to moderate (350°F.) and bake for 10 minutes longer. Invert on rack; remove when cool. Frost with an orange-colored icing and decorate with flowers of whipped cream, cherries, and candied gingerroot.

PUMPKIN ICE CREAM
1 cup canned pumpkin
½ teaspoon each of ground cinnamon and nutmeg
¼ teaspoon salt
½ cup coarsely chopped nuts
½ cup milk
¼ cup sugar
1 cup heavy cream, whipped

Mix pumpkin, spices, salt, and nuts. Heat milk and add sugar, stirring until sugar is dissolved. Stir into pumpkin mixture and chill. Fold in whipped cream. Pour into mold or freezer tray and freeze until firm. Makes 6 servings.

PUMPKIN PRESERVES
5 pounds pumpkin
4 pounds (8 cups) sugar
3 lemons, sliced thin
1 orange, sliced thin
  Few grains of salt

Remove peel and cut raw pumpkin into slices ¼ inch thick and 1 or 2 inches long. Place in stone jar or earthenware utensil and add sugar. Let mixture stand overnight. Drain liquid from pumpkin and boil liquid until it spins a thread. Add sliced pumpkin and remaining ingredients. Cook until thick and clear. Pour into hot sterilized jars and seal. Makes about 8 pints.

FROZEN PUMPKIN TARTS
1 tablespoon cornstarch
¾ cup sugar
½ teaspoon ground cinnamon
¼ teaspoon ground ginger
2 eggs, separated
1 cup milk
¾ cup canned pumpkin
½ cup heavy cream, whipped
⅓ cup chopped pecans
8 baked tart shells

Mix cornstarch, sugar, cinnamon, and ginger. Stir in slightly beaten egg yolks and milk. Cook over hot water in top part of a double boiler until thickened, stirring constantly. Add pumpkin. Freeze. Break into chunks; turn into bowl. Beat smooth with rotary beater; this extra beating adds air, makes a smoother mixture. Fold in stiffly beaten egg whites, whipped cream, and nuts. Pour into tart shells. Freeze firm. Makes 8 servings.

Pumpkins and Philosophy
by Esther E. Wood

When Uncle Frank returned from his sophomore year at the university, he introduced his family to the philosophy of Thoreau. He measured every activity and institution by the yardstick of the Concord thinker. When the neighbors asked him about his year at college, he mystified them by replying, "Education makes a straight-cut ditch out of a free meandering brook." When his sister asked him to dinner at her home, he gave the cool answer, "Such are my engagements to myself that I dare not promise to wend your way." But after he learned that huckleberry pie was to be the dessert of the day, he hastened to accept the invitation. Perhaps he recalled Thoreau's fondness for berries and berry picking.

"Take plenty of time no matter how menial the task," Uncle advised his little sister as she prepared to do the dishes. "Men live like ants," "Silence is the universal refuge," "The only danger in Friendship is that it will end" were but a few of the wise sayings with which he showered his family.

The following summer Uncle's enthusiasm had shifted to Whitman and he quoted *Leaves of Grass* to us. Grandfather, however, did not forget the Thoreau quotations. The one that especially pleased him was "I would rather sit on a pumpkin and have the seat all to myself than be crowded on a velvet cushion."

I suspect that Grandfather was less attracted by the philosophy than by the reference to the pumpkin. He took great pride in raising pumpkins and when he had one of great size, he was sure to say, "There, this one is big enough to seat a Thoreau. Perhaps even an Emerson or an Alcott could be seated also."

It would be more exact to write that Grandfather cherished pumpkins rather than raised them. He set aside the most fertile part of his hillside land as a vine patch. The plot faced the morning sun and got the dampness from the bay. It was near the brook so that in dry weather water could be brought to the water-loving vines. A few of the pumpkin vines received preferential care. The dirt about them was enriched with skim milk; only a few pumpkins on the vines were allowed to mature; when a shower of hail threatened to damage the leaves, the vines were covered with old meal bags. Everyday Grandfather visited his plot to kill the striped bugs, to admire the greenness of the foliage, to pull out encroaching weeds, and to estimate the extent of the harvest.

A few pumpkins were gathered in early September and taken to the exhibition hall at the county fair where they were always awarded a first prize. Grandfather had won the award for so many years that in my childhood he exhibited only every other year. "Nice to give the other fellow a chance," was his comment.

One of the prize pumpkins Grandfather usually gave to the chairman of the fair association. The others were brought home for a special ripening on the granite step by the front door. When they were ripe, Grandfather opened them with swift blows of the ax, scooped out the seeds, and spread the seeds on papers behind the *Home Clarion* range where they were left to dry. After the seeds were dry, some were sealed in tin cans and kept for the May sowing of the hillside plot. Others were poured into a brown bowl and set on Grandfather's

lamp stand. As he read the *New England Homestead* or the *Rural New Yorker,* he ate the sweet kernels that he removed from the paper-white shells. His comment was "Pumpkin seeds are as tasty as nuts."

The final harvesting of the crop came in late September or early October. Grandfather wheeled loads of the orange orbs to the back yard and sorted them into three piles. The least desirable, those irregular in size and those without stems, were set aside for cow fare. A second heap contained the most desirable, those that the grower had earmarked as gifts for his village friends who had no garden plots. The third and the largest pile contained the pumpkins that Grandmother would have for fall and winter use.

The pumpkins, heaped in conical piles, sunned themselves for several weeks beside the barn door. On frosty nights Grandfather covered them with protecting horse blankets. But when the *Old Farmer's Almanac* and local signs agreed in indicating a killing frost, Grandfather brought his orange harvest under cover. The cattle fodder was wheeled to a straw-lined stanchion in the tie-up. The gift pumpkins were stacked in the shed to await village delivery. Grandmother's share was taken to the unfinished ell chamber where they shared winter quarters with pails of red cranberries, strings of dried apples, and bunches of fragrant sage.

The making of the first pumpkin pie was a ceremony over which Grandfather liked to preside. He asked that the pie be baked in a great square pan that reminded him of the tin in which his mother had baked pie for her family of ten children. Grandmother complied with his request but remarked, "We'll never be able to eat a pie of this size unless we have all our relatives in for dinner."

Grandfather hovered near Grandmother as she beat the eggs in a large white ironware bowl, poured in milk, and added the cooked pumpkin. He plied her with questions: "Shouldn't you beat in another egg?" "Why not use cream instead of milk?" When Grandmother poured the sugar and molasses into the pie mixture and added nutmeg and cinnamon, he made a number of suggestions: "I should think it would be well to add just a mite of ginger." "Let's add some vanilla."

Finally Grandmother's patience was gone and she drove him from the kitchen with the dismissal, "You go out in the barn and 'tend to your own affairs. I've been stirring up pies for you for forty years and you've always been able to eat them. You raise the pumpkins and I'll bake the pies. That is a fair division of labor."

The pumpkin pie, brown, sweet, and

flavorful, was served at Sunday dinner when Grandfather's sister, his daughter, and his grandchildren were there to share his favorite dessert. Grandfather was especially happy if his son were there too, because it was largely for his benefit that he remarked,

"There, Frank, if Thoreau had ever tasted a pie as good as this one he would never have talked about sitting on a pumpkin. He would have had it cut up, stewed, and made into a pie."

It would be difficult to duplicate Grandmother's pumpkin pie. I suspect that part of her success came from the fact that she prepared the pumpkin for the pie filling using a process that few today would care to copy. She washed the pumpkin, set it in a pan, and placed it in the oven for a long slow baking. When it was soft, she took a knife and spoon to open it, to remove the seeds, and to take out the dark dry pumpkin. The pumpkin was then sieved. The molasses she used came straight from the West Indies in great hogsheads. Grandfather bought it from the general store a gallon at a time. The pie was baked in the oven of an iron stove.

Today Mother uses canned pumpkin and bakes the pie in a gas stove. She uses Grandmother's recipe. Although she insists that her pumpkin pie does not equal that of her mother, my friends and I rate it as excellent. Here is Grandmother's recipe:

⅔ cup firmly packed brown sugar
½ teaspoon salt
¼ teaspoon ground cinnamon
½ teaspoon ground nutmeg
3 tablespoons molasses
1½ cups mashed cooked pumpkin
2 eggs, beaten
2 cups milk (sometimes she used 1 cup light cream and 1 cup milk)
Pastry for 9-inch pie crust, unbaked

Mix all ingredients except last. Pour into pastry-lined pie pan. Bake in preheated extremely hot oven (500°F.) for 8 minutes. Reduce heat to slow (325°F.) and bake for 55 to 60 minutes longer.

PUMPKIN PIE SPICE—This is a blend of cinnamon, cloves, and ginger ground together to weld the flavors permanently. It is used in pumpkin pie, spice cookies, gingerbread, breakfast buns, and in pumpkin, Hubbard-squash, and sweet-potato dishes.

PUNCH—An alcoholic beverage which can be made with champagne, wine, ale, or liquor, and sometimes with additions of citrus juice, spices, tea, and/or water; or a nonalcoholic beverage made with

PUNCH

fruit juices, The beverage is served from a large punch bowl into small cups. Although an alcoholic punch may be served either hot or cold, the fruit-juice punches are more often served cold.

Punch was introduced to Great Britain from India. The name itself seems to have derived from the Hindi word *panch*, meaning "five," and traditionally, punch was supposed to be made with five ingredients: spirits, water, lemon, sugar, and spice. In practice, however, there is no limit to the number of ingredients a punch may have.

In colonial America, where punch was a favorite beverage, rum was often used as its base. A historian, writing in 1705 of the state of life among the Virginia gentry, comments that one of the most common "Strong" drinks is "Punch, made either of Rum from the Caribee Islands, or Brandy distilled from their own Apples and Peaches."

There are tales of punch bowls in this country large enough to have "swimm'd half a dozen young geese," like that holding the famous Philadelphia Fish House Punch in 1744. The record for huge receptacles certainly must go, however, to an English punch of an earlier day. In the late 16th century a British naval dignitary served to 6,000 guests a punch made of 80 casks of brandy, 9 casks of water, 20,000 large limes, 80 pints of lemon juice, 1,300 pounds of sugar, 5 pounds of nutmeg, and a huge cask of Malaga wine. Understandably an extraordinary container had to be devised for a beverage of such extraordinary proportions. The huge marble basin that was finally settled upon was large enough for a ship's boy to row about in it in a small boat.

CHAMPAGNE PUNCH

    2 cups sugar
    4 cups water
    ½ cup fresh lemon juice
    ½ cup fresh lime juice
    4¼ cups fresh orange juice
    2 cups fresh grapefruit juice
    2 cups Rhine wine
    4/5 quart champagne
       Grenadine (optional)

Combine 2 cups sugar with 2 cups water and the lemon juice. Bring to boil and boil for 1 minute. Add remaining water. Cool. Stir in lime, orange, and grapefruit juices. Pour into punch bowl over ice. Add wine and champagne just before serving. Garnish with fresh lemon slices or sliced fresh strawberries and mint leaves if desired. If more color is desired, add a little grenadine before pouring into punch bowl. Makes approximately 1 gallon.

PHILADELPHIA FISH HOUSE PUNCH

    ¾ pound lump sugar
    2 quarts water
    1 quart fresh lemon juice
    2 quarts dark rum

Fruit Punch

    1 quart brandy
    ½ cup peach brandy

In large punch bowl dissolve sugar and water. When entirely dissolved, add all other ingredients. Mix well. Place a large block of solid ice in punch bowl. Add punch. Let mixture ripen for 2 hours, stirring occasionally. Makes about 1½ gallons, depending on dilution.

HOT MILK PUNCH

    1 teaspoon grated lemon rind
    4 cups milk
    ¾ cup sugar
    3 egg whites, beaten
    ½ cup dark rum
    1 cup brandy
    ½ teaspoon almond extract

Combine lemon rind, milk, and sugar in saucepan. Heat until just scalded. Fold in egg whites, rum, brandy, and almond extract. Serve in punch cups. Makes six 8-ounce servings.

ANNIVERSARY PUNCH

    1 package (12 ounces) frozen sliced
       strawberries*
    2 teaspoons grated lime rind
       Juice of 1 lime
       Block of ice
    1 bottle (4/5 quart) sparkling
       burgundy
    1 bottle (4/5 quart) dry champagne
    1 bottle (4/5 quart) sauterne

Mix strawberries, lime rind, and juice in saucepan. Bring to boil and simmer for 10 minutes. Force through food mill or sieve; cool. Put block of ice in punch bowl and add berry mixture. Just before serving, add wines. If desired, decorate with whole strawberries and lime slices. Makes about 3½ quarts.

* If preferred, 2 cups sliced fresh strawberries, 1 tablespoon water, and ¼ cup sugar may be substituted for the frozen berries.

Champagne Punch

RECEPTION PUNCH

¼ cup sugar
½ cup water
¼ teaspoon ground aniseed
2 cups grape juice
1½ cups light beer
  Lemon slices, whole cloves, and
  cinnamon stick

Combine sugar, water, and aniseed in a saucepan. Bring to a boil and cook for 5 minutes. Cool. Stir sugar syrup into grape juice. Just before serving, add beer and pour over ice. Stud lemon slices with cloves and float over the top of the punch along with cinnamon stick. Makes 3 cups.

FRUIT PUNCH

16 large oranges
16 large lemons
11½ cups (two 46-ounce cans)
  unsweetened pineapple juice
3 cups sugar
2 cups water

6 bottles (29 ounces each) ginger ale
  Ice
1 bunch of mint
1 pint strawberries
2 oranges, sliced

Grate rinds of 3 oranges and 3 lemons; squeeze juice from the 16 oranges and 16 lemons and add grated rinds and pineapple juice. Mix sugar and water; bring to boil, stirring until sugar is dissolved. Cool and add to juices. Add ginger ale, ice, mint, berries, and sliced oranges. Makes 3 gallons.

GOLDEN PUNCH

12 cups (3 quarts) orange-and-grapefruit
  juice, fresh or canned, chilled
½ cup fresh lemon juice, chilled
1 quart ginger ale

Combine orange-and-grapefruit juice and lemon juice. At serving time, add ginger ale. Makes 4 quarts.

APPLE-CRANBERRY PUNCH

Combine 4 cups cranberry juice, 3 cups apple juice, and ½ cup fresh lemon juice. Add 1 lemon, sliced thin, and 1 cup pineapple tidbits. Chill thoroughly. To serve, pour over ice in punch bowl and add 1 bottle (29 ounces) chilled carbonated water. Makes 6 large glasses, 12 small.

PURÉE—A mixture made by pressing a raw or cooked food through a sieve or food mill, or by whirling it in a blender so that it is smooth and thick. The purée is used as is or can be used in sauces, soufflés, soups, or as a garnish.

The word is French, derived from the medieval French *purer*, "to cleanse," which indicates that originally to purée foods meant to remove their impurities.

100 Menus
to help you plan
more varied meals
for your family with
the recipes in this volume

*Recipes for all starred dishes found in this volume.

BREAKFAST

Sliced Peaches and Oranges
Old-Fashioned Oatmeal
Porridge*
Maple Syrup or Honey
Coffee or Tea

Pipérade* (Seasoned Scrambled
Eggs) on Toast Points
Potato or Raised Cake*
Café au Lait

Baked Apples with Cranberry
Sauce
Sherry Posset*
Coffee

Vegetable Juice Cocktail
Canadian Bacon
Broiled Pineapple Slices*
Whole-Wheat Popovers*
Coffee or Tea

Crisp Bacon or Sausage
Sour-Milk Griddle Cakes*
Melted Butter
Dried-Apricot Preserves*
Coffee

Grapefruit or Melon
Danish Pork Balls*
Hashed Brown Potatoes
Sticky Cinnamon Buns*
Beverage

Sauerkraut and Tomato Juice
Fried Scrapple* Topped
with Poached Eggs
Toasted Pumpkin Bread*
Pennsylvania Dutch
Apple Butter*
Coffee

Vanilla Fresh-Plum Compote*
Chinese Pork-Fried Rice*
Almond Popovers*
Coffee or Green Tea

LUNCH or SUPPER

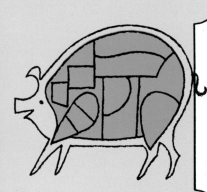

Cranberry Cocktail
Frizzled Ham
Pumpkin Nut Waffles*
Molasses   Butter
Coffee

Pomegranate Nectar*
Cheddar-Cheese Omelet
Buttered Toasted
Prune Bran Bread*
Tea or Coffee

Tangerine Juice
Broiled Pork-Roll Slices
Buckwheat Cakes*
Honey   Butter
Coffee

Fresh or Frozen Raspberries
Creamed Tuna or
Dried Beef on
Potato Waffles*
Crystal Tomato Pickles*
Tea

Old-Fashioned
Pork-Liver Pudding*
Pumpernickel or
Rye Bread
Whipped Sweet Butter
Mustard Pickle*
Sliced Tomatoes
and Onions
Pineapple Ice*

Sliced Salami
Hot Creamy
Potato-Egg Salad*
Rye Wafers
Stewed Fresh Plums*

Celery Sticks
Cherry Tomatoes
Brawn*
Salad Alsace*
Poppy-Seed Coconut Bars*

Potato Soup Parmentier*
Curried Popcorn*
Pineapple-Ham Salad*
Pecan Penuche*

Tuna-Vegetable Pie with
Cheese Pastry*
Fresh-Pineapple and
Avocado Salad*
Minted Iced Tea

Tomato Juice
Potato-Topped
Luncheon Meat*
Sour Green Beans*
California Prune Pudding*

Assorted Raw Relishes
Chicken Rivel Corn Soup*
Lemon Squares with
Apricot Glaze*

Iced Gazpacho with Vegetable,
Crouton, and
Herb Garnish*
Blackberry-Almond
Meringue Pie*

Frankfurters and Noodles*
Pineapple Slaw*
York Hermits*

Hamburger Potato-Cheese
Pie*
Stewed Tomatoes
Honey-Prune Pudding*

Pepper Pot Soup with Dumplings*
Two-Tone Pineapple Salad*
Peppermint Taffy*

◆

Salt-Pork and
Potato Chowder*
Little Pizza*
Applesauce

Indian Pumpkin Soup*
Oriental Pineapple
and Tuna*
Assorted Crisp Breads
Fresh-Coconut Pralines*

◆

Salmagundi Herring Salad*
Rye Wafers
Hungarian Poppy-Seed
Kringle*
Coffee

Celery   Watermelon Pickle*
Oyster-Potato Pie*
Pineapple-Orange Salad*

◆

Krupnik (Barley Soup)*
Pineapple-Cucumber Salad*
Cheese Popovers*
Whipped Butter or Margarine

Clear Fruit Soups,* Croutons
Nóżki Wieprzowe z Grochem
(Pickled or Fresh Pigs'
Knuckles with Split Peas)*
Horseradish
Rye Rolls
Pumpkin Chiffon Cake*

◆

Madras Chicken Pilau*
Fried Apples
Melba Toast
Cottage Pudding*
Foamy Sauce*

Filety z Polędwicy
(Filet Mignon with
Mushrooms)*
Baked Herbed Potatoes*
Sliced Tomato-Endive Salad
Garlic French Bread
Frozen Pistachio Custard*

◆

Curried Potato Soup*
Muskellunge Baked in
Spanish Sauce*
Marinated Cooked Vegetables
Peppermint Chocolate
Chiffon Pie*

Wild Strawberry or
Raspberry Soup*
Polędwica Wieprzowa Duszona
na Winie (Pork Pot Roast
in Wine)*
Pierogi z Kaszy ze Serem
(Buckwheat Dumplings
with Cheese)*
Black-Bottom Pie with
Chocolate Crust*

◆

Pike Baked in Almond Sauce*
Sour-Cream Potatoes*
Marinated Tomatoes
Chocolate Pecan Pie*

Losós do Sosów Goracych
i Zimnych (Poached
Salmon)*
Sos Chrzanowy
(Horseradish Sauce)*
Mizerja II (Cucumber Salad with
Sour Cream)*
Dark Bread
Lemon Strip Pie*

◆

Creole Stuffed Peppers*
Piquant Pineapple
and Beets*
Dinner Rolls   Butter
Marbled Chocolate Rum Pie*

Kura Lub Kurczęta po Polsku
(Roast Chicken or Pullets
à la Polonaise)*
Green Beans
Salatka po Polsku (Salad
Greens à la Polonaise)*
Seeded Rolls   Butter
Mazurek Migdalowy
(Almond Mazurka)*

◆

Puchero (Chicken, Beef, Pork,
Sausage, Vegetable Stew)*
Crusty Rolls   Butter
Banana Pie*

Tapang Baka (Cured Beef)*
Adobong Manok at Baboy
(Chicken and Pork)*
Baked Sweet Potatoes
Fresh Pineapple and
Lettuce Salad
Letse Plan
(Custard Pudding)*

◆

Morcon (Stuffed Rolled Beef)*
Golden Potatoes*
Wilted Spinach Salad
Lemon Ambrosia Pie with
Coconut Crust*

Poakapaka Koala
(Grilled Red Snapper)*
Limu Niu (Coconut Spinach)*
Kumu Niu Pu'Uwai
(Hearts of Palm)*
Maia Kalua (Baked Banana)*
Kona (Coffee)

◆

Papai (Kona Crab)*
Lime Juice
Moa Niu (Coconut Chicken)*
with Spinach
Green Onions   Radishes
Heavenly Pineapple Mousse*
(made with dark rum)

Sardinhas de Caldeirada
(Boatman's Stew)*
Bifes com Azedas
(Sorrel and Spinach
Steaks)*
Sliced Melon Salad
Toucinho-do-Céu
(Bacon from Heaven)*

◆

Roast Pork with Sage Onions*
Pineapple Rice*
Roasted Corn on the Cob*
Mixed Green Salad
Ginger Pear Crumble*

Pescado en Escabeche
(Pickled Fish)*
Sopón de Garbanzos con
Patas de Cerdo
(Chick Pea Soup with
Pigs' Feet)*
Crisp Bread
Sopa Borracha
(Tipsy Cake)*

◆

Lemon-Broiled Pike Fillets*
Corn Pie*
Beet, Onion, Avocado Salad*
Pineapple Meringue Cake*

Baked Fresh Ham,
Southern Style*
Potatoes and Turnips*
Spicy Pickled Peaches*
on Salad Greens
Corn Bread   Butter
Isla Flotante (Floating Island)*

◆

Iced Curried Pea Soup*
Sausage-Leek Pie*
Persimmon, Grapefruit, and
Pomegranate Salad*
with French Dressing
Everyday Rice Pudding*

Pollo en Agridule
(Sweet-and-Sour-Chicken)*
Repollo en Salsa de
Queso (Cabbage in
Cheese Sauce)*
Hojaldre (Sweet Cake)*
Fresh Fruit

◆

Daiquiri-on-the-Rocks*
Pernil con Vino al Caldero
(Pot of Fresh Ham
and Wine)*
Mango and Lettuce Salad
Arroz con Leche
(Creamed Rice)*

Menus

Braised Pork Butt
with Cranberries*
Skillet Potatoes, Onions,
and Beans*
Wilted Lettuce*
Sherry Almond
Snow Pudding*

———

Boiled Beef and Pork Loaf
with Vegetables*
Sour Cream
Potato Pancakes*
Escarole and Onion Salad
Minted Pineapple Cup*

Deep-Dish Ham Pie with
Cheese Pastry*
Pickled Eggs* on Coleslaw
Spicy Sweet-Potato Pudding*

———

Savory Potted Shrimp*
Spareribs Soya*
Cracked-Wheat Pilaf*
Plum Conserve*
Pumpkin Chiffon Meringue*

Baked Pork and Noodles*
Jellied Tomato Salad
on Watercress
Hot Biscuits
Fig Preserves*
Amish Vanilla Pie*

———

Crown Roast of Pork with
Sprouts and Cranberries*
Welsch Kornkuche (Corn Cake)*
Tomato and Cucumber Salad
Ice Cream
Sour-Cream Poundcake*

Tomato Juice with Lemon
Ananas (Pineapple) Pilau*
Dandelion Salad*
Raised Pumpkin Rolls*
Whipped Butter
Peppermint Chiffon Pie*

———

Relyenong Hipon
(Stuffed Shrimps)*
Litsong Baboy (Barbecued
Suckling Pig)*
Liver Sauce*   Rice
Ginatan
(Sweet Fruits and Roots)*

Lamb Shepherd's Pie*
Corn-Stuffed Pimientos*
Cracked-Wheat Bread
Crystal Mixed Pickles*
Individual Plum Shortcakes*

———

Pot-Roasted Breast of
Lamb with Dill Sauce*
Boova Shenkel (Filled Noodles)*
Buttered Swiss Chard
or Spinach
Pickled Apple Slices*
Peanut Crunch Chiffon Pie*

Lamb Serendipity*
Pommes Anna*
Dilly Green Bean Pickles*
on Lettuce
Currant-Glazed Strawberry
Tarts*

———

Clams on Half Shell
Meat Rolls with Pine Nuts*
Potato Gnocchi*
Pepper Cabbage*
Bread Sticks
Low-Calorie
Pineapple Sherbet*

Pot-Roasted Breast of
Lamb, Rosé*
Gratin aux Champignons*
(potatoes)
Asparagus-Radish Salad
Buttered Dinner Rolls
Blueberry Pie*

———

Fresh Pineapple
Mojo Isleño (Fried Fish
with Puerto Rican Sauce)*
Papa Empanada al Horno
(Potato Soufflé)*
Buñuelos de Viento
(Wind Puffs)*

Chicken Bouillon
Veal Pot Roast, Filipino*
Vegetable Pilaf*
Pineapple Apricot
Upside-Down Cake*

———

Jellied Veal*
French Potato Salad with
Onion and Parsley
Dressing*
Cherry Tomatoes
Whole-Wheat Italian
Garlic Bread
Peach Meringue Pie*

Boiled Potpie* (Chicken)
Buttered Green Beans
Jellied Fresh-Plum Salad*
Funny Cake* with
Vanilla Ice Cream

———

Pot-Roasted Duckling,
Spanish Style*
Pumpkin Soufflé*
Green Pepper, Avocado, and
Orange Salad
Toasted Hard Rolls
Frozen Marble Pie*

Barszcz Zimny (Cold Borsch
with Beet Greens)*
Potato-Tuna Casserole*
Philadelphia Vegetable
Relish*
Lebanese Pineapple*

———

Deviled Ocean-Perch Fillets*
Peppers Stuffed with
Rice and Cheese*
Prune-Plum and
Grape Salad*
English Trifle*

Cold Broiled Chicken*
Radishes, Green Onions, and
Carrot Sticks
Salad Lorraine*
Frances Clark's Rolls*
Steamed Strawberry Pudding*

———

Pepper Salad, Italian
Style*
Pot-Roasted Veal Kidneys
au Citron*
Potato Mounds, Amandine*
Broiled Tomatoes
Seeded Hard Rolls
Cantaloupe Chiffon Pie*

Fish Pudding* with Creamed
Eggs and Green Peas
Peppers and Tomatoes*
Assorted Crisp Breads
Butter
Orange-Cranberry-Raisin Pie*

———

Roast Fresh Ham*   Pepper Relish*
Fresh-Corn Pudding*
Broccoli with Pimiento
Salad   Roquefort Dressing
Plum Pudding*
Brandy Hard Sauce*

Pigs' Knuckles, Sauerkraut, and
Biscuit Dumplings*
Dried Corn*   Sliced Beets
Rye Bread   Butter
Red-Cherry Kuchen*
Coffee

Barbecued Pork Chops*
Baked Plantains*   Plain Pilaf*
Green Beans and
Cucumber Salad
Party Pudding*

Smoked Salmon Appetizer
Danish Pot-Roasted
Calf Hearts*
Potato Cakes alla Calabrese*
Buttered Kale or
Brussels Sprouts*
Sliced-Pear-Date Salad
Meringue Cake Pudding*

Spiced Beef Pot Roast*
New Potatoes and
Peas in Cream*
Belgian Endive and
Cucumber Sticks
Southern Pralines*

Biarritz*
Mixed Green Salad
with Tomatoes
French or Italian Bread
Deep-Dish Pantry Apple Pie*

Chicken Broth
Plantain Chips*
Caribbean Loin of Pork
in Black Sauce*
Hearts of Palm Salad
Buttermilk-Coconut-
Cream Pie*
Tea

Brown Pork Hash*
Crisp Bread-and-
Butter Pickles*
Waldorf Salad on Shredded
Red Cabbage*
Pumpernickel Toast
Lemon Cream Rice Pudding*

Spiced Hamburger Balls
with Prunes*
Hot Buttered Noodles
Radishes, Green Onions
Carrot Sticks
Coffee Chiffon Pie*

Apple-Cranberry Punch*
Pike, American Indian Style*
Stewed Potatoes*
Carrot and Green-Pea Salad
Chess Pie*

Gebratene Kalbsleber
(Baked Calf's Liver)*
Potato-Spinach Casserole*
Pickled Okra*
Sliced Tomatoes
Corn Sticks   Butter
Pineapple Fruit Cup Served
in the Half Shell*

Beef Mounds with Noodles*
Piccalilli*
Cooked-Vegetable Salad
Deep-Dish Plum Pie*

Carne de Porco a Alentejana
(Pork with Mussels)*
Cold Carneiro Transmontano
(Lamb from Over the Hills)*
Rice
Onion and Lettuce Salad
Pudim de Bananas
(Banana Pudding)*

Beef Brisket with
Mushroom Gravy*
Leniwe Pierogi
(Lazy Dumplings)*
Asparagus and Stuffed-
Olive Salad
Rhubarb Meringue Pie*

Sliced Ham
Schnitz und Gnepp (Dried
Apples and Raised Dumplings)*
Cauliflower Pickles*
Green-Bean Salad
Poppy-Seed Torte*

Cold Veal-and-Ham Pie*
Sautéed Green Pepper Strips*
Buttered Baby Carrots
Pistachio Fruit Cup*

Kapuśniak
(Cabbage Soup)*
Soufflé ze Śledzia
(Herring Soufflé)*
Pumpernickel Bread
Green Salad
Caramel Apple Pie*

Olive Meat Loaf*
Pineapple Baked Beans*
Spiced Pickled Beets*
Caramel Chiffon Pie*

Barszcz Czysty
(Clear Beet Soup)*
Kotleciki z Mózgu
(Brain Cutlets)*
Lemon Wedges
Parsleyed Potato Balls*
Mizerja I (Cucumber Salad)*
Sour-Cream-Raisin Pie*

Salade Niçoise*
Basil Dressing*
Potato Salad with
Sour Cream*
Crunchy Hard Rolls
Gingered Lemon Pineapple*

Hot Tomato Juice with
Hot Pepper Sauce
Old Homestead Chicken Pie*
Jellied Fruit Salad on
Shredded Escarole
Upside-Down Pudding*

Curried Pork*
Red and Green Tomato Pie*
Coleslaw
Pineapple-Orange Custards*

Bigos Polski
(Polish Bigos)*
Whipped Potatoes
Carrot and
Green Pepper Sticks
Buttered Dark Rye Bread
Deep-Dish Fresh Apple Pie*

Lamb Pie with
Poppy-Seed Crust*
Grilled Green Peppers*
Chowchow*
Coffee Custard Pudding
with Caramel Glaze*

Geś po Polsku (Goose à
la Polonaise)*
Barley Groats
Red Cabbage
Dill Pickles*   Celery
Sweet Cherry Pie*

Green-Pepper and
Beef Oven Stews*
Onion Cheese Pie*
Green Salad
French Dressing
Pumpkin Ice Cream*

Simmered Smoked Picnic (Pork)
Shoulder with Currant-
Mustard Sauce*
Hoppel Poppel*
Buttered Green Cabbage
Sour Rye Bread
Applesauce
Sour-Cream Sugar Cakes*

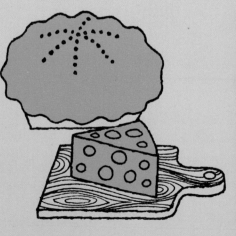

*Recipes for all starred dishes found in this volume.

GENERAL INFORMATION

The Ingredients and Measurements Used in Recipes

All recipes in this book have been tested in the Woman's Day Kitchens with standard American measuring cups (8 ounces = 16 tablespoons), measuring spoons (1 tablespoon = 3 teaspoons), and other standard kitchen equipment. All measurements are level. Liquids are measured in standard 8-ounce glass measuring cups, at eye level.

All sugar is granulated white sugar unless otherwise specified.

All flours, cake and all-purpose, are sifted before measuring unless otherwise specified. No self-rising flour is used.

All baking powder is double-acting baking powder.

All brown sugar is firmly packed when measured.

All confectioners' sugar is sifted before measuring.

All pepper is ground black pepper unless otherwise specified.

Fats and shortening are measured at room temperature, packed firmly into measuring cup and leveled with a straight knife. They are scraped out with a rubber spatula.

Salted butter or margarine, packed in ¼-pound sticks, is used unless otherwise specified. 1 stick = ½ cup = 8 tablespoons = ¼ pound.

1 tall can evaporated milk (14½ ounces) contains 1⅔ cups undiluted evaporated milk. Sweetened condensed milk is an entirely different product, and cannot be used interchangeably with evaporated milk.

⅓ to ½ teaspoon dried herbs can be substituted for each tablespoon fresh herbs. Crumble herbs before using to release flavor.

Before starting to cook or to bake, read the recipes carefully. Assemble all ingredients and equipment. Follow recipe exactly. Do not increase or decrease recipe unless you are a skilled enough cook to recognize what adjustments must be made as to ingredients, pan sizes, and/or cooking time.

Cooking Temperatures and Times

Cooking temperatures and times are approximate for meat. They depend not only on the weight and kind of meat, but also on its shape, temperature, and its bone and fat contents. A meat thermometer was used in testing.

Cooking times for meats are as recommended by the National Live Stock and Meat Board, 36 Wabash Avenue, Chicago, Illinois 60603.

Oven Temperatures

TEMPERATURES (Degree F.)	TERM
250 to 275	VERY SLOW
300 to 325	SLOW
350 to 375	MODERATE
400 to 425	HOT
450 to 475	VERY HOT
500 to 525	EXTREMELY HOT

Important—Preheat oven for 10 to 15 minutes before placing food in it. Many a cake has been spoiled by being placed in a barely heated oven. Baking times are based on the assumption that the oven is already at the stated temperature.

Check the oven temperature control frequently, especially if baking times vary from those given in recipes. (This can be done with a portable oven thermometer.) If a control is consistently off, call your public utility. They should be able to reset the oven temperature control.

Caloric Values

The caloric values, where mentioned, for each food are based on 100 grams, about 3½ ounces edible portion, as mentioned in Composition of Foods, Agriculture Handbook No. 8, Agricultural Service of the United States Department of Agriculture, Washington, D. C., revised December 1963.